DATE DUE

AUG 2 3 2017			

Learning XNA 4.0

Aaron Reed

O'REILLY®

Beijing · Cambridge · Farnham · Köln · Sebastopol · Tokyo

Learning XNA 4.0
by Aaron Reed

Published by O'Reilly Media, Inc., 1005 Gravenstein Highway North, Sebastopol, CA 95472.

O'Reilly books may be purchased for educational, business, or sales promotional use. Online editions are also available for most titles (*http://my.safaribooksonline.com*). For more information, contact our corporate/institutional sales department: (800) 998-9938 or *corporate@oreilly.com*.

Editor: Courtney Nash	**Indexer:** Fred Brown
Production Editor: Kristen Borg	**Cover Designer:** Karen Montgomery
Copyeditor: Genevieve d'Entremont	**Interior Designer:** David Futato
Proofreader: Kristen Borg	**Illustrator:** Robert Romano

Printing History:

December 2010:   First Edition.

ISBN: 978-1-449-39462-2

[LSI]   [2011-05-25]

1306350396

To my mother and father, who, after shelling out $2,500 in the 1980's for a sweet Compaq 286 with a 4-color monitor, 16k internal memory, a 5 1/4" floppy and no internal hard drive, didn't yell at me when they came home and found that I'd taken the thing apart. I've been hooked ever since.

Table of Contents

Preface

I've taught DirectX and XNA game development courses at Neumont University for the past several years, and I've been repeatedly frustrated by my inability to find the right book for these classes. There are numerous books on the subject, but none that I felt fit the goals of my classes (introductory college-level game development courses targeted to an audience familiar with C#) or that presented the material in a style and sequence I felt was appropriate.

Many books required too much previous game or graphics development knowledge. Others assumed too little knowledge of nongame-related development concepts. Still others relied too much on third-party libraries, or presented the material in a sequence that would be counterintuitive to a reader who is new to game development.

I found myself jumping around from Chapter 3 in one book to Chapter 18 in another, then back to the original book for Chapter 7 and Chapter 9, and so forth, while filling in gaps with slides, code samples, and documents I created on my own.

Eventually, I decided to take the content I had developed for my XNA game development course and write some material on the subject for use in the classroom. Initially, I was going to simply create some papers and essays to give to the students. I then realized that a large audience outside of the university would probably benefit from the material as well. I contacted O'Reilly about the book, and the rest is history.

Through my experience teaching XNA game development, I have been able to determine which points typically snag students and which points typically are easily grasped. I've also developed what I feel is a pretty straightforward way of presenting the material in a sequence that makes sense and is easy to follow. This book is designed to follow that sequence and to introduce concepts in a way that will help readers fully understand each individual topic.

Who This Book Is For

This book is meant to be a solid introduction to game development for somebody with basic knowledge of the .NET Framework and C# (or similar technologies). No previous XNA or other game or graphics development experience or knowledge is required.

How This Book Is Organized

This book introduces XNA game development concepts while walking the reader through the development of three different XNA games. Although most of the material generally applies to developing games for any of the available platforms, Chapters 16 and 17 focus on developing games for the Xbox 360 and Windows Phone 7, respectively.

The first portion of the book takes the reader through changes in XNA 4.0 and the development of a 2D game. Here are the chapters that compose this part:

Chapter 1, What's New in XNA 4.0?
>   Takes the reader through the major changes in XNA 4.0 from previous versions.

Chapter 2, Getting Started
>   Walks you through a short introduction to XNA, the tools needed to develop games in XNA, and the installation of XNA Game Studio 4.0.

Chapter 3, Fun with Sprites
>   Introduces 2D sprites, transparency, sort order, movement, framerates, sprite sheets, and animation.

Chapter 4, User Input and Collision Detection
>   Covers user input from keyboards, mice, and Xbox 360 gamepads, as well as the implementation of collision detection.

Chapter 5, Applying Some Object-Oriented Design
>   Discusses and implements game components and applies an object-oriented class hierarchy to the design of your game.

Chapter 6, Sound Effects and Audio
>   Introduces the Microsoft Cross-Platform Audio Creation Tool (XACT) and the new simplified audio API as methods to add sound to your games on the PC, Xbox 360, and Windows Phone 7.

Chapter 7, Basic Artificial Intelligence
>   Explains the nature of the science of artificial intelligence and introduces basic artificial intelligence concepts. This chapter also walks through creating customized derived classes within your class hierarchy to implement different behaviors for your sprites.

Chapter 8, Putting It All Together
>   Puts the finishing touches on the 2D game, including 2D text, scoring, adding different types of sprites, background images, game states, and power-ups.

The next part of the book walks the reader through the development of a 3D game for the PC. At the end of this section, the game is tweaked and deployed to the Xbox 360. Here are the chapters in this part:

Chapter 9, 3D Game Development
Discusses coordinate systems, cameras, and drawing primitive objects, as well as moving, rotating, and scaling objects in 3D space. Culling and texturing surfaces are also discussed.

Chapter 10, 3D Models
Introduces 3D models and discusses drawing, rotating, and moving 3D models in 3D space.

Chapter 11, Creating a First-Person Camera
Walks the reader through the creation of a first-person vector-based camera in 3D, which implements forward and backward movement, strafing, and rotation in yaw, pitch, and roll.

Chapter 12, 3D Collision Detection and Shooting
Delves into the code behind shooting a moving enemy, creating a shot object, moving it in 3D space, and handling collision detection in 3D using bounding spheres. A 3D crosshair HUD (Heads Up Display) and audio effects are also added to the game.

Chapter 13, HLSL Basics
Introduces High Level Shader Language (HLSL) syntax and implementation, as well as the code required to use HLSL effects in XNA. A number of image manipulation effects are implemented using HLSL.

Chapter 14, Particle Systems
Walks the reader through the implementation of a custom vertex and a particle used to create an explosion particle effect.

Chapter 15, Wrapping Up Your 3D Game
Fine-tunes the 3D game, with sections covering splash screens, game states, scoring, and power-ups.

Chapter 16, Deploying to the Xbox 360
Walks the reader through connecting an Xbox 360 to a PC and deploying to the Xbox 360. User input and screen resolution differences between the PC and the Xbox 360 are discussed.

This next part of the book walks you through creating a new game for Windows Phone 7:

Chapter 17, Developing for Windows Phone 7
Walks the reader through the creation of a new game for Windows Phone 7 while discussing key differences between developing for Windows Phone 7 and other platforms.

The last part of the book walks you through creating a network game in XNA. This part assumes knowledge of all previous chapters and comprises only one chapter, which concentrates on networking functionality in XNA while stepping through the creation of a new XNA game:

Chapter 18, Multiplayer Games
> Introduces multiplayer concepts through split-screen functionality as well as networking. Topics include network architectures, network states, communication via packets, and gamer services.

Finally, in the appendix, you'll find the answers to the quizzes at the end of each chapter.

Support

My goal in writing this book is to help the reader gain a true understanding of and passion for game development in XNA. To that end, I'll be supporting the book through my blog, which can be found at:

> *http://www.aaronreed.com/serenitynow/*

On that website you'll find the source code for the book, as well as other XNA-related content (and a fair bit of non-XNA-related content as well). Feel free to chime in on the forums with questions, comments, or even answers.

Conventions Used in This Book

The following typographic conventions are used in this book:

Italic
> Used for emphasis, technical terms where they are defined, URLs, email addresses, filenames, file extensions, and pathnames

`Constant width`
> Used for code samples, methods, functions, variables and their values, objects, and class names

`Constant width bold`
> Used for emphasis in code samples

 This icon signifies a tip, suggestion, or general note.

 This icon indicates a warning or caution.

Using Code Examples

This book is here to help you get your job done. In general, you may use the code in this book in your programs and documentation. You do not need to contact us for permission unless you're reproducing a significant portion of the code. For example, writing a program that uses several chunks of code from this book does not require permission. Selling or distributing a CD-ROM of examples from this book *does* require permission. Answering a question by citing this book and quoting example code does not require permission. Incorporating a significant amount of example code from this book into your product's documentation *does* require permission.

We appreciate, but do not require, attribution. An attribution usually includes the title, author, publisher, and ISBN. For example: "*Learning XNA 4.0*, by Aaron Reed. Copyright 2011 Aaron Reed, 978-0-449-39462-2."

If you feel your use of code examples falls outside fair use or the permission given here, feel free to contact us at *permissions@oreilly.com*.

We'd Like to Hear from You

We have tested and verified the information in this book to the best of our ability, but you might find that features have changed or that we may have made a mistake or two (shocking and hard to believe as that may be). Please let us know about any errors you find, as well as your suggestions for future editions, by writing to:

O'Reilly Media, Inc.
1005 Gravenstein Highway North
Sebastopol, CA 95472
800-998-9938 (in the United States or Canada)
707-829-0515 (international or local)
707-829-0104 (fax)

We have a web page for this book, where we list examples and any plans for future editions. You can access this information at:

http://oreilly.com/catalog/0636920013709/

You can also send messages electronically. To be put on the mailing list or request a catalog, send an email to:

info@oreilly.com

To comment on the book, send an email to:

bookquestions@oreilly.com

For more information about our books, conferences, Resource Centers, and the O'Reilly Network, see our website at:

http://www.oreilly.com

Safari® Books Online

When you see a Safari® Books Online icon on the cover of your favorite technology book, that means the book is available online through the O'Reilly Network Safari Bookshelf.

Safari offers a solution that's better than e-books. It's a virtual library that lets you easily search thousands of top tech books, cut and paste code samples, download chapters, and find quick answers when you need the most accurate, current information. Try it for free at *http://my.safaribooksonline.com*.

Acknowledgments

I explained what drove me to this madness in the first place at the beginning of this preface; that is, the book began from a need I had as an instructor to create a more comprehensive and straightforward way of teaching gaming and graphics. What has driven me to put together a second version of that book? In hindsight, I guess it was driven by some form of insanity. More than anybody, thanks go to my beautiful wife and for her never-ending support through all of this. Spending long nights in front of the keyboard and monitor isn't the best way to keep a marriage going, but my wife puts up with a lot and has always been there for me. I love you so much! Thank you for always being there.

Thank you to my editor (Courtney Nash) and the technical reviewers of the book (Brett Beardall, Ryan Hair, Dan Waters, and others). Without your help, this book would be little more than the misguided ramblings of a boring computer science instructor. Uhh, well...it still might be just that, but either way, your help was invaluable.

Thanks to everybody at Neumont University for allowing me to pursue my two passions: technology and education. And thank you to the hundreds of students who've taken my classes over the years. Watching the lights go on inside students' heads and the smiles on their faces when their graphics come alive on the screen truly is a special experience. It's why I do what I do and, in the end, is the real reason this book exists.

Thanks to my parents for providing a way for me to fall in love with computers, programming, and technology in general. When I was a young teenager, I took apart our family computer to install a new SoundBlaster card. I wanted to pipe the output audio through our living room stereo and blast it throughout the house. I had never installed any hardware before that day and had no idea what I was doing. To my dread, my parents came home before I could finish hooking it all up and found me on the floor, scratching my head, surrounded by parts of our $2,500 computer. After explaining what I was doing, I was shocked that they didn't yell at me and make me fix all the mess I had just created. What thrilled me even more was that when I finished putting it all together and hooked up the stereo, my parents were as excited as I was when I played with the talking parrot program and blasted the audio from a Star Wars game throughout the house. Experiences like that fed my interest in computers, helped me put aside any fear of failure, and instilled in me a passion for building things with technology. Parents of teenagers in America could learn a lot from the example of my parents: embrace your children's interest (in technology or otherwise), funnel it into productive projects (not just *playing* games), encourage them to stretch themselves, and celebrate their successes.

Finally, thank you to Kyle Whittingham and Chris Hill for making University of Utah football such a success. It has nothing to do with this book, but it does make me smile. (Utah 31, Alabama 17.)

CHAPTER 1

What's New in XNA 4.0?

In this chapter, I review major changes that have been made in XNA 4.0. If you're familiar with XNA 3.x or other versions, this is a great place to get started in this book. If you're new to XNA, you should probably skip ahead to the next chapter. You won't be missing out on anything, as all of the information covered in this chapter will be covered throughout the rest of the book.

Revised Project Folder Structure

The first thing you might notice when creating a game project in XNA 4.0 is that the structure of the solution has changed. In previous versions of XNA, the content pipeline picked up game content from a subfolder named *Content*, which was located within the game project you created, as seen in Solution Explorer (see Figure 1-1).

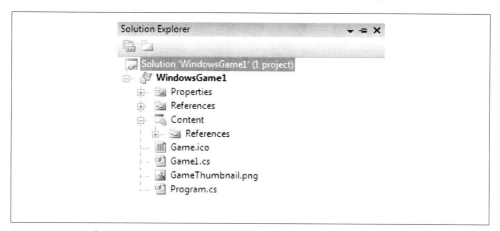

Figure 1-1. Sample XNA 3.x Solution

In XNA 4.0, the *Content* folder has been moved to a new project within your solution. The content project will be listed under the name *GameProjectNameContent* (with the name of your project replacing "GameProjectName") and will be followed with the word "Content" in parentheses (see Figure 1-2).

Figure 1-2. Sample XNA 4.0 Solution

You'll add all your game content (audio, textures, models, etc.) to the content project in the same way you added them to the content folder in XNA 3.x. You will also still use the same code to access the content from the content pipeline, just as you did in XNA 3.x. This move makes working with multiple versions of the same project (e.g., if you built a project for both Windows and Xbox 360) much more user friendly and less confusing.

Develop Games for Windows Phone 7 Series

Just as in previous versions of the XNA Framework, XNA 4.0 is designed for cross-platform development. Developers using XNA 4.0 can write games for Windows, Xbox 360, and now Windows Phone 7 Series. Not only that, but aside from some resource management and screen resolution issues, nearly 100% of the code written for any of those platforms will also work on the other platforms. This gives game developers incredible flexibility to easily create games for each platform.

To learn more about developing games for Windows Phone 7 Series, see Chapter 17.

Graphics Profiles

Between today's top-of-the-line graphics cards, which support DirectX 10 and higher, the powerful Xbox 360, and the introduction of Windows Phone 7 Series, the XNA

Framework supports development on a wide range of devices with different hardware capabilities. In previous versions of XNA, these hardware differences had to be dealt with at runtime, which often led to platform-dependent code. To help facilitate development on these different devices, XNA 4.0 introduces the concept of *profiles*. These profiles allow developers to target certain hardware devices by supporting a specific set of graphics API designated by the profile they choose.

There are two profiles in XNA 4.0: Reach and HiDef. HiDef is designed for high-powered, top-of-the-line hardware, whereas Reach is designed to support a wider range of hardware devices. The Reach profile offers a limited set of graphic features and is a subset of the HiDef profile. When choosing to write a game using the Reach profile, you sacrifice some of the more powerful graphics API, but you'll be assured that your game will work on a variety of devices (specifically Windows, Xbox 360 and Windows Phone), assuming those devices meet the minimum specifications for XNA 4.0.

The HiDef profile is designed to support today's most powerful graphic devices. You can use the HiDef profile to target Xbox 360 hardware as well as Windows-based computers with graphics cards supporting at least DirectX 10.

You can identify which profile is supported by your hardware at runtime by using the `GraphicsAdapter.IsProfileSupported` method. A chart illustrating more detail on the differences between the Reach and HiDef profiles is shown in Table 1-1.

Table 1-1. XNA profile comparison

	Reach	HiDef
Supported Platforms	Windows Phone 7 Series, Xbox 360, and any Windows PC with a DirectX 9 GPU that supports at least shader model 2.0	Xbox 360, and any Windows PC with a DirectX 10 (or higher) GPU
Shader Model	2.0 (but Windows Phone does not support custom shaders)	3.0+ (Xbox 360 supports custom shader extensions such as vfetch, which are not available on Windows)
Maximum Texture Size	2,048	4,096
Maximum Cubemap Size	512	4,096
Maximum Volume Texture Size	Volume textures are not supported	256
Non Power of Two Textures	Yes, but with limitations: no wrap addressing mode, no mipmaps, no DXT compression on non power of two textures	Yes
Non Power of Two Cubemaps	No	Yes
Non Power of Two Volume Textures	Volume textures are not supported	Yes
Maximum Number of Primitives per Draw Call	65,535	1,048,575
Maximum Number of Vertex Streams	16	16
Maximum Vertex Stream Stride	25	255

	Reach	HiDef
Index Buffer Formats	16-bit	16- and 32-bit
Vertex Element Formats	Color, Byte4, Single, Vector2, Vector3, Vector4, Short2, Short4, NormalizedShort2, NormalizedShort4	All of the Reach vertex element formats, plus HalfVector2, HalfVector4
Texture Formats	Color, Bgr565, Bgra5551, Bgra4444, NormalizedByte2, NormalizedByte4, Dxt1, Dxt3, Dxt5	All of the Reach texture formats, plus Alpha8, Rg32, Rgba64, Rgba1010102, Single, Vector2, Vector4, HalfSingle, HalfVector2, HalfVector4; floating-point texture formats do not support filtering
Vertex Texture Formats	Vertex texturing is not supported	Single, Vector2, Vector4, HalfSingle, HalfVector2, HalfVector4
Render Target Formats	Call QueryRenderTargetFormat() to find out what is supported	Call QueryRenderTargetFormat() to find out what is supported
Multiple Render Targets	No	Up to 4; must all have the same bit depth; supports alpha blending and independent write masks per render target
Occlusion Queries	No	Yes
Separate Alpha Blend	No	Yes

Configurable Effects

In previous versions of XNA, the BasicEffect class was a very basic effect, implemented mainly to allow new game developers to build games without in-depth knowledge of complex shader code. The idea was that serious game developers would implement their own shaders and not rely on the BasicEffect class.

Much of that thinking had to change with the onset of Windows Phone 7, which does not support custom shaders. As a result, new configurable effects were added, available on both the Reach and HiDef profiles. These are:

Basic Effects
> The BasicEffect class has been tweaked to include more pixel and vertex shaders to support more realistic lighting and fog effects.

Dual Texture Effects
> This effect allows you to use two different textures with independent texture coordinates. The two textures will be blended together for added complexity and detail.

Alpha Test Effects
> This effect uses a reference alpha and an alpha function to implement alpha testing. This can improve performance by updating only those pixels that are drawn in the scene.

Skinned Effects
> This effect uses bones and weights to determine the vertex positions. The effect is powerful when used for animation and instancing.

Environment Map Effect
> This effect uses textures and a cube map texture to shade objects based on the environment, reflecting the light from objects in the scene.

Built-in State Objects

Some of the state properties that were used in previous versions of XNA to modify the way scenes were drawn on the screen and the way the graphics device processes data sent to it by your game have been moved into state object classes. These classes are:

`BlendState`
> Controls how color and alpha values are blended

`DepthStencilState`
> Controls how the depth buffer and the stencil buffer are used

`RasterizerState`
> Determines how to convert vector data (shapes) into raster data (pixels)

`SamplerState`
> Determines how to sample texture data

Scalars and Orientation

Scalars in XNA 4.0 allow developers to write their games without worrying about the native resolution or screen orientation. The scalars will automatically scale your desired resolution to the resolution supported by the device on which you're playing your game. This enhancement dramatically improves game performance.

Screen orientation is most important on Windows Phone 7 devices, which switch rotation from varieties of landscape to portrait and back when the device rotates. The scalars automatically map your game from one orientation to another, and rotate input such as touch panel input accordingly.

Revised Input API

The `Microsoft.Xna.Framework.Input.Touch` namespace contains classes that enable access to multitouch input on Windows and Windows Phone devices. The namespace adds the `TouchPanel` class and `TouchLocation` class, which enable access to touch points from input devices (such as the touch panel in Windows Phone 7 series devices).

Additional Audio API

Two new classes within the `Microsoft.Xna.Framework.Audio` namespace have been added to improve audio support:

`Microphone`
> This class provides methods, fields, and events for capturing audio with microphones

`DynamicSoundEffectInstance`
> This class provides methods and events for playback of the audio buffer, giving developers the ability to play back synthesized or buffered audio

Music and Picture Enumeration and Video Playback

New audio support has been added to allow developers to use Uniform Resource Identifiers (URI) to play songs and to select, edit, and publish photos.

Use the `Song.FromUri` method to construct a `Song` object based on the specified URI. Use the `MediaLibrary.SavePicture` method to save images to the media library.

Modified and Added Classes and Methods

A fairly large number of classes and methods have been added or modified. You can view a full list on Microsoft's MSDN website at *http://msdn.microsoft.com/en-us/library/bb417503.aspx*.

Test Your Knowledge: Quiz

1. What significant change was made to the XNA folder structure in XNA 4.0?
2. What game platforms are supported with XNA 4.0?
3. What is the difference between the Reach and HiDef profiles in XNA 4.0?
4. Why do the Japanese tourists end up sleeping in a chest of drawers in Kramer's apartment?

CHAPTER 2

Getting Started

Have you ever wanted to write your own video game? I'll assume that because you're reading this book, the answer to that question is yes. (Unless, of course, you're reading this book for its sheer literary goodness, in which case, carry on.) Like many kids, my interest in building games grew the more I played video games. I would spend hours on the computer. It started with *Space Invaders*, *Asteroids*, and *Combat* on the Atari 2600. I then became fascinated by the rich storyline of King Graham of Daventry in Roberta Williams' *King's Quest* series, and my brother and I destroyed several keyboards trying to beat Bruce Jenner in *Decathlon*. But I reached a point where playing the game wasn't enough. I wanted to do more; I wanted to actually build the games. I believe part of what separates a software developer from a software user is that curiosity, a desire to look under the covers and figure out what makes something tick.

For those of us with that innate curiosity and desire to write video games, Microsoft's XNA game development framework is everything we've ever hoped for. With the straightforward layout of the framework and the power it presents to the developer, writing games for the PC has never been easier. On top of that, XNA 4.0 enables developers to develop their own games for the Xbox 360 and Windows Phone 7. Never before has access to software development kits targeting next-gen consoles or the latest handheld media devices been so readily available.

I'm sure you're ready to get started and begin building the next great game, so let's get right to it. This first chapter will help you get everything installed so you can dive in and start developing in XNA 4.0.

System Requirements

This book uses XNA Game Studio 4.0, which is an integrated development environment (IDE) extension to Microsoft's Visual Studio for developing games in XNA. XNA Game Studio 4.0 uses the XNA Framework 4.0, which provides developers with a skeleton XNA game to begin with, and the ability to customize and extend that game in order to create their own games in XNA.

XNA Game Studio 4.0 runs on multiple versions of Microsoft Visual Studio 2010. To install it, you must first install either Visual Studio 2010 Standard Edition or higher (with C# language support installed), or Visual C# 2010 Express Edition.

Visual C# 2010 Express Edition is available at no cost from Microsoft at *http://www .microsoft.com/express/vcsharp/*. It's a great way to get started in XNA if you don't have a license for one of the other versions.

Throughout this book, I'll be using Visual Studio 2010 Professional Edition. The screenshots should look the same (or at least similar) across versions, but you should be aware of the version used to create these examples in case there are discrepancies.

With XNA 4.0, developers can target the following platforms for their games: Windows Vista, Windows 7, Xbox 360, and Windows Phone 7. To run XNA games on Windows, you'll need a graphics card that supports a WDDM 1.1 driver and DirectX 10 or later. A limited API is supported for graphics cards supporting DirectX 9 and at least shader model 2.0.

XNA Game Studio 4.0 is available for download at no charge through the XNA Creator's Club Online at *http://creators.xna.com/en-US/downloads*.

Additional Resources

In addition to this book, you may want to check out the Microsoft Creator's Club Online website (*http://creators.xna.com*). The Creator's Club website is packed full of tutorials, code samples, and other resources to get you started in XNA.

Also, if you're a student, you may want to look at DreamSpark (*https://www.dream spark.com/default.aspx*). DreamSpark is a Microsoft initiative that allows students access to professional versions of Visual Studio and other design and development tools at no cost.

Installation

After you've installed one of the versions of Visual Studio 2010 mentioned previously, install XNA Game Studio 4.0. The setup for XNA Game Studio is fairly straightforward, but I'll walk you through it here. At the EULA screen (Figure 2-1), carefully read the end-user license agreement and click Accept.

Next, click the Install Now button, as shown in Figure 2-2.

If necessary, the installation will then proceed to download any required resources to complete the installation, and will then automatically install Game Studio 4.0 and the Windows Phone Developer Tools.

After the installation is complete, you should see the Setup Complete screen (Figure 2-3). Not too bad, eh? You're now ready to get rolling with XNA!

Figure 2-1. EULA

Figure 2-2. Welcome

Figure 2-3. Setup complete

Creating Your First XNA Application

Now that you have XNA Game Studio 4.0 installed, it's time to create your first XNA application. In Visual Studio, select File→New→Project. Under "Installed Templates" on the left side of the window, select Visual C#→XNA Game Studio 4.0.

On the right side of the window, you'll notice several different options. In this case, you'll want to create a Windows Game (4.0) project. Name the project *Collision*, select the directory in which you want the project saved (creating the project in the default location is perfectly fine), and click OK (see Figure 2-4).

After the project has loaded, select Debug→Start Debugging in Visual Studio. The project will compile and then run, displaying a screen similar to the one in Figure 2-5.

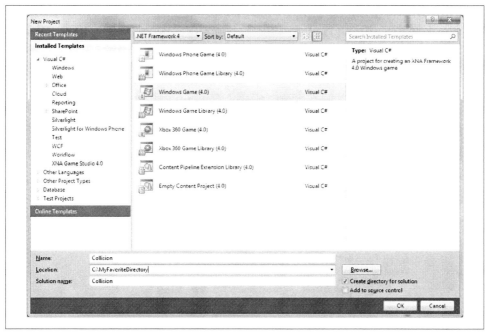

Figure 2-4. New project creation screen

Figure 2-5. Running your Collision project

Note that if you receive the error message shown in Figure 2-6 instead of the game window, you either have a graphics card that doesn't support DirectX 10 or you need to update the drivers for your graphics card. If your graphics card supports DirectX 9 and shader model 2.0, you can adjust your XNA game profile to use a limited API set, which will allow you to develop games using your current graphics card. To adjust the game profile, right-click your Collision project in Solution Explorer and select Properties. Set the Game profile to use "Reach" rather than "HiDef", as shown in Figure 2-7. After setting the profile to "Reach", run your game again, and if your graphics card meets the minimum specs, you should see the game window. Also note that when creating a project for Windows Phone 7, the game profile defaults to Reach. When creating a project for Windows or Xbox 360, it defaults to HiDef.

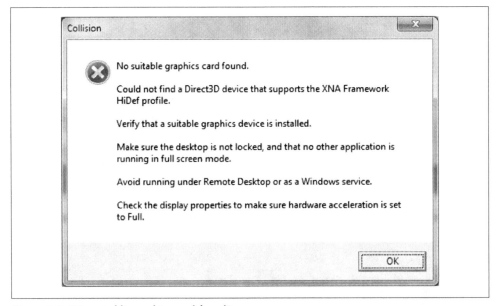

Figure 2-6. "No suitable graphics card found" error

Congratulations! You've just created your first game in XNA! It may not be the most exciting game you've ever played, but make no mistake, this is a 100% genuine XNA 4.0 application—and there's a lot more going on here than meets the eye. Although the project doesn't make use of graphics, sound, or any other cool content, the application is using the XNA Framework to draw, update, and manage resources exactly the way that everything else in this book will. We talk more about what is actually happening behind the scenes in the next chapter.

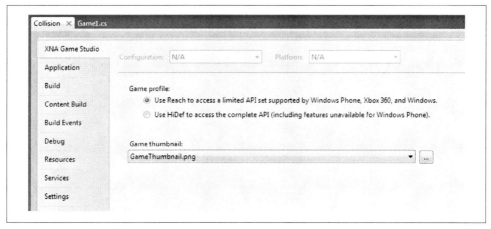

Figure 2-7. Reach profile

What You Just Did

Now you're ready to really get your hands dirty and dive into building your first game. But first, let's review what you accomplished in this chapter:

- You installed XNA Game Studio 4.0 and configured your machine for XNA development.
- You created and ran your first XNA project.

Deploying to the Xbox 360 or Windows Phone 7

If you're chomping at the bit to dive into Xbox 360 or Windows Phone 7 development, you might want to peek ahead at Chapter 17 for information on deployment to Windows Phone 7 or Chapter 16 for deployment to the Xbox 360. Because nearly all of the code you write for the PC is directly portable to these platforms, this book in general covers XNA development on the PC. Chapters 16 and 17 cover specific issues you'll need to consider when targeting each of those platforms.

Summary

- XNA is a powerful framework that facilitates game development on the PC, the Xbox 360, and Windows Phone 7.
- To develop games in XNA, you need to install Visual Studio 2010 Standard Edition or higher, or Visual C# 2010 Express Edition. You must also install XNA Game Studio 4.0.
- XNA development makes us all feel a little bit warmer inside.

Test Your Knowledge: Quiz

1. XNA Game Studio 4.0 allows you to write games for which platforms?
2. Which versions of Visual Studio support XNA Game Studio 4.0?

CHAPTER 3

Fun with Sprites

In the previous chapter, I mentioned that there was actually a lot happening behind the scenes of the simple blue-screen game you built. Let's take a more in-depth look at that code and see what's actually going on. To start, open the game project that you created in Chapter 2.

A Look Behind the Scenes

The *program.cs* file is pretty straightforward. Your Main method, which creates a new object of type Game1 and executes its Run method, is located in this file.

The real guts of your game lie in the *Game1.cs* file. The code for that file will look something like this:

```
using System;
using System.Collections.Generic;
using System.Linq;
using Microsoft.Xna.Framework;
using Microsoft.Xna.Framework.Audio;
using Microsoft.Xna.Framework.Content;
using Microsoft.Xna.Framework.GamerServices;
using Microsoft.Xna.Framework.Graphics;
using Microsoft.Xna.Framework.Input;
using Microsoft.Xna.Framework.Media;

namespace Collision
{
    /// <summary>
    /// This is the main type for your game
    /// </summary>
    public class Game1 : Microsoft.Xna.Framework.Game
    {
        GraphicsDeviceManager graphics;
        SpriteBatch spriteBatch;
```

```csharp
public Game1()
{
    graphics = new GraphicsDeviceManager(this);
    Content.RootDirectory = "Content";
}

/// <summary>
/// Allows the game to perform any initialization it needs to before
/// starting to run. This is where it can query for any required
/// services and load any non-graphic-related content.  Calling
/// base.Initialize will enumerate through any components
/// and initialize them as well.
/// </summary>
protected override void Initialize()
{
    // TODO: Add your initialization logic here

    base.Initialize();
}

/// <summary>
/// LoadContent will be called once per game and is the place to load
/// all of your content.
/// </summary>
protected override void LoadContent()
{
    // Create a new SpriteBatch, which can be used to draw textures.
    spriteBatch = new SpriteBatch(GraphicsDevice);

    // TODO: use this.Content to load your game content here
}

/// <summary>
/// UnloadContent will be called once per game and is the place to unload
/// all content.
/// </summary>
protected override void UnloadContent()
{
    // TODO: Unload any non-ContentManager content here
}

/// <summary>
/// Allows the game to run logic such as updating the world,
/// checking for collisions, gathering input, and playing audio.
/// </summary>
/// <param name="gameTime">Provides a snapshot of timing values.</param>
protected override void Update(GameTime gameTime)
{
    // Allows the game to exit
    if (GamePad.GetState(PlayerIndex.One).Buttons.Back == ButtonState.Pressed)
        this.Exit();
```

```
        // TODO: Add your update logic here

        base.Update(gameTime);
    }

    /// <summary>
    /// This is called when the game should draw itself.
    /// </summary>
    /// <param name="gameTime">Provides a snapshot of timing values.</param>
    protected override void Draw(GameTime gameTime)
    {
        GraphicsDevice.Clear(Color.CornflowerBlue);

        // TODO: Add your drawing code here

        base.Draw(gameTime);
    }
  }
}
```

In this code you'll notice that a couple of class-level variables are provided automatically, as well as a constructor for Game1 and five other methods. The first class-level variable is of the type GraphicsDeviceManager. This is a very important object because it provides you, as a developer, with a way to access the graphics device on your PC, Xbox 360, or Windows Phone 7 device. The GraphicsDeviceManager object has a property called GraphicsDevice that represents the actual graphics device on your machine. Because that graphics device object acts as a conduit between your XNA game and the graphics card on your machine (or more accurately, the *Graphics Processing Unit*, or GPU, on the graphics card), everything you do on the screen in your XNA games will run through this object.

The second variable is an instance of the SpriteBatch class. This is the core object you'll be using to draw sprites. In computer graphics terms, a *sprite* is defined as a 2D or 3D image that is integrated into a larger scene. 2D games are made by drawing multiple sprites in a scene (player sprites, enemy sprites, background sprites, etc.). You'll be using this concept and drawing sprites of your own throughout this chapter.

The Initialize method is used to initialize variables and other objects associated with your Game1 object. Your graphics device object will be instantiated at this point and can be used in the Initialize method to help you initialize other objects that depend on its settings. You'll use this method to initialize score values and other such items in later chapters in this book.

The LoadContent method is called after the Initialize method, as well as any time the graphics content of the game needs to be reloaded (e.g., if the graphics device is reset due to the player changing the display settings, or something like that). The LoadContent method is where you will load all graphics and other content required by your game, including images, models, sounds, and so on. Again, as your current project doesn't really do anything exciting, there isn't much happening in this method.

After the `LoadContent` method finishes, the `Game1` object will enter into something known as a *game loop*. Almost all games use some form of game loop, regardless of whether they are written in XNA. This is one area where game development differs from typical application development, and for some developers it can take a bit of getting used to.

Essentially, a game loop consists of a series of methods that are called over and over until the game ends. In XNA, the game loop consists of only two methods: `Update` and `Draw`. For now, you can think of the game loop in these terms: all logic that affects the actual game play will be done in the `Update` or the `Draw` method. The `Draw` method is typically used, unsurprisingly, to draw things. You should try to do as little as possible in the `Draw` method other than draw your scene. Everything else needed to run your game (which eventually will involve moving objects, checking for collisions, updating scores, checking for end-game logic, etc.) should take place in the `Update` method.

Game Development Versus Polling

Another key difference between game development and typical application development is the concept of polling versus registering for events. Many nongame applications are written solely for events driven by users. For example, if you were writing a widget-naming module for some system, you might build a screen that asks the user for the name of a widget and that has OK and Cancel buttons. Regardless of the language in which the application is written, typically it won't do anything until the user presses the OK or the Cancel button. When the user hits either button, the system will fire an event that the application will catch. That is, the application will wake up and do something only when the user tells it to do so by sending it an event indicating that one of those buttons has been pressed.

In contrast, game development is driven by polling for events, rather than waiting to hear that an event has taken place. Instead of the system telling the game that the user has moved the mouse, for example, your game will have to ask the system whether the mouse has moved. In the meantime, the application is always performing actions, regardless of user input.

Let's say you develop a game where a wizard named Jimmy (yes, there's a big market for Jimmy the Wizard games...) tries to escape from the clutches of an evil pelican warlord (that's right, pelican warlords—scary stuff!). You'll have to account for user events such as the player moving Jimmy to the left or making Jimmy cast an antipelican wing-breaking spell. But rather than XNA telling you that the player has performed these actions via some event, you need to instead poll the input devices (mouse, keyboard, gamepad, etc.) to check for changes in input.

At the same time, regardless of whether the player has interacted with the system in any way, all kinds of things are happening that need to be maintained by the game. For example, maybe the enemy pelican warlord is chasing Jimmy. This will happen regardless of any event caused by the player, and the game will be responsible for constantly changing the position of that enemy object without subscribing to any event. That's the main reason for having a game loop: it provides a way for a game to always be doing something, regardless of what the player is doing.

Of course, much more could be going on than just moving the enemy around the screen. What if the pelican warlord can throw some form of antiwizard bombs in the air? There might be 1, 2, 5, 50, or more bombs flying through the air that need to be moved constantly. You'd also have to constantly check to see whether those bombs hit anything and react accordingly. And what if the player never moves Jimmy, and the pelican warlord catches him? Something should happen in that situation. On top of that, maybe you've set a timer and Jimmy has to escape from the pelican warlord within three minutes. Now you also have some type of timer to keep track of, and some logic to perform if the timer expires or if Jimmy escapes before that happens. In game development, there is always something happening (usually a lot of things), and you're constantly updating animations, moving objects, checking for collisions, updating scores, checking for end-of-game logic, and so on.

In the hypothetical widget-naming application, it would be somewhat difficult to constantly check for some nonuser-generated event, but in XNA development, the method for doing so is built into the application architecture in the form of the game loop. All of these tasks are handled within the Update method of the game loop, and the scene is drawn in the Draw method of the game loop.

 In reality, all applications are built with loops that function in similar ways to a game loop. Windows itself uses a messaging and events system that constantly loops and lets applications know when they need to repaint themselves and perform other functions. Access to these loops is hidden by default, however, because most applications don't require access to such nonuser-driven events.

OK, let's get back to the code we were looking at previously. You'll notice that in the Update method there are a couple of lines of code that tell the game to exit when the player presses the Back button on his gamepad:

```
if (GamePad.GetState(PlayerIndex.One).Buttons.Back ==
  ButtonState.Pressed)
    this.Exit( );
```

This is how the game shuts down on the Xbox 360 or in Windows when an Xbox 360 controller is being used (otherwise, you can click the red X on the window to close it or use Alt-F4 to shut down the application).

As mentioned earlier, the Update method is where you update everything to do with the game. You can update the positions of items on the screen, scores, animation sequences and so on. You'd also check for user input, detect collisions, and adjust any artificial intelligence (AI) algorithms in your Update method.

These changes to the game that are checked for and acted upon in the Update method often correlate to what is known as a *game state*. Game state is a very important concept; it's a way for a game to know what is currently happening in that game. Games typically have several drastically different states, such as showing a splash screen versus actual gameplay versus displaying end-game screens. There may also be more subtle changes in state, such as the user receiving some form of power-up that makes her invincible for a time or some other change in the game behavior. Typically, you'll modify game states in the Update method and then use those states in the Draw method to draw different images, scenes, or other information connected to that particular state.

The Draw method is where you take all of the objects in your game and draw them on the screen itself, using the graphics device object mentioned earlier. In your current application, the only thing in the Draw method is a line of code that uses the graphics device object to clear the display and set the color to CornFlowerBlue (we'll talk about that in more depth momentarily).

Figure 3-1 shows the lifecycle of an XNA game, complete with the Update and Draw methods forming a game loop.

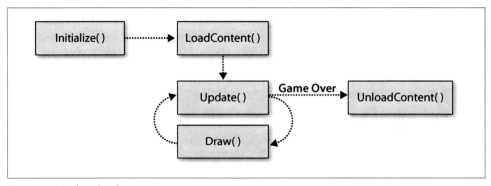

Figure 3-1. Lifecycle of an XNA game

Notice that there are two possible outcomes from the Update method: either it will continue in the game loop and the Draw method will be called or, if the game is over, it will exit the game loop and the UnloadContent method will be called. The game loop ends when you call the Game class's Exit method, just as your game does by default when the user presses the Back button on the Xbox 360 controller. The game will also exit the game loop if the player presses Alt-F4 or hits the red X button to close down the game window.

Your game will typically have some kind of step between when the game loop is exited and when the game ends. For example, if the evil pelican warlord catches Jimmy the Wizard, it would be kind of lame if the game just exited and the game window disappeared. In fact, most users would consider this behavior a bug of some sort. Instead, you'll typically use some game state logic to cause your Draw call to render some type of game-over screen in place of the gameplay scene. Then, after a certain amount of time or when the player presses some key that you determine, the game will actually exit. That may seem like a lot of work right now and may be somewhat confusing, but don't stress about it just yet. You'll be doing that sort of thing throughout this book, and soon you'll understand exactly how to make it happen.

Once the game exits the game loop, UnloadContent is called. This method is used to unload any content loaded in the LoadContent method that requires special unload handling. Typically, XNA (like .NET) will handle all your garbage collection for you, but if you've modified memory in some object that requires special handling, the UnloadContent method will allow you to take care of that here.

Modifying Your Game

All right, enough talk. You're itching to get into game development and ready to put something cool into your game. Let's make it happen.

Take a look at your Draw method. Currently, the method contains the following code:

```
protected override void Draw(GameTime gameTime)
{
    GraphicsDevice.Clear(Color.CornflowerBlue);

    // TODO: Add your drawing code here

    base.Draw(gameTime);
}
```

The first thing to notice here is the parameter that your Draw method receives. The parameter is of the type GameTime and represents the time that has passed during the execution of your game. Why do you need a variable keeping track of time? Because computers do not all run at the same speed. This variable helps you determine when animations and other events should happen based on actual game time rather than processor speed. The gameTime variable will be used throughout this book to gauge things such as framerate, animations, sounds, and other effects. The same parameter is also passed into the Update method, because many of the functions that control those effects need to be performed in the Update method rather than the Draw method.

At the end of the method, you call the Game1 object's base Draw method, which is essential in order to get cascading calls to Draw methods in GameComponents and other objects. That might not make sense to you now, but be assured that you want the base.Draw call in the code, and you should not remove it.

Finally, let's look at the call to Clear using the GraphicsDevice property of the graph ics object. Again, this property represents the actual graphics device on your PC, Xbox 360, or Windows Phone 7 device and allows you to draw different objects on the screen.

The Clear method here actually erases everything on the screen and covers the screen with the color specified (in this case, CornFlowerBlue). Change the color to something like Color.Red and run your game by selecting Debug→Start Debugging. You'll see the same window as before, but now the background color in the window will be red.

Remember when I mentioned that the boring blue screen was actually doing quite a bit behind the scenes? This is what I was talking about. While you see a boring blue (or now, red) screen, XNA is working its tail off to give that screen to you. It's running through its game loop 60 times per second, erasing everything on the screen and painting it red.

In addition, it's also calling the Update method 60 times per second and checking to see whether the Back button on a connected Xbox 360 controller has been pressed. That may not seem like a lot, but XNA is really cruising—and the best part about it is that the game is all set up and ready for you to customize.

So, if the game loop is running at 60 times per second and calling both Update and Draw, why do you want to clear the screen every single time? Although it may sound inefficient to clear the screen and redraw the entire scene and all objects for each new frame, it is far more efficient to do that than the alternative, which would be to try to keep track of everything that moves in a scene from one frame to the next, draw the moved items in their new locations, and draw whatever was behind the object previously in the location from which the object has moved. If you were to remove the Clear call, XNA would not erase the screen before drawing each frame, and will create some unexpected results.

Frames and Framerates

What's a frame? As mentioned previously, by default, XNA will clear the screen and redraw the scene every time Draw is called. A scene that results from one of these Draw calls is referred to as a *frame*. You can think of a 2D game in XNA as a cartoon flipbook, where you draw a character on one page and then the same character, moved slightly, on the next page, and so forth, so that when you flip through the book the character gives the illusion of moving. XNA does exactly the same thing. Every 16 milliseconds (or 60 times per second), the screen is cleared and a new scene is drawn. When that new scene is drawn with a character in a slightly different position, it gives the illusion that the character is animated.

Multiple frames make up an animation in a game, and the number of frames drawn per second represents something called the *framerate* for the game (e.g., 60 fps = 60 frames drawn every second).

Adding a Sprite to Your Project

All right, I said no more talk, and this time I'm serious. Let's get to it. Your project thus far has been fairly boring. Now, let's draw an image on the screen in your game.

All graphics, sounds, effects, and other items are loaded in XNA through something called the *content pipeline*. Essentially, the content pipeline takes things such as *.jpg* files, *.bmp* files, *.png* files, and other formats, and converts them during compilation to an internal format that's friendly to XNA. It also does similar things with other types of resources, such as sound files, 3D models, fonts, etc., which will be explored later in this book. A great benefit of the XNA Framework is that it takes a lot of the guesswork out of importing different file types. If you put an image file into your game and the content pipeline is able to recognize it during compilation, you don't have to worry about the format of the image. (We'll talk more about the content pipeline in later chapters.)

Download the source code for this chapter and place it somewhere on your PC's hard drive. You'll need to do this so that you can access the images that you'll be adding to your project throughout the rest of this chapter.

Open Visual Studio's Solution Explorer and take a look at your solution. You'll see two projects within your solution: a solution named *Collision* and one named *Collision-Content*. All resources you use in your game (images, sounds, models, etc.) should be added to your solution in the project named *CollisionContent*. Because I'm an organization junkie, I recommend creating a subfolder within the *CollisionContent* project for each content type (images, sounds, etc.) and adding each resource to the appropriate folder. To begin, create a new folder within the *CollisionContent* project by right-clicking that project and selecting Add→New Folder. Name the new folder *Images*. Next, right-click the *CollisionContent\Images* folder in Solution Explorer and select Add→Existing Item (see Figure 3-2).

In the file search dialog that opens, navigate to the *logo.png* file within the source code you downloaded for this chapter. The file will be located in the *BasicSprite \Collision\CollisionContent\Images* folder. Once you've selected an image file, you'll see that item within the *Content\Images* folder in your Solution Explorer. It will also have been copied to your own *<Solution>\CollisionContent\Images* directory on your hard drive.

Building your solution at this point (click Debug→Build Solution) will cause the content pipeline to attempt to compile the image file you just added. If you have no build errors, this means the content pipeline recognized the format of the image and was able to convert it to an XNA internal format, and XNA is ready to load and use your image.

The content pipeline uses an asset name to access content resources. Another way of verifying that your image file is recognized by the content pipeline is to view the properties on the newly added item by right-clicking the item in Solution Explorer and selecting Properties, as shown in Figure 3-3.

As you can see in Figure 3-3, the default asset name of the *logo.png* file that you added is logo, or the name of the file without the extension. By default, all asset names will be the name of the file the asset represents without the file extension.

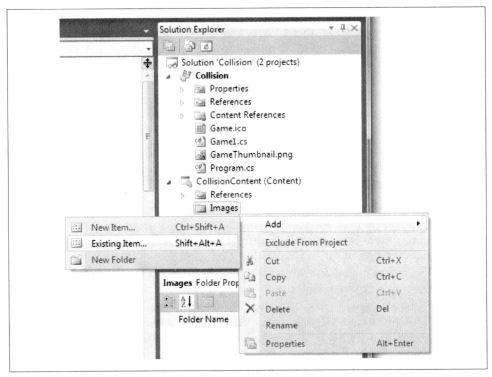

Figure 3-2. Adding an image to your solution

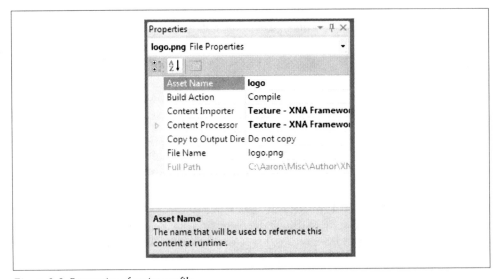

Figure 3-3. Properties of an image file

If you see the `Asset Name` property in the Properties window, you'll know that the content pipeline recognized your image. While you can change the asset names for your resources, the asset names in your project need to be unique. However, asset names need to be unique only within each content folder. This is another benefit of using subfolders within the *CollisionContent* project to organize resources—you can have multiple resources with the same asset name, as long as they are in different folders under the *CollisionContent* project. This may sound like a bad idea that will only complicate things, but it's actually pretty common and very helpful. For example, you may have a font, an effect file, and an image that are all used for an explosion, and it would actually makes things less complicated if you could name them all "Explosion" while keeping them in separate directories dedicated to resources of their respective types.

In Figure 3-3, you may also have noticed two properties below `Asset Name`: `Content Importer` and `Content Processor`. The fact that these properties exist and that they are set to `Texture - XNA Framework` is another sign that the content pipeline has recognized the image that you've added to the project; they are marked as ready to be processed by the content pipeline as *texture* objects. A texture in computer graphics refers to a 2D image that will typically be applied to a surface of some object. We'll be doing exactly that with some image files when we get to the 3D section of this book, but for now we'll be drawing these textures directly onto the screen in a 2D game.

Loading and Drawing Your Sprite

Now that you have an image loaded into your solution that is recognized by the content pipeline, you're ready to draw it on the screen. But before you can access them in code, resources need to be loaded from the content pipeline into variables that you can use to manipulate them.

The default object used to store an image is `Texture2D`. Go ahead and add a `Texture 2D` variable to your game in the *Game1.cs* file near the variable declarations for your `GraphicsDeviceManager` and `SpriteBatch`:

```
Texture2D texture;
```

Now you'll need to load the actual image file into your `Texture2D` variable. To access data from the content pipeline, you use the `Content` property of the `Game` class. This property is of the type `ContentManager` and provides access to all objects loaded in the content pipeline. The `ContentManager` class has a `Load` method that will let you load content into different XNA object formats.

As mentioned previously, all loading of graphics, sounds, and other content resources should be done within the `LoadContent` method. Add the following line to the `LoadContent` method:

```
texture = Content.Load<Texture2D>(@"Images/logo");
```

The parameter passed into the Content.Load method is the path to the image file, starting with the *Content* node in Solution Explorer. When used in relation to strings, the @ symbol causes the string that follows to be interpreted literally, with escape sequences ignored. So, the following two lines of code will create the exact same string:

```
string str1 = @"images\logo";
string str2 = "images\\logo";
```

Notice also in the Content.Load call that the parameter used represents the asset name of the resource, rather than the filename.

The Load method of the ContentManager class is a generic method that requires a type parameter indicating which type of variable you want to access. In this case, you are dealing with an image and are expecting a Texture2D object to be returned.

Your image file is now loaded into the variable texture and is ready for you to use. All drawing in XNA should be done within the Draw method, so add these three lines to your Draw method, after the Clear call:

```
spriteBatch.Begin( );
spriteBatch.Draw(texture, Vector2.Zero, Color.White);
spriteBatch.End( );
```

These three lines of code will draw the image you added to your project in the upper-left corner of the screen. Run your game by selecting Debug→Start Debugging, and you should see something similar to Figure 3-4.

Figure 3-4. The XNA logo image appears in the upper-left corner of the screen

Let's take a look at these three lines of code. The first thing to note is that all three lines use an object called spriteBatch, which is of the type SpriteBatch. This variable is defined in your project when you first create it and is instantiated in the LoadContent method.

Basically, what's happening here is that with the Begin and End calls from the Sprite Batch object, XNA is telling the graphics device that it's going to send it a sprite (or a 2D image). The graphics device will be receiving large amounts of data throughout an XNA game, and the data will be in different formats and types. Whenever you send data to the graphics device, you need to let it know what type of data it is so that it can process it correctly. Therefore, you can't just call SpriteBatch.Draw anytime you want; you first need to let the graphics card know that sprite data is being sent by calling SpriteBatch.Begin.

Your Draw call has three parameters, described in Table 3-1.

Table 3-1. Draw call parameters

Parameter	Type	Description
texture	Texture2D	The Texture2D object that holds the image file you want to draw.
position	Vector2	The position (in 2D coordinates) at which you want to begin drawing the image. The image is always drawn starting from the upper-left corner.
color	Color	The tinting color. Specifying White will not tint the image, whereas specifying any other color will cause the image drawn to be tinted with that color.

Try playing around with the parameters in the Draw call—specifically, with the position and tint color parameters. In 2D, XNA uses the Vector2 struct to define coordinates. Vector2.Zero is a simplified way of specifying a Vector2 with coordinates of 0 for X and Y (i.e., it's the same as saying new Vector2(0,0)).

In 2D XNA games, the X, Y screen coordinate (0, 0) is the upper-left corner of the screen; coordinates move in positive X to the right and positive Y downward.

If you wanted to center your image in the game's window, you'd need to find the center of the window and then offset the upper-left-corner coordinate appropriately. You can find the size of the window by accessing the Window.ClientBounds property of the Game class. When a game is run in Windows, Window.ClientBounds.X and Window. ClientBounds.Y correspond to the upper-left coordinate of the game window, whereas the Width and Height properties of Window.ClientBounds are always equal to the width and height of the window. This is true if the game is running in full-screen or windowed mode. On the Xbox 360 and Windows Phone 7, Window.ClientBounds.X and Y are always 0, while the Width and Height properties of Window.ClientBounds are always equal to the width and height of the display (because Windows Phone 7 and Xbox 360 games are always run in full-screen mode).

Dividing these properties' values by 2 will give you the coordinates for the center of the window. To center your image exactly in the middle of the screen, you'd then need to offset that center coordinate by half the width and height of the image. This is because the position parameter passed to the `Draw` method does not represent the center of the image to be drawn, but rather the upper-left corner of the image. You can access the size of your image via the `Texture2D` variable that holds the image in memory (in this case, `texture`). The `Texture2D` variable has `Width` and `Height` properties that hold the size of the image. Replace your `Draw` call with the one here to see the image centered in the window:

```
spriteBatch.Draw(texture,
    new Vector2(
    (Window.ClientBounds.Width / 2) - (texture.Width / 2),
    (Window.ClientBounds.Height / 2) - (texture.Height / 2)),
    Color.White);
```

Transparency and Other Options

When drawing multiple sprites on the screen, you can (and should, for speed reasons) draw as many of them as possible within one `SpriteBatch` `Begin` and `End` block. In fact, typically you'll want to have one `SpriteBatch` object for your game and draw all your 2D images within that block.

As you saw in Figure 3-4, the XNA logo that I used has a big, ugly white background that would probably look better if it were transparent.

There are two ways to render portions of images transparently: either the image file itself must have a transparent background, or the portion of the image that you want to be transparent must be solid magenta (255, 0, 255) because XNA will automatically render solid magenta as transparent. Transparency can be saved to certain file formats (such as *.png*) that make use of an alpha channel. These formats do not contain only RGB values; instead, each pixel has an additional alpha channel (the *A* in *RGBA*) that determines the transparency of the pixel.

If you have an image-editing tool at your disposal, you can use it to create a transparent background on an image of your choice. Paint.net (*http://paint.net*) is a great free image-editing tool that is actually written in .NET and is available at *http://www.getpaint.net*. For the rest of this example I'll be using another XNA logo image file with a transparent background, which is provided with the source code for this section of the book. The file is named *logo_trans.png*.

Add the transparent XNA logo image to your project in the same way that you added the other image: by right-clicking the *CollisionContent\Images* node in Solution Explorer, selecting Add→Existing Item, and navigating to the *logo_trans.png* file in the Chapter 3 *BasicSprite* source code. The file will be located within the *BasicSprite\Collision\CollisionContent\Images* folder. Don't remove the other XNA logo image from your project, as you'll still be using it to experiment with drawing multiple images.

Once you've added the transparent logo to your project, add another class-level `Texture2D` variable for the new image:

```
Texture2D textureTransparent;
```

Note the asset name of the image file you added, and use it to load the image into your newly added Texture2D variable. Remember that to load the image into your Texture2D variable, you need to use the content pipeline via Content.Load. You should do so in the LoadContent method, by adding the following line:

```
textureTransparent = Content.Load<Texture2D>(@"Images/logo_trans");
```

Now, copy the SpriteBatch.Draw call that used your previous Texture2D variable and paste it on the next line (right above the call to spriteBatch.End). Change the second SpriteBatch.Draw call to use the newly added Texture2D variable (textureTransparent) and change its position coordinate to start drawing in the center of the screen, so that the images are staggered slightly.

Change the background color to Color.Black to make the transparent effect stand out a bit more (do this by changing the color of the Clear call in the Draw method). Your Game1 class should now look something like this:

```
using System;
using System.Collections.Generic;
using System.Linq;
using Microsoft.Xna.Framework;
using Microsoft.Xna.Framework.Audio;
using Microsoft.Xna.Framework.Content;
using Microsoft.Xna.Framework.GamerServices;
using Microsoft.Xna.Framework.Graphics;
using Microsoft.Xna.Framework.Input;
using Microsoft.Xna.Framework.Media;

namespace Collision
{
    /// <summary>
    /// This is the main type for your game
    /// </summary>
    public class Game1 : Microsoft.Xna.Framework.Game
    {
        GraphicsDeviceManager graphics;
        SpriteBatch spriteBatch;
        Texture2D texture;
        Texture2D textureTransparent;

        public Game1()
        {
            graphics = new GraphicsDeviceManager(this);
            Content.RootDirectory = "Content";
        }

        /// <summary>
        /// Allows the game to perform any initialization it needs to before
        /// starting to run. This is where it can query for any required services and
        /// load any non-graphic-related content.  Calling base.Initialize will
        /// enumerate through any components and initialize them as well.
        /// </summary>
```

```csharp
protected override void Initialize()
{
    // TODO: Add your initialization logic here

    base.Initialize();
}

/// <summary>
/// LoadContent will be called once per game and is the place to load
/// all of your content.
/// </summary>
protected override void LoadContent()
{
    // Create a new SpriteBatch, which can be used to draw textures.
    spriteBatch = new SpriteBatch(GraphicsDevice);

    texture = Content.Load<Texture2D>(@"Images/logo");
    textureTransparent = Content.Load<Texture2D>(@"Images/logo_trans");
}

/// <summary>
/// UnloadContent will be called once per game and is the place to unload
/// all content.
/// </summary>
protected override void UnloadContent()
{
    // TODO: Unload any non-ContentManager content here
}

/// <summary>
/// Allows the game to run logic such as updating the world,
/// checking for collisions, gathering input, and playing audio.
/// </summary>
/// <param name="gameTime">Provides a snapshot of timing values.</param>
protected override void Update(GameTime gameTime)
{
    // Allows the game to exit
    if (GamePad.GetState(PlayerIndex.One).Buttons.Back == ButtonState.Pressed)
        this.Exit();

    // TODO: Add your update logic here

    base.Update(gameTime);
}

/// <summary>
/// This is called when the game should draw itself.
/// </summary>
/// <param name="gameTime">Provides a snapshot of timing values.</param>
protected override void Draw(GameTime gameTime)
{
    GraphicsDevice.Clear(Color.CornflowerBlue);

    spriteBatch.Begin();
```

```
            spriteBatch.Draw(texture,
                new Vector2(
                (Window.ClientBounds.Width / 2) - (texture.Width / 2),
                (Window.ClientBounds.Height / 2) - (texture.Height / 2)),
                Color.White);

            spriteBatch.Draw(textureTransparent,
                new Vector2((
                    Window.ClientBounds.Width / 2),
                    (Window.ClientBounds.Height / 2)),
                Color.White);

            spriteBatch.End();

            base.Draw(gameTime);
        }
    }
}
```

Compile and run the game (Debug→Start Debugging), and you should see two images overlapping—one with a transparent background and one with the white block background—as shown in Figure 3-5.

Figure 3-5. Two sprites, one with a transparent background and one without

There are a couple of other drawing options worth noting here. First, you can easily flip images when you draw them and scale them larger or smaller by using an overload of the SpriteBatch.Draw method. To experiment with these options, change the second SpriteBatch.Draw call to the following:

```
spriteBatch.Draw(textureTransparent,
    new Vector2(
    (Window.ClientBounds.Width / 2),
    (Window.ClientBounds.Height / 2)),
    null,
    Color.White,
    0,
    Vector2.Zero,
    1.5f,
    SpriteEffects.FlipHorizontally,
    0);
```

The parameters for this overload are listed in Table 3-2.

Table 3-2. Overloaded Draw method parameters

Parameter	Type	Description
Texture	Texture2D	The texture to be drawn.
Position	Vector2	The coordinate for the upper-left corner of the drawn image.
SourceRectangle	Rectangle	Allows you to draw only a portion of the source image. Use null for now.
Color	Color	The tinting color.
Rotation	float	Rotates the image. Use 0 for now.
Origin	Vector2	Indicates an origin around which to rotate. Use Vector2.Zero for now.
Scale	float	Scales the image. Use 1 to draw the image the same size as the original image. For now, use 1.5f.
Effects	SpriteEffects	Uses the SpriteEffects enum to flip the image horizontally or vertically.
LayerDepth	float	Allows you to specify which images are on top of other images. Use 0 for now.

In this case, you modified the second Draw and applied a scale of 1.5f, which will render the image at 150% of its original size (1.0f = 100% size). You also used the SpriteEffect SpriteEffects.FlipHorizontally to make the image render as flipped in the horizontal direction. Compiling and running your project with the newly modified Sprite Batch.Draw method will display the second XNA logo reversed horizontally and slightly larger than the other XNA logo (Figure 3-6).

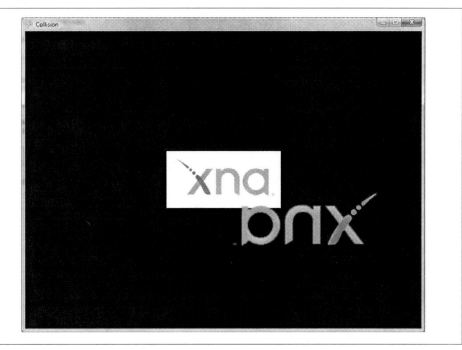

Figure 3-6. Second XNA logo reversed and enlarged

Layer Depth

You may have noticed that the second XNA logo is drawn overlapping the original logo. By default, XNA will draw each image on top of any previously drawn image, but there are some things you can do to affect the order in which images appear on the screen. The ordering of these overlapping images is referred to as the *Z order*, or the *layer depth*, of the images.

You may not care at this point which XNA logo is on top, but sometimes you'll want a certain image to always be on top of other images. For example, in most games, you'll typically want to show the moving characters on top of any background image. One way to do this is to make sure that whatever image you want on top is always drawn last. This method will work, but as the number of images you use in your game increases, organizing and staggering your `Draw` calls to achieve the desired results will become excruciatingly cumbersome.

Thankfully, XNA lets you specify a layer depth for each individual image, which allows you to always place images in the right Z order. To modify the layer depth, you need to convert both `SpriteBatch.Draw` method calls to the overloaded method used in the previous example. Convert your first `Draw` call to this overload as follows:

```
spriteBatch.Draw(texture,
    new Vector2(
    (Window.ClientBounds.Width / 2) - (texture.Width / 2),
    (Window.ClientBounds.Height / 2) - (texture.Height / 2)),
    null,
    Color.White,
    0,
    Vector2.Zero,
    1,
    SpriteEffects.None,
    0);
```

This code will draw your first sprite exactly the same way as the previous `Draw` call, as at this point you aren't passing anything to the extra parameters other than the default values.

However, this particular overload of the `Draw` method accepts a value for the layer depth of the image to be drawn as its final parameter. The layer depth parameter is represented by a float value that must be between 0 and 1. The value 0 corresponds to what XNA calls the *front* of the Z order; the value 1 represents the *back* of the Z order.

If you change the layer depth parameters and run the project as is, you won't see anything changing at this point. This is because you still need to tell XNA that you want it to stagger the images according to their layer depth properties. In order for XNA to recognize the images' layer depth properties, you need to add a parameter to the `SpriteBatch.Begin` method call by using one of the overloads for that method.

Until now you've used an overload of `SpriteBatch.Begin` that requires no parameters, but in order to use layer depth values to sort your images, you need to use an overload of `Begin` that takes a parameter of the type `SpriteSortMode`. The best option here is an overload that requires two parameters, as shown in Table 3-3.

Table 3-3. Parameter list for SpriteBatch.Begin overload

Parameter type	Description
SpriteSortMode	Defines the sorting options of rendered sprites. There are five options:
	• Deferred: sprites are not drawn until SpriteBatch.End is called. Calls are then forwarded to the graphics device in the order in which they were made. Multiple SpriteBatch objects can make Draw calls without conflict in this mode. (This is the default mode.)
	• Immediate: the Begin call immediately sets the graphics device settings and new Draw calls are immediately drawn. Only one SpriteBatch object can be active at a given time. This is the fastest mode.
	• Texture: same as Deferred mode, but sprites are sorted by texture prior to being drawn.
	• BackToFront: same as Deferred mode, but sprites are ordered in front-to-back order based on the layer depth parameter in the Draw call.
	• FrontToBack: same as Deferred mode, but sprites are ordered in back-to-front order based on the layer depth parameter in the Draw call.

Parameter type	Description
BlendState	Determines how sprite colors are blended with background colors. There are four options:

- AlphaBlend: source and destination data are blended using the alpha value. This is the default, and it enables transparency, as discussed earlier. If you have images with transparent backgrounds, you should use AlphaBlend.
- Additive: alpha blend; adds the destination data to the source data without using alpha.
- NonPremultiplied: blends source and destination data using alpha while assuming the color data contains no alpha information.
- Opaque: opaque blend; overwrites the source with the destination data.

Modify your SpriteBatch.Begin method call to include both of these parameters. Set the first parameter to SpriteSortMode.FrontToBack. This option will draw sprites staggered in the order specified by their layer depth properties in the Draw call, with objects whose layer depth values are closer to the front (0) on top of objects whose layer depth properties are closer to the back (1). Because this is a floating-point value, you have a huge number of possible layer depth values to deal with (any valid floating-point number between 0.0 and 1.0). Next, because one of your images uses transparency, set the second parameter to BlendState.AlphaBlend.

The last thing you need to do is change the final parameter of each of the Draw calls to different values, remembering that the values must be in the range 0–1 but can include float values between 0 and 1. Given that your sort mode is FrontToBack, the object that has the smaller layer depth value will be drawn first. Leave the final parameter of the first Draw call 0, and make the final parameter of the second Draw call 1. At this point, your Draw method should look something like this:

```
protected override void Draw(GameTime gameTime)
    {
        GraphicsDevice.Clear(Color.CornflowerBlue);

        spriteBatch.Begin(SpriteSortMode.FrontToBack, BlendState.AlphaBlend);

        spriteBatch.Draw(texture,
            new Vector2(
            (Window.ClientBounds.Width / 2) - (texture.Width / 2),
            (Window.ClientBounds.Height / 2) - (texture.Height / 2)),
            null,
            Color.White,
            0,
            Vector2.Zero,
            1,
            SpriteEffects.None,
            0);

        spriteBatch.Draw(textureTransparent,
            new Vector2(
            (Window.ClientBounds.Width / 2),
            (Window.ClientBounds.Height / 2)),
```

```
                null,
                Color.White,
                0,
                Vector2.Zero,
                1.5f,
                SpriteEffects.FlipHorizontally,
                1);

            spriteBatch.End();

            base.Draw(gameTime);
    }
```

Run the game at this point, and the transparent image will still be on top of the non-transparent image. Next, switch the layer depth values for each image (use 1 for the first image drawn and 0 for the second) and run it again. The transparent image will now display behind the nontransparent image.

Go ahead and play around with different SpriteSortModes, BlendStates, and layer depth parameters to get a feel for how they function in different scenarios.

Let's Move

Drawing different sort modes and layer depths is fun and all, but it really isn't all that exciting. Now, let's make the two images that you've drawn move and bounce off the edges of the screen. To move the objects, you are going to need to change the positions at which they are drawn. Right now, they are both being drawn at constant positions, one with its upper-left corner at the exact center of the window and the other offset from the center so that the image itself is centered in the middle of the screen.

 The code for this section of the chapter is available with the source code for the book under Chapter 3 and is titled *MovingSprites*.

To move something around the screen, you have to modify the position of that object between frames. Therefore, the first thing you need to do is start using a variable in place of the constant values you've been using to specify the objects' positions. Add two class-level Vector2 variable definitions (called pos1 and pos2) at the top of your class, and initialize both objects to Vector2.Zero:

```
Vector2 pos1 = Vector2.Zero;
Vector2 pos2 = Vector2.Zero;
```

You'll also need to have a speed variable for each object. This variable will be used to determine how far you move each object between frames. Add two float variables (called speed1 and speed2) below the Vector2 variables you just added:

```
float speed1 = 2f;
float speed2 = 3f;
```

Now, change the position parameters in each `Draw` method to use `pos1` and `pos2`, respectively. Just to clean things up, set the second `Draw` call's `SpriteEffects` parameter to `SpriteEffects.None` and change the scale parameter (third from the end) from `1.5f` to `1`. This will remove the scaling and horizontal flipping that you implemented previously.

Your two `Draw` calls now should look like this:

```
spriteBatch.Draw(texture,
    pos1,
    null,
    Color.White,
    0,
    Vector2.Zero,
    1,
    SpriteEffects.None,
    0);

spriteBatch.Draw(textureTransparent,
    pos2,
    null,
    Color.White,
    0,
    Vector2.Zero,
    1,
    SpriteEffects.None,
    1);
```

Compiling and running the project at this point will result in both sprites being drawn in the upper-left corner of the window, one on top of the other. Now all you have to do is get the objects to move.

While drawing is handled in the `Draw` method provided in your `Game1` class, all updating of objects (including position, speed, collision detection, artificial intelligence algorithms, etc.) should take place in the `Update` method.

To update the position at which you draw the objects, you need to modify the values of your position variables, `pos1` and `pos2`. Add the following lines of code to your `Update` method in the place of the TODO comment line:

```
pos1.X += speed1;
if (pos1.X > Window.ClientBounds.Width - texture.Width ||
    pos1.X < 0)
    speed1 *= -1;

pos2.Y += speed2;
if (pos2.Y > Window.ClientBounds.Height - textureTransparent.Height ||
    pos2.Y < 0)
    speed2 *= -1;
```

There's nothing too complicated going on here. You update the X property of the pos1 Vector2 object by adding the value in the variable speed1. The if statement that follows checks to see whether the new position will result in placing the image off the right or left edge of the screen. If it is determined that the image will be drawn off the edge of the screen, the value of speed1 is multiplied by –1. The result of that multiplication is that the image reverses direction. The same steps are then taken with the other image, but in the vertical direction rather than horizontally.

Compile and run the project now and you'll see both images moving, one horizontally and the other vertically. Both images "bounce" and reverse direction when they run into the edges of the window, as shown in Figure 3-7.

Figure 3-7. Nothing says excitement like moving, bouncing XNA logos

Animation

As mesmerizing as it is to sit and watch moving, bouncing XNA logos, that's not exactly the reason you're reading this book. Let's get to something a little more exciting by animating some sprites.

The code for this section of the chapter is available with the source code for the book under Chapter 3 and is titled *AnimatedSprites*.

As discussed earlier in this chapter, animation in 2D XNA games is done much like a cartoon flipbook. Animations are made up of a number of standalone images, and flipping through the images in a cycle causes them to appear animated.

Typically, sprite animations are laid out in a single sheet, and you pull out individual images from that sheet and draw them on the screen in a specific order. These sheets are referred to as *sprite sheets*. An example of a sprite sheet is included in the source for this chapter, in the *AnimatedSprites\AnimatedSprites\AnimatedSpritesContent\Images* folder. The sprite sheet is named *threerings.png* and is shown in Figure 3-8.

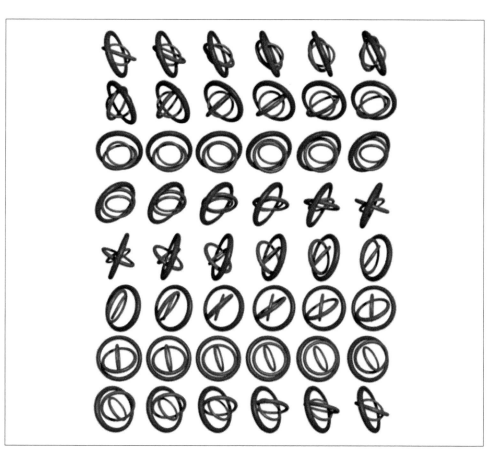

Figure 3-8. Sample sprite sheet (threerings.png)

In each of the previous examples, you have drawn a sprite by loading the image into a `Texture2D` object and then drawing the entire image. With a sprite sheet, you need to be able to load the entire sheet into a `Texture2D` object and then pull out individual sprite frames to draw as you cycle through the animation. The overload for `Sprite Batch.Draw` that you've used in the past few examples has a parameter (the third in the list) that allows you to specify a source rectangle, causing only that portion of the source `Texture2D` object to be drawn. Until now you've specified `null` for that parameter, which tells XNA to draw the entire `Texture2D` image.

To get started with the animation, create a new project (File→New→Project...). In the New Project window, select the Visual C#→XNA Game Studio 4.0 node on the left. On the right, select Windows Game (4.0) as the template for the project. Name the project *AnimatedSprites*.

Once you've created the project, add a subfolder to the *AnimatedSpritesContent* project in Solution Explorer by right-clicking the *AnimatedSpritesContent* project and selecting Add→New Folder. Name the folder *Images*. Next, you'll need to add the image shown previously in Figure 3-8 to your project by right-clicking the new *Content\Images* folder in Solution Explorer and selecting Add→Existing Item.... Navigate to the *threerings.png* image from the previously downloaded Chapter 3 source code from this book (the image is located in the *AnimatedSprites\AnimatedSprites\Animated-SpritesContent\Images* folder).

Load the image into a `Texture2D` object the same way you've done previously with other images. First, add a class-level variable to your `Game1` class:

```
Texture2D texture;
```

Then, add the following line of code to the `LoadContent` method of the `Game1` class:

```
texture = Content.Load<Texture2D>(@"images\threerings");
```

Now that you have the image loaded into a `Texture2D` object, you can begin to figure out how you are going to rotate through the images on the sheet. There are a few things that you'll need to know in order to create an algorithm that will cycle through each image:

- The height and width of each individual image (or frame) in the sprite sheet
- The total number of rows and columns in the sprite sheet
- An index indicating the current row and column of the image in the sprite sheet that should be drawn next

For this particular image, the size of each individual frame is 75 pixels in width × 75 pixels in height. There are six columns and eight rows, and you'll start by drawing the first frame in the sequence. Go ahead and add some class-level variables to reflect this data:

```
Point frameSize = new Point(75, 75);
Point currentFrame = new Point(0, 0);
Point sheetSize = new Point(6, 8);
```

The `Point` struct works well for each of these variables because they all require a datatype that can represent a 2D coordinate (X and Y positions).

Now you're ready to add your `SpriteBatch.Draw` call. You'll use the same `Draw` call that you used in previous examples, with one difference: instead of passing in `null` for the source rectangle in the third parameter of the call, you have to build a source rectangle based on the current frame and the frame size. This can be done with the following code, which should be added to the `Draw` method of your `Game1` class just before the call to `base.Draw`:

```
spriteBatch.Begin(SpriteSortMode.FrontToBack, BlendState.AlphaBlend);

spriteBatch.Draw(texture, Vector2.Zero,
    new Rectangle(currentFrame.X * frameSize.X,
        currentFrame.Y * frameSize.Y,
        frameSize.X,
        frameSize.Y),
    Color.White, 0, Vector2.Zero,
    1, SpriteEffects.None, 0);

spriteBatch.End();
```

If you're confused about the logic used to create the source rectangle, consider this: with a zero-based current frame—meaning that you're initializing your `CurrentFrame` variable to (0, 0) instead of (1, 1), or, in other words, that the upper-left image in your sprite sheet will be referred to as (0, 0) rather than (1, 1)—the X coordinate of the upper-left corner of the current frame will always be the current frame index's X value multiplied by the width of each individual frame. Likewise, the Y coordinate of the upper-left corner of the current frame will always be the current frame index's Y value multiplied by the height of each individual frame.

The width and height values of the source rectangle are always the same, and you can use the frame size X and Y values to represent the width and height of the rectangle.

Next, change the background color to white by changing the color passed to the `GraphicsDevice.Clear` method within the `Draw` method of your `Game1` class. Then, compile and run the project. You should see the first sprite in the three rings sprite sheet being drawn in the upper-left corner of the game window.

The sprite still isn't animating, though, because you are continuously drawing only the first image in the sheet. To get the image to animate, you need to update the current frame index to cycle through the images in the sheet. Where should you add the code to move the current frame index from one frame to the next? Remember that you draw in the `Draw` method, and you do everything else in `Update`. So, add the following code to your `Update` method, before the `base.Update` call:

```
++currentFrame.X;
if (currentFrame.X >= sheetSize.X)
{
    currentFrame.X = 0;
    ++currentFrame.Y;
    if (currentFrame.Y >= sheetSize.Y)
        currentFrame.Y = 0;
}
```

All this code does is increment the X property of the CurrentFrame object and then check to make sure it isn't greater than or equal to the number of frame columns. If it is greater than the number of columns, it resets the X property to 0 and increments the Y value to draw the next row of sprites in the sheet. Finally, if the Y value exceeds the number of rows in the sheet, it resets Y to 0, which starts the entire animation sequence over, starting with frame (0, 0).

Compile and run the project at this point and you should see your three rings image spinning in the upper-left corner of the window, as shown in Figure 3-9.

Figure 3-9. Three spinning rings…nothing better than that!

It's about time you saw the fruits of your efforts in XNA. Although the spinning rings isn't exactly the next great game, it does look really good, and you should be starting to get a sense of how easy XNA is to use and just how powerful it can be. As you can see, by cycling through images in a sprite sheet it becomes fairly straightforward to create any kind of animation that can be drawn in sprite sheet format.

Adjusting the Framerate

Although the three rings animation looks pretty decent when you run the project, there may be a time when your animation runs too quickly or too slowly and you want to change the speed at which it animates.

I mentioned the framerate earlier, but here's a quick reminder: *framerate* generally refers to how many times per second a game redraws the entire scene. In XNA, the default is 60 frames per second (fps) for PC and Xbox360 games, and 30 fps for Windows Phone 7 games. Unless you're running the current project on a very slow machine, you're most likely seeing the three rings image project being drawn at 60 fps.

There is also a different type of framerate, related to individual animations. This framerate (often referred to as the *animation speed*) reflects the rate at which a given animation cycles through images in the sprite sheet. Right now, your animation speed for the three rings image is 60 fps because you are drawing a new image from the sprite sheet every time you redraw the scene (which is happening at 60 fps).

There are a few different ways you can change the animation speed of your three rings animation. XNA's Game class has a property called TargetElapsedTime that tells XNA how long to wait between calls to the Game.Update method. Essentially, this represents the amount of time between each frame being drawn. By default, this is set to 1/60 of a second, which gives XNA the default 60 fps.

To change the framerate of your project, add the following line of code at the end of the Game1 constructor:

```
TargetElapsedTime = new TimeSpan(0, 0, 0, 0, 50);
```

This tells XNA to call Game.Update only every 50 milliseconds, which equates to a framerate of 20 fps. Compile the game and run it, and you should see the same three rings animation, but animating at a much slower speed. Experiment with different values in the TimeSpan constructor (for example, 1 millisecond) and see how fast the animation cycles through the sprite sheet.

Ideally, you'll want to keep the framerate at around 60 fps, which means you can typically leave the default framerate alone. Why is 60 frames per second the standard? This is the minimum refresh rate of a monitor or television set that won't render as flickering when viewed by the human eye.

If you push the framerate too high, XNA can't guarantee that you'll have the kind of performance you're expecting. The speed of the graphics card GPU, the speed of the computer's processor, the number of resources you consume, and the speed of your code all go a long way toward determining whether your game will have that peak performance.

Luckily, XNA has provided a way to detect if your game is suffering from performance issues. The GameTime object, which is passed in as a parameter in both the Update and the Draw methods, has a Boolean property called IsRunningSlowly. You can check this property at any time within those methods; if its value is true, XNA isn't able to keep up with the framerate you have specified. In this case, XNA will actually skip Draw calls in an effort to keep up with your intended speed. This probably isn't the effect that you desire in any game, so if this ever happens you'll probably want to warn the user that her machine is having a hard time keeping up with your game.

Adjusting the Animation Speed

Although adjusting the framerate of the game itself does affect the three rings animation speed, it's not the ideal way to do so. Why is that? When you change the framerate for the project, it will affect the animation speed of all images, including things such as the speed of moving objects and so on. If you wanted one image to animate at 60 fps and another to animate at 30 fps, you wouldn't be able to accomplish that by adjusting the overall game's framerate.

Remove the line you added in the previous section that set the TargetElapsedTime member of the Game1 class, and let's try a different route.

When adjusting a sprite's animation speed, you typically want to do so for that sprite alone. This can be done by building in a way to move to the next frame in the sprite sheet only when a specified time has elapsed. To do this, add two class-level variables, which you'll use to track the time between animation frames:

```
int timeSinceLastFrame = 0;
int millisecondsPerFrame = 50;
```

The timeSinceLastFrame variable will be used to track how much time has passed since the animation frame was changed. The millisecondsPerFrame variable will be used to specify how much time you want to wait before moving the current frame index.

The actual cycling of animation frames happens in your Update method. So, the next step is to check the elapsed time between animation frames and run the code that moves the current frame only if the desired elapsed time has been reached. Modify the code you've added to the Update method to include the surrounding if statement shown here (changes are in bold):

```
timeSinceLastFrame += gameTime.ElapsedGameTime.Milliseconds;
if (timeSinceLastFrame > millisecondsPerFrame)
{   timeSinceLastFrame -= millisecondsPerFrame;
    ++currentFrame.X;
    if (currentFrame.X >= sheetSize.X)
    {
        currentFrame.X = 0;
        ++currentFrame.Y;
        if (currentFrame.Y >= sheetSize.Y)
            currentFrame.Y = 0;
    }
}
```

As you can see here, you use the `gameTime.ElapsedGameTime` property to determine how much time has passed since the previous frame change. This property indicates how much time has passed since the previous call to `Update`. You add the `Milliseconds` property of that object to your `TimeSinceLastFrame` variable. When the value of that variable is greater than the number of milliseconds you want to wait between frame changes, you enter the `if` statement, adjust the `TimeSinceLastFrame` variable by subtracting the value in `MillisecondsPerFrame`, and then change the animation frame.

Compile and run the project now, and you should see the three rings image animating slowly. The important thing to note here is that the animation speed of the three rings is running at a different framerate (20 fps) than the game itself (60 fps). With this method, you're able to run any number of images at different framerates without sacrificing the framerate of your game as a whole.

What You Just Did

Good times are here to stay because you now know how to animate in 2D XNA at will! Let's take a minute and review what you accomplished this chapter:

- You investigated what happens behind the scenes in an XNA game, including the XNA program flow and the XNA game loop.
- You drew your first sprite on the screen.
- You learned a little bit about the content pipeline and its purpose.
- You moved a sprite around the screen.
- You played with sprite transparency, horizontal flipping, and other options.
- You drew sprites in different Z orders based on the layer depth property.
- You drew an animated sprite using a sprite sheet.
- You adjusted the framerate of an XNA game.
- You adjusted the individual animation speed of a sprite.

Summary

- When you create a new XNA project, it has a game loop and program flow built in. The game loop consists of an Update/Draw cycle, whereas the program flow adds steps at which the programmer can set game settings (Initialize), load graphics and sounds and other content (LoadContent), and perform special unload operations (UnloadContent).

- To draw an image on the screen, you need a Texture2D object that will hold the image in memory. The content pipeline prepares the image at compile time by converting it to an internal XNA format. You then use a SpriteBatch object to draw the object on the screen.

- All sprites must be drawn between a SpriteBatch.Begin and a SpriteBatch.End call. These calls inform the graphics device that sprite information is being sent to the card. The Begin method has several overloads that allow you to change the way transparency is handled and the way sprites are sorted.

- Animating sprites typically is done via a sprite sheet (a sheet containing multiple frames of sprite images drawn flipbook-style). Cycling through those images allows the sprite to appear animated.

- The default framerate of an XNA game is 60 fps. Changing that value will affect sprite animations that do not use a separate timer to determine animation speed as well as the overall game speed.

- To adjust the animation speed of an individual sprite, you can set a counter to keep track of the last time you changed frames and change frames only every X number of milliseconds.

- There are only two kinds of pixels on a computer monitor: pixels that have tried to draw an animated sprite of Chuck Norris getting beaten up by a bad guy, and pixels that still work.

Test Your Knowledge: Quiz

1. What are the steps in an XNA game loop?

2. If you wanted to load a Texture2D object, in which method should you do that?

3. What line of code should you use to change the framerate of an XNA game to 20 fps?

4. What should you pass in as the parameter of Content.Load when loading a Texture2D object?

5. Fact or fiction: the content pipeline will let you know at compile time if you add an image to your project that it cannot parse.

6. You're drawing a sprite, and you want the background to be transparent. What steps do you need to take to draw it with a transparent background?

7. You have two sprites (A and B), and when they collide, you always want A to be drawn on top of B. What do you need to do?

8. What are the things you need to keep track of to cycle through a sprite sheet?

9. What was the first television series to command more than $1 million per minute for advertising?

Test Your Knowledge: Exercise

In this chapter, you built an example where two XNA logo images moved around the screen and bounced off the edges. Take the animated sprite example that you built at the end of this chapter, and make the animated sprite move and bounce in a similar fashion—but in this case, make the animated sprite move in both X and Y directions and bounce off of all four edges of the screen.

CHAPTER 4

User Input and Collision Detection

As cool as it was to see a nice-looking set of rings spinning around and realize that you'd made that happen yourself, there's a long way to go with XNA. Although the animated object looked nice, it didn't do anything, and you had no control over its movement. What fun is a game where there's no interaction on the part of the player? In this chapter, we explore user input and collision detection as ways to make your game actually do something besides look nice and pretty.

This chapter uses the code that you built at the end of Chapter 3 (the animated three rings sprite). Open that project and make the changes discussed in this chapter there.

More Sprites

If you're going to have a user-controlled object and build in some collision detection against other objects, you're going to need at least one more object on the screen. Let's add another animated sprite to your project.

Instead of using the same three rings image, we'll use a different image for the second animated sprite. Along with the source code for this book, you'll find the code for this chapter. In the *AnimatedSprites\AnimatedSprites\AnimatedSpritesContent\Images* folder, you'll find an image called *skullball.png*. Add that image file to the project in the same way you've added previous image files (right-click the *Content\Images* folder in Solution Explorer, select Add→Existing Item, and then browse to the *skullball.png* image and add it to the solution).

Next, you'll need to create a number of variables that will allow you to draw and animate the skull ball sprite. These variables should look somewhat familiar to you, as they are very similar to the ones you used in Chapter 3 to draw and animate the three rings sprite. Add the following class-level variables at the top of your Game1 class:

```
Texture2D skullTexture;
Point skullFrameSize = new Point(75, 75);
Point skullCurrentFrame = new Point(0, 0);
Point skullSheetSize = new Point(6, 8);
```

```
int skullTimeSinceLastFrame = 0;
const int skullMillisecondsPerFrame = 50;
```

The skull ball image frames are 75 × 75 pixels, and there are six columns and eight rows in the sprite sheet. You'll want to change the names for the variables you're using in this game to draw and animate the three rings now, to avoid confusion due to having multiple sprites in your game. Add the word "rings" at the beginning of each variable name, and change all the references to those variables; this will help you keep things straight as you move through this chapter. The rings variables should now be declared as:

```
Texture2D ringsTexture;
Point ringsFrameSize = new Point(75, 75);
Point ringsCurrentFrame = new Point(0, 0);
Point ringsSheetSize = new Point(6, 8);
int ringsTimeSinceLastFrame = 0;
int ringsMillisecondsPerFrame = 50;
```

Compile the project and make sure that you don't have any compilation errors due to the renaming of these variables. If you do, remember that the variable names should be the same as in the previous project; you've just added the word "rings" to the beginning of each name. Fix any errors until the game compiles properly.

Chapter 5 will walk you through some basic object-oriented design principles that will make adding new sprites much easier. For now, you just want to get to some user input and collision detection, so let's add the code for the skull ball animation.

Load your skull ball image into the skullTexture variable in the LoadContent method in the same way you loaded your three rings image:

```
skullTexture = Content.Load<Texture2D>(@"Images\skullball");
```

Next, add the code that will move the current frame through the sequence of frames on the sprite sheet. Remember, this is done in the Update method. Because you're already doing this with the three rings sprite, you can just copy the code for the three rings animation and rename the variables to make it work:

```
skullTimeSinceLastFrame += gameTime.ElapsedGameTime.Milliseconds;
if (skullTimeSinceLastFrame > skullMillisecondsPerFrame)
{
    skullTimeSinceLastFrame -= skullMillisecondsPerFrame;
    ++skullCurrentFrame.X;
    if (skullCurrentFrame.X >= skullSheetSize.X)
    {
        skullCurrentFrame.X = 0;
        ++skullCurrentFrame.Y;
        if (skullCurrentFrame.Y >= skullSheetSize.Y)
            skullCurrentFrame.Y = 0;
    }
}
```

Finally, you need to draw the sprite on the screen. Remember that all drawing takes place in the Draw method. Once again, you already have code in that method that draws the three rings sprite, and you can just copy that code and change the variable names to draw the skull ball image. So that the two sprites aren't drawn on top of each other, change the second parameter of the skull ball's Draw call to draw the image at (100, 100) rather than at (0, 0). Your skull ball Draw call should look like this:

```
spriteBatch.Draw(skullTexture, new Vector2(100, 100),
    new Rectangle(skullCurrentFrame.X * skullFrameSize.X,
        skullCurrentFrame.Y * skullFrameSize.Y,
        skullFrameSize.X,
        skullFrameSize.Y),
        Color.White, 0, Vector2.Zero,
        1, SpriteEffects.None, 0);
```

Compile and run the application at this point and you'll see both images animating, as shown in Figure 4-1.

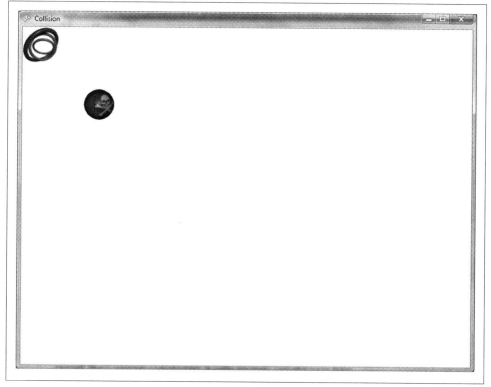

Figure 4-1. Two animated sprites doing their thing

Not bad! In only a few moments, you've added a completely new animated sprite to your game. Software development often yields moments of excitement and accomplishment, but that feeling seems to be amplified with game development because of the added visual (and later auditory) senses involved. These two animating objects look pretty cool, but things are only just getting interesting. Now you'll learn how to control the objects on the screen and give your application some user interaction.

User input in XNA is done via a combination of multiple device options: the keyboard, the mouse, the Xbox 360 controller, Xbox 360 peripherals, and the Windows Phone 7 Series touch screen and accelerometer. Mouse input is never available on the Xbox 360 or Windows Phone 7.

In this chapter, you'll add support for the keyboard, the mouse, and the Xbox 360 controller into your game.

In the previous chapter, we discussed polling versus registering for events. The difference between the two strategies is really never more visible than when dealing with input devices. Traditional Windows programmers are used to registering for events such as key-down events or mouse-move events. With this programming model, the application performs some actions and then, when the application has idle time, the messages are pumped into the application and the events are processed.

In game development, there is no idle time, so it would be too expensive to enable developers to register for events. Instead, it is up to you as the developer to constantly poll input devices asking whether the player has performed any actions on those devices.

That's a slightly different way of looking at input and other messages and events, but once you figure it out, game development will make a lot more sense.

Keyboard Input

Keyboard input is handled via the `Keyboard` class, which is in the `Microsoft.XNA.Frame work.Input` namespace. The `Keyboard` class has a static method called `GetState` that retrieves the current state of the keyboard in the form of a `KeyboardState` structure.

The `KeyboardState` structure contains three key methods that will give you most of the functionality you'll need, as shown in Table 4-1.

Table 4-1. Key methods in the KeyboardState structure

Method	Description
`Keys[] GetPressedKeys( )`	Returns an array of keys pressed at the time of the method call
`bool IsKeyDown(Keys key)`	Returns `true` or `false` depending on whether or not the key represented by the parameter is down at the time of the method call
`bool IsKeyUp(Keys key)`	Returns `true` or `false` depending on whether the key represented by the parameter is up at the time of the method call

As an example of the use of the Keyboard class, if you wanted to check to see whether the "A" key was pressed, you'd use the following line of code:

```
if(Keyboard.GetState( ).IsKeyDown(Keys.A))
    // BAM!!! A is pressed!
```

In this game, you'll modify the code to allow the user to control the three rings sprite, moving it up, down, left, or right with the arrow keys.

The three rings sprite is currently hardcoded to be drawn at (0, 0), but to move it around the screen, you need to be able to change the position at which you draw the sprite. You'll need to use a Vector2 variable to represent the current position at which to draw the three rings sprite. You'll also want to add a variable to represent the speed at which the three rings sprite will move. Because the speed at which you move the three rings sprite won't change during the course of the game, you can make that variable a constant. Add these class-level variables at the top of your class:

```
Vector2 ringsPosition = Vector2.Zero;
const float ringsSpeed = 6;
```

Also, make sure that you change the second parameter of the SpriteBatch.Draw method you're using to draw the three rings sprite to use your new ringsPosition variable rather than the hardcoded position indicated by Vector2.Zero. The second parameter of that Draw method represents the position at which to draw the sprite.

Now you'll need to add code to check whether the up, down, left, or right arrow keys are pressed and, if any of them are, move the sprite's position by changing the value of the ringsPosition variable.

Where should you put the code to check for input? Remember that there are only two methods to choose from when determining where to put certain logic into an XNA game loop: Draw, which is for drawing objects, and Update, which is essentially for everything else (keeping score, moving objects, checking collisions, etc.). So, go ahead and add the following code to the end of your Update method, just before the call to base.Update:

```
KeyboardState keyboardState = Keyboard.GetState( );
if (keyboardState.IsKeyDown(Keys.Left))
    ringsPosition.X -= ringsSpeed;
if (keyboardState.IsKeyDown(Keys.Right))
    ringsPosition.X += ringsSpeed;
if (keyboardState.IsKeyDown(Keys.Up))
    ringsPosition.Y -= ringsSpeed;
if (keyboardState.IsKeyDown(Keys.Down))
    ringsPosition.Y += ringsSpeed;
```

What about the code itself? Wouldn't an if/else statement be more efficient than four if statements? Well, yes, it would. But an if/else statement would only allow you to move in one direction at a time, whereas using four separate if statements allows you to move diagonally as well (for example, combining the up and left key inputs).

Also note that instead of calling the GetState method of the Keyboard class in each if statement, you're calling it only once and then reusing the result from that call. This is because the call to GetState is fairly expensive, and this approach reduces the number of times you have to make that call.

Compile the project and run it. You should see that now you can move your three rings sprite object around the screen, as shown in Figure 4-2.

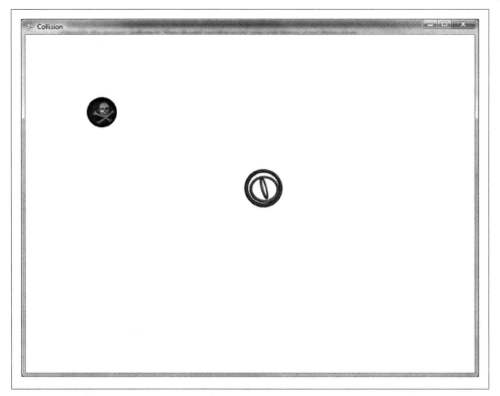

Figure 4-2. Look out—spinning rings on the move!

Mouse Input

XNA provides a Mouse class to interact with the mouse that behaves very similarly to the Keyboard class. The Mouse class also has a GetState method that you can use to get data from the mouse in the form of a MouseState struct. The Mouse class also has another method worthy of note: void SetPosition(int x, int y). This method will— you guessed it—allow you to set the position of the mouse. This position is relative to the upper-left corner of the game window.

The `MouseState` struct has several properties that will help you understand what is happening with the mouse at the particular moment in time when you called `Get State`. These properties are detailed in Table 4-2.

Table 4-2. Important properties of the MouseState struct

Property	Type	Description
LeftButton	Button State	Returns the state of the left mouse button.
MiddleButton	Button State	Returns the state of the middle mouse button.
RightButton	Button State	Returns the state of the right mouse button.
ScrollWheel Value	int	Returns the total accumulated movement of the scroll wheel since the game started. To find out how much the scroll wheel has moved, compare this value to the previous frame's scroll wheel value.
X	int	Returns the value of the horizontal position of the mouse in relation to the upper-left corner of the game window. If the mouse is to the left of the game window, the value is negative. If the mouse is to the right of the game window, the value is greater than the width of the game window.
XButton1	Button State	Returns the state of additional buttons on some mice.
XButton2	Button State	Returns the state of additional buttons on some mice.
Y	int	Returns the value of the vertical position of the mouse in relation to the upper-left corner of the game window. If the mouse is above the game window, the value is negative. If the mouse is below the game window, the value is greater than the height of the game window.

You may have noticed that by default the mouse cursor is hidden when the mouse is dragged over an XNA game window. If you want to display the cursor in an XNA window, you can do so by setting the `IsMouseVisible` property of the `Game` class to `true`.

Regardless of whether or not the mouse is visible, the `MouseState` struct returned from a call to `GetState` will always hold the current state of the mouse device.

Let's make the movement of the mouse control the three rings sprite's movement around the game window. Leave the keyboard controls added in the previous section in place, and you'll end up with multiple ways to control the sprite.

Because the `MouseState`'s X and Y properties tell you the current position of the mouse cursor, you can just assign the position of the three rings sprite to the current position of the mouse.

However, because you're allowing the player to use the keyboard as well, you can't always just set the three rings sprite's position to the position of the mouse. If you did, the three rings sprite would stay where the mouse is, regardless of whether the player moved the mouse.

In order to determine whether the mouse has moved, add a class-level `MouseState` variable at the top of your class:

```
MouseState prevMouseState;
```

This variable will keep track of the mouse state from the previous frame. You'll use it to compare the previous state to the current state of the mouse in each frame. If the values of the `X` and/or `Y` properties are different, you know the player has moved the mouse and you can move the three rings sprite to the new mouse position.

Add the following code to the end of your `Update` method, just before the call to `base.Update`:

```
MouseState mouseState = Mouse.GetState(   );
if(mouseState.X != prevMouseState.X ||
    mouseState.Y != prevMouseState.Y)
    ringsPosition = new Vector2(mouseState.X, mouseState.Y);
prevMouseState = mouseState;
```

This code will move the three rings sprite to the position of the mouse, but only if the mouse has been moved. If you compile and run at this point, you should see that you are now able to control the rings sprite with the mouse or the keyboard.

Gamepad Input

If you're developing a game for Windows, you can still program for an Xbox 360 controller. You'll have to have a wired controller, or you can purchase an Xbox 360 Wireless Receiver for around $20, which will allow you to connect up to four wireless controllers to a PC.

 The wireless Xbox 360 controller actually does come with a wire if you buy the charge pack for that controller. However, there is no data transfer over that cable, so even when it's plugged in, it's still a wireless controller. The cable on the charge pack transfers electricity for the charge and nothing more.

Just as XNA provides a `Mouse` class for mouse input and a `Keyboard` class for keyboard input, it provides a `GamePad` class for reading input from an Xbox 360 gamepad. And yes, that's right, there's a `GetState` method for the `GamePad` class, just as there is for the other devices. There's something to be said for standards, and Microsoft's XNA Framework is, for the most part, a superb example of how standardization across a large-scale system (in this case, a framework and API) can be of such great benefit. Most of the time, you can tell how to use an object just by understanding the type of the object and knowing how similarly typed objects function. That's a tribute to a great design by the XNA team—kudos to them.

The GetState method for the GamePad class accepts an enum parameter called Player Index that indicates which player's controller you want to access, and it returns a GamePadState struct that you can use to get data from the selected controller. Key properties of the GamePadState struct are listed in Table 4-3.

Table 4-3. Key properties of the GamePadState struct

Property	Type	Description
Buttons	GamePadButtons	Returns a struct that tells which buttons are currently pressed. Each button is represented by a ButtonState enum that specifies whether the button is pressed or not pressed.
DPad	GamePadDPad	Returns a struct that tells which directions on the DPad are pressed. The DPad struct has four buttons (up, down, left, and right), each of which is represented by a ButtonState enum that specifies whether the button is pressed or not pressed.
IsConnected	boolean	Indicates whether the controller is currently connected to the Xbox 360.
ThumbSticks	GamePadThumbSticks	Returns a struct that determines the directions of the thumbsticks. Each thumbstick (left and right) is a Vector2 object with X and Y values that have limits of –1 to 1 (e.g., for the left thumbstick, if you push it all the way left, its X value will be –1; if you don't push it at all, the X value will be 0; and if you push it all the way to the right, the X value will be 1).
Triggers	GamePadTriggers	Returns a struct that tells whether the triggers are pressed. The Triggers struct contains two float values (left and right). A value of 0 means the trigger is not pressed at all, whereas a value of 1 means the trigger is fully pressed.

The GamePadState struct contains two methods that will give you most of the functionality you need. These methods are listed in Table 4-4.

Table 4-4. Key methods of the GamePadState struct

Method	Description
bool IsButtonDown(Buttons)	Pass in a button or multiple buttons with a bitwise OR. Returns true if all buttons are down, and false otherwise.
bool IsButtonUp(Buttons)	Pass in a button or multiple buttons with a bitwise OR. Returns true if all buttons are up, and false otherwise.

Looking at the properties in Table 4-3, you'll notice that some of the controls are represented by Boolean or two-state values (either on or off), and others are represented by values that fluctuate between a range of numbers (0 to 1, or –1 to 1). These ranged properties are referred to as *analog controls*, and because they don't have a simple on or off value, they offer more accuracy and more precision in a gaming control. You might have noticed that in some games on an Xbox 360 you can move at different speeds with the triggers or thumbsticks. This is because as you press either button in a given direction, the controller will send a signal to the application in varying strengths. This is an important concept to remember when programming against an Xbox 360 controller and a feature that you'll want to incorporate into games that you develop. We cover how to do that in this section.

All right, let's add some code that will let you control your sprite with your Xbox 360 gamepad. Just as before, leave the code for the mouse and keyboard there, too, and you'll have three ways to control your sprite.

Because the thumbsticks can contain X and Y values ranging from -1 to 1, you'll want to multiply those values of the ThumbSticks property by the ringsSpeed variable. That way, if the thumbstick is pressed all the way in one direction, the sprite will move at full speed in that direction; if the thumbstick is only slightly pushed in one direction, it will move more slowly in that direction.

The following code will adjust your sprite's position according to how much and in which direction the left thumbstick on player one's controller is pressed. Add this code to the Update method, just below the code for the keyboard and mouse input:

```
GamePadState gamepadState = GamePad.GetState(PlayerIndex.One);
ringsPosition.X += ringsSpeed * gamepadState.ThumbSticks.Left.X;
ringsPosition.Y -= ringsSpeed * gamepadState.ThumbSticks.Left.Y;
```

Compile and run the application now, and you'll have full control of your three rings sprite using your Xbox 360 controller.

Let's spice things up a bit. Using an Xbox 360 controller should be a bit more fun than it currently is. Let's add a turbo functionality that doubles your movement speed when active. Of course, when moving so rapidly around the screen in turbo mode, you should feel some vibration in your controller due to the dangerous velocity at which you'll be moving your sprite. You've probably felt the vibrations in an Xbox 360 controller before. This type of mechanism is referred to as *force feedback*, and it can greatly enhance the gameplay experience because it adds yet another sense that pulls the user into the game.

The method SetVibration will set vibration motor speeds for a controller. The method returns a Boolean value indicating whether it was successful (false means that either the controller is disconnected or there is some other problem). The method accepts a player index, and a float value (from 0 to 1) for the left and right motors of the controller. Set the values to zero to stop the controller from vibrating. Anything above zero will vibrate the controller at varying speeds. Modify the code you just added to move the sprite with the Xbox 360 controller to include the following:

```
GamePadState gamepadState = GamePad.GetState(PlayerIndex.One);
if (gamepadState.Buttons.A == ButtonState.Pressed)
{
    ringsPosition.X += ringsSpeed * 2 * gamepadState.ThumbSticks.Left.X;
    ringsPosition.Y -= ringsSpeed * 2 * gamepadState.ThumbSticks.Left.Y;
    GamePad.SetVibration(PlayerIndex.One, 1f, 1f);
}
else
{
    ringsPosition.X += ringsSpeed * gamepadState.ThumbSticks.Left.X;
    ringsPosition.Y -= ringsSpeed * gamepadState.ThumbSticks.Left.Y;
    GamePad.SetVibration(PlayerIndex.One, 0, 0);
}
```

The code first checks to see if the A button on the controller is pressed. If it is, turbo mode is activated, which means that you'll move the sprite at twice the normal speed and activate the vibration mechanism on the controller. If A is not pressed, you deactivate the vibration and move at normal speed.

Compile and run the game to get a sense of how it works.

As you can see, the gamepad adds a different dimension of input and gives a different feel to the game itself. It's a powerful tool, but it won't work well with all game types. Make sure you think about what type of input device is best for the type of game you are creating, because the input mechanism can go a long way toward determining how fun your game is to play.

Keeping the Sprite in the Game Window

You have probably noticed that the rings sprite will disappear off the edge of the screen if you move it far enough. It's never a good idea to have the player controlling an object that is offscreen and unseen. To rectify this, update the position of the sprite at the end of the Update method. If the sprite has moved too far to the left or the right or too far up or down, correct its position to keep it in the game window. Add the following code at the end of the Update method, just before the call to base.Update:

```
if (ringsPosition.X < 0)
    ringsPosition.X = 0;
if (ringsPosition.Y < 0)
    ringsPosition.Y = 0;
if (ringsPosition.X > Window.ClientBounds.Width - ringsFrameSize.X)
    ringsPosition.X = Window.ClientBounds.Width - ringsFrameSize.X;
if (ringsPosition.Y > Window.ClientBounds.Height - ringsFrameSize.Y)
    ringsPosition.Y = Window.ClientBounds.Height - ringsFrameSize.Y;
```

Compile and run the game at this point, and you should be able to move the rings sprite around the screen just as before; however, it should always stay within the game window rather than disappearing off the edge of the screen.

Collision Detection

So, you have a pretty good thing going thus far. Players can interact with your game and move the three rings around the screen—but still there's not a lot to do. You need to add some collision detection in order to take the next step.

Collision detection is a critical component of almost any game. Have you ever played a shooter game where you seem to hit your target but nothing happens? Or a racing game where you seem to be far away from a wall but you hit it anyway? This kind of gameplay is infuriating to players, and it's a result of poorly implemented collision detection.

Collision detection can definitely make or break a gameplay experience. The reason it's such a make-or-break issue is because the more precise and accurate you make your collision-detection algorithms, the slower your gameplay becomes. There is a clear trade-off between accuracy and performance when it comes to collision detection.

One of the simplest and fastest ways to implement collision detection is through the bounding-box algorithm. Essentially, when using a bounding-box algorithm, you "draw" a box around each object on the screen and then check to see whether the boxes themselves intersect. If they do, you have a collision. Figure 4-3 shows the three rings and skull ball sprites with these invisible boxes surrounding the two objects.

Figure 4-3. Bounding boxes around your objects

To implement the bounding-box algorithm in the current game, you'll need to create a rectangle for each sprite based on the position of the sprite and the width and height of the frames for that sprite. The code will make more sense if you change the position of the skull ball sprite to a variable, as you've done with the rings sprite. Add the following class-level variable, which will be used to hold the position of the skull ball sprite. Also, initialize the variable to the value that you're currently setting as the position of the sprite when you draw it, (100, 100):

```
Vector2 skullPosition = new Vector2(100, 100);
```

Next, pass the `skullPosition` variable as the second parameter to the `sprite Batch.Draw` call where you actually draw the skull ball.

OK, now that you have a variable representing the position of the skull ball sprite, you can create a rectangle using that variable and the size of the skull ball frame and check to see whether it intersects with a similarly created rectangle for the rings sprite.

Add the following method to your Game1 class, which will create rectangles for each sprite using the XNA Framework Rectangle struct. The Rectangle struct has a method called Intersects that can be used to determine whether two rectangles intersect:

```
protected bool Collide( )
{
    Rectangle ringsRect = new Rectangle((int)ringsPosition.X,
        (int)ringsPosition.Y, ringsFrameSize.X, ringsFrameSize.Y);
    Rectangle skullRect = new Rectangle((int)skullPosition.X,
        (int)skullPosition.Y, skullFrameSize.X, skullFrameSize.Y);

    return ringsRect.Intersects(skullRect);

}
```

Next, you need to use the new Collide method to determine whether the objects have collided. If so, you'll want to perform some action. In this case, you're just going to close down the game by calling the Exit method if the sprites collide. Obviously, this isn't something you'd want to do in a real game, because just quitting the game when something like a collision occurs will seem like a bug to a player. But because we just want to see collision detection in action, this will work for now.

Add the following code to the end of your Update method, just before the call to base.Update:

```
if (Collide( ))
    Exit( );
```

Compile and run the game. If you move your rings object too close to the ball, the application will shut down.

You may notice that the ball and the rings never actually touch. Any idea why this is? If you look at the sprite sheet for the rings (see Figure 4-4), you'll see that there's a fair amount of space between the images of each frame. The distance is compounded even further when the large ring rotates horizontally. All that whitespace gets added to the collision check because you're using your frame size variable as the size of the object when building the rectangle for your collision check.

One way to rectify this is to adjust your sprite sheet to not have so much whitespace. Another way is to create a smaller rectangle for use in the collision detection. This smaller rectangle must be centered on the sprite and therefore needs to be offset slightly from each edge of the actual frame.

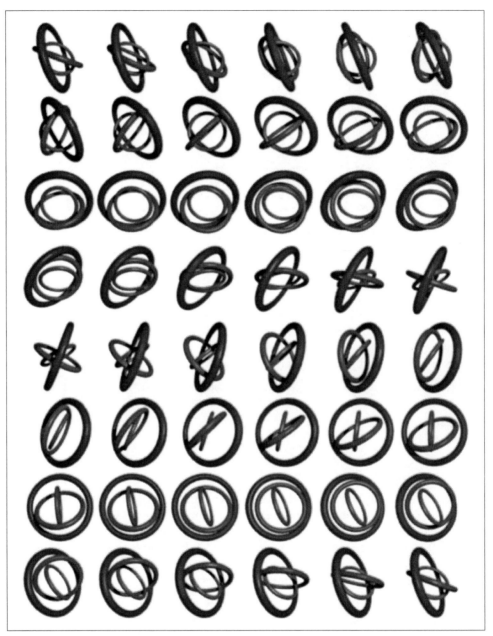

Figure 4-4. All the whitespace in the rings image creates a less-than-accurate collision check when using the frame size for collision detection

To create a smaller rectangle, define an offset variable for each sprite, which will indicate how much smaller in each direction the collision check rectangle is than the overall frame. Add these two class-level variables to your project:

```
int ringsCollisionRectOffset = 10;
int skullCollisionRectOffset = 10;
```

Next, you'll use these variables to construct a rectangle that is slightly smaller than the actual frame size. Adjust your Collide method as shown here, and you'll have more accurate collision detection:

```
protected bool Collide(  )
{
    Rectangle ringsRect = new Rectangle(
        (int)ringsPosition.X + ringsCollisionRectOffset,
        (int)ringsPosition.Y + ringsCollisionRectOffset,
        ringsFrameSize.X - (ringsCollisionRectOffset * 2),
        ringsFrameSize.Y - (ringsCollisionRectOffset * 2));
    Rectangle skullRect = new Rectangle(
        (int)skullPosition.X + skullCollisionRectOffset,
        (int)skullPosition.Y + skullCollisionRectOffset,
        skullFrameSize.X - (skullCollisionRectOffset * 2),
        skullFrameSize.Y - (skullCollisionRectOffset * 2));

    return ringsRect.Intersects(skullRect);

}
```

Compile and run the game to try out the new collision detection. It should be much more accurate using this method.

 There is a closely related algorithm that uses a sphere instead of a box. You could use that here as well, especially given that your current objects are circular; however, you'll be using some noncircular objects in future chapters, so stick with the bounding-box method for now.

Even now that you've fine-tuned the algorithm a bit, running the application will show that the collision detection is not 100% accurate. In this limited test, the deficiencies are easy to see. The goal in any game, however, is not necessarily to get collision detection 100% accurate, but rather to get it accurate to the point where the player won't know the difference.

This may sound like cheating, but in reality, it boils down to a performance issue. For example, let's say you're working with a sprite that's not circular, such as an airplane. Drawing a single box around an airplane will yield some very inaccurate collision detection. You can get around that by adding multiple, smaller boxes to your airplane and checking for collisions between each of these smaller boxes and any other object in the game. Such a bounding-box layout is shown in Figure 4-5.

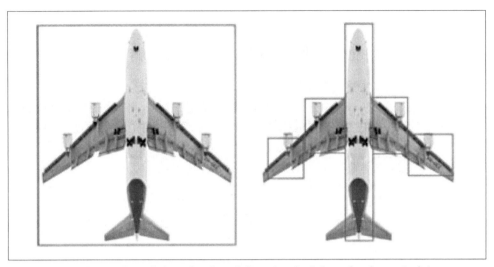

Figure 4-5. Airplane with single bounding box (left) and multiple bounding boxes (right)

The example on the left will be fairly inaccurate, whereas the one on the right will greatly improve the accuracy of the algorithm. But what problem will you run into? Let's say you have two planes in your game and you want to see whether they collide. Instead of one set of calculations for the two planes, you now have to compare each box in each plane against each box in the opposite plane. That's 25 sets of calculations to compare two planes! If you added more planes to your code, the calculations required would go up exponentially and could eventually affect the speed of your game.

There is a way to improve performance by merging the two methods. That is, you can first check for collisions against objects using a box surrounding the entire object, such as the one shown on the left in Figure 4-5. Then, if that collision check comes back as a potential collision, you can dig deeper into the subboxes like the ones on the right in Figure 4-5 and compare those boxes for collisions.

You can tell that collision detection really is a balancing act between performance and accuracy. In spite of all the extra effort, even collision checks made with all the boxes surrounding the plane on the right side of Figure 4-5 won't be 100% accurate. The goal once again is to make the collision-detection close enough to not adversely affect game-play or performance.

There is yet another way to speed up collision detection that I should mention. Dividing the game window into a grid-based coordinate system allows you to do a very simple check to determine whether two objects are even close enough to warrant running a collision check. If you keep track of the current grid cell in which each object is positioned, you can check to make sure one object is in the same grid cell as another object before running the collision-detection algorithm on those two objects. This method will save a good number of calculations in each frame and can also positively affect the speed of the game.

What You Just Did

Great job! You have some cool animation, and now you're checking for collisions while moving the sprites around the screen. Very impressive. Here's a recap of what you did in this chapter:

- You implemented a sprite controlled by a user via a keyboard, a mouse, and an Xbox 360 gamepad.
- You implemented force feedback using the Xbox 360 controller.
- You implemented collision detection for two animated sprites.
- You learned about the balance between accuracy and performance in collision detection.

Summary

- Input devices supported in XNA include the keyboard, mouse, and Xbox 360 controller.
- The Xbox 360 has several analog inputs that allow for varying degrees of input from a single button.
- Collision detection is a constant balance between performance and accuracy. The more accurate an algorithm is, the more of a performance hit is usually incurred.
- The bounding-box algorithm for collision detection is one of the simplest and most straightforward algorithms. If you "draw" an imaginary box around each object, you can easily tell which box is colliding with another box.
- You can speed up collision detection while improving accuracy by combining methods. Use a large box to determine whether it's worth the time to check the smaller boxes surrounding sections of an object, or implement a grid-based system to avoid unnecessary collision checks between objects that are not close together.
- Do you notice anything that tyrannical dictators, drug lords, and gangbangers have in common? That's right, typically they don't use XNA. That's proof right there that XNA spreads world peace. Make XNA, not war.

Test Your Knowledge: Quiz

1. What object is used to read input from a mouse?
2. Fact or fiction: the X and Y coordinates from a mouse as read in an XNA application represent how much the mouse has moved since the previous frame.
3. What is the difference between an analog input control and a digital input control?
4. Describe the bounding-box collision-detection algorithm.

5. Describe the pros and cons of the bounding-box collision-detection algorithm.

6. What is the ratio of unicorns to leprechauns?

Test Your Knowledge: Exercise

Let's combine some aspects of this chapter and the previous one. Take the code where we left off at the end of this chapter and modify it to include another nonuser-controlled sprite (use the *plus.png* image, which is located with the source code for this chapter in the *AnimatedSprites\AnimatedSprites\AnimatedSpritesContent\Images* folder). Add movement to both nonuser-controlled sprites, as you did in Chapter 3, so that each sprite moves in both the X and Y directions and bounces off the edges of the screen. Add collision detection to the newly added sprite as well. The end result will be a game where you try to avoid two moving sprites. When you hit either sprite, the game ends.

For clarity in working with the *plus.png* image, the frame size of the sprite sheet is 75 × 75 pixels, and it has six columns and four rows (note that the rings and skull ball sprite sheets each had six columns and eight rows).

Applying Some Object-Oriented Design

Congratulations! You built the beginnings of a rudimentary game at the end of the previous chapter. You're making some real progress here. However, the way that we've done things thus far, though good for educational purposes, is very inefficient from a design standpoint. A sound design will always increase development efficiency.

You probably noticed how painful it was to add a new sprite object to your project. Especially if you need to add an object that will animate, use collision detection, and move, there are a lot of variables and other code that must be duplicated, and as a result your code is becoming quite a mess. If you continue down this path, things will quickly get out of hand. So, let's take a few minutes to apply some sound object-oriented design to your system. This will make things a lot easier for you down the road.

Designing Your Classes

If you were doing serious game development, you'd want to expand further on the design in this chapter and fine-tune it to meet your needs. We don't have time to tweak your design to how you'd want it for a commercial-quality application, but there are some changes you can make that will result in a huge improvement over what you have thus far.

First things first, let's look at your objects. The basic visual object in a 2D game is a sprite. Based on the code you put together in previous chapters, you have two different types of objects: objects that are controlled by the player, and objects that are not. Aside from that, all other functionality of the animated sprites you've worked on thus far is exactly the same.

Think about what type of functionality those two objects share. They both get drawn on the screen, and they both animate using a sprite sheet. Thinking about that more in depth, you'd probably agree that all animated sprites will have those two functional elements. Based on that logic, it would make sense to create a base class that represents a standard sprite and has the ability to draw itself and animate via a sprite sheet. For more customized functionality, you could then look at deriving from that base class to create classes with added behavior. Based on the examples you've run through thus far, you can anticipate that your class hierarchy eventually will look something like the image in Figure 5-1.

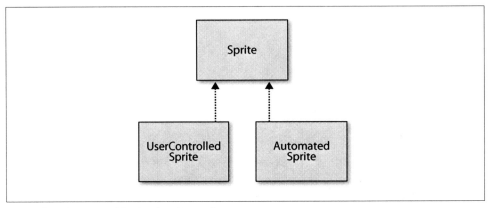

Figure 5-1. Anticipated Sprite class hierarchy

Creating a Sprite Class

Now you can go ahead and get started on your `Sprite` base class. What might you want to include in that class? Table 5-1 lists the members, and Table 5-2 lists the methods.

Table 5-1. Members of your Sprite class

Member	Type	Description
textureImage	Texture2D	Sprite or sprite sheet of image being drawn
position	Vector2	Position at which to draw sprite
frameSize	Point	Size of each individual frame in sprite sheet
collisionOffset	int	Offset used to modify frame-size rectangle for collision checks against this sprite
currentFrame	Point	Index of current frame in sprite sheet
sheetSize	Point	Number of columns/rows in sprite sheet
timeSinceLastFrame	int	Number of milliseconds since last frame was drawn
millisecondsPerFrame	int	Number of milliseconds to wait between frame changes
speed	Vector2	Speed at which sprite will move in both X and Y directions

Table 5-2. Methods of your Sprite class

Method	Return type	Description
Sprite(...) (multiple constructors)	Constructor	Sprite constructor method
Update(GameTime, Rectangle)	void	Handles all collision checks, movement, user input, and so on
Draw(GameTime, SpriteBatch)	void	Draws the sprite

This chapter will build upon the code that you created in Chapter 4. Open the code from that chapter and add a new class to your project by right-clicking on the project in Solution Explorer and selecting Add→Class. Name the new class file *Sprite.cs*.

Because you'll probably never find a reason to create an instance of the Sprite class, it makes sense to mark the class as abstract, forcing you to use one of the derived classes to instantiate objects. Make the base Sprite class abstract by adding the keyword abstract to the definition of the class:

```
abstract class Sprite
```

Add two XNA namespaces to your new class, which you'll need to enable the use of XNA objects:

```
using Microsoft.Xna.Framework;
using Microsoft.Xna.Framework.Graphics;
```

Then, add the following variables, which correspond to the members of the class shown in Table 5-1. Make sure you mark the protected variables appropriately, or the subclasses you build later will not work properly:

```
Texture2D textureImage;
protected Point frameSize;
Point currentFrame;
Point sheetSize;
int collisionOffset;
int timeSinceLastFrame = 0;
int millisecondsPerFrame;
const int defaultMillisecondsPerFrame = 16;
protected Vector2 speed;
protected Vector2 position;
```

In addition to the variables listed in Table 5-1, you're defining a constant that will represent the default animation speed if no animation speed is specified.

Next, add the two constructors, as follows:

```
public Sprite(Texture2D textureImage, Vector2 position, Point frameSize,
    int collisionOffset, Point currentFrame, Point sheetSize, Vector2 speed)
    : this(textureImage, position, frameSize, collisionOffset, currentFrame,
    sheetSize, speed, defaultMillisecondsPerFrame)
{
}
```

```
public Sprite(Texture2D textureImage, Vector2 position, Point frameSize,
    int collisionOffset, Point currentFrame, Point sheetSize, Vector2 speed,
    int millisecondsPerFrame)
{
    this.textureImage = textureImage;
    this.position = position;
    this.frameSize = frameSize;
    this.collisionOffset = collisionOffset;
    this.currentFrame = currentFrame;
    this.sheetSize = sheetSize;
    this.speed = speed;
    this.millisecondsPerFrame = millisecondsPerFrame;
}
```

The only difference between the two constructors is that the second one requires a
millisecondsPerFrame variable, used to calculate the animation speed. Hence, the first
constructor will just call the second constructor (using the this keyword) and pass to
that constructor all of its parameters, as well as the constant representing the default
animation speed.

At a minimum, all animated sprites do two things: animate by moving a current frame
index through the images on a sprite sheet, and draw the current image from the animation on the screen. Beyond that, you might want to add additional functionality to
this class, or you may prefer to add it to a derived class to create a more specialized
object. At the very least, though, you'll want to animate and draw in all animated
sprites, so let's add the functionality to do that in the base Sprite class.

You've already written the code to animate and draw in previous chapters. All you need
to do now is take that same code, which uses variables from the Game1 class, and apply
it to the variables that you've defined in your Sprite base class. Once again, to perform
the animation, all you do is move a current frame index through a sprite sheet, making
sure to reset the index once it's passed through the entire sheet.

The following code, which should be familiar from previous chapters, does just that.
Code the Update method of your Sprite base class as follows:

```
public virtual void Update(GameTime gameTime, Rectangle clientBounds)
{
    timeSinceLastFrame += gameTime.ElapsedGameTime.Milliseconds;
    if (timeSinceLastFrame > millisecondsPerFrame)
    {
        timeSinceLastFrame = 0;
        ++currentFrame.X;
        if (currentFrame.X >= sheetSize.X)
        {
            currentFrame.X = 0;
            ++currentFrame.Y;
            if (currentFrame.Y >= sheetSize.Y)
                currentFrame.Y = 0;
        }
    }
}
```

You probably noticed the keyword virtual in the method declaration. This marks the method itself as virtual, which enables you to create overrides for this method in subclasses so you can modify its functionality in those classes if needed.

You may also have noticed the Rectangle parameter. This parameter represents the game window's client rectangle and will be used to detect when objects cross the edges of the game window.

Just as you've previously written code for animation, you've also already written code to draw a single frame of an animated sprite. Now you just need to take that code and plug it into your Sprite class, changing it to use the variables you've defined here.

The one difference between the drawing code from previous chapters and the code you need to add to your Sprite class is that in this case you have no access to a Sprite Batch object (which, as you hopefully remember, is required to draw Texture2D objects). To get around that, you need to accept a GameTime parameter and add a SpriteBatch parameter to the Draw method of your Sprite base class.

Your Sprite base class's Draw method should look something like this:

```
public virtual void Draw(GameTime gameTime, SpriteBatch spriteBatch)
{
    spriteBatch.Draw(textureImage,
        position,
        new Rectangle(currentFrame.X * frameSize.X,
            currentFrame.Y * frameSize.Y,
            frameSize.X, frameSize.Y),
        Color.White, 0, Vector2.Zero,
        1f, SpriteEffects.None, 0);
}
```

In addition to the Update and Draw methods, you're going to want to add a property to this class that represents the direction in which this sprite is moving. The direction will always be a Vector2, indicating movement in the X and Y directions, but it will also always be defined by the subclasses (i.e., automated sprites will move differently than user-controlled sprites). So, this property needs to exist in the base class, but it should be abstract, meaning that in the base class it has no body and therefore must be defined in all subclasses.

Add the abstract direction property to the base class as follows:

```
public abstract Vector2 direction
{
    get;
}
```

There's one more thing to add to your Sprite base class: a property that returns a rectangle that can be used for collision detection. Add the following property to your Sprite class:

```
public Rectangle collisionRect
{
```

```
    get
    {
        return new Rectangle(
            (int)position.X + collisionOffset,
            (int)position.Y + collisionOffset,
            frameSize.X - (collisionOffset * 2),
            frameSize.Y - (collisionOffset * 2));
    }
}
```

Your base class is pretty well ironed out at this point. The class will draw itself via the
Draw method and will cycle through a sprite sheet via the Update method. So, let's turn
our attention to the user-controlled sprite for a moment.

Creating a User-Controlled Sprite Class

Now you'll create a class that derives from your base Sprite class, adding functionality
to let the user control the sprite. Add a new class to your project by right-clicking on
the project in Solution Explorer and selecting Add→Class. Name the new class file
UserControlledSprite.cs. Once the file is ready, mark this class as a subclass of the
Sprite class:

```
class UserControlledSprite: Sprite
```

Next, you'll need to add some XNA using statements. Use the same ones as you did in
the Sprite base class, plus an additional one (Microsoft.Xna.Framework.Input) that will
allow you to read data from input devices:

```
using Microsoft.Xna.Framework;
using Microsoft.Xna.Framework.Graphics;
using Microsoft.Xna.Framework.Input;
```

Next, add the constructors for the UserControlledSprite class. These will be basically
the same as the constructors for the Sprite class and will just pass the parameters on
to the base class:

```
public UserControlledSprite(Texture2D textureImage, Vector2 position,
    Point frameSize, int collisionOffset, Point currentFrame, Point sheetSize,
    Vector2 speed)
    : base(textureImage, position, frameSize, collisionOffset, currentFrame,
    sheetSize, speed)
{
}


public UserControlledSprite(Texture2D textureImage, Vector2 position,
    Point frameSize, int collisionOffset, Point currentFrame, Point sheetSize,
    Vector2 speed, int millisecondsPerFrame)
    : base(textureImage, position, frameSize, collisionOffset, currentFrame,
    sheetSize, speed, millisecondsPerFrame)
{
}
```

Then, you need to add the code for the overloaded direction property. The direction property will be used in the Update method to modify the position of the sprite (or in other words, to move the sprite in the direction indicated by this property). Direction in the case of the UserControlledSprite class will be defined as a combination of the speed member of the base class and the direction in which the player is pressing the gamepad's left thumbstick, or the arrow keys the user is pressing.

Users will also be able to control the sprite using the mouse, but mouse input will be handled a bit differently. When the mouse is being used to control the sprite, you are going to move the sprite to the position of the mouse on the screen. So, there's really no need for a direction property when dealing with mouse movement. This property, therefore, will reflect player input only from the keyboard or the Xbox 360 gamepad. To build the direction property from the data read from the thumbstick and keyboard, code the property as follows:

```
public override Vector2 direction
{
    get
    {
        Vector2 inputDirection = Vector2.Zero;

        if (Keyboard.GetState(  ).IsKeyDown(Keys.Left))
            inputDirection.X -= 1;
        if (Keyboard.GetState(  ).IsKeyDown(Keys.Right))
            inputDirection.X += 1;
        if (Keyboard.GetState(  ).IsKeyDown(Keys.Up))
            inputDirection.Y -= 1;
        if (Keyboard.GetState(  ).IsKeyDown(Keys.Down))
            inputDirection.Y += 1;

        GamePadState gamepadState = GamePad.GetState(PlayerIndex.One);
        if(gamepadState.ThumbSticks.Left.X != 0)
            inputDirection.X += gamepadState.ThumbSticks.Left.X;
        if(gamepadState.ThumbSticks.Left.Y != 0)
            inputDirection.Y -= gamepadState.ThumbSticks.Left.Y;

        return inputDirection * speed;
    }
}
```

This property will return a Vector2 value indicating the movement direction (in the X and Y planes), multiplied by the speed member of the base class. Notice that the keyboard and gamepad inputs are combined, allowing the player to control the sprite with either input device.

To deal with mouse movement, you're essentially going to detect whether the mouse has moved from frame to frame. If so, you'll assume that the user wants to control the sprite with the mouse, and move the sprite to the location of the mouse cursor. If the mouse does not move from one frame to another, the keyboard and gamepad input will affect the movement of the sprite.

To determine whether the mouse has moved from one frame to the next, add the following class-level variable to your `UserControlledSprite` class:

```
MouseState prevMouseState;
```

Now you can go ahead and code the `Update` method of your `UserControlledSprite` class. You'll need to override the `Update` method from the base class and add to that method the code that will move the sprite based on the `direction` property as well as mouse movement (if the mouse has been moved). In addition, you'll add some logic in that method to keep the user-controlled sprite in play if the sprite is moved off the screen. Your `Update` method should look like this:

```
public override void Update(GameTime gameTime, Rectangle clientBounds)
{
    // Move the sprite based on direction
    position += direction;

    // If player moved the mouse, move the sprite
    MouseState currMouseState = Mouse.GetState();
    if (currMouseState.X != prevMouseState.X ||
        currMouseState.Y != prevMouseState.Y)
    {
        position = new Vector2(currMouseState.X, currMouseState.Y);
    }
    prevMouseState = currMouseState;

    // If sprite is off the screen, move it back within the game window
    if (position.X < 0)
        position.X = 0;
    if (position.Y < 0)
        position.Y = 0;
    if (position.X > clientBounds.Width - frameSize.X)
        position.X = clientBounds.Width - frameSize.X;
    if (position.Y > clientBounds.Height - frameSize.Y)
        position.Y = clientBounds.Height - frameSize.Y;

    base.Update(gameTime, clientBounds);
}
```

There you have it. Your `UserControlledSprite` class is ready to go! You don't have to do anything with the `Draw` method in this class, because your base class will take care of drawing the individual frames of your sprite. Nice job!

Creating an Automated Sprite Class

Now that you have a class that allows the user to control a sprite, it's time to add a class that will generate an animated sprite that moves on its own. Add a new class to your project by right-clicking on the project in Solution Explorer and selecting Add→Class. Name the class file *AutomatedSprite.cs*. Once the file is ready, mark the new class as a subclass of your `Sprite` class:

```
class AutomatedSprite: Sprite
```

Add the same XNA namespaces as before, but without the input namespace because you won't be gathering input from any devices in this class:

```
using Microsoft.Xna.Framework;
using Microsoft.Xna.Framework.Graphics;
```

Next, add two constructors for the AutomatedSprite class. These constructors will be identical to the ones used for the UserControlledSprite class:

```
public AutomatedSprite(Texture2D textureImage, Vector2 position, Point frameSize,
    int collisionOffset, Point currentFrame, Point sheetSize, Vector2 speed)
    : base(textureImage, position, frameSize, collisionOffset, currentFrame,
    sheetSize, speed)
{
}

public AutomatedSprite(Texture2D textureImage, Vector2 position, Point frameSize,
    int collisionOffset, Point currentFrame, Point sheetSize, Vector2 speed,
    int millisecondsPerFrame)
    : base(textureImage, position, frameSize, collisionOffset, currentFrame,
    sheetSize, speed, millisecondsPerFrame)
{
}
```

Your automated sprite will use the speed member of the base class to move around the screen. This will be done through an overridden direction property because that property is abstract in the base class and therefore must be defined in this class. Create the override for the direction property as follows:

```
public override Vector2 direction
{
    get { return speed; }
}
```

Now you need to add the code that will make your automated sprite move. Because the direction property is represented by a Vector2 value, this property represents direction and speed for your automated sprite. Any direction in 2D space can be represented by a Vector2 value, and the magnitude (or length) of that vector indicates the speed of the object: the longer the vector is, the faster the automated sprite will move.

All you have to do is add the vector represented by the direction property to the position of your sprite, and the sprite will move in the direction of that vector at the speed indicated by the length of that vector. An illustration of how this vector math works is shown in Figure 5-2.

Add to your AutomatedSprite class an overridden Update method that will move the sprite based on the direction property:

```
public override void Update(GameTime gameTime, Rectangle clientBounds)
{
    position += direction;

    base.Update(gameTime, clientBounds);
}
```

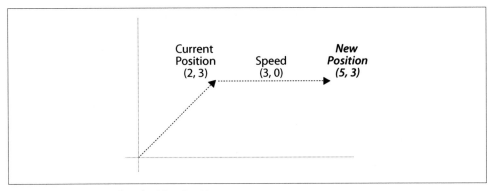

Figure 5-2. Position + Speed = New Position

That's all there is to it! You now have an automated sprite class that will draw itself and update its position based on a 2D vector.

Artificial Intelligence?

So, this sprite is moving by itself—but is that what we call artificial intelligence? Well, what is artificial intelligence? That's a tough question. Artificial intelligence refers to the science of making a computer act as if it is intelligent. The problem with that definition is that there really is no clear definition of intelligence. Therefore, it's extremely difficult to define artificial intelligence.

The class you've just coded allows your sprite to move on its own, so you could argue that you've just created an artificial intelligence algorithm—a very weak and unimpressive one, but an artificial intelligence algorithm nonetheless. On the other hand, you could argue that your sprite is no more intelligent than a bullet flying through the air, because all it does is move in a constant direction with a constant velocity. And not many people would argue that bullets are intelligent!

In later chapters, we look at different ways to make your automated sprites and 3D objects act more and more intelligent, but in the meantime, intelligent or not, you've made a good start.

So far you have two different types of sprites, both deriving from a base class representing a generic animated sprite. In previous chapters, when you wanted to add a new sprite you had to add a number of variables and different settings to implement that new sprite. With this model, you can add a new sprite to your application with the addition of one new variable (either an `AutomatedSprite` or a `UserControlledSprite`).

However, thinking beyond just adding a few variables here and there for different sprites, let's look at a more modular approach. XNA provides us with a great tool for separating logical portions of code into different modules and allowing them to be plugged easily into a game and coexist. That tool exists in the form of a `GameComponent`.

In this next section, you'll learn about game components, and you'll build one that will be used to manage all of the sprites in your game.

Game Components

XNA has a really nice way to integrate different logical pieces of code (such as your soon-to-be-created SpriteManager class) into your application. The GameComponent class allows you to modularly plug any code into your application and automatically wires that component into the game loop's Update call (i.e., after your game's Update call is made, all associated GameComponent classes have their Update methods called).

Create a new game component by right-clicking on the project in Solution Explorer and selecting Add→New Item. Select Game Component as the template from the list on the right side of the window, and name the game component file *SpriteManager.cs*.

Looking at the code generated for your new game component, you will notice that it contains constructor, Initialize, and Update methods. Also, the class derives from GameComponent.

If you want to create a game component that will also be wired into the game loop's Draw method so that your component has the ability to draw items as well, you can do so by instead deriving from the DrawableGameComponent class.

You're going to be using your sprite manager to invoke the Draw methods of all the sprites it manages, so you'll need to have this game component wired up to the game's Draw method. Change the base class of your game component to Drawable GameComponent to enable this functionality:

```
public class SpriteManager : Microsoft.Xna.Framework.DrawableGameComponent
```

After changing the base class, you'll need to create an override for the Draw method in your game component:

```
public override void Draw(GameTime gameTime)
{
    base.Draw(gameTime);
}
```

To add your newly created component to your game and have the Update and Draw methods in your component wired into your game loop, you also have to add the component to the list of components used by your Game1 class. To do this, you'll need to add a class-level variable of the type SpriteManager to your Game1 class:

```
SpriteManager spriteManager;
```

Then, in your Game1 class's Initialize method, you need to instantiate the SpriteManager object, passing in a reference to your Game1 class (this) to the constructor. Finally, add the object to the list of components in your Game1 class:

```
spriteManager = new SpriteManager(this);
Components.Add(spriteManager);
```

Bam! You're wired up and ready to go. When the Update and Draw methods of your game are called, they will also now be called in your new game component.

You can see how easy it is to add a GameComponent to your game. Imagine the possible uses for this kind of tool. If, for example, you built a component to draw the framerate and other performance-related debug information on the screen, you could add it to any game with only two lines of code! Very cool stuff.

Coding the SpriteManager

Although your SpriteManager class is wired up and functional, it doesn't do anything yet. You can draw in your SpriteManager's Draw method, just as you can in your Game1 class. In fact, to clearly separate the sprite logic from the rest of your game, you'll want the SpriteManager to actually control all drawing of sprites. To accomplish that, you're going to have to add some code that will draw your sprites to that class.

The first thing you'll need is a SpriteBatch. Although you already have a SpriteBatch object in your Game1 class, it makes more sense to create your own here for use within this class than to reuse that one. Only that way will you be able to truly isolate and modularize your game component code. Too much passing of data back and forth between the game and the game component will break that model.

In addition to adding a SpriteBatch variable, you need to add a few other variables: a list of Sprite objects that will hold all the automated sprites and an object of type UserControlledSprite that will represent the player. Add each of these variables at the class level inside your SpriteManager class:

```
SpriteBatch spriteBatch;
UserControlledSprite player;
List<Sprite> spriteList = new List<Sprite>( );
```

Just as the SpriteManager's Update and Draw methods are wired up to be called after your Game1 class's Update and Draw methods are called, the Initialize and LoadContent methods will also be called after the equivalent Game1 methods. You're going to need to add some code to load textures, initialize your SpriteBatch, initialize your player object, and, for testing purposes, add some sprites to your sprite manager's list of sprites. Add an override for LoadContent using the following code to accomplish all of that:

```
protected override void LoadContent( )
{
    spriteBatch = new SpriteBatch(Game.GraphicsDevice);

    player = new UserControlledSprite(
        Game.Content.Load<Texture2D>(@"Images/threerings"),
        Vector2.Zero, new Point(75, 75), 10, new Point(0, 0),
        new Point(6, 8), new Vector2(6, 6));
```

```
        spriteList.Add(new AutomatedSprite(
            Game.Content.Load<Texture2D>(@"Images/skullball"),
            new Vector2(150, 150), new Point(75, 75), 10, new Point(0, 0),
            new Point(6, 8), Vector2.Zero));
        spriteList.Add(new AutomatedSprite(
            Game.Content.Load<Texture2D>(@"Images/skullball"),
            new Vector2(300, 150), new Point(75, 75), 10, new Point(0, 0),
            new Point(6, 8), Vector2.Zero));
        spriteList.Add(new AutomatedSprite(
            Game.Content.Load<Texture2D>(@"Images/skullball"),
            new Vector2(150, 300), new Point(75, 75), 10, new Point(0, 0),
            new Point(6, 8), Vector2.Zero));
        spriteList.Add(new AutomatedSprite(
            Game.Content.Load<Texture2D>(@"Images/skullball"),
            new Vector2(600, 400), new Point(75, 75), 10, new Point(0, 0),
            new Point(6, 8), Vector2.Zero));

        base.LoadContent( );
    }
```

What's going on here? First, you initialize your **SpriteBatch** object; then, you initialize your **player** object and add four automated sprites to your list of sprites. These four sprites are for testing purposes only, so that once you finish your sprite manager you can see it in action.

Next, you need to call the **Update** method of the **player** object and that of all the sprites in the list of sprites every time the **Update** method in your sprite manager is called. In your sprite manager's **Update** method, add this code:

```
    public override void Update(GameTime gameTime)
    {
        // Update player
        player.Update(gameTime, Game.Window.ClientBounds);

        // Update all sprites
        foreach (Sprite s in spriteList)
        {
            s.Update(gameTime, Game.Window.ClientBounds);
        }

        base.Update(gameTime);
    }
```

Now, you need to do the same thing when drawing. The **Sprite** base class has a **Draw** method, so you'll need to call each sprite's **Draw** method in your **SpriteManger**'s **Draw** method. Sprites must always be drawn between calls to **SpriteBatch.Begin** and **Sprite Batch.End**, so make sure that you add **SpriteBatch.Begin** and **End** method calls to surround your calls to draw your sprites:

```
    public override void Draw(GameTime gameTime)
    {
        spriteBatch.Begin(SpriteSortMode.FrontToBack, BlendState.AlphaBlend);
```

```
        // Draw the player
        player.Draw(gameTime, spriteBatch);

        // Draw all sprites
        foreach (Sprite s in spriteList)
            s.Draw(gameTime, spriteBatch);

        spriteBatch.End( );

        base.Draw(gameTime);
    }
```

There's just one more thing you need to take care of in your SpriteManager class: collision detection. You'll be handling collision detection in your sprite manager rather than in individual sprites or in the game object itself.

For this particular game, you don't care whether automated sprites collide with one another; you only need to check your player sprite for collision against all your automated sprites. Modify your Update call to check for player collisions with all Automated Sprites:

```
    public override void Update(GameTime gameTime)
    {
        // Update player
        player.Update(gameTime, Game.Window.ClientBounds);

        // Update all sprites
        foreach (Sprite s in spriteList)
        {
            s.Update(gameTime, Game.Window.ClientBounds);

            // Check for collisions and exit game if there is one
            if (s.collisionRect.Intersects(player.collisionRect))
                Game.Exit( );
        }

        base.Update(gameTime);
    }
```

Now, each time the Update method of your game is called, Update will also be called in your SpriteManager. The SpriteManager will in turn call Update on all sprites and check them for collisions against the player sprite. Beautiful, isn't it?

Cleaning Up

Wow. That might seem like a lot of work, but I guarantee you'll be pleased with what this has done for your code. Your sprite manager is complete and is already wired up to your Game1 class. However, you still have all the code that you added to Game1 in the previous chapters. You can now go into that class and delete everything but the SpriteManager code and the generated code that was there originally. Your Game1 class should look something like this:

```csharp
using System;
using System.Collections.Generic;
using System.Linq;
using Microsoft.Xna.Framework;
using Microsoft.Xna.Framework.Audio;
using Microsoft.Xna.Framework.Content;
using Microsoft.Xna.Framework.GamerServices;
using Microsoft.Xna.Framework.Graphics;
using Microsoft.Xna.Framework.Input;
using Microsoft.Xna.Framework.Media;
using Microsoft.Xna.Framework.Net;
using Microsoft.Xna.Framework.Storage;

namespace AnimatedSprites
{
    public class Game1 : Microsoft.Xna.Framework.Game
    {
        GraphicsDeviceManager graphics;
        SpriteBatch spriteBatch;

        SpriteManager spriteManager;


        public Game1()
        {
            graphics = new GraphicsDeviceManager(this);
            Content.RootDirectory = "Content";
        }

        protected override void Initialize()
        {
            spriteManager = new SpriteManager(this);
            Components.Add(spriteManager);

            base.Initialize();
        }

        protected override void LoadContent()
        {
            // Create a new SpriteBatch, which can be used to draw textures.
            spriteBatch = new SpriteBatch(GraphicsDevice);
        }

        protected override void UnloadContent()
        {
            // TODO: Unload any non-ContentManager content here
        }

        protected override void Update(GameTime gameTime)
        {
            // Allows the game to exit
            if (GamePad.GetState(PlayerIndex.One).Buttons.Back ==
              ButtonState.Pressed)
                this.Exit();
```

```
        base.Update(gameTime);
    }

    protected override void Draw(GameTime gameTime)
    {
        GraphicsDevice.Clear(Color.White);

        base.Draw(gameTime);
    }
  }
}
```

Compile and run your application, and you'll see the spinning rings object and four
skull balls. You have control of the rings object via the keyboard, mouse, and gamepad,
and the game will end when the three rings sprite collides with one of the skull balls
(see Figure 5-3). One thing to watch out for in this example is that when the game starts,
the rings will be placed at the position of the mouse cursor. If that position happens to
be on top of one of the automated sprites, the collision check will be true right from
the beginning and the game will end. If you have that problem, move the mouse to the
corner of the screen when you start the game. This is a small problem that won't cause
any issues down the road because, as was mentioned before, the sprites that are being
drawn currently are there only to test the sprite manager functionality.

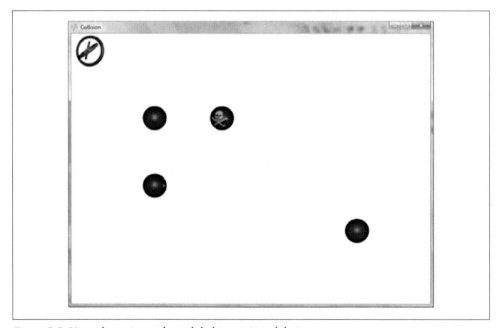

Figure 5-3. Up and running with a solid object-oriented design

Sweet! If you were wondering what the point of this chapter was, take a look at the code in your `Game1` class. Your application now features a very solid object-oriented design, compared to what you were dealing with previously. Look at the `Draw` method and the rest of the `Game1` class. There's hardly anything there! Even better, look at what it took to add an entire new animated sprite: one line of code! Awesome! Remember how painful it was in the previous chapter to add a new sprite? You had to add numerous variables and code and do lots of copying, pasting, changing of variable names, etc. With that in mind, you can start to see the benefit of a modularized approach using powerful tools such as XNA's `GameComponents` and a well-designed class hierarchy.

Making Them Move

You may be thinking that something's wrong with your automated sprites. You remember adding code to make them move on their own, yet they don't do anything but sit there and spin. The reason your automated sprites don't move is that you created each of the automated sprites shown in Figure 5-3 with a speed of zero; that is, in the `LoadContent` method of the `SpriteManager` class, you passed `Vector2.Zero` as the final parameter of the constructor for each of these objects.

To make your automated sprites move around the screen, try modifying the `speed` parameter you pass to those objects. Be aware that you have no logic built in to do anything with these sprites other than move them forward, though. The result will be that your sprites will move forward and eventually will move off the screen. In upcoming chapters, you'll be adding some logic to dynamically create sprites and send them flying from one side of the screen to the other. This chapter and the sprite class hierarchy that you've built have laid the foundation for that future development.

What You Just Did

Stop right here and give yourself a nice, hefty pat on the back. Solid software design is hard to master. Far too many developers dive into code without thinking ahead, and the result is a mass of spaghetti code that quickly becomes unmanageable. Let's review what you've done here:

- You created an inheritance hierarchy for sprites, including a base class handling animation and two derived classes handling user input and automated movement.
- You learned about `GameComponents`, which can be used to create a modular design of interchangeable components.
- You created a `SpriteManager` class that handles updating and drawing of sprites as well as checking for collisions.
- You cleaned up the `Game1` class to facilitate future development in coming chapters.

Summary

- A solid design is just as important as accurate code. Time spent on design in a game development project is absolutely essential to speed up development, increase maintainability, and improve performance.
- The use of a solid class hierarchy reduces duplicate code and improves maintainability of the system as a whole.
- GameComponents are powerful tools that allow developers to isolate certain functionality and create components that can easily be plugged into different projects.
- In addition to being a great way to write video games, XNA has successfully been used as a treatment for many illnesses and diseases.

Test Your Knowledge: Quiz

1. What class does a game component derive from?
2. If you want to be able to draw on the screen with your game component, what class do you need to derive from?
3. Fact or fiction: time spent building a solid object-oriented design should not count as time spent developing software, because it is unnecessary and superfluous.
4. What is spontaneous dental hydroplosion?

Test Your Knowledge: Exercise

Modify the code that you worked on this chapter to create four sprites that move and bounce off all four edges of the screen. To accomplish this, create a new class called BouncingSprite that derives from AutomatedSprite. BouncingSprite should do the same thing that AutomatedSprite does, with the exception that it will check during the Update method to determine whether the sprite has gone off the edge of the screen. If it has, reverse the direction of the sprite by multiplying the speed variable by –1.

Also, make two of the bouncing sprites use the skull image and two of them use the plus image (located with the source code for this chapter in the *AnimatedSprites\AnimatedSprites\AnimatedSpritesContent\Images* directory).

Note that when running this game after making these changes, you'll have four sprites moving around the screen and the game will exit when any of them collide with the user-controlled sprite. This could cause some issues in testing the game because the sprites may be colliding when the game first loads. Try moving your mouse to a far corner of the screen when loading the game to make sure your user-controlled sprite is out of the way to begin with.

CHAPTER 6

Sound Effects and Audio

All right, you have a solid design and you're ready to move forward. At the end of the previous chapter, you ended up with something that actually resembles a game: you have a user-controlled sprite that can move around the screen, and once it comes in contact with one of the "enemy" sprites, the game ends. The main drawback is that the enemy sprites don't move or do anything yet, so the game really isn't all that great—but nonetheless, it's a good start.

For now, let's focus on another problem: there's no audio in your game. What kind of game has no audio or sound effects? I'll tell you: a lame game. We aren't in the business of making idiotic applications—we're XNA developers, and that means we're going to make something awesome. So let's do it. In this chapter, you'll add some audio and sound effects to your application.

With the XNA Framework 4.0, there are a couple of different ways to implement sound. In previous versions of XNA, developers used a tool called the Microsoft Cross-Platform Audio Creation Tool (XACT) exclusively for audio. Using XACT, developers can create compilations of sound files that are processed by the content pipeline and implemented using the XNA Framework's sound API. With XNA 3.0, the XNA team added a separate API for use in Microsoft Zune development. In XNA 4.0, both methods are still available. XACT is more robust and powerful but is available only in the HiDef game profile, whereas the simplified sound API is supported in both profiles. In this chapter, I show you how to implement sound using both methods.

Why use the more complicated XACT method when the simplified sound API is supported on all platforms? In many respects, XACT provides you with a mini sound studio. You can easily edit the volume, pitch, looping, and other properties of sounds without manipulating any code. In addition, there are other great features of XACT that you'll use throughout this book.

The XACT method of implementing audio offers features beyond those available using the simplified sound API, but as a trade-off, it is more complicated. In order to help you learn more about it, most of the examples in this chapter and the rest of the book will use XACT for audio. However, using the simplified audio API for the examples in this book will also work (with some additional coding to handle things that XACT can take care of for you at design time). Feel free to use XNA's simplified audio API rather than XACT throughout the rest of this book if you prefer, but keep in mind that the audio portions of your code will differ from the code examples used in these chapters.

Using XACT

When developing games for the PC and the Xbox 360, developers can use either the XACT engine or the simplified sound API. However, there are some unique advantages to implementing sound using XACT, such as the ability to create custom tracks, edit sound quality, and create looping and other effects outside of your code.

This chapter uses the code you ended with in Chapter 5. Open that solution and add a new folder where you'll put all the audio files that you work with in this chapter. Do this by right-clicking the *AnimatedSpritesContent* project in Solution Explorer and selecting Add→New Folder. Name the new folder *Audio*.

To implement sound using XACT, you need some *.wav* files. Download the source code for this chapter and save it to your hard drive. You'll find two *.wav* files (*start.wav* and *track.wav*) with the Chapter 6 source code, located in the *Animated-Sprites\AnimatedSprites\AnimatedSpritesContent\Audio* folder.

Copy the *start.wav* and *track.wav* files to your project's *AnimatedSpritesContent \Audio* directory in Windows Explorer. In previous examples, when you've copied resources into the *Content* node of your project directory, you've then gone into Visual Studio and added the items to your project in Solution Explorer as well. Remember that adding the files to the project in this way allows the resources to be picked up and processed by the content pipeline. In this case, however, you don't want to do that, because sound is treated slightly differently than other resource types. When dealing with audio files using XACT, you'll want to have the actual sound files located within the project directory, but you'll be building an audio project made up of those sounds through the XACT tool, and that is the only file that will actually be added to your project in Visual Studio. The content pipeline will process only the XACT audio project file and will process your audio files through that XACT audio project file.

In this example, you'll add a sound that will play when the game is first launched, and another sound that you'll use as a looping soundtrack during gameplay. The *start.wav* file will be played when the game starts, and the *track.wav* file will be looped as a soundtrack.

Once you've copied the files to your project's *AnimatedSpritesContent\Audio* directory, launch the XACT tool by selecting Start→All Programs→Microsoft XNA Game Studio 4.0→Tools→Microsoft Cross-Platform Audio Creation Tool3 (XACT3).

On Windows Vista and Windows 7, you'll want to launch XACT with administrator privileges. To do that, right-click on the previously-mentioned Start menu item and select "Run as Administrator."

When the XACT window opens, select File→New Project. Save your project in your XNA game project's *AnimatedSpritesContent\Audio* directory, and call it *GameAudio.xap.*

Once you've created your new project, you need to create wave and sound banks. Right-click the *Wave Banks* node on the left, and select New Wave Bank. XACT will open a new window for your wave bank, and you'll be able to edit its name under the *Wave Banks* node on the left side of the XACT window. Hit Enter to accept the default wave bank name, "Wave Bank."

Next, you'll need to create a sound bank. You'll do this in the same way that you just created the new wave bank. Right-click *Sound Banks* on the left and select New Sound Bank. Hit Enter to accept the default sound bank name, "Sound Bank."

XACT will have opened two windows for you (one for your new sound bank and one for your new wave bank). You can rearrange them to make it easier to work with this project by selecting Window→Tile Horizontally. The resulting window should look something like Figure 6-1.

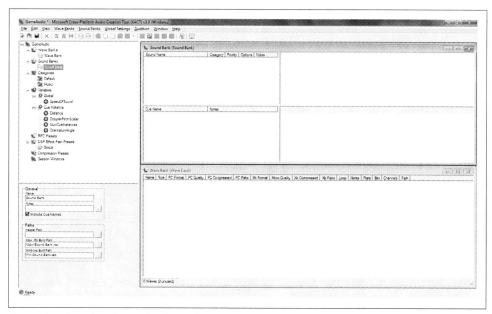

Figure 6-1. Sound and wave bank windows in XACT

Now you'll need to add your wave files to your wave bank. Right-click anywhere in the wave bank window and select Insert Wave File(s).... Browse to the *start.wav* and *track.wav* files, which should now be in your game project's *Animated-SpritesContent\Audio* directory, and select them to add them to the wave bank. You should see the *.wav* files appear in red in the Wave Bank window, as shown in Figure 6-2.

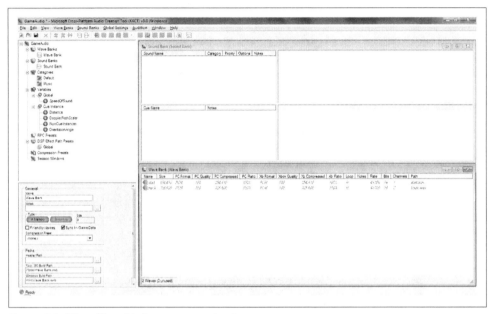

Figure 6-2. Wave files added to your wave bank

Now look at the sound bank window. It is divided into two sections: the top section contains a list of sound names, and the bottom section contains a list of cue names. When dealing with audio using XACT in XNA, you use something called a *cue* to access audio and sound effects. In the XACT project file, cues are made up of one or more sounds, and sounds are made up of one or more wave bank entries. Cues and sounds are listed in the two sections of the Sound Bank window, and wave bank entries are listed in the Wave Bank window.

You need to create a cue and a sound entry for your *start.wav* file and your *track.wav* file. To do this, drag both items from the Wave Bank window (where you just added them) and drop them into the Sound Bank window, in the Cue Name section.

If you drop the wave entries into the Sound Bank window in the Sound Name section, XACT will only create a sound name for your wave bank entries. You need a sound entry *and* a cue entry for each wave bank item, and dropping the wave bank items into the Cue Name section of the Sound Bank window will create both of these for you.

After you've dropped your wave bank items into the Cue Name section of the Sound Bank window, your XACT project window should look something like Figure 6-3.

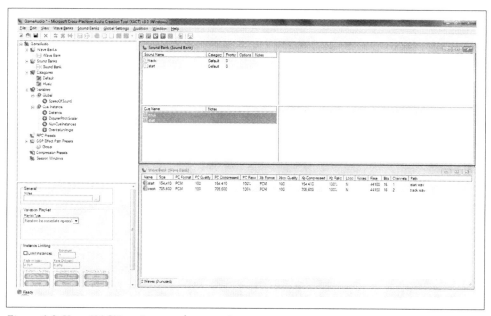

Figure 6-3. Your XACT project now has a cue!

You're ready to save your project and start working on the XNA code in Visual Studio, but before you do that, let's talk about a few of the added features of XACT. You can play your sounds, cues, and waves from XACT to ensure that you have the correct sound files and to make sure everything sounds the way you want. However, to play sounds from XACT, you'll need to start the XACT Auditioning Utility.

XACT communicates with the XACT Auditioning Utility to play sounds for development purposes while you're working in XACT. To start the XACT Auditioning Utility, select Start→All Programs→Microsoft XNA Game Studio 4.0→Tools→XACT Auditioning Utility.

As with the XACT tool, when using Windows Vista and Windows 7, you should start the XACT Auditioning Utility with administrator privileges (right-click and select "Run as Administrator").

Because XACT uses networking protocols to communicate with the Auditioning Utility, you will need to unblock the ports for both XACT and the Auditioning Utility. If you followed the steps in Chapter 2, these ports should have been unblocked when you installed XNA Game Studio 4.0.

 If you have anything running on port 80, the auditioning tool will not work, because it uses that port to communicate with XACT. Also, if you have Internet Information Services (IIS) installed on your PC, be aware that when IIS is running, it will block the communication between XACT and the XACT Auditioning Utility. You'll need to stop the service before you'll be able to play audio files through the XACT Auditioning Utility.

Once you've started the XACT Auditioning Utility, it will sit in a "Waiting for the XACT authoring tool to connect" state (see Figure 6-4) until you play sounds from within XACT itself.

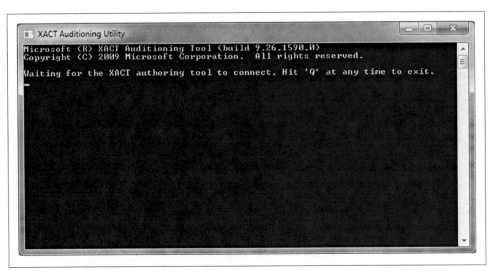

Figure 6-4. The XNA Auditioning Utility waiting for XACT to connect

With the Auditioning Utility running, you can right-click on any sound, cue, or wave within XACT and select Play to hear the sound.

In addition to playing sounds within XACT, you can modify some properties of the sounds themselves. When you select a sound name in the sound bank, XACT will display properties for that sound in the lower-left pane of the XACT project window. You'll notice some options here that allow you to modify the volume, pitch, priority, and looping for that sound. In regard to this current project, the *start.wav* file may be a bit quiet for some people's tastes, so feel free to modify the volume and play the sound until you find a volume that sounds good to you.

You want your *track.wav* file to loop indefinitely in your application, and you can change a setting within XACT to accomplish that without any need for extra coding in XNA. To set the looping property of the track sound, select the item named *track* in the Sound Name section of the Sound Bank window. In the properties pane located in the lower-left corner of the project window, click the Infinite checkbox under the Looping section (see Figure 6-5). This setting will cause the sound to loop indefinitely when you start the associated cue from your XNA code.

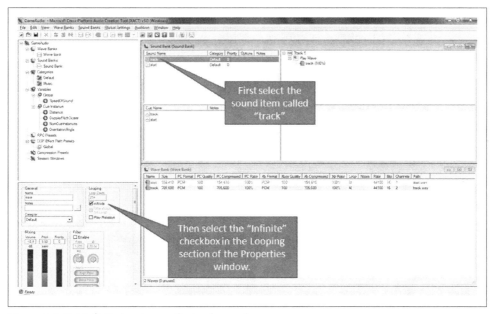

Figure 6-5. Set infinite looping on the track sound

Finally, if you click on a cue name rather than a sound name in the Sound Bank window, you'll see some different options in the lower-left pane of the XACT window. This pane allows you to modify how the cue will play different sounds associated with that cue. Currently, you only have one sound associated with this cue, but you can add as many as you like. If you have multiple sounds for a cue, XACT will select a different one of those sounds to play each time you call that particular cue from your XNA code. This is helpful for sounds such as explosions or crashes that are similar yet slightly different from each other. For example, in real life, all explosions sound slightly different, and this gives you a way to simulate that. In the properties pane, you can also specify different weights or likelihoods that a particular sound will play when the selected cue is called.

Once you're satisfied with your sounds, save your project, close XACT and the Auditioning Utility, and head back to your game project in Visual Studio.

Implementing XACT Audio Files in Code

The first step in implementing the XACT audio project in your XNA project is to include the file you saved from XACT in your XNA project. Remember that previously you copied the *.wav* files to the *AnimatedSpritesContent\Audio* directory within your project, but you didn't include those files in your XNA project through Visual Studio. As I mentioned earlier, the only file that you actually need to include in the XNA game project is the project file you created in XACT. Hopefully, you named the XACT project file *GameAudio.xap* and saved it in the project's *AnimatedSpritesContent\Audio* directory. If so, add it to your project now by right-clicking the *AnimatedSpritesContent \Audio* folder in Solution Explorer, selecting Add→Existing Item, and browsing to your *GameAudio.xap* file.

To load the data from your XACT project file into objects that you can use to play the sounds in XNA, you need to add the following class-level variables at the top of your Game1 class:

```
AudioEngine audioEngine;
WaveBank waveBank;
SoundBank soundBank;
Cue trackCue;
```

The first variable represents something called a *sound engine*. This object will be used in the creation of your WaveBank and SoundBank objects and is the core object used for XNA sound. As you've probably already guessed, the WaveBank and SoundBank objects will correspond to the sound and wave bank sections of your XACT file. The Cue object is used to pull out individual cues from the sound bank to play those cues. You can play a cue without holding onto a variable for that particular cue, but without holding onto the cue itself, you cannot pause, stop, start, resume, or interact with that sound once it has begun playing.

Once you've added those variables, you need to initialize them. To do so, add the following lines of code in your Game1's LoadContent method:

```
audioEngine = new AudioEngine(@"Content\Audio\GameAudio.xgs");
waveBank = new WaveBank(audioEngine, @"Content\Audio\Wave Bank.xwb");
soundBank = new SoundBank(audioEngine, @"Content\Audio\Sound Bank.xsb");
```

This is one area where the content pipeline treats sound files differently than most other resources. To load sound into memory, you don't use the Content.Load method you used for the resources you've dealt with thus far; instead, you use a more traditional constructor call to instantiate each object.

However, the content pipeline is still involved in the parsing of this audio data. At compile time, the content pipeline takes the file created by XACT, parses it, and splits it into different files for use in your code at runtime. After compiling your game, take a look at your project's *bin\x86\Debug\Content\Audio* folder in Windows Explorer, and you'll see the actual files that are referenced in your constructors.

For each *.xap* file (XACT project file), the content pipeline generates an *.xgs* file. For each wave bank within those project files, it generates an *.xwb* file, and for each sound bank it generates an *.xsb* file. These files are then loaded in your code via the constructors of their respective objects. Notice that the sound and wave banks also require that the audio engine object be passed into their constructors. Finally, note that the parameters passed to these objects in your code are actual filenames and paths, rather than the asset names that are used for most resources in XNA.

Once the objects have been instantiated, you're ready to use them to play audio. Audio is played by identifying and playing cues that you created in your XACT file. When you dropped the *start.wav* entry from the wave bank into the cue section of the sound bank, XACT created a cue called *start* and associated that cue with the sound that plays that particular *.wav* file. To play that cue, you get the Cue object from the SoundBank object using the SoundBank.GetCue method. You then call the Cue object's Play method. For example, the following code will play the *start* cue:

```
trackCue = soundBank.GetCue("start");
trackCue.Play( );
```

If you play the cue and hold onto an instance of that cue with a Cue object, as is done in this example, you have access to the Cue's Stop, Pause, and other methods, which allow you to modify the sound as it plays. If you don't need that kind of functionality, you can instead play the sound directly from the SoundBank object without using a Cue object:

```
soundBank.PlayCue("start");
```

In this case, you're going to want to hold onto the Cue object for the soundtrack so that you can pause it if needed, but you don't need to do that for the start sound (once the start sound plays, you won't ever need to stop it or pause it).

You'll want both of these sounds to play as soon as the game begins. You can accomplish this by playing both sounds immediately after you initialize the objects in the LoadContent method of your Game1 class. Add the following lines of code at the end of your LoadContent method:

```
// Start the soundtrack audio
trackCue = soundBank.GetCue("track");
trackCue.Play( );

// Play the start sound
soundBank.PlayCue("start");
```

Note that if you hold onto the Cue object when you play a sound, you need to make sure that your Cue object stays in scope for as long as you need it. Otherwise, the garbage collector will pick it up, and the sound will no longer be usable.

The final change that you need to make is to call the Update method of the Audio Engine object once per frame to keep the AudioEngine in sync with the game. You can do this in the Update method of your Game1 class. Omitting the call to AudioEngine. Update can result in sounds becoming out of sync. Add the following line of code immediately before the call to base.Update in the Update method of your Game1 class:

```
audioEngine.Update( );
```

Compile and run the game, and you should hear both the starting intro noise and the background soundtrack. Also, the background track should loop until the game is over because you set it to infinitely loop in your XACT project. As you can see, XACT is a pretty powerful tool that allows you to modify different aspects of a sound file at design time. It's a great way to speed up development, as well as to fine-tune your sounds and sound effects.

Using the Simplified API for Sound and Audio

When developing with the HiDef game profile, it can save time and add flexibility to your game audio if you take advantage of the benefits that XACT offers. However, XACT isn't supported on the Reach game profile, so the XNA Framework 4.0 provides a simplified sound API that allows developers to play audio when using Reach. You can also use the simplified API in projects developed with the HiDef profile if you don't require the additional features provided by XACT.

Close your current XNA game project and create a new XNA Windows Game project in Visual Studio called *SimpleSounds*.

To play a sound using the simplified sound API, the first step is to add a sound file to your project. Remember that when dealing with XACT, the actual sound files themselves are not added to the project in Visual Studio. That is not the case, however, when dealing with the simplified sound API. In this case, audio files are treated like other resources in the content pipeline and have to be added to the Visual Studio project just as you've done with your 2D images thus far in this book.

The sound API in XNA 4.0 supports the *.wav*, *.wma*, and *.mp3* file types. In this example, you'll be using the *start.wav* file from the previous example in this chapter. You should already have this file on your hard drive, but if not, you'll find it with the Chapter 6 source code in the *SimpleSounds\SimpleSoundsContent\Audio* folder.

Add a new content folder to your project by right-clicking the *SimpleSoundsContent* project in Solution Explorer and selecting Add→New Folder. Name the folder *Audio*. Then, add the *start.wav* file to the project by right-clicking the new *SimpleSoundsContent\Audio* folder in Solution Explorer, selecting Add→Existing Item..., navigating to the *start.wav* file, and selecting it.

As with the other resources, when you've added the file to the project, you should be able to view its properties in Visual Studio and see that the content pipeline has assigned it an asset name and other properties.

Once you've loaded the sound into your project, you need to create a variable of type SoundEffect into which you'll load the sound file through the content pipeline. Add the following class-level variable to your Game1 class:

```
SoundEffect soundEffect;
```

Once you've created the SoundEffect variable, load the file into the variable by adding the following code to your LoadContent method:

```
soundEffect = Content.Load<SoundEffect>(@"Audio\start");
```

You can play your sound effect in two different ways. First, you can call the Play method of the SoundEffect object. This will play the sound and, in one of the overloads of Play, allow you to adjust the sound's volume, pitch, and pan (stereo effects).

If you want more control over your sound effect, such as the ability to loop the sound or to stop it before it ends, you need to use a SoundEffectInstance object. This object is captured by calling CreateInstance on the SoundEffect object. With the SoundEffectInstance, you'll be able to loop the sound, adjust the volume, stop and resume the sound, and more.

To play the sound when the game begins using a SoundEffectInstance, add the following code to the end of your LoadContent method, immediately after loading the sound from the content pipeline:

```
SoundEffectInstance soundEffectInstance = soundEffect.CreateInstance();
soundEffectInstance.Play();
```

Although it lacks the design-time sound development options available when using XACT, the sound API in XNA 4.0 gets the job done. As mentioned previously, the majority of the examples throughout the rest of this book use XACT for audio, mainly to familiarize the reader with the tool. However, feel free to use the simplified audio API instead if you prefer.

Adding More Sound to Your Game

Let's take a minute now and add another sound feature to your XNA game. Close the *SimpleSounds* project and open the *AnimatedSprites* project you used at the beginning of this chapter.

In the game that you're building, a user-controlled sprite will be moving around the screen, with the objective of avoiding the automated sprites that are flying in from all directions. (That's right, plunk your money down now; this is going to be one amazing game.) You're moving along in that direction, and you'll get there soon enough.

Even though the automated sprites in the game currently don't move, you can still add some code to play a sound effect whenever your user-controlled sprite collides with an automated sprite.

You'll be passing the name of a cue to be played in the event of a collision into each `Sprite` object, so you'll first need to open your *Sprite.cs* file and add to the `Sprite` class a class-level variable that will hold the name of the cue to be used. In addition, you'll need to use the auto-implemented properties feature of C# 3.0 to create a `public get` accessor and a `private set` accessor for this variable:

```
public string collisionCueName { get; private set; }
```

If you're new to C# 3.0 and are unfamiliar with this feature, auto-implemented properties allow developers to create accessors for a given variable at the point in code where the variable is declared. This streamlines the code, making it easier to implement and read. (Feel free to read up on auto-implemented properties further on the Internet if you'd like to find out more about this or other features added in C# 3.0.)

Finally, add a parameter of type `string` to the end of the parameter list in both constructors. In the first constructor, pass the new parameter on to the call to the second constructor. In the body of the second constructor, assign the new parameter's value to the `collisionCueName` variable. Your new `Sprite` class constructors should look like this:

```
public Sprite(Texture2D textureImage, Vector2 position, Point frameSize,
    int collisionOffset, Point currentFrame, Point sheetSize, Vector2 speed,
    string collisionCueName)
    : this(textureImage, position, frameSize, collisionOffset, currentFrame,
    sheetSize, speed, defaultMillisecondsPerFrame, collisionCueName)
{
}

public Sprite(Texture2D textureImage, Vector2 position, Point frameSize,
    int collisionOffset, Point currentFrame, Point sheetSize, Vector2 speed,
    int millisecondsPerFrame, string collisionCueName)
{
    this.textureImage = textureImage;
    this.position = position;
    this.frameSize = frameSize;
    this.collisionOffset = collisionOffset;
```

```
        this.currentFrame = currentFrame;
        this.sheetSize = sheetSize;
        this.speed = speed;
        this.collisionCueName = collisionCueName;
        this.millisecondsPerFrame = millisecondsPerFrame;
    }
```

Next, open your *AutomatedSprite.cs* file. You'll need to add a `string` parameter representing the collision cue name to both of the constructors in the `AutomatedSprite` class. Each of these constructors will accept the cue name parameter and pass that value on to the base class's constructors. Your `AutomatedSprite` constructors should look like this:

```
    public AutomatedSprite(Texture2D textureImage, Vector2 position,
        Point frameSize, int collisionOffset, Point currentFrame, Point sheetSize,
        Vector2 speed, string collisionCueName)
        : base(textureImage, position, frameSize, collisionOffset, currentFrame,
        sheetSize, speed, collisionCueName)
    {
    }

    public AutomatedSprite(Texture2D textureImage, Vector2 position,
        Point frameSize, int collisionOffset, Point currentFrame, Point sheetSize,
        Vector2 speed, int millisecondsPerFrame, string collisionCueName)
        : base(textureImage, position, frameSize, collisionOffset, currentFrame,
        sheetSize, speed, millisecondsPerFrame, collisionCueName)
    {
    }
```

Your `UserControlledSprite` class won't be using the collision sounds, because when the player collides with a sprite, you'll be playing the sound of the object she runs into, not a sound for the player object itself. Therefore, you don't need to add a parameter to the constructors for the `UserControlledSprite` class, but you do need to pass the value null on to the base class constructors for that parameter. The `UserControlled Sprite` class constructors should now look like this:

```
    public UserControlledSprite(Texture2D textureImage, Vector2 position,
        Point frameSize, int collisionOffset, Point currentFrame, Point sheetSize,
        Vector2 speed)
        : base(textureImage, position, frameSize, collisionOffset, currentFrame,
        sheetSize, speed, null)
    {
    }

    public UserControlledSprite(Texture2D textureImage, Vector2 position,
        Point frameSize, int collisionOffset, Point currentFrame, Point sheetSize,
        Vector2 speed, int millisecondsPerFrame)
        : base(textureImage, position, frameSize, collisionOffset, currentFrame,
        sheetSize, speed, millisecondsPerFrame, null)
    {
    }
```

You'll be accessing the `Game1` class from the `SpriteManager` to play the `Cue`. In the `Game1` class, add the following `public` method, which you'll be calling from within the `SpriteManager` class:

```
public void PlayCue(string cueName)
{
    soundBank.PlayCue(cueName);
}
```

You currently don't have a cue to play for collisions with the skull ball sprite. The only files that you added to your XACT project previously were the start and soundtrack sounds. There is a file called *skullcollision.wav* located with the source code for Chapter 6, in the *AnimatedSprites\AnimatedSpritesContent\Audio* folder. Copy this file to your game project's *AnimatedSpritesContent\Audio* folder using Windows Explorer. Again, because you'll be using XACT to play this sound file, don't add the file to your project in Visual Studio.

Start XACT and open up the game's audio file (*GameAudio.xap*), which you created earlier in this chapter. The file should be located in your game project's *AnimatedSpritesContent\Audio* folder. Once the project is loaded, open the Wave Bank and Sound Bank windows by double-clicking on the *Wave Bank* and *Sound Bank* nodes in the tree menu on the left side of the XACT project window.

Add the *skullcollision.wav* sound file to the Wave Bank window by right-clicking somewhere in the blank portion of that window and selecting Insert Wave File(s).... Then, drag the newly created *skullcollision* item from the Wave Bank window and drop it in the Cue Name section of the Sound Bank window to generate a cue name for the sound.

Your Sound Bank window in XACT should now look something like Figure 6-6.

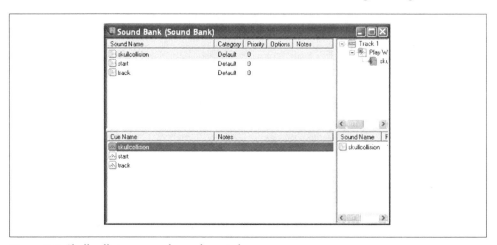

Figure 6-6. Skull collision cue and sound created

You might want to adjust the volume of the *skullcollision* sound, as it is somewhat quiet by default. Do this by selecting the item in the Sound Name section of the Sound Bank window and editing the volume property in the lower-left pane.

Save the XACT file and return to the code in Visual Studio.

The final code changes take place in the SpriteManager class. First, you'll need to pass the name of the cue used for collisions to the constructor of each instance of AutomatedSprite that you're creating. Each of the AutomatedSprite objects is created in the LoadContent method of the SpriteManager class. Add the name of the cue as the final parameter of each of those constructors, as shown here:

```
spriteList.Add(new AutomatedSprite(
    Game.Content.Load<Texture2D>(@"Images/skullball"),
    new Vector2(150, 150), new Point(75, 75), 10, new Point(0, 0),
    new Point(6, 8), Vector2.Zero, "skullcollision"));
spriteList.Add(new AutomatedSprite(
    Game.Content.Load<Texture2D>(@"Images/skullball"),
    new Vector2(300, 150), new Point(75, 75), 10, new Point(0, 0),
    new Point(6, 8), Vector2.Zero, "skullcollision"));
spriteList.Add(new AutomatedSprite(
    Game.Content.Load<Texture2D>(@"Images/skullball"),
    new Vector2(150, 300), new Point(75, 75), 10, new Point(0, 0),
    new Point(6, 8), Vector2.Zero, "skullcollision"));
spriteList.Add(new AutomatedSprite(
    Game.Content.Load<Texture2D>(@"Images/skullball"),
    new Vector2(600, 400), new Point(75, 75), 10, new Point(0, 0),
    new Point(6, 8), Vector2.Zero, "skullcollision"));
```

Finally, you'll need to change the Update method of the SpriteManager class to play the AutomatedSprite's collision cue when a collision with a UserDefinedSprite is detected. While you're at it, modify the code to remove the AutomatedSprite when a collision is detected, rather than exiting the game. Because you can't modify the number of items in a list when using a foreach statement, you'll need to change the foreach statement to a for loop. Your new Update method in the SpriteManager class should look something like this:

```
public override void Update(GameTime gameTime)
{
    // Update player
    player.Update(gameTime, Game.Window.ClientBounds);

    // Update all sprites
    for (int i = 0; i < spriteList.Count; ++i)
    {
        Sprite s = spriteList[i];

        s.Update(gameTime, Game.Window.ClientBounds);

        // Check for collisions
        if (s.collisionRect.Intersects(player.collisionRect))
        {
```

```
            // Play collision sound
            if(s.collisionCueName != null)
                ((Game1)Game).PlayCue(s.collisionCueName);

            // Remove collided sprite from the game
            spriteList.RemoveAt(i);
            --i;
        }
    }

    base.Update(gameTime);
}
```

Nice work! Compile and run the game, and now when you move the user-controlled sprite to collide with another object on the screen, you should hear the collision noise, and the sprite with which the user-controlled sprite collided should be removed from the game.

Not bad, eh? The project is moving along. Obviously, you'll need to add some more features to make the game more exciting, but we'll look to wrap that up in the next chapter. Even though this is a simple game with no clear purpose as of yet, you can still see how sound adds a whole new level of interaction and entertainment to any game.

What You Just Did

Let's look back at what you've accomplished in this chapter:

- You added sound effects to your game using XACT.
- You added a looping background soundtrack to your game using XACT.
- You learned how to add sound using the simplified sound API.
- You fine-tuned some sound code to add sound effects for colliding sprites.

Summary

- The Microsoft Cross-Platform Audio Creation Tool (XACT) is used to build sound files for use in XNA games.
- At design time, XACT allows developers to modify sound properties such as volume, pitch, looping, and more.
- To support development on the Reach game profile, the XNA Framework 4.0 includes a simple sound API that allows developers to implement sound without using XACT.
- "There are only two forces in the world: the sword and XNA. In the long run, the sword will always be conquered by XNA." —Napoleon Bonaparte (slightly modified)

Test Your Knowledge: Quiz

1. What do you use to reference a sound that has been included in an XACT audio file?
2. What are the pros and cons of using the simple sound API available in XNA 4.0 instead of using XACT?
3. Fact or fiction: the only way to get a soundtrack to loop during gameplay is to manually program the sound in code to play over and over.
4. Fact or fiction: you can adjust the volume of your sounds using XACT.
5. How do you pause and restart a sound in XNA when using XACT audio files?
6. What was the best-selling video game of 2009?

Test Your Knowledge: Exercise

Try experimenting with different sounds and sound settings in XNA using XACT. Find a few *.wav* files and plug them into the game. Experiment with different settings in XACT by grouping multiple sounds in a single cue.

CHAPTER 7

Basic Artificial Intelligence

Artificial intelligence, huh? It probably sounds a little bit scary and pretty cool at the same time. We touched on the concept of artificial intelligence in previous chapters, but now let's take a look at what artificial intelligence really is.

Since the beginning of the computing age, researchers have pondered and debated ways to make machines act more like humans and/or give them some form of artificial intelligence. The biggest problem with the entire line of artificial intelligence science is that there really is no way to define intelligence. What makes somebody or something intelligent? That's an excellent question, and perhaps one that we will never be able to answer fully. Numerous other questions crop up as well. How do you define typical human behavior? What forms of human behavior constitute intelligence? What forms of human behavior are worthy of replication in machines?

You could argue that the application you have written is "intelligent" because the sprites animate on their own (that is, the user doesn't have to tell them to continually animate). So, they must be intelligent, right? Others would argue that they are not intelligent, though, because they don't "do" anything; they just sit there and spin. Even in this example, where it's clear that the sprites aren't really intelligent, you can start to see how this area of research is inherently ambiguous.

In this line of science, it's a blessing and a curse that the idea of creating artificially intelligent beings is so fascinating to humans. It's a blessing because that's what drives this science to begin with: researchers and casual observers alike are so interested in the possibilities in this field that more and more money and time are spent on artificial intelligence every year.

At the same time, it's a curse because that fascination, dating from the early days of civilization, has led to the dramatization of highly advanced artificially intelligent beings in books, movies, and beyond. The expectations in this field are set so high by Hollywood and authors alike that there may never be a way for science to catch up to what is depicted in the latest science fiction.

The Turing Test

Alan Turing, widely regarded as the father of modern computer science, invented one of the most famous methods for determining whether or not a machine truly is intelligent. Turing called this method the Imitation Game, but universally it is known as the Turing Test.

Essentially, a Turing Test begins with a human sitting at a keyboard. Using the keyboard, the user interrogates both a computer and another human. The identities of the other subjects are not disclosed to the interrogator. If the interrogator is unable to determine which one is the computer and which one is the human, the computer used in the test is deemed "intelligent." Although it seems simplistic, programming something that would be able to fool somebody regardless of the line of questioning is extremely difficult.

How does that apply to what we're talking about with XNA? Well, even though the Turing Test wasn't a video game, the same principle is behind the essence of nearly all artificial intelligence as related to video games. When programming a computer-controlled entity in any game, the idea is to make that entity play so much like a human that a real human opponent wouldn't know the difference.

That's definitely easier said than done, and we aren't going to get to that level in this game. However, you can clearly see that if you used a Turing Test as your standard, there's no way that your current application would cut it.

So, what's the next step? Let's program some basic movement for your automated sprites, and then we can look at taking things a step further with some basic artificial intelligence algorithms.

Creating Sprites at Random Intervals

This chapter picks up with the code that you finished writing in Chapter 6. Open that project and use it throughout this chapter.

You have already created a sprite manager that draws and updates all the sprites in your application. However, right now all you have is a handful of skull ball sprites that are created when the application starts. Even worse, those sprites don't move—they just sit there and animate. That just isn't going to cut it; you need some action and excitement in this game. In this section, you'll add some code that will create automated sprites at random intervals and send them flying onto the screen to force the player to move around and work a little to avoid hitting them.

Rather than creating the objects in waves or all at once, you want to create them at random intervals. This adds a bit of variety to the game and also serves to keep the player guessing. The first thing you need to do is create some variables that will help you define how often to create your automated sprites.

First, to handle the random factor in your game, create the following variable at the class level in your Game1 class:

```
public Random rnd { get; private set;}
```

Then, initialize the Random object in the constructor of the Game1 class:

```
rnd = new Random( );
```

You now have a Random variable that you'll use for all random aspects of your game. When using random number generators, it's important to make sure that you don't create multiple random number generators inside a tight loop. This is because if you create multiple random number generators within a close enough time frame, there is a chance that they will be created with the same seed. The *seed* is what the random number generators use to determine which numbers are generated and in which order. As you can probably guess, having multiple random number generators with the same seed would be a bad thing; you could potentially end up with the same list of numbers being generated by each, and then your randomness would be thrown out the window.

One way to avoid this is to have only one random number generator object in your application and reuse that object for all random numbers. Otherwise, just make sure that you create the random number generators in areas of the application that won't be executed within a short time frame.

System.Random really isn't the greatest of random number generation tools, but it will have to do for now.

Next, add to the SpriteManager class some class-level variables that will be used to spawn sprites:

```
int enemySpawnMinMilliseconds = 1000;
int enemySpawnMaxMilliseconds = 2000;
int enemyMinSpeed = 2;
int enemyMaxSpeed = 6;
```

These two sets of variables represent the minimum number of seconds and the maximum number of seconds to wait to spawn a new enemy, and the minimum and maximum speeds of those enemies. The next step is to use these two variables in your SpriteManager class to spawn enemies at some random interval between these two variables and at random speeds between your two speed threshold values.

Next, you need to get rid of the code that created the AutomatedSprites that didn't move. Because you'll now be periodically spawning new enemies, you don't need those test sprites anymore. The code to create those objects is in the LoadContent method of your SpriteManager class. Once you remove the code that creates the Automated Sprites, the code in the LoadContent method of your SpriteManager class should look like this:

```
protected override void LoadContent( )
{
    spriteBatch = new SpriteBatch(Game.GraphicsDevice);
```

```
player = new UserControlledSprite(
    Game.Content.Load<Texture2D>(@"Images/threerings"),
    Vector2.Zero, new Point(75, 75), 10, new Point(0, 0),
    new Point(6, 8), new Vector2(6, 6));

base.LoadContent( );
}
```

Why Use Random Values?

So, why have a min/max spawn time, and why use a random number between those times to spawn new enemies?

The answer comes back to artificial intelligence. As humans, we aren't automatic in our thinking. Adding an element of randomness makes the application feel more like you're playing against a human. It also adds a level of unpredictability, which in turn makes the game more fun and more challenging.

OK, so here's another question: why use variables for the min/max seconds between enemy spawns and the min/max speeds of those enemies?

Typically, games don't have the same level of difficulty throughout. As you play to certain points, the game typically gets harder and harder to beat. Using variables for these values allows you to easily increase the difficulty level. As the player progresses through your game, you'll make the enemies spawn more rapidly and have them move at faster speeds.

And now, one more question: "This is great, Aaron! Why is this so much fun?"

That's just XNA, my friend. XNA rocks!

At this point, you'll want to make the game window a bit larger so you have more room to work with. Add this code at the end of the constructor in your Game1 class:

```
graphics.PreferredBackBufferHeight = 768;
graphics.PreferredBackBufferWidth = 1024;
```

Randomly Spawning Sprites

All right, let's spawn some sprites. You want to make your sprites spawn at somewhat random intervals, and you want them to spawn from the top, left, right, and bottom sides of the screen. For now, you'll just have them traveling in a straight direction across the screen, but they'll do so at varying speeds.

You need to let your SpriteManager class know when to spawn the next enemy sprite. Create a class-level variable in your SpriteManager class to store a value indicating the next spawn time:

```
int nextSpawnTime = 0;
```

Next, you need to initialize the variable to your next spawn time. Create a separate method that will set the next spawn time to some value between the spawn time

---

thresholds represented by the class-level variables you defined previously in the SpriteManager class:

```
private void ResetSpawnTime( )
{
    nextSpawnTime = ((Game1)Game).rnd.Next(
        enemySpawnMinMilliseconds,
        enemySpawnMaxMilliseconds);
}
```

You'll then need to call your new ResetSpawnTime method from the Initialize method of your SpriteManager class, so the variable is initialized when the game starts. Add the following line at the end of the Initialize method of the SpriteManager class, just before the call to base.Initialize:

```
ResetSpawnTime( );
```

Now you need to use the GameTime variable in the SpriteManager's Update method to determine when it's time to spawn a new enemy. Add this code to the beginning of the Update method:

```
nextSpawnTime -= gameTime.ElapsedGameTime.Milliseconds;
if (nextSpawnTime < 0)
{
    SpawnEnemy( );

    // Reset spawn timer
    ResetSpawnTime( );
}
```

This code first subtracts the elapsed game time in milliseconds from the NextSpawn Time variable (i.e., it subtracts the amount of time that has passed since the last call to Update). Once the NextSpawnTime variable is less than zero, your spawn timer expires, and it's time for you to unleash the fury of your new enemy upon the pitiful human player—err...I mean...it's time to spawn an AutomatedSprite. You spawn a new enemy via the SpawnEnemy method, which you'll write in just a moment. Then, you reset the NextSpawnTime to determine when a new enemy will spawn again.

The SpawnEnemy method will need to, well, spawn an enemy. You'll be choosing a random starting position for the enemy, at the left, right, top, or bottom of the screen. You'll also be choosing a random speed for the enemy based on the speed threshold variables in the Game1 class. To add the enemy sprite to the game, all you need to do is add a new AutomatedSprite to your SpriteList variable. Add the SpawnEnemy to your code as follows:

```
private void SpawnEnemy( )
{
    Vector2 speed = Vector2.Zero;
    Vector2 position = Vector2.Zero;

    // Default frame size
    Point frameSize = new Point(75, 75);
```

```
// Randomly choose which side of the screen to place enemy,
// then randomly create a position along that side of the screen
// and randomly choose a speed for the enemy
switch (((Game1)Game).rnd.Next(4))
{
    case 0: // LEFT to RIGHT
        position = new Vector2(
            -frameSize.X, ((Game1)Game).rnd.Next(0,
            Game.GraphicsDevice.PresentationParameters.BackBufferHeight
            - frameSize.Y));

        speed = new Vector2(((Game1)Game).rnd.Next(
            enemyMinSpeed,
            enemyMaxSpeed), 0);
        break;

    case 1: // RIGHT to LEFT
        position = new
            Vector2(
            Game.GraphicsDevice.PresentationParameters.BackBufferWidth,
            ((Game1)Game).rnd.Next(0,
            Game.GraphicsDevice.PresentationParameters.BackBufferHeight
            - frameSize.Y));

        speed = new Vector2(-((Game1)Game).rnd.Next(
            enemyMinSpeed, enemyMaxSpeed), 0);
        break;

    case 2: // BOTTOM to TOP
        position = new Vector2(((Game1)Game).rnd.Next(0,
            Game.GraphicsDevice.PresentationParameters.BackBufferWidth
            - frameSize.X),
            Game.GraphicsDevice.PresentationParameters.BackBufferHeight);

        speed = new Vector2(0,
            -((Game1)Game).rnd.Next(enemyMinSpeed,
            enemyMaxSpeed));
        break;

    case 3: // TOP to BOTTOM
        position = new Vector2(((Game1)Game).rnd.Next(0,
            Game.GraphicsDevice.PresentationParameters.BackBufferWidth
            - frameSize.X), -frameSize.Y);

        speed = new Vector2(0,
            ((Game1)Game).rnd.Next(enemyMinSpeed,
            enemyMaxSpeed));
        break;
}

// Create the sprite
spriteList.Add(
    new AutomatedSprite(Game.Content.Load<Texture2D>(@"images\skullball"),
```

```
            position, new Point(75, 75), 10, new Point(0, 0),
            new Point(6, 8), speed, "skullcollision"));
    }
```

First, this method creates variables for the speed and position of the soon-to-be-added sprite. Next, the `speed` and `position` variables are set by randomly choosing in which direction the new sprite will be heading. Then, the sprite is created and added to the list of sprites. The `frameSize` variable defined at the top of the method is used to determine how far to offset the sprite from all sides of the window.

Compile and run the application at this point, and you'll find that it's looking more and more like a real game. The enemy sprites are spawned from each edge of the screen, and they head across the screen in a straight line at varying speeds (see Figure 7-1).

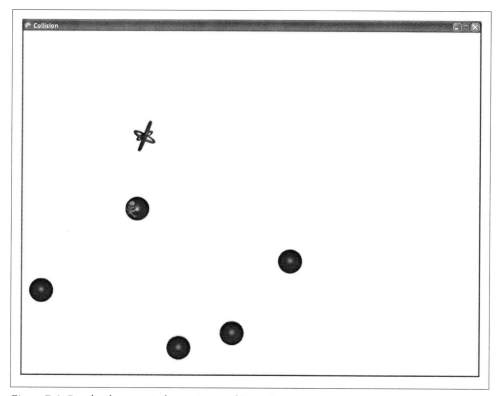

Figure 7-1. Randomly generated enemies attacking us!

OK, quiz time. Let's see how well you understand what's going on here, and what problems you might run into. Let the game run for a minute or so without user input. Some objects may hit the user-controlled sprite and disappear, but most of them will fly harmlessly off the edge of the screen. What's the problem, and how can you fix it?

If you said that you're not deleting your objects, you're really picking this up and understanding game concepts—great job! If you're confused by that, let me explain: when an automated sprite hits the user-controlled sprite, the automated sprite is removed from the list of sprites and destroyed. However, when an automated sprite makes it all the way across the screen, it simply disappears; you aren't doing anything with that object to destroy it and the player can no longer collide with the object to destroy it, either. The result is that these objects will continue forever outside the field of play, and in every frame, you will continue to update and draw each of them—not to mention running pointless collision checks on them. This problem will grow worse and worse until at some point it affects the performance of your game.

Irrelevant Objects

This brings us to a fundamental element of game development. One thing that is absolutely essential to any game is the definition of what makes an object "irrelevant." An object is considered irrelevant when it can no longer affect anything in the game.

Irrelevancy is handled differently in each game. Some games allow objects to leave the screen and then ultimately return. Other games destroy objects before they ever leave the screen. An example of the latter is seen in most renditions of the game *Asteroids*. In most versions of *Asteroids*, when shooting from one side of the screen to the other, a ship's bullet actually disappears before it leaves the screen. This is because the shot has a maximum distance that it can travel before it is deleted from the game. Although I'm not a huge fan of that functionality (yeah, I like guns that can shoot as far as I can see), the developers made the call that a bullet wouldn't be able to reach from one side of the screen to the other. You can argue the merits of that choice, but that's not the point. The point is that the developers decided what constituted irrelevancy for those bullets, and when they reached that point, they deleted them.

It's interesting to look at the *Asteroids* game further, because while its developers decided to remove bullets before they hit the edge of the screen, they did the opposite with the asteroids themselves: the asteroids are recycled immediately when they leave the screen, and they pop into view on another side of the screen. Again, you can argue about whether you like this behavior and whether it's realistic, but that's not the point. One of the great things about game development is that you control the world, and you can do whatever you want. The developers of *Asteroids* made that call, and hey, who can argue with one of the best classic games ever made, right?

Currently, you aren't doing anything about your irrelevant sprites. Your sprites leave the screen and never have any chance to return (you only have logic for the sprites to move forward, not to turn or double back), and therefore at that point they become irrelevant. Once one of your automated sprites leaves the screen, you need to detect that and get rid of it so that you don't waste precious processor time updating and drawing objects that will never come into play in the game again.

To do this, you need to add a method in your Sprite base class that will accept a Rectangle representing the window rectangle and return true or false to indicate whether the sprite is out of bounds. Add the following method to your Sprite class:

```
public bool IsOutOfBounds(Rectangle clientRect)
{
    if (position.X < -frameSize.X ||
        position.X > clientRect.Width ||
        position.Y < -frameSize.Y ||
        position.Y > clientRect.Height)
    {
        return true;
    }

    return false;
}
```

Next, you'll need to add to the Update method of your SpriteManager class some code that will loop through the list of AutomatedSprites and call the IsOutOfBounds method on each sprite, deleting those that are out of bounds. You already have code in the Update method of your SpriteManager class that loops through all your Automated Sprite objects. The current code should look something like this:

```
// Update all sprites
for (int i = 0; i < spriteList.Count; ++i)
{
    Sprite s = spriteList[i];

    s.Update(gameTime, Game.Window.ClientBounds);

    // Check for collisions
    if (s.collisionRect.Intersects(player.collisionRect))
    {
        // Play collision sound
        if(s.collisionCueName != null)
            ((Game1)Game).PlayCue(s.collisionCueName);

        // Remove collided sprite from the game
        spriteList.RemoveAt(i);
        --i;
    }
}
```

Add some code to check whether the sprite is out of bounds. If the sprite is out of bounds, remove it from the game. The preceding loop should now look like this (added lines are in bold):

```
// Update all sprites
for (int i = 0; i < spriteList.Count; ++i)
{
    Sprite s = spriteList[i];

    s.Update(gameTime, Game.Window.ClientBounds);
```

```
    // Check for collisions
    if (s.collisionRect.Intersects(player.collisionRect))
    {
        // Play collision sound
        if(s.collisionCueName != null)
            ((Game1)Game).PlayCue(s.collisionCueName);

        // Remove collided sprite from the game
        spriteList.RemoveAt(i);
        --i;
    }

    // Remove object if it is out of bounds
    if (s.IsOutOfBounds(Game.Window.ClientBounds))
    {
        spriteList.RemoveAt(i);
        --i;
    }

}
```

Now your irrelevant objects will be deleted after they leave the screen. Your game will have to update, draw, and run collision checks only on objects that are on the screen, and this will greatly improve performance, especially as the game progresses.

Creating a Chasing Sprite

As mentioned previously, when it comes to computer-controlled objects, the goal of any game is to make those objects appear intelligent to the point where a user may not be able to tell the difference between an object controlled by a human and an object controlled by a computer. We clearly aren't even close to that.

The automated sprites you've added do nothing more than move forward in a straight line. You've done some great work on your SpriteManager, but we haven't discussed how to do anything to improve the movement of your automated sprites.

Let's create a couple of different objects that do something a little more intelligent than simply moving in a straight line.

In this section, you'll create a new sprite type that will chase your user-controlled object around the screen. You'll do this with the following very simple chase algorithm:

```
if (player.X < chasingSprite.X)
    chasingSprite.X -= 1;
else if (player.X > chasingSprite.X)
    chasingSprite.X += 1;

if (player.Y < chasingSprite.Y)
    chasingSprite.Y -= 1;
else if (player.Y > chasingSprite.Y)
    chasingSprite.Y += 1;
```

Essentially, the algorithm compares the position of the player with that of the chasing sprite. If the player's X coordinate is less than the chasing sprite's X coordinate, the chasing sprite's coordinate is decremented. If the player's X coordinate is greater than the chasing sprite's X coordinate, the chasing sprite's X coordinate is incremented. The same is done with the Y coordinate.

To implement the chasing sprite, you'll want to create a new class that derives from `Sprite`. But before you do that, you can see from the preceding algorithm that the new class is going to need to know the position of the player object. Looking at your current `Sprite` class and its derived classes, there is no way to get that information. So, you'll need to add a public accessor to the `Sprite` base class that will return the position of the sprite object:

```
public Vector2 GetPosition
{
    get { return position; }
}
```

Then, add a method in your `SpriteManager` class that will return the position of the player object:

```
public Vector2 GetPlayerPosition(  )
{
    return player.GetPosition;
}
```

That done, you'll need to create a new class within your project (right-click on the project in the Solution Explorer and select Add→Class...). Name it *ChasingSprite.cs*, and replace the code that's generated with the following:

```
using System;
using Microsoft.Xna.Framework;
using Microsoft.Xna.Framework.Graphics;

namespace AnimatedSprites
{
    class ChasingSprite : Sprite
    {
        // Save a reference to the sprite manager to
        // use to get the player position
        SpriteManager spriteManager;

        public ChasingSprite(Texture2D textureImage, Vector2 position,
            Point frameSize, int collisionOffset, Point currentFrame,
            Point sheetSize, Vector2 speed, string collisionCueName,
            SpriteManager spriteManager)
            : base(textureImage, position, frameSize, collisionOffset,
            currentFrame, sheetSize, speed, collisionCueName)
        {
            this.spriteManager = spriteManager;
        }
```

```
public ChasingSprite(Texture2D textureImage, Vector2 position,
    Point frameSize, int collisionOffset, Point currentFrame,
    Point sheetSize, Vector2 speed, int millisecondsPerFrame,
    string collisionCueName, SpriteManager spriteManager)
    : base(textureImage, position, frameSize, collisionOffset,
    currentFrame, sheetSize, speed, millisecondsPerFrame,
    collisionCueName)
{
    this.spriteManager = spriteManager;
}

public override Vector2 direction
{
    get { return speed; }
}

public override void Update(GameTime gameTime, Rectangle clientBounds)
{
    // Use the player position to move the sprite closer in
    // the X and/or Y directions
    Vector2 player = spriteManager.GetPlayerPosition( );

    // Because sprite may be moving in the X or Y direction
    // but not both, get the largest of the two numbers and
    // use it as the speed of the object
    float speedVal = Math.Max(
        Math.Abs(speed.X), Math.Abs(speed.Y));

    if (player.X < position.X)
        position.X -= speedVal;
    else if (player.X > position.X)
        position.X += speedVal;

    if (player.Y < position.Y)
        position.Y -= speedVal;
    else if (player.Y > position.Y)
        position.Y += speedVal;

    base.Update(gameTime, clientBounds);
}
}
}
```

There are a couple of things to note about this code. First, the namespace that you're using is AnimatedSprites. This was what you should have named your project way back in the first couple of chapters in this book. If the namespace is giving you problems, you most likely named your project something else. Look at the namespace in your Game1 class, and use the same namespace that you have listed there in this file.

Next, notice that the constructor is essentially the same as the one in your Automated Sprite class, with one key exception: here, you've added a SpriteManager parameter and set a local SpriteManager variable to keep track of the object passed in via that parameter. During the Update method call, this object is used to retrieve the position of the player via the method you added previously.

The other important thing to understand is what's going on in the Update method. You're retrieving the position of the player and then running your chasing algorithm using the largest of the two coordinates specified in the speed member of the Sprite base class (because the sprites will be moving only in the X or the Y direction, not both).

The final thing that you'll need to change in order to get a functional chasing sprite is the SpriteList.Add call in your SpriteManager's SpawnEnemy method. You'll need to change the type of sprite you're creating to ChasingSprite instead of AutomatedSprite. This will result in creating ChasingSprite objects at random intervals rather than AutomatedSprites, and when you run your application, they should give you a good run for your money. Your SpriteList.Add call, which is at the end of the SpawnEnemy method in the SpriteManager class, should look like this:

```
spriteList.Add(
    new ChasingSprite (Game.Content.Load<Texture2D>(@"images\skullball"),
    position, new Point(75, 75), 10, new Point(0, 0),
    new Point(6, 8), speed, "skullcollision", this));
```

Run the application, and get ready to run for your life. You can try to avoid the objects, but eventually there'll be too many of them and you'll hit them. Try using a gamepad or the keyboard rather than the mouse for an even tougher challenge. Your application should, at this point, look something like Figure 7-2.

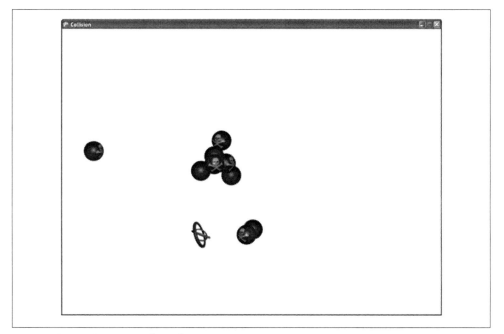

Figure 7-2. I can't get away from those sprites!!!

You can easily increase or decrease the difficulty of this algorithm by multiplying the speed member of the base class by some value. Increasing the speed will make your sprites chase the player faster, whereas decreasing the speed will slow them down. As it is, the objects definitely chase the player around the screen, but we're going to tweak them a little bit for the purposes of this game. Instead of having the objects chase the player indefinitely all over the screen, you're going to program them to continue on their course across the screen while veering toward the player. This will cause the chasing sprites to continue their course off the screen toward deletion from the game if the player successfully avoids them.

To accomplish this, you'll first need to figure out which direction a given sprite is moving in (remember that the sprites only move in one direction—up, down, left, or right). If the sprite is moving horizontally, you'll adjust only the sprite's vertical movement to chase the player. If the sprite is moving vertically, you'll adjust only the horizontal movement to chase the player. This will make the sprites continue in their original direction (horizontal or vertical) while chasing the player at the same time.

Replace the Update method of your ChasingSprite class with this one:

```
public override void Update(GameTime gameTime, Rectangle clientBounds)
{
    // First, move the sprite along its direction vector
    position += speed;

    // Use the player position to move the sprite closer in
    // the X and/or Y directions
    Vector2 player = spriteManager.GetPlayerPosition(  );

    // If player is moving vertically, chase horizontally
    if (speed.X == 0)
    {
        if (player.X < position.X)
            position.X -= Math.Abs(speed.Y);
        else if (player.X > position.X)
            position.X += Math.Abs(speed.Y);
    }

    // If player is moving horizontally, chase vertically
    if (speed.Y == 0)
    {
        if (player.Y < position.Y)
            position.Y -= Math.Abs(speed.X);
        else if (player.Y > position.Y)
            position.Y += Math.Abs(speed.X);
    }

    base.Update(gameTime, clientBounds);
}
```

This is a slightly modified chasing algorithm that will chase in only one direction. The method starts by adding the speed member to the sprite's position member. This will move the sprite forward in the direction of the speed vector.

After the position is updated, the player object's position is retrieved. Recall from when you wrote the code that generates the automated sprites that the code generates a `Vector2` for speed that will have a zero value in the X or Y coordinate (i.e., sprites move only vertically or horizontally, not diagonally). Because of this, the algorithm next detects whether the `ChasingSprite` is moving horizontally or vertically by determining which coordinate in the `Speed` variable is zero. If the X coordinate is zero, that means that the object is moving vertically, and the algorithm will then adjust only the X coordinate of the `ChasingSprite` to "chase" the player in only the horizontal direction. The result is that the sprite will continually move up or down across the screen, but while doing so, will sway to the left or the right to chase the player. The algorithm then runs the same checks and calculations for objects moving horizontally.

Compile and run the game now, and you'll see that the sprites move horizontally or vertically across the screen, but bend slightly to chase the player. As you'll probably notice when playing, the sprites that move more quickly are definitely more difficult to evade than the slower ones. That's because your objects are chasing the player at the same speed at which they are cruising across the screen (i.e., you're using the `speed` member variable to chase the player by using `Math.Abs(speed.X)` and `Math.Abs(speed.Y)`).

Congratulations! Now you're really getting somewhere. Not only does your game actually look and feel more like a real game, but you've just written an artificial intelligence algorithm that makes the sprites respond to the movements of the real human player. Pretty cool!

Creating an Evading Sprite

You now have two types of automated sprites in your application: one that moves across the screen without changing direction and one that moves across the screen but changes direction slightly to chase the player.

In this section, you'll build one more type of sprite that is similar to the chasing sprite, but this one will actually try to avoid the player. Why would you want to write a sprite that avoids the player? This sprite type will be used for something that the player will *want* to run into (maybe a power-up, or extra life, or something), so the sprite will tease the player by letting her get close to it but then, when she gets too close, taking off in another direction. This should add a nice different element to the game, as well as making it more challenging.

Let's get started. Add a new class to your project, and call it *EvadingSprite.cs*. The code for this sprite will be very similar to the code you just wrote for the `ChasingSprite`—so similar, in fact, that it will be easier to start with that code than to start from scratch. Remove the code generated for you in the `EvadingSprite` class and replace it by copying the code in the `ChasingSprite` class and pasting that code into the *EvadingSprite.cs* file. You'll need to change the name of the class from `ChasingSprite` to `EvadingSprite` and also change the names of the constructors. Your *EvadingSprite.cs* file should now look like this:

```
using System;
using Microsoft.Xna.Framework;
using Microsoft.Xna.Framework.Graphics;

namespace AnimatedSprites
{
    class EvadingSprite : Sprite
    {
        // Save a reference to the sprite manager to
        // use to get the player position
        SpriteManager spriteManager;

        public EvadingSprite(Texture2D textureImage, Vector2 position,
            Point frameSize, int collisionOffset, Point currentFrame,
            Point sheetSize, Vector2 speed, string collisionCueName,
            SpriteManager spriteManager)
            : base(textureImage, position, frameSize, collisionOffset,
            currentFrame, sheetSize, speed, collisionCueName)
        {
            this.spriteManager = spriteManager;
        }

        public EvadingSprite(Texture2D textureImage, Vector2 position,
            Point frameSize, int collisionOffset, Point currentFrame,
            Point sheetSize, Vector2 speed, int millisecondsPerFrame,
            string collisionCueName, SpriteManager spriteManager)
            : base(textureImage, position, frameSize, collisionOffset,
            currentFrame, sheetSize, speed, millisecondsPerFrame,
            collisionCueName)
        {
            this.spriteManager = spriteManager;
        }

        public override Vector2 direction
        {
            get { return speed; }
        }

        public override void Update(GameTime gameTime, Rectangle clientBounds)
        {
            // First, move the sprite along its direction vector
            position += speed;

            // Use the player position to move the sprite closer in
            // the X and/or Y directions
            Vector2 player = spriteManager.GetPlayerPosition(  );

            // If player is moving vertically, chase horizontally
            if (speed.X == 0)
            {
```

```
            if (player.X < position.X)
                position.X -= Math.Abs(speed.Y);
            else if (player.X > position.X)
                position.X += Math.Abs(speed.Y);
        }

        // If player is moving horizontally, chase vertically
        if (speed.Y == 0)
        {
            if (player.Y < position.Y)
                position.Y -= Math.Abs(speed.X);
            else if (player.Y > position.Y)
                position.Y += Math.Abs(speed.X);
        }

        base.Update(gameTime, clientBounds);
    }

  }
}
```

Because this code is exactly the same as the code you used for your ChasingSprite object, creating an object of this type at this point will create an object that will chase the user while moving across the screen. However, you want to program this class to actually run *away* from the player.

First, you'll need to tell the SpriteManager to create objects of the type EvadingSprite rather than ChasingSprite. To do this, modify the SpriteList.Add call in the Sprite Manager's SpawnEnemy method:

```
spriteList.Add(
    new EvadingSprite (Game.Content.Load<Texture2D>(@"images\skullball"),
    position, new Point(75, 75), 10, new Point(0, 0),
    new Point(6, 8), speed, "skullcollision", this));
```

Now you're ready to get to work on the evasion algorithm. The algorithm is really simple. In fact, it's essentially the opposite of the chasing algorithm: if the X coordinate of the player's position is less than the X coordinate of the evading sprite's position, rather than decreasing the value of the X coordinate of the evading sprite's position to move the sprite closer to the player, you'll increase the value to move the sprite farther away from the player.

You can do this by swapping the additions and subtractions in your chasing algorithm. Also, because you are now evading the player, you don't care about continuing in a straight line across the screen, so you can remove the two if statements detecting the direction in which the sprite is traveling. After making these changes, your Evading Sprite's Update method should look like this:

```
public override void Update(GameTime gameTime, Rectangle clientBounds)
{
    // First, move the sprite along its direction vector
    position += speed;
```

```
        // Use the player position to move the sprite closer in
        // the X and/or Y directions
        Vector2 player = spriteManager.GetPlayerPosition( );

        // Move away from the player horizontally
        if (player.X < position.X)
            position.X += Math.Abs(speed.Y);
        else if (player.X > position.X)
            position.X -= Math.Abs(speed.Y);

        // Move away from the player vertically
        if (player.Y < position.Y)
            position.Y += Math.Abs(speed.X);
        else if (player.Y > position.Y)
            position.Y -= Math.Abs(speed.X);

        base.Update(gameTime, clientBounds);
    }
```

Compile and run your project at this point, and you'll see that the objects are nearly impossible to catch. Instead of traveling across the screen, they veer off to one side to avoid even coming close to the player.

Although the sprites are effectively avoiding the player, this really isn't very fun. You're losing at your own game, and that's just lame. Let's modify the new sprite so that it travels across the screen just like an AutomatedSprite object, but then, when the player gets within a certain range of the object, the evasion algorithm turns on and the sprite turns and runs.

Add a few variables to your EvadingSprite class: one that will be used to detect when to activate the evasion algorithm, one that will determine the speed at which the sprite runs from the player, and one that will keep track of the sprite's state (possible states are evading and not evading). By default, you want this variable to indicate that your sprite is in a not-evading state:

```
float evasionSpeedModifier;
int evasionRange;
bool evade = false;
```

Why use a separate speed for evasion? You don't have to do this, but the evasion tactic will be somewhat unexpected for the user. All of the other sprites in the game either move forward only or actually chase after the player. Having a sprite turn and book it in a different direction will be a bit of a surprise and therefore will be a little harder for the player to handle. Using a modifier like this will enable you to increase or decrease the speed of the sprite while in evasion mode. You'll be able to play with the numbers and find a speed that feels right to you as a player/developer.

Next, update your constructors to accept parameters for the evasionSpeedModifier and evasionRange variables. You'll want to assign the values from those parameters to your member variables in the body of your constructors as well:

```
public EvadingSprite(Texture2D textureImage, Vector2 position,
    Point frameSize, int collisionOffset, Point currentFrame,
    Point sheetSize, Vector2 speed, string collisionCueName,
    SpriteManager spriteManager, float evasionSpeedModifier,
    int evasionRange)
    : base(textureImage, position, frameSize, collisionOffset,
    currentFrame, sheetSize, speed, collisionCueName)
{
    this.spriteManager = spriteManager;
    this.evasionSpeedModifier = evasionSpeedModifier;
    this.evasionRange = evasionRange;
}

public EvadingSprite(Texture2D textureImage, Vector2 position,
    Point frameSize, int collisionOffset, Point currentFrame,
    Point sheetSize, Vector2 speed, int millisecondsPerFrame,
    string collisionCueName, SpriteManager spriteManager,
    float evasionSpeedModifier, int evasionRange)
    : base(textureImage, position, frameSize, collisionOffset,
    currentFrame, sheetSize, speed, millisecondsPerFrame,
    collisionCueName)
{
    this.spriteManager = spriteManager;
    this.evasionSpeedModifier = evasionSpeedModifier;
    this.evasionRange = evasionRange;
}
```

Now you'll need to modify your Update method to add some logic that will make the sprite operate just like an AutomatedSprite would until the distance between the player's position and the sprite's position is less than the value in the evasionRange variable. You can use the Vector2.Distance method to determine the distance between two vectors.

Once the sprites are closer than the evasionRange, you need to reverse the direction of the sprite and activate the evasion algorithm. That algorithm should continue to run until the sprite is destroyed.

Your Update method should look something like this:

```
public override void Update(GameTime gameTime, Rectangle clientBounds)
{
    // First, move the sprite along its direction vector
    position += speed;

    // Use the player position to move the sprite closer in
    // the X and/or Y directions
    Vector2 player = spriteManager.GetPlayerPosition( );

    if (evade)
    {
        // Move away from the player horizontally
        if (player.X < position.X)
            position.X += Math.Abs(speed.Y);
        else if (player.X > position.X)
            position.X -= Math.Abs(speed.Y);
```

```
        // Move away from the player vertically
        if (player.Y < position.Y)
            position.Y += Math.Abs(speed.X);
        else if (player.Y > position.Y)
            position.Y -= Math.Abs(speed.X);
    }
    else
    {
        if (Vector2.Distance(position, player) < evasionRange)
        {
            // Player is within evasion range,
            // reverse direction and modify speed
            speed *= -evasionSpeedModifier;
            evade = true;
        }
    }

    base.Update(gameTime, clientBounds);
}
```

Finally, you'll need to change the `SpriteList.Add` call in the `SpriteManager`'s `Spawn Enemy` method once again, adding the two parameters to the constructor for the `EvadingSprite` object. For starters, pass in `.75f` as the modifier for the evasion speed and `150` for the evasion range. These values will cause the sprite to begin evading the player when the two are within a range of 150 units, and the sprite will evade at three quarters of its normal speed:

```
spriteList.Add(
    new EvadingSprite (Game.Content.Load<Texture2D>(@"images\skullball"),
    position, new Point(75, 75), 10, new Point(0, 0),
    new Point(6, 8), speed, "skullcollision", this, .75f, 150));
```

Compile and run the game now, and you'll see that the sprites seem to have a bit more "intelligence." They detect when the player is near, and they turn and head off in the opposite direction. Also, you'll find that you probably can catch most of them, but they're still a bit tricky. Once you add the other sprites floating around that the player actually has to avoid, this evasion technique will be just enough to represent a good challenge.

So that's it? Is that artificial intelligence?

Well, not quite. We haven't even scratched the surface of true artificial intelligence algorithms. In fact, many hardcore AI experts would argue that this isn't artificial intelligence at all—and they might be right. Again, the science is somewhat ambiguous, and who's to say whether what you've done here truly represents intelligence or not?

The point here is that you can definitely go overboard in the name of science sometimes. True artificial intelligence research and algorithms absolutely have a place in the world, but probably not in a 2D sprite-avoidance game. When programming artificially intelligent objects—especially in video games—there is a certain level of "intelligence" that is typically "good enough." You could spend months or years fine-tuning an algorithm for this game so you could argue that it is truly intelligent, but at what cost, and at what advantage to the player?

Unfortunately, there is no right or wrong answer in relation to the degree or quality of artificial intelligence that should be implemented, and it comes down to a decision that you as the developer must make. Ultimately, it's up to you to decide when your algorithm needs improvement and at what point it's good enough for what you're trying to accomplish.

What You Just Did

You're now very close to having something worthy of your newly developed XNA prowess. In the next chapter, you'll fine-tune the game and wrap up your 2D development. In the meantime, let's reflect on what you just accomplished:

- You learned some background to artificial intelligence.
- You created a factory for sprites that creates sprites at random intervals.
- You learned about irrelevant objects and what to do with them to improve game performance.
- You created a chasing sprite that follows a player across the screen.
- You created an evading sprite that runs from a player.
- You drank from the fount of XNA goodness.

Summary

- Artificial intelligence means many different things, mainly because the term "intelligence" itself is ambiguous and difficult to define.
- Alan Turing made great strides in the field of artificial intelligence. Much of his work is directly relevant to what game developers attempt to accomplish.
- Irrelevant objects are objects that will no longer affect gameplay (e.g., a bullet that's shot into the sky and doesn't hit anything). These objects must be removed and deleted in order to not negatively impact performance as they accrue.
- To implement a chase algorithm, detect the position of the player in relation to the chaser's current position, and then move the chasing object in the direction of the player.
- Implementing an evasion algorithm is the opposite of the chase algorithm: detect the position of the player, and move the evading object in the opposite direction.
- "Artificial intelligence is no match for natural stupidity." —Anonymous

Test Your Knowledge: Quiz

1. What is the Turing Test?
2. Why is artificial intelligence so difficult to perfect?
3. What constitutes irrelevancy for an object in a video game? What should be done with irrelevant objects, and why?
4. If you have a player whose position is stored in a `Vector2` object called `PlayerPos` and a chasing object whose position is stored in a `Vector2` object called `ChasePos`, what algorithm will cause your chasing object to chase after your player?
5. In the beginning, what was created that made a lot of people very angry and has been widely regarded as a bad move?

Test Your Knowledge: Exercise

Take what you've learned in this chapter and make yet another type of sprite object, one that moves randomly around the screen. To do this, you'll want to create a random timer that signifies when the object should change directions. When the timer expires, have the object move in a different direction, and then reset the random timer to a new random time at which the object will again shift its direction.

CHAPTER 8

Putting It All Together

All right, you've built a solid design and have the start of what could become a pretty cool game. Again, the concept of the game is that a player will control one sprite and try to avoid hitting the chasing sprites as they fly across the screen, while also trying to catch the evading sprites. Now you need to add some scoring and some game logic and do some other fine-tuning to get your game to where you want it.

The first thing you'll do in this chapter is add some scoring to your game. The first step when you're writing a game and you start to look at scoring is to decide what events will trigger a change in score. Sometimes scores will change when a weapon of some kind hits the player. At other times, you'll change the score when the player hits something herself. Still other times, you'll want to change the score when the user accomplishes something (e.g., answers a question, solves a puzzle, etc.).

In this game, you're going to change the score when an enemy sprite leaves the screen without having run into the player (meaning that the player successfully avoided that sprite).

It would make sense, given that scoring mechanism, for you to add a score value to each individual sprite. Some sprites might be worth more than others, based on their speed or some other factor that you determine.

In addition to deciding how to calculate the score, you need to be able to draw the score on the screen. We'll tackle that side of the scoring problem first, and then see how to adjust the score whenever a sprite crosses the screen without hitting the player.

In addition to adding scoring to your game and learning to draw text using Sprite Fonts in this chapter, you'll also add some variety to your sprites by introducing different sprite images and different sounds for each sprite type. You'll also add a background image, look at game states, and add a power-up to the game.

Drawing 2D Text

This chapter builds on the code that you finished writing in Chapter 7. Open that game project and use it throughout this chapter.

First, you'll need to add an integer variable representing a sprite's score value to the Sprite base class (note the addition of the public get accessor as well, via auto-implemented properties):

```
public int scoreValue {get; protected set;}
```

Modify both constructors in the Sprite class to receive an integer value for the score value for that sprite. The first constructor should pass the value to the second constructor, and the second constructor should use that value to set the scoreValue member variable. The constructors for the Sprite class should now look like this:

```
public Sprite(Texture2D textureImage, Vector2 position, Point frameSize,
    int collisionOffset, Point currentFrame, Point sheetSize, Vector2 speed,
    string collisionCueName, int scoreValue)
    : this(textureImage, position, frameSize, collisionOffset, currentFrame,
    sheetSize, speed, defaultMillisecondsPerFrame, collisionCueName,
    scoreValue)
{
}

public Sprite(Texture2D textureImage, Vector2 position, Point frameSize,
    int collisionOffset, Point currentFrame, Point sheetSize, Vector2 speed,
    int millisecondsPerFrame, string collisionCueName, int scoreValue)
{
    this.textureImage = textureImage;
    this.position = position;
    this.frameSize = frameSize;
    this.collisionOffset = collisionOffset;
    this.currentFrame = currentFrame;
    this.sheetSize = sheetSize;
    this.speed = speed;
    this.collisionCueName = collisionCueName;
    this.millisecondsPerFrame = millisecondsPerFrame;
    this.scoreValue = scoreValue;
}
```

You'll also have to change the constructors for the derived classes (AutomatedSprite, ChasingSprite, EvadingSprite, and UserControlledSprite) to accept an integer parameter for the score value and to pass that value on to the base class constructor. The constructors for those sprites should look like this:

Constructors for the AutomatedSprite *class*

```
public AutomatedSprite(Texture2D textureImage, Vector2 position,
    Point frameSize, int collisionOffset, Point currentFrame, Point sheetSize,
    Vector2 speed, string collisionCueName, int scoreValue)
    : base(textureImage, position, frameSize, collisionOffset, currentFrame,
    sheetSize, speed, collisionCueName, scoreValue)
{
```

```
    }

    public AutomatedSprite(Texture2D textureImage, Vector2 position,
        Point frameSize, int collisionOffset, Point currentFrame, Point sheetSize,
        Vector2 speed, int millisecondsPerFrame, string collisionCueName,
        int scoreValue)
        : base(textureImage, position, frameSize, collisionOffset, currentFrame,
        sheetSize, speed, millisecondsPerFrame, collisionCueName, scoreValue)
    {
    }
```

Constructors for the ChasingSprite *class*

```
    public ChasingSprite(Texture2D textureImage, Vector2 position,
        Point frameSize, int collisionOffset, Point currentFrame,
        Point sheetSize, Vector2 speed, string collisionCueName,
        SpriteManager spriteManager, int scoreValue)
        : base(textureImage, position, frameSize, collisionOffset,
        currentFrame, sheetSize, speed, collisionCueName, scoreValue)
    {
        this.spriteManager = spriteManager;
    }

    public ChasingSprite(Texture2D textureImage, Vector2 position,
        Point frameSize, int collisionOffset, Point currentFrame,
        Point sheetSize, Vector2 speed, int millisecondsPerFrame,
        string collisionCueName, SpriteManager spriteManager,
        int scoreValue)
        : base(textureImage, position, frameSize, collisionOffset,
        currentFrame, sheetSize, speed, millisecondsPerFrame,
        collisionCueName, scoreValue)
    {
        this.spriteManager = spriteManager;
    }
```

Constructors for the EvadingSprite *class*

```
    public EvadingSprite(Texture2D textureImage, Vector2 position,
        Point frameSize, int collisionOffset, Point currentFrame,
        Point sheetSize, Vector2 speed, string collisionCueName,
        SpriteManager spriteManager, float evasionSpeedModifier,
        int evasionRange, int scoreValue)
        : base(textureImage, position, frameSize, collisionOffset,
        currentFrame, sheetSize, speed, collisionCueName, scoreValue)
    {
        this.spriteManager = spriteManager;
        this.evasionSpeedModifier = evasionSpeedModifier;
        this.evasionRange = evasionRange;
    }

    public EvadingSprite(Texture2D textureImage, Vector2 position,
        Point frameSize, int collisionOffset, Point currentFrame,
        Point sheetSize, Vector2 speed, int millisecondsPerFrame,
        string collisionCueName, SpriteManager spriteManager,
        float evasionSpeedModifier, int evasionRange,
        int scoreValue)
```

```
        : base(textureImage, position, frameSize, collisionOffset,
        currentFrame, sheetSize, speed, millisecondsPerFrame,
        collisionCueName, scoreValue)
    {
        this.spriteManager = spriteManager;
        this.evasionSpeedModifier = evasionSpeedModifier;
        this.evasionRange = evasionRange;
    }
```

Constructors for the UserControlledSprite *class*

```
    public UserControlledSprite(Texture2D textureImage, Vector2 position,
        Point frameSize, int collisionOffset, Point currentFrame, Point sheetSize,
        Vector2 speed)
        : base(textureImage, position, frameSize, collisionOffset, currentFrame,
        sheetSize, speed, null, 0)
    {
    }

    public UserControlledSprite(Texture2D textureImage, Vector2 position,
        Point frameSize, int collisionOffset, Point currentFrame, Point sheetSize,
        Vector2 speed, int millisecondsPerFrame)
        : base(textureImage, position, frameSize, collisionOffset, currentFrame,
        sheetSize, speed, millisecondsPerFrame, null, 0)
    {
    }
```

 The UserControlledSprite will not have a score value associated with it, because the player can't be awarded points for avoiding himself. Therefore, you won't need to add a new parameter to the constructor for this class, but you will need to pass a 0 to the score Value parameter of the constructors for the base class.

Finally, in the SpriteManager class, you'll need to add the score value as the final parameter in the constructor when initializing new Sprite objects. You're currently creating objects only of type EvadingSprite, and you're doing this at the end of the SpawnEnemy method. Add a zero as the score value for the EvadingSprites you're creating. (You'll be adding some logic later in this chapter that will create different types of sprites and assign different score values to those sprites based on their types.) The code that creates your EvadingSprite objects in the SpawnEnemy method should now look like this:

```
    spriteList.Add(
        new EvadingSprite (Game.Content.Load<Texture2D>(@"images\skullball"),
        position, new Point(75, 75), 10, new Point(0, 0),
        new Point(6, 8), speed, "skullcollision", this, .75f, 150, 0));
```

You now have a way to calculate the score during the game based on events with different sprites. Even though you're currently only using zeros as the score values, the underlying code is now there, so you can start to write some scoring logic for the game. First, you'll need to add to the Game1 class a variable that represents the total score of the current game:

```
int currentScore = 0;
```

Now you're ready to draw the score on the screen. Drawing text in 2D is done in a very similar manner to the way that you draw sprites. For every frame that is drawn, you will draw text on that frame using a `SpriteBatch` and an object called a `SpriteFont`. When drawing 2D images on the screen, you specify an image file to use and a `Texture2D` object to hold that image. XNA then takes the image from memory and sends the data to the graphics card.

The same thing happens when drawing with `SpriteFont` objects. In this case, a sprite-font file is created. This is an XML file defining the characteristics of a given font: font family, font size, font spacing, etc. A `SpriteFont` object is used in memory to represent the spritefont. When the `SpriteFont` object is drawn, XNA will build a 2D image using the text you want to draw and the font specified in the XML file. The image is then sent to the graphics device to be drawn on the screen.

When drawing the game score, you'll want to use the value of the `currentScore` variable. As the variable's value changes, the score on the screen will be updated.

To draw text on the screen using a `SpriteFont`, you need to add a `SpriteFont` resource to your project. First, add a new resource folder to your project for font objects. Right-click the *AnimatedSpritesContent* project in Solution Explorer and select Add→New Folder. Name the folder *Fonts*. Now, add the actual spritefont resource. Right-click the new *AnimatedSpritesContent\Fonts* folder in Solution Explorer and select Add→New Item.... On the left side of the Add New Item window, select the Visual C# category. Select Sprite Font for the template and name the spritefont *Score.spritefont* (see Figure 8-1).

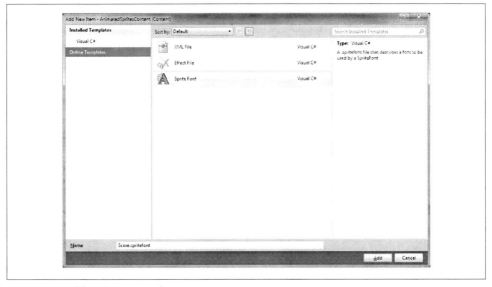

Figure 8-1. Adding Score.spritefont to your project

Spritefonts are resources that are picked up and processed by the content pipeline. As such, they must be created within the *AnimatedSpritesContent* project of your project.

By default, XNA 4.0 uses a font named "Kootenay" when creating a new spritefont. You can change the type of font used in your spritefont by editing the file and changing the name of the font found in the line of code that reads `<FontName>Kootenay</Font Name>`. It is recommended that you select a font from the Redistributable Font Pack, which can be found at *http://creators.xna.com/en-us/contentpack/fontpack*.

Once you click the Add button, the spritefont file will be created and will open in Visual Studio. You'll notice that it's an XML file that contains information such as the font name, size, spacing, style, and so on. You can modify these values to customize your font as needed.

Next, you need to add a `SpriteFont` variable, which will store your spritefont in memory. Add the following class-level variable at the top of your `Game1` class:

```
SpriteFont scoreFont;
```

Now, load your `SpriteFont` object via the content pipeline, the same way that you've loaded most other game assets. You'll retrieve the font from the content pipeline using the `Content.Load` method. Add the following line of code to the `LoadContent` method in your `Game1` class:

```
scoreFont = Content.Load<SpriteFont>(@"fonts\score");
```

The next step is to actually draw the text on the screen. As mentioned earlier, this is done via a `SpriteBatch` object. Instead of using the `SpriteBatch`'s `Draw` method, you'll use a method called `DrawString` to draw text using a `SpriteFont`. Add the following code to the `Draw` method of your `Game1` class, between the call to `GraphicsDevice.Clear` and the call to `base.Draw`:

```
spriteBatch.Begin( );

// Draw fonts
spriteBatch.DrawString(scoreFont, "Score: " + currentScore,
    new Vector2(10, 10), Color.DarkBlue, 0, Vector2.Zero,
    1, SpriteEffects.None, 1);

spriteBatch.End( );
```

Notice that the font needs to be drawn between calls to `SpriteBatch.Begin` and `Sprite Batch.End`, because XNA treats spritefonts just like any other 2D image resources.

The `DrawString` method has parameters that are similar to the parameters used in calls to `SpriteBatch.Draw` for 2D images. You can adjust the position, color, scale, etc. of the font to be drawn. The first parameter passed into the `DrawString` method is the `Sprite Font` object you wish to use to draw with, and the second parameter is the actual text you wish to draw.

In XNA 2.0, monospaced fonts did not render properly. XNA treated them as regular fonts (losing the benefit of a monospaced font). In XNA 4.0 this issue was fixed, and monospaced fonts now render properly.

Compile and run the game at this point and you should see the score drawn at the upper-left corner of the screen, as shown in Figure 8-2.

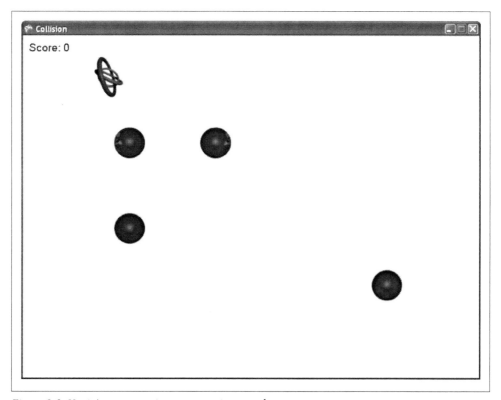

Figure 8-2. Yay! A score...wait...my score is zero...hmmm...

Excellent work! You now have an overall game score, and that means you're one step closer to completing your game. However, the problem you have now is that you never update the game score. Before you do that, you need to add logic to create different types of sprites at random intervals rather than always creating the same type of sprite. Once you've implemented those changes, you can add scoring for the different sprite types.

Randomly Generating Different Sprite Types

To randomly generate sprites of different types, you first need to determine the likelihood that each type will be created. Most of the sprites in this game will be Automated Sprites. ChasingSprites will be the next most common, and EvadingSprites will show up only occasionally. In this section, you'll be assigning a percentage likelihood to each type of sprite. Each time a new sprite is spawned, you'll determine which type of sprite to create based on those percentages. The exact percentage likelihood for each sprite type is something that you can play with as you test your game, and you can adjust the values to the point where they feel right to you, the developer.

To begin, open the SpriteManager class and add three new class-level variables representing the likelihood that each sprite type will be spawned:

```
int likelihoodAutomated = 75;
int likelihoodChasing = 20;
int likelihoodEvading = 5;
```

You'll notice that the values added equal 100 (representing 100%). Essentially, 75% of the time you'll generate an AutomatedSprite, 20% of the time a ChasingSprite, and 5% an EvadingSprite.

Now you have to add some code that will generate a random number and, based on the value of that random number, create one of the three sprite types. Open your SpriteManager class and replace this call to SpriteList.Add, which is at the end of the SpawnEnemy method:

```
spriteList.Add(
    new EvadingSprite (Game.Content.Load<Texture2D>(@"images\skullball"),
    position, new Point(75, 75), 10, new Point(0, 0),
    new Point(6, 8), speed, "skullcollision", this, .75f, 150, 0));
```

with the following code:

```
// Get random number
int random = ((Game1)Game).rnd.Next(100);
if (random < likelihoodAutomated)
{
    // Create AutomatedSprite
    spriteList.Add(
        new AutomatedSprite(Game.Content.Load<Texture2D>(@"images\skullball"),
        position, new Point(75, 75), 10, new Point(0,0), new Point(6, 8),
        speed, "skullcollision", 0));
}
else if (random < likelihoodAutomated +
    likelihoodChasing)
{
    // Create ChasingSprite
    spriteList.Add(
        new ChasingSprite(Game.Content.Load<Texture2D>(@"images\skullball"),
        position, new Point(75, 75), 10, new Point(0,0), new Point(6, 8),
        speed, "skullcollision", this, 0));               }
```

```
    else
    {
        // Create EvadingSprite
        spriteList.Add(
            new EvadingSprite(Game.Content.Load<Texture2D>(@"images\skullball"),
                position, new Point(75, 75), 10, new Point(0, 0), new Point(6, 8),
                speed, "skullcollision", this, .75f, 150, 0));
    }
```

This code first generates a number between 0 and 99, and then compares that generated number to the value representing how often an AutomatedSprite should be generated. If the generated number is less than that value, an AutomatedSprite is created. If the randomly generated number is not less than that value, it is then compared against the sum of the value representing how often an AutomatedSprite should be generated and the value representing how often a ChasingSprite should be generated. If the generated value is less than the sum of those two values, a ChasingSprite is generated. If it isn't less than that value, an EvadingSprite is generated.

If that doesn't make sense, think of it this way: using the values from our current example, the random number (some value between 0 and 99) is first evaluated to see whether it is less than 75. If it is, an AutomatedSprite is generated. This represents a 75% chance that an AutomatedSprite will be created, which is exactly what you want. If the random number is greater than 75, it is then checked to see whether it is less than 95 (i.e., the sum of the chance of creating an AutomatedSprite, which is 75%, and the chance of creating a ChasingSprite, which is 20%). Because this comparison would never have been performed if the random number had been less than 75, this is essentially checking to see whether the value is between 75 and 94—which represents a 20% chance that a ChasingSprite will be created (again, this is exactly what you want). Finally, an EvadingSprite will be generated if neither case is true—in other words, if the random value is between 95 and 99, of which there is a 5% chance, as you wanted.

Oh yeah! This is all starting to come together. Compile and run the game, and you should notice that the majority of the sprites generated are AutomatedSprites, some ChasingSprites are mixed in, and an occasional EvadingSprite shows up. Good times!

The problem that your game has at this point is that while the sprites have different behaviors, they all look the same. Not only does that make things somewhat boring, but it's also confusing to the player because one would expect similar-looking sprites to behave similarly. You need to add some diversity to these different types of sprites.

Adding Some Variety to Your Sprites

First things first, you need some more images. If you haven't already done so, download the source code for this chapter of the book. Within this chapter's source code (in the *AnimatedSprites\AnimatedSpritesContent\Images* folder), you'll find some sprite sheet files for the different types of sprites.

Right-click the *Content\Images* folder in Solution Explorer and select Add→Existing Item.... Navigate to the *AnimatedSprites\AnimatedSpritesContent\Images* folder of the source code for this chapter and add the *bolt.png, fourblades.png, threeblades.png*, and *plus.png* images to your project.

In addition to a new image for each of the new sprites, you'll want some different sounds for collisions with each type. Also with the source code for this chapter, in the *Anima-tedSprites\AnimatedSpritesContent\Audio* folder, you'll find some *.wav* files. Copy the *boltcollision.wav, fourbladescollision.wav, pluscollision.wav*, and *threebladescolli-sion.wav* files from that folder to your own project's *AnimatedSpritesContent\Audio* folder using Windows Explorer. Remember that when dealing with actual sound files, you don't add them to the project in Visual Studio. You need to copy them to your project's *AnimatedSpritesContent\Audio* directory, but you'll add them to the project using XACT rather than within Visual Studio.

Once you've copied the files, start XACT so that you can add these new *.wav* files to your XACT project file.

In XACT, load the sound project for this game (the file should be called *GameAudio.xap* and should be located in your project's *AnimatedSpritesContent\Au-dio* folder). Open the Wave Bank and Sound Bank windows for your XACT project by double-clicking on the *Wave Bank* and *Sound Bank* nodes in the tree menu on the left.

In the Wave Bank window, right-click and select Insert Wave File(s).... Select the four new *.wav* files that you've copied to your project's *Content\Audio* directory, as shown in Figure 8-3.

When you click Open, the *.wav* files will be added to your Wave Bank window, which should now look something like Figure 8-4.

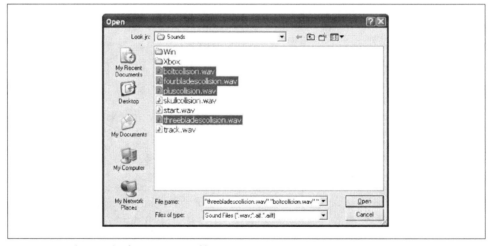

Figure 8-3. Selecting the four new .wav files

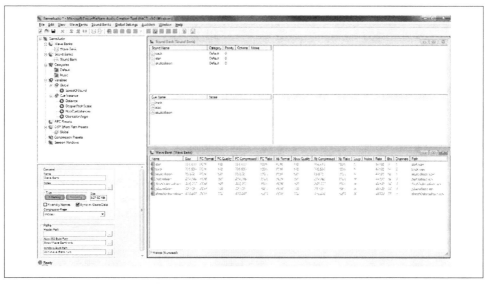

Figure 8-4. The four new .wav files are added to the Wave Bank and will appear highlighted in red

Next, drag the items you just added from the Wave Bank window into the Cue Name section of the Sound Bank window. You need to drop them in the Cue Name section rather than the Sound Name section because you need cue names for each of these sounds in order to play them from your code. Your window should now have the new sounds listed in the Wave Bank window and in the Sound Name and Cue Name sections of the Sound Bank window, as shown in Figure 8-5.

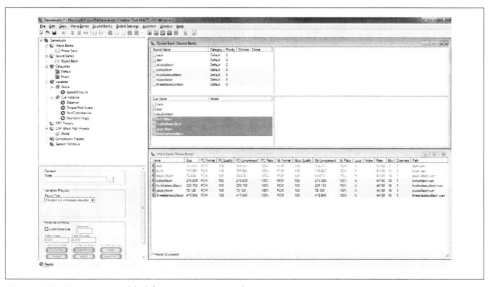

Figure 8-5. Cue names added for your new sounds

You can adjust the volume levels of the sounds to your liking, as described in Chapter 6. Once you're satisfied, save your project, exit XACT, and return to Visual Studio.

Now you'll need to assign the new images and sounds to the different types of sprites when they spawn. Luckily, because of the way you've designed your SpriteManager class, this will be easy. You are already randomly creating different types of sprites, and now all you need to do is apply the different images and sounds to those sprites.

You may be wondering about some of the files you've just added, because currently you have only three types of sprites. However, there are actually six different sprite sheets in your project. Take a look at Table 8-1 to see the intended use for each of the sprites in this game.

Table 8-1. Sprite images and their purposes

Sprite image	Name	Purpose
	Three rings	Used for the player-controlled sprite.
	Three blades	This saw image (as well as the four-blade image) is used in AutomatedSprites and represents the enemy of the player. The player must avoid getting hit by these objects, or the game will end. You'll add "lives" to the game later in this chapter, allowing the player to get hit a number of times before the game ends.
	Four blades	This saw image (as well as the three-blade image) is used in AutomatedSprites and represents the enemy of the player. The player must avoid getting hit by these objects, or the game will end. You'll add "lives" to the game later in this chapter, allowing the player to get hit a number of times before the game ends.
	Skull ball	Used in ChasingSprites that pursue the player. If an object of this type hits the player sprite, the player's movement speed will be cut by 50% for a short time, making it harder to avoid the AutomatedSprites.
	Plus	Used in ChasingSprites that pursue the player. If an object of this type hits the player sprite, the player sprite will double in size for a short time, making it harder to avoid AutomatedSprites.
	Bolt	Used in EvadingSprites. This is the only type of sprite object the player will actually want to collide with. Colliding with a bolt will increase the player's movement speed for a short time, allowing him to avoid AutomatedSprites more easily.

In the SpriteManager class's SpawnEnemy method, you added the code that randomly generates different types of sprites. You'll need to change that code to create one of the five nonplayer sprite types mentioned in the preceding table. If the random-number comparison indicates that you need to create an AutomatedSprite, you'll need to do another random calculation to determine whether you'll be creating a three-blade object or a four-blade object (both should have a 50% probability).

Likewise, if a ChasingSprite is chosen, you'll need to do a random calculation to determine whether to create a plus or a skull ball (again, with a 50% chance for either one). Finally, if an `EvadingSprite` is to be created, you'll create the bolt sprite. Replace the following code that you just added to the end of the `SpawnEnemy` method:

```
// Get random number
int random = ((Game1)Game).rnd.Next(100);
if (random < likelihoodAutomated)
{
    // Create AutomatedSprite
    spriteList.Add(
        new AutomatedSprite(Game.Content.Load<Texture2D>(@"images\skullball"),
        position, new Point(75, 75), 10, new Point(0,0), new Point(6, 8),
        speed, "skullcollision", 0));
}
else if (random < likelihoodAutomated +
    likelihoodChasing)
{
    // Create ChasingSprite
    spriteList.Add(
        new ChasingSprite(Game.Content.Load<Texture2D>(@"images\skullball"),
        position, new Point(75, 75), 10, new Point(0,0), new Point(6, 8),
        speed, "skullcollision", this, 0));          }
else
{
    // Create EvadingSprite
    spriteList.Add(
        new EvadingSprite(Game.Content.Load<Texture2D>(@"images\skullball"),
        position, new Point(75, 75), 10, new Point(0, 0), new Point(6, 8),
        speed, "skullcollision", this, .75f, 150, 0));
}
```

with this code:

```
// Get random number between 0 and 99
int random = ((Game1)Game).rnd.Next(100);
if (random < likelihoodAutomated)
{
    // Create an AutomatedSprite.
    // Get new random number to determine whether to
    // create a three-blade or four-blade sprite.
    if (((Game1)Game).rnd.Next(2) == 0)
    {
        // Create a four-blade enemy
        spriteList.Add(
            new AutomatedSprite(
                Game.Content.Load<Texture2D>(@"images\fourblades"),
                position, new Point(75, 75), 10, new Point(0, 0),
                new Point(6, 8), speed, "fourbladescollision", 0));
    }
    else
    {
        // Create a three-blade enemy
        spriteList.Add(
            new AutomatedSprite(
                Game.Content.Load<Texture2D>(@"images\threeblades"),
                position, new Point(75, 75), 10, new Point(0, 0),
                new Point(6, 8), speed, "threebladescollision", 0));
```

```
        }
    }
    else if (random < likelihoodAutomated +
        likelihoodChasing)
    {
        // Create a ChasingSprite.
        // Get new random number to determine whether
        // to create a skull or a plus sprite.
        if (((Game1)Game).rnd.Next(2) == 0)
        {
            // Create a skull
            spriteList.Add(
                new ChasingSprite(
                    Game.Content.Load<Texture2D>(@"images\skullball"),
                    position, new Point(75, 75), 10, new Point(0, 0),
                    new Point(6, 8), speed, "skullcollision", this, 0));
        }
        else
        {
            // Create a plus
            spriteList.Add(
                new ChasingSprite(
                    Game.Content.Load<Texture2D>(@"images\plus"),
                    position, new Point(75, 75), 10, new Point(0, 0),
                    new Point(6, 4), speed, "pluscollision", this, 0));
        }
    }
    else
    {
        // Create an EvadingSprite
        spriteList.Add(
            new EvadingSprite(
                Game.Content.Load<Texture2D>(@"images\bolt"),
                position, new Point(75, 75), 10, new Point(0, 0),
                new Point(6, 8), speed, "boltcollision", this,
                .75f, 150, 0));
    }
```

One important thing to note is that the sprite sheet for the plus ChasingSprite has six columns and only four rows, whereas all the others have six columns but eight rows. If you run your game and the plus sprite animates, disappears, and reappears, that most likely is the cause of your issue.

Compile and run the game now, and you should see a variety of objects running around the screen with different behaviors, as shown in Figure 8-6. These objects should also make different sounds when they collide with the player.

You probably received a compilation warning about the likelihoodEvading variable in the AnimatedSprite class. This variable is assigned but never used. If you look at your code, you'll see that the variable really only exists to show the percentage likelihood of creating an evading sprite. The value isn't used in the code. To avoid the warning, you can comment out that line (don't remove it, though, as it's useful for maintenance

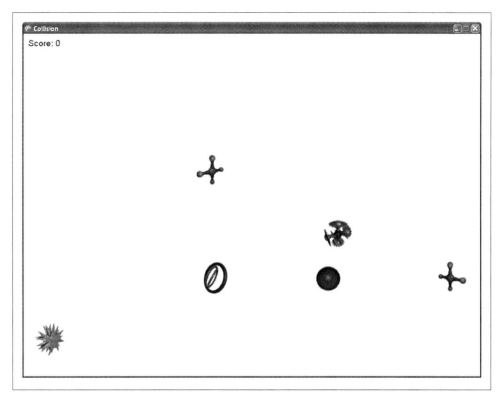

Figure 8-6. A variety of sprites—sweet!

purposes—this variable quickly shows the percentage likelihood of an evading sprite being created).

Adding a Background Image

Next, you'll add a little more spice to your game by adding a background image. With the source code for this chapter (again, in the *AnimatedSprites\Animated-SpritesContent\Images* folder), you'll find an image named *background.jpg*. Add the image to the project the same way you added the other images (right-click the *AnimatedSpritesContent\Images* folder, select Add→Existing Item..., and navigate to the *background.jpg* image included with the source code).

Your `SpriteManager` class was built to handle animated sprites and derived classes. Something as simple as a background image can just be added to your `Game1` class. You'll need to add a `Texture2D` variable for the image:

```
Texture2D backgroundTexture;
```

and load the `Texture2D` image in the `LoadContent` method:

```
backgroundTexture = Content.Load<Texture2D>(@"Images\background");
```

Next, you'll need to add the code to draw the image. Because you'll now have multiple sprites being drawn within your `Game1` class (the `SpriteFont` counts as a sprite, so you'll be drawing a score sprite as well as a background sprite), you need to make sure that the score text is always on top of the background image. Typically, when trying to ensure that one sprite is on top of another, you modify the `SpriteBatch.Begin` call to include an appropriate `SpriteSortMode`. However, this is a case where you're drawing only two items, and you know that you'll always want to draw the score on top of the background. As such, you can forego the overhead involved in specifying a sort mode in the `Begin` method, and instead always draw the background first and then the score.

Modify the `Draw` method of your `Game1` class to look like this:

```
protected override void Draw(GameTime gameTime)
{
    GraphicsDevice.Clear(Color.White);

    spriteBatch.Begin( );

    // Draw background image
    spriteBatch.Draw(backgroundTexture,
        new Rectangle(0, 0, Window.ClientBounds.Width,
        Window.ClientBounds.Height), null,
        Color.White, 0, Vector2.Zero,
        SpriteEffects.None, 0);

    // Draw fonts
    spriteBatch.DrawString(scoreFont, "Score: " + currentScore,
        new Vector2(10, 10), Color.DarkBlue, 0, Vector2.Zero,
        1, SpriteEffects.None, 1);

    spriteBatch.End( );

    base.Draw(gameTime);
}
```

Compile and run the game, and you'll see the impact that a background image can have on the overall look of the game (Figure 8-7). This is getting exciting—things are really starting to come together!

Nice job. You have a background and multiple types of sprites with varying behaviors. Now let's take a look at finishing up the game scoring logic.

Game Scoring

As you'll recall from our earlier discussion of this topic, the first thing you need to do is determine what event(s) will trigger a change in score. For this game, you'll be updating the score whenever the user successfully avoids a three-blade, four-blade, skull ball, or plus sprite. You actually have already added the logic to determine when one of those sprites has been successfully avoided; it lies in the code that deletes the sprites when they disappear off the edge of the screen. If a sprite makes it across the screen

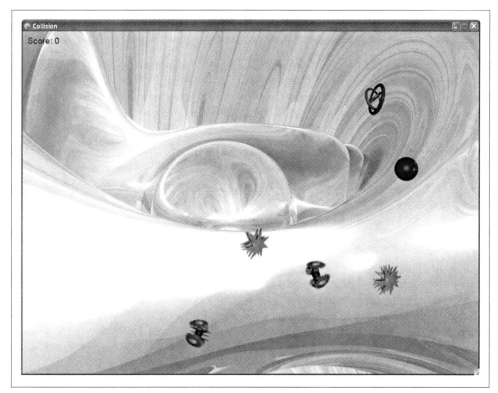

Figure 8-7. The game in progress with a sprite background

and needs to be deleted, that means the user has avoided that sprite, and if it was a three-blade, four-blade, skull ball, or plus sprite, you need to give some points to the user.

 Any time you're developing a game, scoring rules and calculations are things you'll need to think about. You'll most likely formulate an idea, implement it, and then tweak it while testing your game to see whether it feels right and plays the way you want it to. For the purposes of this book, the scoring calculations and rules are laid out for you to learn. However, as you begin to feel more comfortable with the concepts in this book and this chapter specifically, feel free to change the rules and tweak the game to whatever feels right to you as both the developer and a player.

In the `SpriteManager` class, add three new class-level variables representing the three types of sprites you'll be sending at the player, as well as public properties for each variable:

```
int automatedSpritePointValue = 10;
int chasingSpritePointValue = 20;
int evadingSpritePointValue = 0;
```

The chasing sprites are tougher than the automated ones, which just move in a straight line across the screen. As such, they are worth more points. The evading objects will be used for power-ups, and whereas the player will want to track them down to gain a performance bonus, there will be no scoring penalty or bonus for not colliding with those sprites.

You now need to add to your `Game1` class a public method that will allow your `Sprite Manager` to add to the game score. Because the deletion of sprites takes place in the `SpriteManager`, it makes sense to calculate the score at that point in the program. Add the following method to your `Game1` class:

```
public void AddScore(int score)
{
    currentScore += score;
}
```

Next, you'll need to locate the code that deletes the sprites when they go off the edge of the screen. This code resides in the `Update` method of your `SpriteManager` class. The method actually has two different places where sprites are deleted: one for sprites that are deleted because they have gone off the screen and one for sprites that are deleted because they have collided with the player object. Both cases use `SpriteList.Remove At(i)` to remove the sprite from the list of sprites in the game.

Find the code that removes sprites because they have gone off the edge of the screen. Currently, the code should look something like this:

```
// Remove object if it is out of bounds
if(s.IsOutOfBounds(Game.Window.ClientBounds))
{
    spriteList.RemoveAt(i);
    --i;
}
```

You'll need to modify the code to add the score for that sprite before removing it. Change the code as shown here (the added line is shown in bold):

```
// Remove object if it is out of bounds
if(s.IsOutOfBounds(Game.Window.ClientBounds))
{
    ((Game1)Game).AddScore(spriteList[i].scoreValue);
    spriteList.RemoveAt(i);
    --i;
}
```

So you can verify that you placed the line in the correct place, your `Update` method should now look something like this (the changed code section is highlighted in bold):

```
public override void Update(GameTime gameTime)
{
    // Update player
    player.Update(gameTime, Game.Window.ClientBounds);

    // Check to see if it's time to spawn a new enemy
    nextSpawnTime -= gameTime.ElapsedGameTime.Milliseconds;
    if (nextSpawnTime < 0)
    {
        SpawnEnemy(  );

        // Reset spawn timer
        nextSpawnTime = ((Game1)Game).GetRandom.Next(
            ((Game1)Game).EnemySpawnMinMilliseconds,
            ((Game1)Game).EnemySpawnMaxMilliseconds);
    }

    // Update all sprites
    for (int i = 0; i < spriteList.Count; ++i)
    {
        Sprite s = spriteList[i];

        s.Update(gameTime, Game.Window.ClientBounds);

        // Check for collisions
        if (s.collisionRect.Intersects(player.collisionRect))
        {
            // Play collision sound
            if(s.GetCollisionCueName != null)
                ((Game1)Game).PlayCue(s.GetCollisionCueName);

            // Remove collided sprite from the game
            spriteList.RemoveAt(i);
            --i;
        }

        // Remove object if it is out of bounds
        if(s.IsOutOfBounds(Game.Window.ClientBounds))
        {
            ((Game1)Game).AddScore(spriteList[i].GetScoreValue);
            spriteList.RemoveAt(i);
            --i;
        }
    }

    base.Update(gameTime);
}
```

The Update method of your SpriteManager class is getting pretty hairy now, so it's time
for a little refactoring. Create a method called UpdateSprites that takes a parameter of
type GameTime. Remove from the Update method the section of code that updates your
sprites (player and nonplayer), and place it in the UpdateSprites method. In the place
of the original code in the Update method, call UpdateSprites. Your Update method
should now look like this:

```
public override void Update(GameTime gameTime)
{
    // Time to spawn enemy?
    nextSpawnTime -= gameTime.ElapsedGameTime.Milliseconds;
    if (nextSpawnTime < 0)
    {
        SpawnEnemy(  );

        // Reset spawn timer
        ResetSpawnTime(  );
    }

    UpdateSprites(gameTime);

    base.Update(gameTime);
}
```

Ahhh, yes...much better. Your UpdateSprites method, in turn, should look like this:

```
protected void UpdateSprites(GameTime gameTime)
{
    // Update player
    player.Update(gameTime, Game.Window.ClientBounds);

    // Update all nonplayer sprites
    for (int i = 0; i < spriteList.Count; ++i)
    {
        Sprite s = spriteList[i];

        s.Update(gameTime, Game.Window.ClientBounds);

        // Check for collisions
        if (s.collisionRect.Intersects(player.collisionRect))
        {
            // Play collision sound
            if (s.collisionCueName != null)
                ((Game1)Game).PlayCue(s.collisionCueName);

            // Remove collided sprite from the game
            spriteList.RemoveAt(i);
            --i;
        }

        // Remove object if it is out of bounds
        if (s.IsOutOfBounds(Game.Window.ClientBounds))
        {
            ((Game1)Game).AddScore(spriteList[i].scoreValue);
            spriteList.RemoveAt(i);
            --i;
        }

    }
}
```

Finally, you'll need to add the appropriate score values to the constructors used to create each new sprite. For each AutomatedSprite that is generated, the final parameter (which represents the score value for that sprite) should be the automatedSpritePoint Value member variable. Likewise, for each ChasingSprite generated, the final parameter should be the chasingSpritePointValue, and the final parameter for each Evading Sprite should be the evadingSpritePointValue property.

You'll have to change these values in the constructors for each sprite type in the SpawnEnemy method of the SpriteManager class. To find the constructors easily, search in the *SpriteManager.cs* file for each instance of spriteList.Add. Each time sprite List.Add is called, you're passing in a new Sprite object whose constructor you'll need to modify. For clarification purposes, your SpawnEnemy method should now look something like this (the only changes are the final parameters in the constructors for each of the sprite types):

```
private void SpawnEnemy()
{
    Vector2 speed = Vector2.Zero;
    Vector2 position = Vector2.Zero;

    // Default frame size
    Point frameSize = new Point(75, 75);

    // Randomly choose which side of the screen to place enemy,
    // then randomly create a position along that side of the screen
    // and randomly choose a speed for the enemy
    switch (((Game1)Game).rnd.Next(4))
    {
        case 0: // LEFT to RIGHT
            position = new Vector2(
                -frameSize.X, ((Game1)Game).rnd.Next(0,
                Game.GraphicsDevice.PresentationParameters.BackBufferHeight
                - frameSize.Y));
            speed = new Vector2(((Game1)Game).rnd.Next(
                enemyMinSpeed,
                enemyMaxSpeed), 0);
            break;
        case 1: // RIGHT to LEFT
            position = new
                Vector2(
                Game.GraphicsDevice.PresentationParameters.BackBufferWidth,
                ((Game1)Game).rnd.Next(0,
                Game.GraphicsDevice.PresentationParameters.BackBufferHeight
                - frameSize.Y));

            speed = new Vector2(-((Game1)Game).rnd.Next(
                enemyMinSpeed, enemyMaxSpeed), 0);
            break;
        case 2: // BOTTOM to TOP
            position = new Vector2(((Game1)Game).rnd.Next(0,
            Game.GraphicsDevice.PresentationParameters.BackBufferWidth
                - frameSize.X),
                Game.GraphicsDevice.PresentationParameters.BackBufferHeight);
```

```
                    speed = new Vector2(0,
                        -((Game1)Game).rnd.Next(enemyMinSpeed,
                        enemyMaxSpeed));
                    break;
            case 3: // TOP to BOTTOM
                    position = new Vector2(((Game1)Game).rnd.Next(0,
                        Game.GraphicsDevice.PresentationParameters.BackBufferWidth
                        - frameSize.X), -frameSize.Y);

                    speed = new Vector2(0,
                        ((Game1)Game).rnd.Next(enemyMinSpeed,
                        enemyMaxSpeed));
                    break;
        }

    // Get random number between 0 and 99
    int random = ((Game1)Game).rnd.Next(100);
    if (random < likelihoodAutomated)
    {
        // Create an AutomatedSprite.
        // Get new random number to determine whether to
        // create a three-blade or four-blade sprite.
        if (((Game1)Game).rnd.Next(2) == 0)
        {
            // Create a four-blade enemy
            spriteList.Add(
            new AutomatedSprite(
                Game.Content.Load<Texture2D>(@"images\fourblades"),
                position, new Point(75, 75), 10, new Point(0, 0),
                new Point(6, 8), speed, "fourbladescollision",
                automatedSpritePointValue));
        }
        else
        {
            // Create a three-blade enemy
            spriteList.Add(
            new AutomatedSprite(
                Game.Content.Load<Texture2D>(@"imageshreeblades"),
                position, new Point(75, 75), 10, new Point(0, 0),
                new Point(6, 8), speed, "threebladescollision",
                automatedSpritePointValue));
        }
    }
    else if (random < likelihoodAutomated +
    likelihoodChasing)
    {
        // Create a ChasingSprite.
        // Get new random number to determine whether
        // to create a skull or a plus sprite.
        if (((Game1)Game).rnd.Next(2) == 0)
        {
            // Create a skull
            spriteList.Add(
            new ChasingSprite(
```

```
                    Game.Content.Load<Texture2D>(@"images\skullball"),
                    position, new Point(75, 75), 10, new Point(0, 0),
                    new Point(6, 8), speed, "skullcollision", this,
                    chasingSpritePointValue));
            }
            else
            {
                // Create a plus
                spriteList.Add(
                new ChasingSprite(
                    Game.Content.Load<Texture2D>(@"images
lus"),
                    position, new Point(75, 75), 10, new Point(0, 0),
                    new Point(6, 4), speed, "pluscollision", this,
                    chasingSpritePointValue));
            }
        }
        else
        {
            // Create an EvadingSprite
            spriteList.Add(
            new EvadingSprite(
                Game.Content.Load<Texture2D>(@"images·olt"),
                position, new Point(75, 75), 10, new Point(0, 0),
                new Point(6, 8), speed, "boltcollision", this,
                .75f, 150, evadingSpritePointValue));
        }
    }
}
```

Oh yeah! Compile and run the game now, and you'll see that as the sprites are successfully avoided and move off the screen, the point values for those sprites are added to the game score, as shown in Figure 8-8.

Awesome! You have some sprites running around, and the game actually keeps score! You're all done now, right? Er...uh, wait a minute...the game never ends. That means every time you play you can potentially get a high score by just sitting there and watching. Hmmm, on second thought, we have a ways to go. Let's add some logic to create different game states and end the game when a player gets hit a given number of times.

Game States

Your game is coming along, but there has to be a way to end the game. Typically, when a game ends, the game window doesn't just disappear; usually there's some kind of game-over screen that displays your score or at least lets you know that you've failed (or succeeded) in your mission. That's what you need to add next. While you're at it, it's also common to have the same kind of thing at the beginning of the game (perhaps a menu enabling the player to select options, or at least a splash screen presenting instructions and maybe displaying your name as the author of this great game). In the following sections, you'll add both an introductory splash screen and a closing game-over screen.

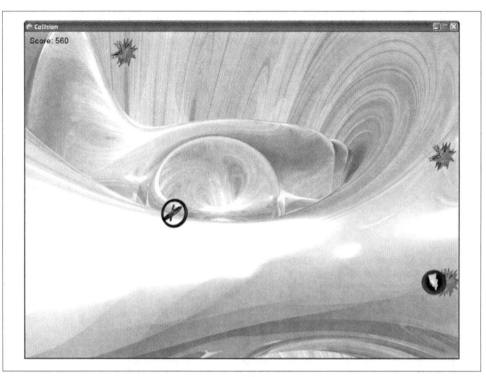

Figure 8-8. 560 points!!! That's amazing!!!

Throughout the life of any game, the game will go through different states. Sometimes these states indicate that the player has moved to a different level in the game or a different area. Sometimes the game state depicts a status change for a player (like in *Pac-Man*, when you turn on the ghosts and begin to chase them rather than being chased). Regardless of the specifics, the game moves through different states, and in those different states the game behaves differently. One way to implement splash screens and game-over screens is by making use of these states.

To define some states for your game, you'll need to enumerate the different possible states that the game can have. Create an enum variable at the class level in your Game1 class. Currently, you have only three states in your game: Start (where you display your splash screen), InGame (where the game is actually running), and GameOver (where you'll display your game over screen). You'll also need to create a variable of that enum type that will hold the current state of the game. You'll want to initialize that current state variable to the game state representing the start of the game:

```
enum GameState { Start, InGame, GameOver };
GameState currentGameState = GameState.Start;
```

Currently in your Game1 class, you have Update and Draw methods that let you draw things on the game screen and update objects in the game. When you place code in one of those methods (such as code to draw the score and the background image), that code runs every time the method is called (i.e., in every frame throughout the life of the game). You're going to want to separate the logic in the Update and Draw methods to allow you to write specific code that will run only in certain situations, depending on the current state of the game. You can do this by adding a switch statement to both methods with different case statements for each possible game state. Then, when you want to write specific code to update or draw items that should take place only in a given game state, you add that code to the Update or Draw methods within the case for that particular game state.

First, add a switch statement to the Update method of your Game1 class. The Update method should now look like this:

```
protected override void Update(GameTime gameTime)
{
    // Only perform certain actions based on
    // the current game state
    switch (currentGameState)
    {
        case GameState.Start:
            break;
        case GameState.InGame:
            break;
        case GameState.GameOver:
            break;
    }

    // Allows the game to exit
    if (GamePad.GetState(PlayerIndex.One).Buttons.Back ==
      ButtonState.Pressed)
        this.Exit( );

    audioEngine.Update( );

    base.Update(gameTime);
}
```

Next, do the same thing with the Draw method. Your Draw method already has logic in it to draw the score and the background image, but this stuff should be drawn only when the game is in the GameState.InGame state, so you'll need to put that code in the appropriate case of the switch statement. Your Draw method should now look like this:

```
protected override void Draw(GameTime gameTime)
{
    // Only draw certain items based on
    // the current game state
    switch (currentGameState)
    {
        case GameState.Start:
            break;

        case GameState.InGame:
            GraphicsDevice.Clear(Color.White);
            spriteBatch.Begin( );
```

```
            // Draw background image
            spriteBatch.Draw(backgroundTexture,
                new Rectangle(0, 0, Window.ClientBounds.Width,
                Window.ClientBounds.Height), null,
                Color.White, 0, Vector2.Zero,
                SpriteEffects.None, 0);

            // Draw fonts
            spriteBatch.DrawString(scoreFont,
                "Score: " + currentScore,
                new Vector2(10, 10), Color.DarkBlue,
                0, Vector2.Zero,
                1, SpriteEffects.None, 1);

            spriteBatch.End( );
            break;

        case GameState.GameOver:
            break;
    }

    base.Draw(gameTime);
}
```

If you were to compile and run the application at this point, it would look kind of cool but a bit messed up. The score and background would be missing from the game window, and the animated sprites would not be erased from frame to frame, which would result in trails being left for the animations.

The score and background would be missing because the current game state is set to GameState.Start by default, and in that game state you aren't drawing those items. Likewise, you'd see the trails because you don't call GraphicsDevice.Clear in the Game State.Start state (you only do that in the GameState.InGame state).

The reason you'd still see your animated sprites is because the SpriteManager class isn't affected by the game state logic you just added. You only added that code to the Game1 class; the SpriteManager is a game component and is not affected by the switch statement you just added.

To get all of this to work correctly, you'll need to add some logic to disable your SpriteManager game component in certain game states and enable it in other states.

Enabling/Disabling GameComponents

By default, when you create an instance of a GameComponent and add it to the list of components in a game, the GameComponent is wired into the game loop. When the game's Update method is called, so is the Update method of the GameComponent, and so on.

There are two properties that can be used to enable and disable a GameComponent. The Enabled property of a GameComponent will determine whether its Update method is called when the game's own Update method is called. Likewise, the Visible property of a DrawableGameComponent will determine whether its Draw method is called when the game's Draw method is called. Both of these properties are set to true by default. Go to the Initialize method in your Game1 class and set both properties to false immediately after adding the component to your list of game components (added lines are in bold):

```
spriteManager = new SpriteManager(this);
Components.Add(spriteManager);
spriteManager.Enabled = false;
spriteManager.Visible = false;
```

 Why start the SpriteManager in a disabled state? Remember that the game starts in the GameState.Start state, which will be used for a splash screen of some sort. You're not going to want sprites flying in and out of the screen at this point in the game. Hence, you'll start the game with a disabled SpriteManager, and then, when the splash screen closes, you'll move to a game playing state and activate the SpriteManager.

Next, add some code to show some text when the game is in the GameState.Start state. This will serve as your splash screen, and you can add graphics, text, and even animations or other effects to it, just as you would during the game itself. For now, you'll just be adding some simple text that will tell the user that he needs to avoid the blade objects. In your Draw method, add to the GameState.Start case of your switch statement some code to display these simple instructions to the user:

```
case GameState.Start:
    GraphicsDevice.Clear(Color.AliceBlue);

    // Draw text for intro splash screen
    spriteBatch.Begin( );
    string text = "Avoid the blades or die!";
    spriteBatch.DrawString(scoreFont, text,
        new Vector2((Window.ClientBounds.Width / 2)
        - (scoreFont.MeasureString(text).X / 2),
        (Window.ClientBounds.Height / 2)
        - (scoreFont.MeasureString(text).Y / 2)),
        Color.SaddleBrown);

    text = "(Press any key to begin)";
    spriteBatch.DrawString(scoreFont, text,
        new Vector2((Window.ClientBounds.Width / 2)
        - (scoreFont.MeasureString(text).X / 2),
        (Window.ClientBounds.Height / 2)
        - (scoreFont.MeasureString(text).Y / 2) + 30),
        Color.SaddleBrown);

    spriteBatch.End( );
    break;
```

This code should be pretty straightforward; there's nothing you haven't seen before, other than the use of the `SpriteFont`'s `MeasureString` method. This method will return a `Vector2` object indicating the size of the string being measured. This is helpful when trying to center a spritefont in the middle of the screen, which is exactly what is being done in this code. To center the text exactly in the middle of the screen, you divide the value of the `Window.ClientBounds.Width` property by two to find the horizontal middle of the screen, and then offset the text by subtracting half the width of the spritefont text you're about to draw. You determine the width of the text you're about to draw by using the `SpriteFont.MeasureString` method.

If you compile and run the code at this point, you're going to be somewhat disappointed. After all the work you've put into this game, it doesn't work! All you have now is a message telling you to avoid the blades or die; worse yet, the game screen says to press any key to get started, but no matter how hard you press those keys, nothing happens. That's because you haven't yet added any functionality to move from the `GameState.Start` state to the `GameState.InGame` state.

To move to the `GameState.InGame` state, add some code to the `GameState.Start` case of the `switch` statement in the `Update` method of the `Game1` class. The following code will detect any key presses from the user and, when the player presses a key, change the game to the `GameState.InGame` state and activate your `SpriteManager`, which will allow sprites to start flying around the screen:

```
case GameState.Start:
    if (Keyboard.GetState().GetPressedKeys( ).Length > 0)
    {
        currentGameState = GameState.InGame;
        spriteManager.Enabled = true;
        spriteManager.Visible = true;
    }
    break;
```

If you wanted to, you could also add support here for the player clicking a mouse button or pressing a button on the gamepad to start the game. In this case, you'd probably want to instruct the player to press any key, click a mouse button, or press a button on the gamepad to continue. It's always a good idea to let players know what controls they can use so they don't have to guess. Making players guess will always lead to unsatisfied gamers.

Compile and run the application now, and you'll see a very simple splash screen (shown in Figure 8-9) that disappears when you press any key, at which point the game begins. Great job!

Now that you have a fancy, schmancy splash screen, it's time to add the same type of screen at the end of the game. Before you do that, however, you'll need to add logic that will actually make the game end.

Figure 8-9. A very simple splash screen with a very scary message

Game-Over Logic and the Game-Over Screen

So, now you have to determine how your game will end. You already have an objective for the game: avoid the three- and four-blade sprites. But when is the game actually over? It seems a bit rough to end the game as soon as the user hits a single blade sprite. Instead, it might make the game a bit more enjoyable if the player had a certain number of lives to play with.

To accomplish this, first you'll need to create a class-level variable in your Game1 class to keep track of the number of lives remaining, as well as a public property with get and set accessors to allow the SpriteManager to access and modify the value:

```
int numberLivesRemaining = 3;
public int NumberLivesRemaining
{
    get { return numberLivesRemaining; }
    set
    {
        numberLivesRemaining = value;
        if (numberLivesRemaining == 0)
        {
```

```
            currentGameState = GameState.GameOver;
            spriteManager.Enabled = false;
            spriteManager.Visible = false;
        }
    }
}
```

Notice that when the property is set, its value is assigned to the `numberLivesRemain ing` variable, and then that variable is checked to see whether its value is zero. If the value is zero, the game state is changed to `GameState.GameOver` and the `SpriteManager` is disabled and hidden. This allows you to decrement this value from the `Sprite Manager` class and then, when the player is out of lives, have the game automatically shut down and enter a state in which you can display a game-over screen.

Now, not only do you want to keep track of the number of lives that a player has, but the player also needs to be able to see how many lives he has left at any given time.

 Why show the number of lives remaining on the screen?

Again, this comes down to trying to make the game a more enjoyable experience for the player. If the player has to constantly keep track of the number of lives she has left on her own, it will detract from the gameplay experience. Anything you can do to help the player out by displaying important data (such as the score and the number of lives remaining) will go a long way toward letting her focus on the most important thing: having fun playing your game.

To display the number of lives remaining, you'll draw one animated three rings sprite in the upper-left corner of the screen (below the score) for each life that the player has remaining.

To avoid confusion, you won't want the sprites to be the same size as the actual sprite being controlled by the player, so you'll have to add some code that will allow you to scale the sprites. Because these sprites won't move on their own and the player won't interact with them, you can use the `AutomatedSprite` class and specify a speed of (0, 0) to draw these objects.

In the `Sprite` class, add a class-level variable to represent the scale at which the sprite is supposed to be drawn:

```
protected float scale = 1;
```

Specifying a scale value of 1 will cause the object to be drawn at the original size of the sprite, so you should initialize it to that value. Next, you'll need to change the `Draw` method in your `Sprite` class to use your newly added `Scale` variable for the scale parameter. Your `Draw` method should look like this:

```
public virtual void Draw(GameTime gameTime, SpriteBatch spriteBatch)
{
    spriteBatch.Draw(textureImage,
```

```
        position,
        new Rectangle(currentFrame.X * frameSize.X,
            currentFrame.Y * frameSize.Y,
            frameSize.X, frameSize.Y),
        Color.White, 0, Vector2.Zero,
        scale, SpriteEffects.None, 0);
}
```

Finally, you'll need to add to the Sprite class a new constructor that will accept a scale value as a parameter:

```
public Sprite(Texture2D textureImage, Vector2 position, Point frameSize,
    int collisionOffset, Point currentFrame, Point sheetSize, Vector2 speed,
    string collisionCueName, int scoreValue, float scale)
    : this(textureImage, position, frameSize, collisionOffset, currentFrame,
    sheetSize, speed, defaultMillisecondsPerFrame, collisionCueName,
    scoreValue)
{
    this.scale = scale;
}
```

and add to the AutomatedSprite class a new constructor that will accept a scale parameter and pass that value on to the base class:

```
public AutomatedSprite(Texture2D textureImage, Vector2 position,
    Point frameSize, int collisionOffset, Point currentFrame, Point sheetSize,
    Vector2 speed, string collisionCueName, int scoreValue, float scale)
    : base(textureImage, position, frameSize, collisionOffset, currentFrame,
    sheetSize, speed, collisionCueName, scoreValue, scale)
{
}
```

Your AutomatedSprite class is now ready to be used to create the sprites that will display the number of lives remaining for the player. In the SpriteManager class, add a class-level variable to keep track of the sprites used for player lives:

```
List<AutomatedSprite> livesList = new List<AutomatedSprite>( );
```

In the SpriteManager's LoadContent method, you'll need to fill the livesList list with a number of sprites equaling the number of lives a player begins with. In each frame, you'll draw the list of items in the livesList variable in the upper-left corner of the screen. This will be a visual indicator to show the player how many lives she has remaining. To fill the list, create a loop that runs as many times as the player has lives, adding a new AutomatedSprite object to the list each time through the loop:

```
for (int i = 0; i < ((Game1)Game).NumberLivesRemaining; ++i)
{
    int offset = 10 + i * 40;
    livesList.Add(new AutomatedSprite(
        Game.Content.Load<Texture2D>(@"images\threerings"),
        new Vector2(offset, 35), new Point(75, 75), 10,
        new Point(0, 0), new Point(6, 8), Vector2.Zero,
        null, 0, .5f));
}
```

The only complex thing going on in this code is the second parameter, which represents the position of the sprite. The parameter is of the type `Vector2`. Your goal in this list is to create a set of sprites that do not move and that are staggered in a row across the upper-left corner of the screen. The X portion of the parameter is first offset by 10 (so that the leftmost image is offset slightly from the edge of the screen) and then multiplied by 40 (so each image is drawn 40 units to the right of the previous image). The Y portion of the parameter is set to 35, to offset it just below the score text.

Now all that's left to do is update your `livesList` objects each time `Update` is called in the `SpriteManager` class and draw your objects each time `Draw` is called.

To do this, add the following code at the end of the `UpdateSprites` method in your `SpriteManager` class:

```
foreach (Sprite sprite in livesList)
    sprite.Update(gameTime, Game.Window.ClientBounds);
```

and add the following code to the `Draw` method, just above the call to `spriteBatch.End`:

```
foreach (Sprite sprite in livesList)
    sprite.Draw(gameTime, spriteBatch);
```

Compile and run the game at this point, and you'll see three sprites in the upper-left corner of the screen, indicating the number of lives the player has left (see Figure 8-10).

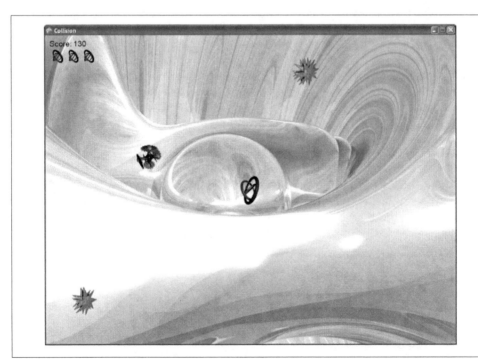

Figure 8-10. Three lives left!

Good job! Now you just need to add some logic to remove a life when the player collides with a blade sprite and to display a game-over screen when the game ends.

Removing one of the life sprites is pretty straightforward. You have code that detects collisions between the player and the moving sprites on the screen. When such a collision occurs, you need to check the type of the sprite that collided with the player: if the type is AutomatedSprite, you'll remove a life sprite from the end of the list of life sprites. Make sure you remove the sprite from the end of the list, because you inserted them in order from left to right.

In addition to removing a sprite from the list of sprites representing lives remaining, you'll need to decrement the value of the numberLivesRemaining variable from the Game1 class by using its accessor.

The code for the collision checks is located in your SpriteManager's UpdateSprites method. In that method, you have logic to remove sprites in two cases: when a sprite collides with the player and when a sprite leaves the game screen. Both cases use the spriteList.RemoveAt method to remove the sprite from the game. Search for the two instances of spriteList.RemoveAt within the UpdateSprites method of the Sprite Manager class, and find the one used for collisions (you'll see code used to play collision sounds nearby). Add the following code to the method, just before the code to remove the sprite when a collision occurs:

```
if (s is AutomatedSprite)
{
    if (livesList.Count > 0)
    {
        livesList.RemoveAt(livesList.Count - 1);
        --((Game1)Game).NumberLivesRemaining;
    }
}
```

For clarity, the entire UpdateSprites method is posted here, with the added code marked in bold so you can see exactly where to put that code:

```
protected void UpdateSprites(GameTime gameTime)
{
    // Update player
    player.Update(gameTime, Game.Window.ClientBounds);

    // Update all nonplayer sprites
    for (int i = 0; i < spriteList.Count; ++i)
    {
        Sprite s = spriteList[i];

        s.Update(gameTime, Game.Window.ClientBounds);

        // Check for collisions
        if (s.collisionRect.Intersects(player.collisionRect))
        {
```

```
// Play collision sound
if (s.collisionCueName != null)
    ((Game1)Game).PlayCue(s.collisionCueName);

// If collided with AutomatedSprite,
// remove a life from the player
if (s is AutomatedSprite)
{
    if (livesList.Count > 0)
    {
        livesList.RemoveAt(livesList.Count - 1);
        --((Game1)Game).NumberLivesRemaining;
    }
}

// Remove collided sprite from the game
spriteList.RemoveAt(i);
--i;
        }

        // Remove object if it is out of bounds
        if (s.IsOutOfBounds(Game.Window.ClientBounds))
        {
            ((Game1)Game).AddScore(spriteList[i].scoreValue);
            spriteList.RemoveAt(i);
            --i;
        }

    }

    // Update lives-list sprites
    foreach (Sprite sprite in livesList)
        sprite.Update(gameTime, Game.Window.ClientBounds);

}
```

If you run the game now, you'll notice that a life is removed every time you run into a three- or four-blade sprite. When all your lives are used up, the game will appear to freeze. It actually isn't frozen, though; it's simply entered a game state in which you aren't doing anything (GameState.GameOver). The last step in this section is to create a game-over screen, similar to the splash screen you created earlier.

First, in the Update method of the Game1 class, add some code that will allow the player to close the game window when the game is in the game-over state. Here, you'll close the game when the player presses the Enter key. Add the following code to detect when the Enter key is pressed and to call the Exit( ) method, which will shut down the game entirely (if you added support for starting the game by pressing a mouse or gamepad button, you should probably add similar input support here to close the game as well):

```
case GameState.GameOver:
    if (Keyboard.GetState( ).IsKeyDown(Keys.Enter))
        Exit( );
    break;
```

To clarify, your `Game1` class's `Update` method should now look something like this (changes are in bold):

```
protected override void Update(GameTime gameTime)
{
    // Only perform certain actions based on
    // the current game state
    switch (currentGameState)
    {
        case GameState.Start:
            if (Keyboard.GetState().GetPressedKeys().Length > 0)
            {
                currentGameState = GameState.InGame;
                spriteManager.Enabled = true;
                spriteManager.Visible = true;
            }
            break;
        case GameState.InGame:
            break;
        case GameState.GameOver:
            if (Keyboard.GetState().IsKeyDown(Keys.Enter))
                Exit();
            break;
    }

    // Allows the game to exit
    if (GamePad.GetState(PlayerIndex.One).Buttons.Back ==
      ButtonState.Pressed)
        this.Exit();

    //Update audio
    audioEngine.Update();

    base.Update(gameTime);
}
```

Now add some code that will draw a game-over message when the game is in the game-over state. Of course, because you're going to be drawing, you'll do this in the `Draw` method of the `Game1` class. In the game-over `case` of the `switch` statement, add the following code:

```
case GameState.GameOver:
    GraphicsDevice.Clear(Color.AliceBlue);

    spriteBatch.Begin(  );
    string gameover = "Game Over! The blades win again!";
    spriteBatch.DrawString(scoreFont, gameover,
        new Vector2((Window.ClientBounds.Width / 2)
        - (scoreFont.MeasureString(gameover).X / 2),
        (Window.ClientBounds.Height / 2)
        - (scoreFont.MeasureString(gameover).Y / 2)),
        Color.SaddleBrown);
```

```
gameover = "Your score: " + currentScore;
spriteBatch.DrawString(scoreFont, gameover,
    new Vector2((Window.ClientBounds.Width / 2)
    - (scoreFont.MeasureString(gameover).X / 2),
    (Window.ClientBounds.Height / 2)
    - (scoreFont.MeasureString(gameover).Y / 2) + 30),
    Color.SaddleBrown);

gameover = "(Press ENTER to exit)";
spriteBatch.DrawString(scoreFont, gameover,
    new Vector2((Window.ClientBounds.Width / 2)
    - (scoreFont.MeasureString(gameover).X / 2),
    (Window.ClientBounds.Height / 2)
    - (scoreFont.MeasureString(gameover).Y / 2) + 60),
    Color.SaddleBrown);

spriteBatch.End( );
break;
```

This code will draw three lines of text on the screen: a message indicating that the game is over, a message indicating that to exit the player should press the Enter key, and a message showing the player's final score. The game-over screen will look something like Figure 8-11.

Figure 8-11. 100 points—not too shabby!

Fine-Tuning Gameplay

With any game that you develop, you will want to tweak things during game testing to ensure that the game plays the way that you intend and is challenging but fun at the same time. The biggest factor is to make sure that the game is entertaining to play. If you're just making the game for yourself, obviously that will be your call. If, however, you're developing it for a wider audience, it's important to get feedback from that user base sooner rather than later.

In this case, one thing you might want to tweak is related to the mouse movement that you've built into the game. You may have noticed that playing with the mouse is much easier than playing with the keyboard keys. To make the game more challenging and to force the user to use an input form that maintains a constant speed for the player sprite, try removing mouse support (I'd recommend leaving support for the gamepad and keyboard input in place).

To remove support for the mouse, comment out or delete the mouse-movement code located in the `Update` method of the `UserControlledSprite` class:

```
// COMMENTED-OUT MOUSE SUPPORT
// If the mouse moved, set the position of the sprite to the mouse position
// MouseState currMouseState = Mouse.GetState(  );
// if (currMouseState.X != prevMouseState.X ||
//      currMouseState.Y != prevMouseState.Y)
// {
//      position = new Vector2(currMouseState.X, currMouseState.Y);
// }
// prevMouseState = currMouseState;
```

You should also comment out the class-level `prevMouseState` variable in the `User ControlledSprite` class:

```
// COMMENTED-OUT MOUSE SUPPORT
// MouseState prevMouseState;
```

Prior to removing the mouse support for the game, the initial player sprite position was set to the position of the mouse cursor. That won't work anymore, so you'll want to start the player in the middle of the screen. You create the `player` object in the `Load Content` method of the `SpriteManager` class, and in the constructor for the `player` object you pass in `Vector2.Zero` as the parameter for the position of the object (the second parameter in the list). Change that code so you pass in the middle of the screen as the initial position of the `player` object. Your initialization code for the `player` object in the `LoadContent` method of the `SpriteManager` class should now look like this:

```
player = new UserControlledSprite(
    Game.Content.Load<Texture2D>(@"Images/threerings"),
    new Vector2(Game.Window.ClientBounds.Width / 2,
        Game.Window.ClientBounds.Height / 2),
    new Point(75, 75), 10, new Point(0, 0),
    new Point(6, 8), new Vector2(6, 6));
```

Another aspect of the gameplay experience that you'll probably want to tweak is to make the game increasingly more difficult to play. As the game stands at this point, players can play virtually forever because the game just isn't very challenging.

How do you make the game more difficult? Well, there are a lot of ways. You could make the blade sprites in the game move progressively faster, or you could spawn different types of sprites that are more and more difficult to avoid. Or you could use a combination of those approaches, or do something totally different. The key here is to be creative. This is video game development, and fresh and new ideas are what make great games. Feel free to play with the game and think about what you could do to make the experience more entertaining.

For the purposes of this book, we're going to make the sprites spawn more and more often in order to make the game progressively harder. You already have two variables that determine a minimum and maximum spawn time for each new sprite (enemySpawn MinMilliseconds and enemySpawnMaxMilliseconds in the Game1 class). These variables are set to 1,000 and 2,000 milliseconds, respectively (in other words, a new sprite is spawned every 1 to 2 seconds).

You don't want to decrease the spawn times every frame, because with the game running at 60 frames per second, the rate of change would be too quick to make things interesting. Instead, create a couple of new class-level variables in the SpriteManager class that you can use to decrease the spawn time every so often (in this case, every second):

```
int nextSpawnTimeChange = 5000;
int timeSinceLastSpawnTimeChange = 0;
```

These variables may look familiar because this is the same concept you used when experimenting with animation speeds. Basically, you'll add some code in the Update method of the Game1 class that will add the elapsed time to the timeSinceLastSpawn TimeChange variable. When that variable's value is greater than the value of the nextSpawnTimeChange variable (which will occur after every 5 seconds of gameplay because nextSpawnTimeChange is set to 5,000 milliseconds), you'll decrease the values of both of the spawn timer variables (enemySpawnMinMilliseconds and enemy SpawnMaxMilliseconds).

However, you don't want to decrease these values indefinitely. If the spawn time values reached zero, a new sprite would be generated every frame—that's 60 sprites generated every second. There's no way anybody could ever keep up with that. To avoid this scenario, you'll cap off the spawn time at 500 milliseconds.

Create a new method in the SpriteManager class that will adjust the spawning frequency variables, making enemy sprites spawn more and more frequently as the game progresses:

```
protected void AdjustSpawnTimes(GameTime gameTime)
{
    // If the spawn max time is > 500 milliseconds,
    // decrease the spawn time if it is time to do
    // so based on the spawn-timer variables
    if (enemySpawnMaxMilliseconds > 500)
    {
        timeSinceLastSpawnTimeChange += gameTime.ElapsedGameTime.Milliseconds;
        if (timeSinceLastSpawnTimeChange > nextSpawnTimeChange)
        {
            timeSinceLastSpawnTimeChange -= nextSpawnTimeChange;
            if (enemySpawnMaxMilliseconds > 1000)
            {
                enemySpawnMaxMilliseconds -= 100;
                enemySpawnMinMilliseconds -= 100;
            }
            else
            {
                enemySpawnMaxMilliseconds -= 10;
                enemySpawnMinMilliseconds -= 10;
            }
        }
    }
}
```

In this code, the interior if/else statement causes the spawning increments to be decreased rapidly (subtracting 100 each time the spawn times are decremented) until the max spawn time is less than 1 second (1,000 milliseconds). After that, the spawn time continues to decrease until it reaches a max spawn time of 500 milliseconds, but it decreases at a much slower rate (subtracting only 10 each time the spawn times are decremented). Again, this is just another part of tweaking the gameplay experience. This particular method of changing the spawn time will cause the game to get tougher and more interesting fairly quickly, and then slowly get harder and harder until the game is tough enough to pose a challenge to most players.

You'll need to add a call to the new AdjustSpawnTimes method from within the Update method of your SpriteManager class. Add the following line to the Update method immediately before the call to base.Update:

```
AdjustSpawnTimes(gameTime);
```

Compile and run the game at this point, and you'll find that the longer you stay alive, the harder the game will become. At some point, you will no longer be able to keep up, and the game will end. See Figure 8-12 for a view of how convoluted the game can get once it really starts rolling.

Figure 8-12. Ahhh!!! It's getting crowded in here!

Creating Power-Ups

We'll add one last thing to the game in this chapter, and then it will be up to you to fine-tune and tweak it further. You have three sprites that don't do anything at this point: the skull ball, the plus, and the bolt. These sprites are meant not to take away a player's life when they collide with the player's object, but rather to have some positive or negative effect on the player.

As in previous sections in this chapter, we're really getting into the creative aspect of game development here, and if there's something you feel would add a great deal of entertainment to the game, you should look at adding that functionality. As you consider implementing things like power-ups, there really is no limit to what you can do.

For the purposes of this book, the effects that these objects will have when they collide with the player object are as follows:

- The bolt causes the player object to move at 200% of its current speed for 5 seconds.
- The skull ball causes the player object to move at 50% of its current speed for 5 seconds.
- The plus causes the player object to be 200% larger than its current size for 5 seconds.

Essentially, a power-up (or power-down, if the effect is negative to the player) will run for a given number of seconds, and then the effect will wear off. In this game, the effects will stack, meaning that you can be influenced by more than one effect at a given time, and you can be influenced by the same effect multiple times (for instance, if you hit two skull balls back to back, you'll be running at 25% of your normal speed).

 Should the effects always stack? That's completely your call. You're the developer, and you own this virtual world. You want to make the game fun to play and challenging. Again, experiment with different effects and decide what you like and what works for you.

To create these effects, you'll need to add some code to your Sprite base class. First, you'll need to add a variable that will hold the initial value of the scale property. Currently, you're initializing scale to 1, but if the player collides with a plus sprite, the value of scale will double. After that power-up expires, you'll have to set scale back to its original value. Rather than hardcoding the value 1 in at that point, it would be better to use a variable representing the original value. Add the following class-level variable to the Sprite class:

```
protected float originalScale = 1;
```

Next, you'll need to add a method that will allow the SpriteManager to increase or decrease the value of the scale variable, as well as a method that the SpriteManager can call to reset the scale variable to its original value. Add the following methods to the Sprite class:

```
public void ModifyScale(float modifier)
{
    scale *= modifier;
}
public void ResetScale( )
{
    scale = originalScale;
}
```

Pause here for a second and answer this question: what effect will changing the scale have on your collision detection? That's right, it's going to get messed up. You'll have changed the scale, but the collision detection will still be using the frameSize and collisionOffset properties, which hold the original values for the size of the frame and the collision offset. What can you do about this? Luckily, your SpriteManager uses an accessor called CollisionRect that builds a Rectangle for collision detection. You can modify that accessor to use the scale property to correctly build the Rectangle when a different scale factor is applied. Change the collisionRect property in your Sprite base class as follows:

```
public Rectangle collisionRect
{
```

```
    get
    {
        return new Rectangle(
            (int)(position.X + (collisionOffset * scale)),
            (int)(position.Y + (collisionOffset * scale)),
            (int)((frameSize.X - (collisionOffset * 2)) * scale),
            (int)((frameSize.Y - (collisionOffset * 2)) * scale));
    }
}
```

Now you'll need to do the same sort of thing for the Speed variable. First, add to the Sprite class a class-level variable that will hold the original speed:

```
Vector2 originalSpeed;
```

Because you're initializing speed in the constructors via a parameter rather than instantiating it to a constant value, you don't need to initialize the originalSpeed variable to anything specific. You will, however, need to initialize it in the constructor that sets the speed variable. Add the following code just below the line in the constructor that reads this.speed = speed:

```
originalSpeed = speed;
```

Next, add two methods (just as you did for the scale variable) that will allow the SpriteManager to modify and reset the Speed variable of the Sprite class:

```
public void ModifySpeed(float modifier)
{
    speed *= modifier;
}
public void ResetSpeed( )
{
    speed = originalSpeed;
}
```

Oh yeah, that's good stuff so far. Now you're ready to make the final changes. Open the SpriteManager class, as you'll be making some changes in that class next.

Every time the player hits one of these special sprites, a power-up timer needs to be set to let that power-up run for 5 seconds. Add a class-level variable to the SpriteManager class to keep track of when power-ups should expire:

```
int powerUpExpiration = 0;
```

Next, find the UpdateSprites method. In that method, you check to see whether the player has collided with a sprite. Previously, you added a check to see whether a collision with an AutomatedSprite object had occurred and, if so, you removed a life from the player. Now you're going to handle the other types of collisions that are possible. The easiest way to determine the type of sprite that was hit if it wasn't an AutomatedSprite is by examining the CollisionCue property of the sprite. Remember that a sprite's CollisionCue property determines which sound is played in a collision with that object, and therefore that sound property is unique for each different type of sprite.

Your code should have an `if` statement that looks like the following:

```
if (s is AutomatedSprite)
{
    if (livesList.Count > 0)
    {
        livesList.RemoveAt(livesList.Count - 1);
        --((Game1)Game).NumberLivesRemaining;
    }
}
```

Add the following code after that first `if` statement (the `if(s is AutomatedSprite)` statement, not the `if(LivesList.Count > 0)` statement) to create the power-up effect and set the power-up expiration timer to 5 seconds (5,000 milliseconds):

```
else if (s.collisionCueName == "pluscollision")
{
    // Collided with plus - start plus power-up
    powerUpExpiration = 5000;
    player.ModifyScale(2);
}
else if (s.collisionCueName == "skullcollision")
{
    // Collided with skull - start skull power-up
    powerUpExpiration = 5000;
    player.ModifySpeed(.5f);
}
else if (s.collisionCueName == "boltcollision")
{
    // Collided with bolt - start bolt power-up
    powerUpExpiration = 5000;
    player.ModifySpeed(2);
}
```

This code will perform some action that starts a power-up effect on the player based on the collision cue of the colliding sprite. In addition, it will set the `powerUpExpira` `tion` variable to `5000` to indicate that the power-up timer has started and has 5 seconds remaining.

The last thing you'll need to do is decrement the expiration timer every time the `Update` method of the `SpriteManager` class is called. Add the following method to the `SpriteManager` class:

```
protected void CheckPowerUpExpiration(GameTime gameTime)
{
    // Is a power-up active?
    if (powerUpExpiration > 0)
    {
        // Decrement power-up timer
        powerUpExpiration -=
            gameTime.ElapsedGameTime.Milliseconds;
        if (powerUpExpiration <= 0)
        {
            // If power-up timer has expired, end all power-ups
            powerUpExpiration = 0;
```

```
                player.ResetScale( );
                player.ResetSpeed( );
            }
        }
    }
```

Then, call that method from within your Update method, just before the base.Update call:

```
    CheckPowerUpExpiration(gameTime);
```

This new method will subtract the elapsed game time from the power-up timer at every frame, and when the power-up timer reaches zero, it will reset the scale and speed of the player.

Compile and run the game now, and you'll find that you have a complete 2D game written in XNA. It's basic, but pretty fun. Again, you can tweak gameplay issues such as speeds, spawn rates, power-ups, and so on to your liking and customize the game to make it play the way you feel it should.

While playing, notice how the power-up effects stack. For example, if you hit a plus sprite and then hit a skull sprite before the plus effect wears off, both effects are added to your player sprite. The same thing happens with similarly typed sprites; for instance, if you hit a plus and then another plus before the effect from the first plus wears off, your player sprite will now be at 400% of its normal size (normal size × 2 × 2).

The tricky thing is that even though you can stack power-up effects, there is only one power-up timer. This means that if you have two or three or more effects on your player sprite, they won't expire at different times. Instead, every time you hit a power-up, the power-up timer will be reset to 5 seconds. Only if 5 seconds pass without you hitting any other power-ups will all the accumulated power-up effects expire.

This is by design, but again, this is a great place for you to examine how you think the game should be played. If you think a different rule for power-ups should be in place, make it happen! You're the developer, and you're the king of this virtual world, right? You might as well take advantage of that and make the game play exactly how you think it should.

What You Just Did

Wow. Maybe this should say, "What didn't you do?" This was a long chapter, but you did some great stuff. Let's take a look:

- You learned how to draw 2D text on the screen.
- You randomly generated sprites of different types.
- You added a background image.
- You fleshed out a system to keep score.

- You experimented with game states and implemented three states (start, in-game, and end).
- You added splash and game-over screens using game states.
- You added power-up effects and fine-tuning logic to your game.

Summary

- 2D fonts are drawn on the screen just the same as any `Texture2D` object.
- 2D fonts are built using the `SpriteFont` object.
- Background images are added to games by using a sprite that covers the entire screen.
- Game states are breaks in gameplay or transitions in gameplay from one state to another (for example, moving from one level to another, accomplishing a mission, losing the game, or something similar in concept).
- Game development is a very creative business. While the mechanics are very scientific, as in all programming, the actual fine-tuning of the game is a very art-oriented craft that is heavily centered on how the gameplay feels to a user. As a developer, you should play with your game as early and often as possible so that you can tweak the experience into something that you enjoy and that you envision others will enjoy as well.
- "Our mental discipline is matched only by our skill in XNA...I only hope these are enough to withstand this awful trial." —Akara

Test Your Knowledge: Quiz

1. What type of object is used to draw 2D text in XNA?
2. How is a background image different from an image used to represent a player or object in the game?
3. What are game states and how are they used?
4. In the *Flight of the Conchords* episode "Mugged," what do the muggers steal from Jemaine?

Test Your Knowledge: Exercise

Change the behavior of the skull power-up (or power-down, if you prefer) to freeze the player for 2 seconds rather than reduce the player's speed by 50% for 5 seconds. Use different power-up timers for the skull, bolt, and plus sprites.

CHAPTER 9

3D Game Development

As you have seen throughout this book, there are a lot of really cool things that you can do with 2D graphics in XNA. However, given the strength of today's graphics cards and processors, recently there have been huge advancements in the area of 3D graphics. Load up any of the latest first-person shooters and, as long as you have the hardware to support it, you'll be amazed at the level of detail in the game and the number of objects flying around the screen at any given time. 3D graphics truly are the way of the future, and if you want to do serious game development, they're probably where you'll want to focus most of your time and attention.

So, let's get started. Because 2D and 3D graphics are treated so differently in XNA, go ahead and create a new project from scratch for this section. Open Visual Studio and select File→New→Project. When the New Project window appears, select Visual C#→XNA Game Studio 4.0 in the menu tree on the left side of the window, and then select Windows Game 4.0 for the template on the right side of the window. Name your project *3D Madness*, choose the location for the project, and click OK (see Figure 9-1).

Now that you've created your project and you're ready to go, let's look at some of the key differences between 2D and 3D game programming in XNA.

Coordinate Systems

The first difference you'll notice when dealing with 3D graphics rather than 2D is the addition of an extra dimension. Yeah...that's right. Who would have thought? I know I probably didn't blow your mind with that one, but the transition from 2D to 3D takes a bit of getting used to, and it can often be downright confusing.

Programming 2D games in XNA is very similar to painting a picture on a canvas: you're drawing in two-dimensional space; the coordinate (0, 0) sits at the upper-left corner of the screen; and X moves positively to the right, whereas Y moves positively downward.

If drawing in 2D is like painting a picture, drawing in 3D is like recording a video with a handheld camera. Coordinates in 3D are based on a three-dimensional coordinate

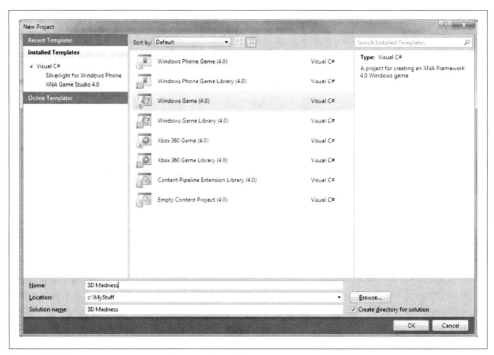

Figure 9-1. Create a new project for your first 3D game

system. This coordinate system, sometimes referred to as *world space*, centers around an origin at the coordinate $(0, 0, 0)$. However, unlike when drawing in 2D, when drawing something at the origin in 3D, you can't guarantee that that object will be viewed at the center of the screen, the upper-left corner, or anywhere at all. Why is that? Because in 3D, there are two basic components to drawing a scene: placing objects in the world, and placing a camera in the world and specifying a direction in which that camera will point. Only objects that the camera sees will be visible on the screen.

Depending on where the camera is and what direction it's pointing in, an object that you draw at the origin in a 3D game could be in the middle of the screen, at the bottom of the screen, somewhere else on the screen, or even off the screen entirely.

Before we get too deep into that, let's talk a bit about the 3D coordinate system. If you're familiar with 3D coordinate systems, you'll realize that typically the X-axis moves positively to the right and the Y-axis moves positively upward. However, the Z-axis is not so clearly defined. Two different types of 3D coordinate systems exist, each with the Z-axis moving positively in an opposite direction. The direction in which Z moves positively determines the orientation, or *handedness*, of the coordinate system. The two possible orientations are *left-handed* and *right-handed* coordinate systems.

One way to distinguish between a left-handed coordinate system and a right-handed coordinate system is to place your hands, palms up, with the fingers pointing in the direction of positive X and curled up toward positive Y. The direction in which your thumb points indicates the direction of positive Z for that hand's coordinate system (see Figure 9-2).

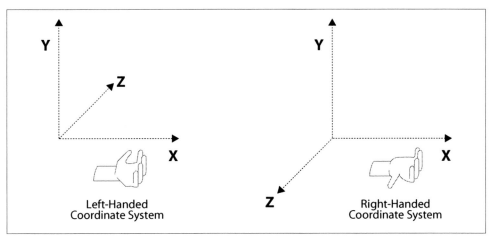

Figure 9-2. Left-handed versus right-handed coordinate systems

XNA uses a right-handed coordinate system, which means that when you're looking at the origin from a traditional angle where X moves positively to the right and Y moves positively upward, Z moves positively toward you.

Cameras

So, now that you understand coordinate systems, let's talk about cameras. As mentioned previously, drawing a scene in 3D is much like recording a movie with a handheld camera. You have to define where the camera is located, what it's pointing at, and various other properties.

These properties are stored in a `Matrix` object. Matrices are fairly complex mathematical entities that are well beyond the scope of this chapter and this book in general. Suffice it to say that matrices are at the heart of almost everything you do in 3D graphics. Fortunately, XNA handles all the hairy matrix details behind the scenes, and at this point, you really don't need to concern yourself with how it all unfolds. For now, just understand that a matrix or two can represent a camera.

There are two `Matrix` objects that make up a camera in XNA: the *view* and *projection* matrices. The view matrix holds information that determines where the camera sits in the world, what direction it's pointing in, and what its orientation is. The projection matrix holds information that determines properties of the camera based on the angle of the view, how far the camera can see, and so forth. This matrix represents the transformation from the 3D world to the 2D plane of the screen.

To create a view matrix, you use a static method from the **Matrix** class called **Create LookAt**. This method returns a **Matrix** object and accepts the parameters listed in Table 9-1.

Table 9-1. Parameters of Matrix.CreateLookAt

Parameter	Type	Description
cameraPosition	Vector3	Coordinate of the camera's position
cameraTarget	Vector3	Coordinate of the point at which the camera is looking
cameraUpVector	Vector3	Vector indicating which direction is up

First, notice the data type of each of these parameters. What's a **Vector3**? Just as you used a **Vector2** in 2D development to represent an (X, Y) coordinate, a **Vector3** represents a 3D coordinate (X, Y, Z).

Next, notice the third parameter to the **CreateLookAt** method. Although you can specify a position for a camera and a direction, that still doesn't determine how objects are drawn on the screen. With a handheld video camera, you can turn the camera sideways or even upside down, and the direction it's facing will affect the way things are recorded. The same is true with a camera in XNA. You specify an up vector for the camera so that XNA knows not only how to place the camera in the world, but also what the orientation of the camera is.

To create a projection matrix, use another static method from the **Matrix** class called **Matrix.CreatePerspectiveFieldOfView**. This method also returns a **Matrix** object and accepts the parameters listed in Table 9-2.

Table 9-2. Parameters of Matrix.CreatePerspectiveFieldOfView

Parameter	Type	Description
fieldOfView	float	Angle of the camera view in radians. This is typically 45 degrees, or π/4.
aspectRatio	float	Aspect ratio of the camera. This is typically the width of the screen divided by the height of the screen.
nearPlaneDistance	float	How close to the camera an object can be before it can no longer be seen.
farPlaneDistance	float	How far away from the camera an object can be before it can no longer be seen.

The projection matrix builds what's called a *viewing frustum*, or *field of view* for your camera. Essentially, it defines an area in 3D space that is viewable by the camera and will be drawn on the screen. Objects that exist within that area are drawn on the screen, unless they're obscured by other objects between them and the camera. Objects that are outside the viewing frustum are not drawn on the screen.

In Figure 9-3, you can see a drawing of a hypothetical viewing frustum, or field of view. The three-dimensional box represents the area that will be drawn on the screen. Any object outside of this box will not be drawn, regardless of whether it is drawn in front of, behind, or to the side of the box. The `nearPlaneDistance` and `farPlaneDistance` parameters define the front and back of the box and are also referred to as the *near clipping plane* and the *far clipping plane*. Nothing in front of the near clipping plane will be drawn, and nothing behind the far clipping plane will be drawn.

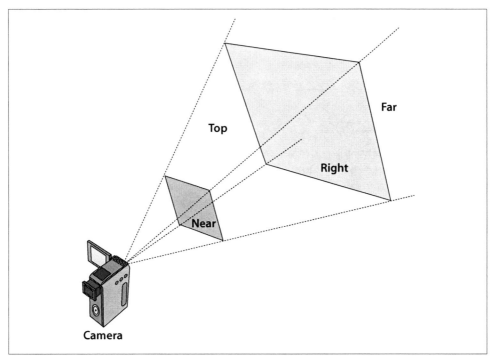

Figure 9-3. A three-dimensional viewing frustum, or field of view

Defining the Field of View

You need to be somewhat careful when choosing which values to use to represent your near and far planes. Most beginning XNA developers will choose a very small number (like 1) for the near plane and a very large number (like 10,000) for the far plane. Keep in mind that this means that everything within those planes (and within the other bounds of the field of view) will be drawn on the screen. If there's a lot going on in your game, you may encounter performance issues if your near and far planes are too far apart.

Ever notice in a land-based game that you're walking around in the wilderness, and all of a sudden a somewhat distant mountain just pops into view? This is because the mountain was previously behind the far plane, and as you moved toward it, it entered the field of view. If such games didn't have that functionality and instead always drew everything in the world, performance would crawl and the game would be unplayable. Make sure that you show enough of the world to make the game playable but exclude enough to avoid performance issues.

In my experience in teaching students how to develop in XNA, when a developer expects to see something drawn on the screen in 3D and the object doesn't appear, the problem has something to do with the field of view of the camera or the position and direction of the camera.

The most common mistakes I see in this area are that an object isn't drawn because the camera is pointing in the wrong direction, and that objects aren't visible on the screen because they are either in front of the near clipping plane or behind the far clipping plane.

Creating a 3D Camera

OK, let's put together some code. When dealing with cameras, it often makes sense to create a game component for your camera. This makes it really easy to add cameras to new games (just add the component to the project, and then add it in code to the game) and to update the camera and move it around. Create a new game component in your 3D project by right-clicking the project name and selecting Add→New Item.... In the templates list on the right side of the Add New Item screen, select Game Component. Name the component *Camera.cs*, and click Add (see Figure 9-4).

In the Camera.cs class, add two class-level variables (and appropriate auto-implemented properties) to represent your camera's view and projection matrices:

```
public Matrix view {get; protected set;}
public Matrix projection { get; protected set; }
```

Then, change the constructor to accept three Vector3 variables representing the initial position, target, and up vectors for the camera. Also, in your constructor, initialize the view by calling Matrix.CreateLookAt and the projection by calling Matrix.Create PerspectiveFieldOfView. Here's the complete code for the constructor of the Camera class:

```
public Camera(Game game, Vector3 pos, Vector3 target, Vector3 up)
    : base(game)
{
    view = Matrix.CreateLookAt(pos, target, up);

    projection = Matrix.CreatePerspectiveFieldOfView(
        MathHelper.PiOver4,
        (float)Game.Window.ClientBounds.Width /
        (float)Game.Window.ClientBounds.Height,
        1, 100);
}
```

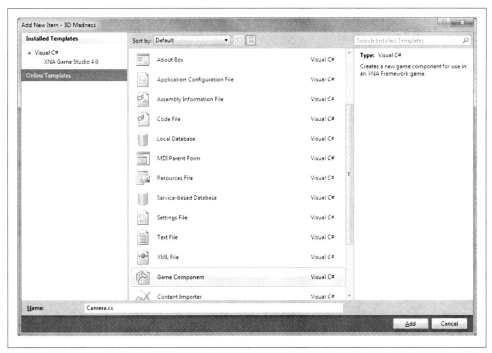

Figure 9-4. Creating a camera game component

 Make sure that you cast the screen width and height to floating-point values when calculating the aspect ratio, as shown here. Not doing so will divide int by int, which can cause information loss and may make your graphics look squished.

The only tricky thing here is the use of the `MathHelper.PiOver4` value to represent π divided by 4. We'll talk a lot more about this later in this chapter, but for now, you just need to know that angles in XNA are measured in radians. In radians, π equals 180°. Hence, π/4 is 45°, which is a standard field of view angle. The `MathHelper.PiOver4` value is a constant that is handy to access rather than having to compute π/4 every time you want to use that value.

Next, you'll need to add your camera component to the list of components in your `Game1` class. Create a class-level `Camera` variable in your `Game1` class:

```
Camera camera;
```

Then, in the `Initialize` method of the `Game1` class, add the following code to instantiate the camera and add it to the list of `Game1`'s components:

```
// Initialize camera
camera = new Camera(this, new Vector3(0, 0, 5),
    Vector3.Zero, Vector3.Up);
Components.Add(camera);
```

So, what's going on here? You're creating your camera at position (0, 0, 5), telling it to look at the origin (`Vector3.Zero` returns an empty `Vector3` representing the point (0, 0, 0), or the origin), and specifying that (0, 1, 0) is up (`Vector3.Up` returns a `Vector3` of (0, 1, 0), which represents up, by default).

Compile and run the game now, and you'll see some amazing camera work. Well... maybe not. You might be thinking, "Well, this sure is lame." And in a sense, you might be right. But on the other hand, although there's nothing shown on the screen, you're actually "filming" in 3D right now. You have a camera ready to go; you just don't have anything on the set to "film" (see Figure 9-5). We'll take care of that next.

Figure 9-5. Sweet! Er...uh...wait...this is lame.

Drawing Primitives

Now that you have a camera set up and ready to go, you need to draw something on the screen. The root of all 3D drawings is the triangle. If you draw enough triangles, you can render almost any shape possible. Put enough triangles next to each other and make them all small enough, and you can even get a smooth, round surface.

This actually isn't unlike the world in which we live. If you took a perfectly smooth surface and looked at it on a microscopic level, the surface would not be smooth at all; it would be full of microscopic ridges and valleys. Our computers aren't powerful enough to mimic that level of detail, but they're definitely improving. Curved and shiny surfaces are amazingly more detailed and realistic today than they were even a few years ago.

Actually, while we're on the subject, much of 3D graphics is built to mimic real life. Lighting effects are meant to act as much like real-world light as possible (or at least, real-world light as far as we currently understand it), and so on. For the most part, games in general are more enjoyable the more they act and feel like real life. For example, games such as *Half-Life 2* have greatly benefited from having advanced physics engines that allow players to interact with objects in ways that conform as much as possible to the real-world laws of physics.

To draw your first triangle, you need to define some points, or *vertices*, to represent each of the corners of the triangle. You'll also need an object called a VertexBuffer in which you'll store your vertex information for use on the graphics device. In your Game1 class, create an array of VertexPositionColor objects at the class level as well as a variable of type VertexBuffer:

```
VertexPositionColor[] verts;
    VertexBuffer vertexBuffer;
```

You'll also need something called a BasicEffect in order to draw your primitives. Essentially, everything in XNA 3D must be drawn using effects (typically high-level shaders). The BasicEffect class will be explained in more detail later, but basically it allows you to draw in 3D by using default shader code:

```
BasicEffect effect;
```

You'll use these objects to create those points. A VertexPositionColor object represents a vertex that has both a position and a color. You specify these values in the constructor for the objects when you create them. In the LoadContent method of your Game1 class, initialize the points with this code:

```
// Initialize vertices
verts = new VertexPositionColor[3];
verts[0] = new VertexPositionColor(new Vector3(0, 1, 0), Color.Blue);
verts[1] = new VertexPositionColor(new Vector3(1, -1, 0), Color.Red);
verts[2] = new VertexPositionColor(new Vector3(-1, -1, 0), Color.Green);
```

After you've added the code to initialize your vertices, you need to add code to fill your VertexBuffer with the vertex information. Add the following code directly after the vertex initialization code you just added in your LoadContent method:

```
// Set vertex data in VertexBuffer
vertexBuffer = new VertexBuffer(GraphicsDevice, typeof(VertexPositionColor),
    verts.Length, BufferUsage.None);
vertexBuffer.SetData(verts);
```

Finally, after setting the data on your `VertexBuffer`, initialize your effect by adding the following code at the end of your `LoadContent` method:

```
// Initialize the BasicEffect
effect = new BasicEffect(GraphicsDevice);
```

Next, in the `Draw` method of your `Game1` class, you need to tell the `GraphicsDevice` which vertex buffer you'll be drawing from. Essentially, what this does is tell the graphics device on your PC that you're about to send it some information and specifies what type of information you will be sending. In this case, you're going to tell the graphics device that you're about to send it some `VertexPositionColor` data (the type of data you assigned to your `vertexBuffer` in your `LoadContent` method). Add this line just after the `GraphicsDevice.Clear` call in the `Draw` method:

```
GraphicsDevice.SetVertexBuffer(vertexBuffer);
```

Next, after the `VertexDeclaration`, add the following code to draw your triangle:

```
//Set object and camera info
effect.World = Matrix.Identity;
effect.View = camera.view;
effect.Projection = camera.projection;
effect.VertexColorEnabled = true;

// Begin effect and draw for each pass
foreach (EffectPass pass in effect.CurrentTechnique.Passes)
{
    pass.Apply();

    GraphicsDevice.DrawUserPrimitives<VertexPositionColor>
        (PrimitiveType.TriangleStrip, verts, 0, 1);
}
```

Running the game at this point should display a pretty cool-looking triangle (Figure 9-6). Notice how the colors on each vertex of the triangle blend into each other toward the center of the triangle. This is because behind the scenes the GPU measures the distance of each pixel from each vertex and builds the color for that particular pixel based on a calculation involving the distance from each of the vertices and the colors of those vertices. Pretty cool, huh?

How did you end up with a triangle like that? The coordinates that you used for the three vertices were, in order, (0, 1, 0), (1, –1, 0), and (–1, –1, 0). You specified the colors blue, red, and green for those vertices, respectively. XNA takes those coordinates and builds a triangle. Take a look at Figure 9-7 to see how this would look if you overlaid the triangle image with the coordinate system.

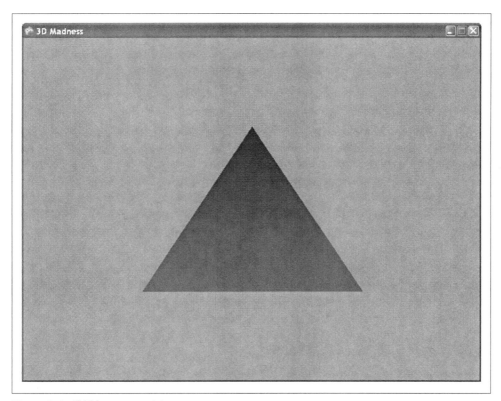

Figure 9-6. Ahhhh…mesmerizing…

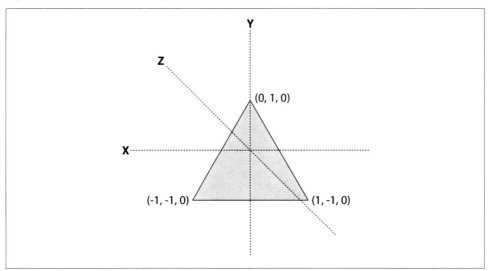

Figure 9-7. Triangle with coordinate system overlaid

As you can see in this figure, the triangle's vertices correspond to the points that you created in your vertex array. XNA does the color shading automatically by mixing the colors between the vertices; the closer a pixel is to a given vertex, the more of that vertex's color is included in the coloring of that particular pixel.

Let's review that last bit of code you added. That's a lot of code for one little triangle—imagine how much code it would take to build *Quake 3* this way!

Don't let this discourage you. Let me explain what's going on here. First, you need to understand how 3D graphics are rendered in XNA. Everything in XNA 3D is drawn using something called High Level Shader Language (HLSL). HLSL is based on the C development language and allows developers to easily create incredibly powerful effects such as water ripples, reflective surfaces, and other eye candy. You don't need to worry about it too much at this point; we cover HLSL in detail in a later chapter. All you need to know for now is that everything in XNA 3D is drawn using HLSL, via something called an `Effect`.

The `Effect` class allows you to interface with HLSL code, to pass data to HLSL, and so forth. The XNA team was kind enough to include a class that derives from `Effect`, called `BasicEffect`. Using `BasicEffect`, you can effectively use default HLSL code without having to know anything about HLSL beforehand. This means you can concentrate on getting your triangle to display without having to deal with the headaches of complicated HLSL code. Thanks, XNA team!

Now, back to the code. First, you set the `world` property on your `BasicEffect` object. This property essentially represents the position at which the object will be drawn. You're drawing at the origin, so for now, you'll use `Matrix.Identity`.

 Don't freak out about `Matrix.Identity` just yet. We'll cover more basics of matrix multiplication later in this chapter. For now, just think of `Matrix.Identity` as being a default location for an object to be drawn, and that default location is around the origin.

Next, you set the view and the projection of the effect using the information from your camera component. Then, you set the `VertexColorEnabled` property of the effect to `true`. Without this, the color will not be drawn and your triangle will show up on the screen completely white.

A little more information about effects is in order here. Every effect has one or more *techniques*. Every technique has one or more *passes*. The `for` loop that comes next in your code loops through the passes of the technique you'll use to draw this triangle. To begin a pass when drawing a technique, you must call `EffectPass.Apply()`. This will all make more sense later, when we cover HLSL in depth, but for now, consider this `EffectPass.Apply()` call similar to the calls to `SpriteBatch.Begin` and `End` that you made in earlier chapters. With the `SpriteBatch`, all sprites had to be drawn between `Begin` and End calls. The same applies with this code: all passes must be executed after their own Apply call.

The code that actually draws the triangle on the screen, which is after the call to Effect Pass.Apply, is a call to GraphicsDevice.DrawUserPrimitives. Let's look at that method more closely:

```
GraphicsDevice.DrawUserPrimitives<VertexPositionColor>
    (PrimitiveType.TriangleStrip, verts, 0, 1);
```

DrawUserPrimitives is a generic method, and therefore you must specify the type of vertex that you're going to draw (in this case, VertexPositionColor). The first parameter is a method for drawing triangles that we'll cover in a moment. For now, just realize that when given three vertices, passing PrimitiveType.TriangleStrip for this parameter will cause XNA to build a triangle out of those three vertices. The next parameter is the vertex array where you've stored your vertex info. The third parameter is the offset into that array, or the index at which to start drawing vertices on the screen. You want to start at the beginning of your verts array, so you specify 0 for this parameter. The final parameter is a primitive count, or how many primitives you are expecting to draw in this method call. A triangle is one primitive, and you're expecting to draw one triangle, so you pass in the value 1 for this parameter.

Matrix Multiplication

All right, you have yourself a fancy, schmancy triangle. You probably want to make it do something else now, right? Well, let's talk about rotations and translations. As mentioned previously, matrices are behind essentially everything you do in 3D graphics. This is especially the case when you're trying to move, rotate, or scale an object. You saw in the previous code that you had to set the World property of the BasicEffect to Matrix.Identity. Let's see if we can make a little more sense out of that now.

You can think of the World property of a BasicEffect as a matrix that tells XNA where to draw what you're about to tell it to draw and how to position it in the world with an appropriate rotation and scale. It's similar to a coordinate at which to draw the item (in fact, a 3D coordinate is contained within the matrix), but it's much more than that, holding all the information for the rotation and scale as well. We're not going to go into all the details here, but if you're interested in investigating further, there are a lot of resources in mathematical textbooks and on the Internet that will teach you all that you want to know about matrix multiplication.

For the purposes of this book and as an introduction to XNA, you really just need to know that matrix multiplication is behind all rotations, scales, translations (movement), etc. in 3D graphics. The matrix represented by Matrix.Identity is what's known as the *identity matrix*. The identity matrix is a special matrix that, when it comes to multiplication, behaves just like the number one; that is, any matrix multiplied by the identity matrix yields itself as the product of that multiplication.

What that means to you is that the identity matrix represents a fresh starting point. If you wanted to draw an object at the origin, you'd set its `World` property to `Matrix.Identity`. You did that in this first triangle example, and the triangle was drawn around the origin.

So, why do you care about all of this? Well, it's good to understand at some level what's going on behind the scenes. Luckily for us, though, XNA handles most of the matrix calculations itself via the `Matrix` class.

Movement and Rotation

In this section, we'll look at how to move and rotate objects in 3D. In your project, you have a cool triangle. If you want to move this object to the left a little bit, you can do so via the `Matrix.CreateTranslation` method.

A *translation* moves an object or a point in a direction specified by a vector. Thus, the `CreateTranslation` method takes a `Vector3` as a parameter. It also has an override that accepts float values for X, Y, and Z.

Now, if you want to actually move your object and/or rotate it continuously rather than just have it change positions and sit still, you'll need a variable to represent your object's world. Create a `Matrix` variable at the class level in your `Game1` class and initialize it to `Matrix.Identity`:

```
Matrix world = Matrix.Identity;
```

Then, modify the line of code in your `Draw` method where you set the `BasicEffect.World` property to use this new variable:

```
effect.World = world;
```

Next, add the following code to your `Update` method, just above the call to `base.Update`:

```
// Translation
KeyboardState keyboardState = Keyboard.GetState( );
if (keyboardState.IsKeyDown(Keys.Left))
    world *= Matrix.CreateTranslation(-.01f, 0, 0);
if (keyboardState.IsKeyDown(Keys.Right))
    world *= Matrix.CreateTranslation(.01f, 0, 0);
```

Compile and run the game now, and you'll notice that when you press the left and right arrow keys, the object moves accordingly.

What's Happening?

So, what's going on here? Am I moving the object or am I moving the entire world?

Don't let the variable name "world" confuse you. I would have had you name the variable you added differently, but you end up setting it to the `World` property of the `BasicEffect` class, so it really wouldn't have made any more sense to name your variable something else.

The world matrix doesn't represent the entire world, though. Think of the variable as a matrix representing how the world looks to a given object that you draw. Why is it called a world matrix? Perhaps the reason is because the world matrix takes an object and places it into the world.

In this particular case, the world matrix places your triangle into the world. Inside the world matrix variable is a coordinate that tells XNA to start drawing the object and supplies it with a rotation at which to draw, a scale at which to draw, and a lot more. In short, it describes how a particular object will be drawn.

If you were to draw a second triangle, you'd want to create a different world matrix for that triangle and apply different settings to it (perhaps rotating it a little, scaling it, and/ or moving it). When you drew that second triangle, it would be drawn according to its world matrix; the first triangle's world matrix would have nothing to do with the second's, and vice versa.

What about rotating the object? Well, there are several methods that can be used to rotate objects, and which one you should use depends on the axis around which you want to rotate the object. Similar to the earth rotating around its axis, every rotation in XNA revolves around an axis. Thus, when performing a rotation, you must specify an axis to rotate around.

Add the following line of code below the code you just added for the translation:

```
// Rotation
world *= Matrix.CreateRotationY(MathHelper.PiOver4 / 60);
```

This code uses one of the basic rotation methods provided by the `Matrix` class: `Matrix.CreateRotationY`. This method rotates an object around the Y-axis to the number of degrees specified in the parameter. Note that the degrees are in radians, not degrees, and in radians, π is 180 degrees. The parameter `MathHelper.PiOver4 / 60` will rotate the object .75 degrees. There's no science as to why I picked that number; it just looks smooth in the application. Feel free to play with the rotation speed and get different results.

Notice the use of *= instead of just = when setting the `world` variable. This is important not only because it will incrementally add values to the rotation and the translation at each frame, which will cause the objects to move and rotate continually, but also because the `Matrix` variable holds multiple aspects related to how an object sits in the world (a position, a rotation, a scale, etc.).

You set the position via the `Matrix.CreateTranslation`, and if you used = instead of *= when setting the rotation via `Matrix.CreateRotationY`, you'd lose the translation that was done previously.

Compile and run the game at this point, and you'll see the triangle rotating continuously around the Y-axis (as shown in Figure 9-8). You'll also still be able to control its horizontal movement with the left and right arrow keys.

You may notice when you move the triangle that not only are you moving it, but you're changing the center of rotation. Actually, technically you're not changing the center of rotation (whenever you rotate using `Matrix.CreateRotationY`, you are rotating an object around the origin); what you are doing is modifying where the triangle sits in relation to that center of rotation. When the game begins, the triangle is drawn centered around the origin, which means that when `Matrix.CreateRotationY` is called, the triangle appears to rotate in place (around the origin, which it is currently centered around). When you move the object to the right, the triangle now appears to orbit around the origin. However, what's actually happening is that the triangle moves to the right, and then you rotate it around the origin with the call to `Matrix.CreateRotationY`.

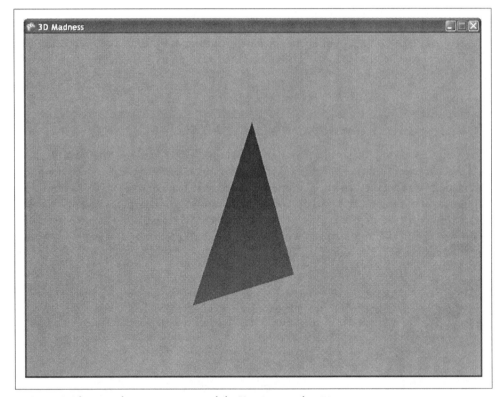

Figure 9-8. The triangle is rotating around the Y-axis...woohoo!!!

But wait a minute! When the triangle rotates 180 degrees, it disappears, and then it reappears after it has made a complete rotation. What gives?

Backface Culling

What you're seeing when the triangle disappears is a process called *backface culling*. Culling is a process in 3D graphics that limits the number of things drawn on the screen to improve performance. Essentially, the goal of backface culling is to draw only the side of a primitive that is facing the camera. In this application, only one side of your triangle is drawn.

By default, XNA will cull primitives that are drawn in a counterclockwise fashion. Remember when you created the vertices for this triangle? You drew your vertices in a clockwise fashion, as shown in Figure 9-9.

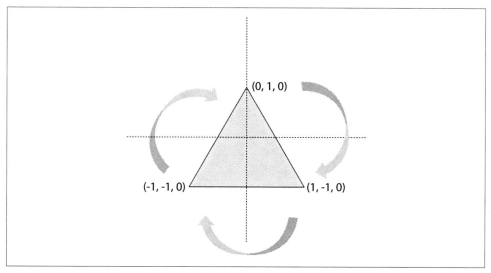

Figure 9-9. Drawing vertices in a clockwise fashion

If you were to draw those vertices in a counterclockwise order and run the game, you'd see that the triangle actually starts out culled and therefore invisible. In this case, only when it has rotated 180° will you see it.

So, what does culling do for you? It enhances the performance of your game. Imagine a soccer ball. What does the inside of the ball look like? Do you care? Does anybody care? The obvious answer is no. So, why waste valuable processor time drawing the inside of a soccer ball when nobody will ever see it?

Just as a real-life soccer ball is hollow, all objects in 3D graphics are hollow. All they really consist of is a "skin" drawn around some empty space using a series of triangles. Nobody cares what the inside of those skins looks like, so there's no point in drawing them.

Thanks to the culling process, your game will automatically determine what should not be drawn, based on the orientation of the vertices that are drawn.

You can turn off culling by placing the following line of code at the bottom of your LoadContent method call in your Game1 class:

```
// Set cullmode to none
RasterizerState rs = new RasterizerState();
rs.CullMode = CullMode.None;
GraphicsDevice.RasterizerState = rs;
```

Typically you would never want to turn off culling because it's an extremely powerful performance booster, but it can be helpful for debugging purposes. For example, if you think you should see something on screen but it's not showing up, you can turn off culling to see whether the object really is there but is being culled for some reason.

More on Rotations

Another thing you may have noticed when playing around with your triangle is that when the application first starts, the triangle appears to be spinning in place. If you move the triangle to the left, it still rotates, but now it appears to be orbiting the origin rather than spinning in place. This is because the order of the translation and the rotation makes a big difference in the resulting effect.

When a rotation is applied, the rotation always rotates the object around the origin. In your code, you are applying the translation first and then the rotation during every frame. So, when the application first loads, the object is drawn at the origin and the rotation causes it to rotate around the origin, which gives the effect of it spinning in place.

However, once you move the object to the left, adding the rotation to the object so that it rotates around the origin (which now is to the right of the object) causes it to have an orbiting effect.

To get your object to spin in place regardless of where it is, you'll need to apply the rotation first, and then the translation. This will cause the rotation to be applied while the object is at the origin (giving it the effect of spinning in place), and the translation will then move the object and its rotation to the specified location.

For this to work, instead of having a single object representing the world for the triangle, you'll need to add two variables to represent the world of the object (you can also remove the Matrix variable called world that you added earlier):

```
Matrix worldTranslation = Matrix.Identity;
Matrix worldRotation = Matrix.Identity;
```

Next, modify the code in the Update method to apply the rotations and translations only to the desired matrices. Change the following code:

```
// Translation
KeyboardState keyboardState = Keyboard.GetState( );
if (keyboardState.IsKeyDown(Keys.Left))
    world *= Matrix.CreateTranslation(-.01f, 0, 0);
```

```
if (keyboardState.IsKeyDown(Keys.Right))
    world *= Matrix.CreateTranslation(.01f, 0, 0);

// Rotation
world *= Matrix.CreateRotationY(MathHelper.PiOver4 / 60);
```

to this:

```
// Translation
KeyboardState keyboardState = Keyboard.GetState(  );
if (keyboardState.IsKeyDown(Keys.Left))
    worldTranslation *= Matrix.CreateTranslation(-.01f, 0, 0);
if (keyboardState.IsKeyDown(Keys.Right))
    worldTranslation *= Matrix.CreateTranslation(.01f, 0, 0);

// Rotation
worldRotation *= Matrix.CreateRotationY(MathHelper.PiOver4 / 60);
```

This will allow the game to keep your rotations separate from your translations and allow you to apply them in the order you want when you draw your object. To do that, change the code in the Draw method that sets the BasicEffect.World parameter to this:

```
effect.World = worldRotation * worldTranslation;
```

Each rotation, translation, and scale added in this manner will have a different effect on the object being drawn, depending on the order in which you apply them. For example, see what happens when you change the preceding code to this:

```
effect.World = Matrix.CreateScale(.5f) * worldRotation * worldTranslation;
```

Applying a scale of .5f at the front of the sequence causes your triangle to be drawn at half the normal size. However, see if you can tell the difference between that code and this code:

```
effect.World = worldRotation * worldTranslation * Matrix.CreateScale(.5f);
```

This is a subtle change, but it has an important effect. The latter line of code will apply the scale of .5 to everything to the left of Matrix.CreateScale in the sequence. This means the triangle will move half as fast in the second example because the scale will affect the translation. In the first example the scale also affects everything to its left, but as there's nothing there, the scale will be applied only to the drawing of the triangle, not to the translation.

What if you wanted to simulate something like a planet orbiting the sun? How would you do that? Well, think about what a planet orbiting the sun does. Typically, it spins in place while orbiting, right? To make the object spin in place, you'd first apply a rotation. You'd then need to move the object a certain distance away from the sun (the origin, in this case). Finally, to make the object "orbit" the origin, you'd apply another rotation that would rotate the object around the origin.

Try this by changing the line of code that sets the World to the line that follows:

```
effect.World = worldRotation * worldTranslation * worldRotation;
```

Compile and run the game at this point. Move the object to the right or left, and you should see it rotating in place while orbiting the origin. Pretty cool, huh? I recommend that you take some time to play around with rotations and translations now to get a good feel for what happens when you apply them in different orders.

Even More Rotations

So far, you've seen how to translate, rotate, and scale objects, but you've only rotated using a method called `CreateRotationY`, which rotates an object around the Y-axis.

There are other rotations that are worth noting here. You've probably guessed that as there's a `CreateRotationY`, there will also be `CreateRotationX` and `CreateRotationZ` methods. That's a pretty good guess, and as it turns out, you're right. These methods can be used to rotate an object around the Y-, X-, or Z-axis, respectively.

Another method used to apply rotations is `Matrix.CreateFromYawPitchRoll`. Essentially, this method allows you to create a rotation that combines rotations around the X-, Y-, and Z-axes simultaneously. As pictured in Figure 9-10, a *yaw* rotates an object around the Y-axis, a *pitch* rotates around the X-axis, and a *roll* rotates around the Z-axis.

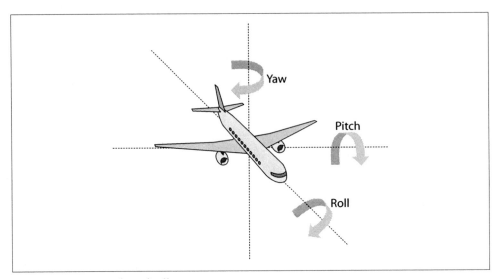

Figure 9-10. Yaw, pitch, and roll

There's another method that should be mentioned here as well: `Matrix.CreateFrom AxisAngle`. This method takes a parameter in the form of a `Vector3` that represents an axis upon which to rotate an object (rather than specifying X, Y, or Z), as well as an angle at which to rotate the object. For example, imagine you're building a model of the solar system. You'll want to specify some arbitrary axis for the Earth to spin on, because the Earth's axis is tilted and doesn't line up exactly with X, Y, or Z.

I'd recommend that you pause here and take some time to apply different types of rotations to your object to get a good feel for what they each do. Try applying a rotation using `CreateFromYawPitchRoll` by changing the rotation code in your `Update` method from this:

```
// Rotation
worldRotation *= Matrix.CreateRotationY(MathHelper.PiOver4 / 60);
```

to this:

```
// Rotation
worldRotation *= Matrix.CreateFromYawPitchRoll(
    MathHelper.PiOver4 / 60,
    0,
    0);
```

Then experiment with different versions of this code by putting in different values for each of the three parameters.

Primitive Types

So, you're cruising along, enjoying the ride through XNA 3D land...but it still isn't that exciting. You've created a cool-looking triangle and moved it around, but that's about it. Although the triangle has a cool effect with the blended colors, you'll probably never see a full game done completely with colors like this. Typically, when drawing in 3D you'll be drawing primitives and then applying textures to those primitives.

 Applying a texture? What's that? As you've learned in previous chapters of this book, a texture represents a 2D bitmap or other image. Textures in 3D graphics are often mapped to 3D surfaces on objects (such as your triangle in the previous example). This process of mapping a 2D texture to a 3D surface is referred to as applying a texture.

So, in the rest of this chapter, we focus on applying a texture to your triangle. However, you're going to use a rectangular texture, so you'll need to convert your triangle to a rectangle. How can this be done? Well, you can't just start drawing rectangles, because you need to draw using triangles. However, two triangles next to each other can form a square or rectangle.

Change the code in your `LoadContent` method that initializes your vertex array to the following:

```
verts = new VertexPositionColor[4];
verts[0] = new VertexPositionColor(new Vector3(-1, 1, 0), Color.Blue);
verts[1] = new VertexPositionColor(new Vector3(1, 1, 0), Color.Yellow);
verts[2] = new VertexPositionColor(new Vector3(-1, -1, 0), Color.Green);
verts[3] = new VertexPositionColor(new Vector3(1, -1, 0), Color.Red);
```

Next, in your `Draw` method, you'll need to change the last parameter of the `Graphics Device.DrawUserPrimitives` call to 2. Remember, this parameter is not a vertex count, but rather a primitive count; it tells the graphics device how many primitives you expect to draw in this call. You're now expecting to draw two triangles, so you'll need to set the parameter appropriately:

```
GraphicsDevice.DrawUserPrimitives<VertexPositionColor>
    (PrimitiveType.TriangleStrip, verts, 0, 2);
```

Compile and run the game now, and you'll see that the triangle has changed to a rectangle (see Figure 9-11).

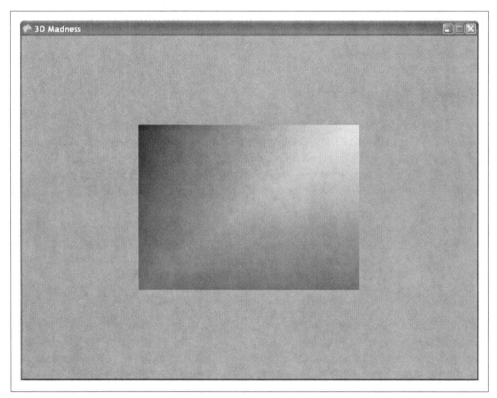

Figure 9-11. Wow! Sweet rectangle goodness!

How does this awe-inspiring rectangle work? The magic is in the first parameter of the call to `GraphicsDevice.DrawUserPrimitives`. There are three different ways to draw primitive triangles in XNA: you can draw using a triangle list, a triangle strip, or a triangle fan. In your call to `GraphicsDevice.DrawUserPrimitives`, you're currently telling the graphics device to draw your vertices using a `PrimitiveType.TriangleStrip`. Let's take a look at the different options.

A triangle list will take the first three vertices specified and build a triangle out of them. It will then build an additional triangle out of each additional set of three vertices, as shown in Figure 9-12. The triangle list is perhaps the least complicated way to draw triangles, but it's also the least efficient, as you have to specify three new vertices for each triangle drawn.

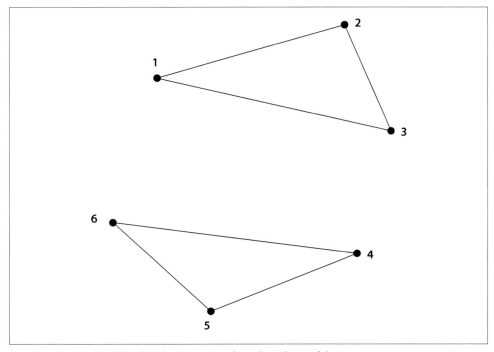

Figure 9-12. A triangle list builds a new triangle with each set of three vertices

A triangle strip will also build a triangle out of the first three vertices specified, but it will then build a new triangle with each additional vertex by using the new vertex and the previous two vertices. Look at Figure 9-13, and notice how different the triangles look, even though you used the exact same points and specified them in the same order as in the previous example of a triangle list.

A triangle fan will similarly build a new triangle with the first three vertices specified and will build a new triangle with each additional vertex, but to do so it uses the new vertex, the previous vertex, and the first vertex. Thus, a fan formation is built, as seen in Figure 9-14 (again using the same points from the previous examples).

Take some time now to familiarize yourself with the different primitive types. Try just changing the primitive type from `PrimitiveType.TriangleStrip` to `PrimitiveType.TriangleList` and `PrimitiveType.TriangleFan` with the four points you currently have, and make sure you understand what's happening in each case.

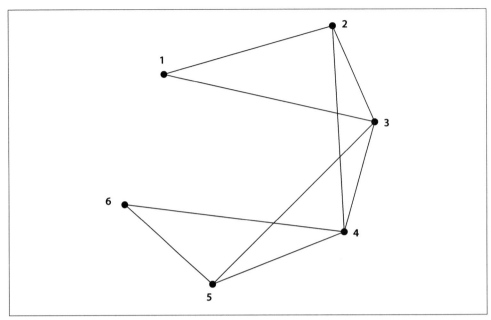

Figure 9-13. A triangle strip builds a triangle out of the first three vertices and a new triangle with each additional vertex, using the new vertex and the previous two vertices

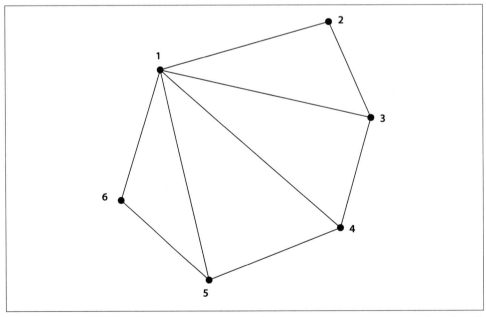

Figure 9-14. A triangle fan builds a triangle out of the first three vertices and a new triangle with each additional vertex using the new vertex, the previous vertex, and the first vertex

Whoa!!! Wait a minute! When you run the game using a triangle list, the game crashes. What's up?

Triangle lists require three vertices for each primitive, so the graphics device expects to receive six vertices, and you're only providing four. To fix this, you can change the final parameter of the DrawUserPrimitives call to 1 (meaning you only want to draw one primitive); XNA will then draw only one triangle, using the first three vertices in the array.

You can also fix this issue by adding two more vertices to your array; in this case, XNA will draw two triangles with the six vertices provided.

Applying Textures

OK, now that you have a rectangular shape, you're ready to apply a texture to your rectangle. First, you'll have to tell the graphics device that you're going to be using textures with your vertices. Currently, the type of object you're using to represent your vertices is VertexPositionColor, which tells XNA that you want to use a position and a color for your vertices. You'll need to change this to use a different object type called VertexPositionTexture, which represents a vertex that has both a position and a texture. Change the type for your vertex array variable at the top of the class to this:

```
VertexPositionTexture[] verts;
```

Next, change the code in the LoadContent method that initializes the vertices. The constructor for a VertexPositionTexture takes two parameters: a Vector3 representing the position of the vertex and a Vector2 representing a texture coordinate.

Wait a minute! What's a "texture coordinate"? That's an excellent question. A texture coordinate is a way for XNA to map a coordinate on a texture to a vertex of a primitive. When texturing a primitive in this way, you identify points of a texture that correspond to vertices, and then XNA handles grabbing the specified portion of the texture and mapping it accordingly on the primitive.

A texture coordinate is represented by a two-dimensional (U, V) coordinate, where U is horizontal and V is vertical. The upper-left corner of an image is represented by texture coordinate (0, 0), and the lower-right corner of an image is represented by texture coordinate (1, 1), regardless of the size of the image. To specify a point in the exact middle of a texture, you would use the texture coordinate (0.5, 0.5).

You can think of both U and V as percentages of the size of a texture, with 1 equaling 100% height or width and 0 equaling 0%. The (U, V) coordinates of the corners of any given texture are shown in Figure 9-15.

When initializing your vertices, you need to determine which point on the texture will map to which vertex and assign the appropriate (U, V) coordinate to that vertex. Then, when you draw the primitives, XNA will map the texture appropriately onto those primitives.

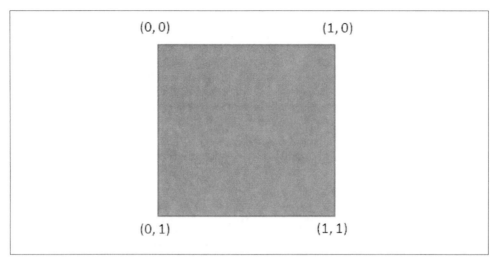

Figure 9-15. (U, V) coordinates of a texture

Change your vertex initialization code in the LoadContent method to use Vertex PositionTexture objects and to set the (U, V) coordinates as shown here:

```
verts = new VertexPositionTexture[4];
verts[0] = new VertexPositionTexture(
    new Vector3(-1, 1, 0), new Vector2(0, 0));
verts[1] = new VertexPositionTexture(
    new Vector3(1, 1, 0), new Vector2(1, 0));
verts[2] = new VertexPositionTexture(
    new Vector3(-1, -1, 0), new Vector2(0, 1));
verts[3] = new VertexPositionTexture(
    new Vector3(1, -1, 0), new Vector2(1, 1));
```

Next, change the line of code that initializes your VertexBuffer in the LoadContent method to also use VertexPositionTexture. Remember, you'll essentially be telling the graphics device what type of information you're about to send it through the Vertex Buffer, so you'll need to update that line to indicate that you're now using VertexPosi tionTexture for your vertex information. The new line of code that initializes your VertexBuffer should look like this:

```
vertexBuffer = new VertexBuffer(GraphicsDevice, typeof(VertexPositionTexture),
    verts.Length, BufferUsage.None);
```

You're also specifying the VertexPositionColor generic method type in your DrawUser Primitives call in your Draw method. Change that to use VertexPositionTexture:

```
GraphicsDevice.DrawUserPrimitives<VertexPositionTexture>
    (PrimitiveType.TriangleStrip, verts, 0, 2);
```

Nice. Now you're ready to draw VertexPositionTexture vertices, which will let you apply a texture to your rectangle. All you need to do now is create a texture and apply it.

Just as you did with the sprites in 2D, you'll need to add an image file to your project. If you haven't already, download the source code for this chapter. With the source code, in the *3D Madness\3D MadnessContent\Textures* folder, you'll find a file called *trees.jpg*.

Right-click the *Content* folder in Solution Explorer, select Add→New Folder, and name the new folder *Textures*. Then, right-click the new *Textures* folder, select Add→Existing Item..., and navigate to the *trees.jpg* file. Select that file to add it to your project.

Next, you'll have to add a new class-level variable to your Game1 class for your texture:

```
Texture2D texture;
```

and load the texture in your LoadContent method. Make sure that you use the asset name for your image in the parameter to the Content.Load method (if you used an image of your own, odds are that the name won't be "trees"):

```
texture = Content.Load<Texture2D>(@"Textures\trees");
```

Finally, in your Draw method, you'll need to tell BasicEffect which texture to use and enable the texture. Change the code in the Draw method from this (which enables the color of the vertices):

```
effect.VertexColorEnabled = true;
```

to this (which enables the texture):

```
effect.Texture = texture;
effect.TextureEnabled = true;
```

OK, now you're ready to go. Compile and run the application, and you'll see the same rotating rectangle that you had previously, but now the texture is applied to the primitives instead of the blend of colors you saw previously. Depending on the image you chose to add to your project, you should see something similar to Figure 9-16.

Nice job! Now that's a pretty cool game you've made. You've created a spinning, rotating, moving, tree picture thing...awesome! Well, things are about to get a whole lot better. In the next chapter we'll start using 3D models rather than just a triangle or a rectangle, and that's when 3D development really gets fun.

 If you're going to do development that will require you to draw numerous vertices in the way described in this chapter, there are some things you can do to make things significantly easier for yourself. We won't be covering this in depth in this book, as we'll be focusing on drawing with 3D models rather than drawing individual vertices, as shown here, but by using an IndexBuffer, you can reuse single points in 3D space for multiple vertices in your game. There are great resources on Index Buffers online; check out the sources listed in "Additional Resources" on page 8, if you'd like to look into them further.

Figure 9-16. Oh yeah! Those are some cool trees that are spinning around on my screen!

What You Just Did

There was a lot of information in this chapter. Let's take a quick look back at what you just did:

- You built your first 3D project and added a camera to that project using a GameComponent.
- You drew a triangle on the screen by specifying vertices for the points, and you colored the triangle.
- You learned about the very exciting world of matrix multiplication and a little bit about how it applies to 3D graphics programming.
- You learned about rotations, translations, and scale.
- You experimented with different primitive types, such as triangle lists, strips, and fans.
- You applied a texture to a set of triangles forming a rectangle.

Summary

- 3D development uses a coordinate system with X-, Y-, and Z-axes. XNA uses a right-handed coordinate system.

- Creating a game in 3D differs from 2D development in ways similar to how painting on a canvas differs from recording a video with a camcorder. In 3D development, you place objects at different points in the world and create a camera that you move around that world.

- A camera defines a viewing frustum, or field of view, that determines which portions of a 3D world are visible on the screen. Anything that exists inside the viewing frustum is visible; if an object is not in the viewing frustum, it won't be visible on the screen.

- XNA uses High Level Shader Language (HLSL) to draw objects in 3D. The `Effect` class is used to draw objects from XNA code and allows developers to modify parameters of the HLSL effect being used. The `BasicEffect` class derives from `Effect` and allows you to draw objects without having to code the HLSL yourself.

- Nearly everything in XNA 3D is drawn using primitives. Triangles are one such primitive, and you draw them by specifying a series of vertices. The `VertexPositionColor` and `VertexPositionTexture` objects are two objects used to draw different types of primitives.

- When a triangle is drawn in 3D, the back side of it is not drawn. This is because, to improve performance, only the parts of an object that are facing the camera are drawn (this is called backface culling). Objects drawn in counterclockwise fashion in XNA are culled by default.

- Matrix multiplication is behind most calculations in 3D graphics. Translations, rotations, and scaling operations all use matrix multiplication.

- The order in which translations, rotations, and scaling operations are applied to an object is important when determining what type of effect is desired. Objects will behave differently when the order of these operations is changed.

- Triangle lists, triangle strips, and triangle fans are all different ways of drawing triangle primitives. Each will draw different types of triangles based on a series of vertices.

- When applying a texture to a primitive, you specify (U, V) coordinates for each vertex and the texture is mapped accordingly.

- XNA 3D is among man's top five inventions of all time; fire, the wheel, football, and peanut butter round out the rest of the top five.

Test Your Knowledge: Quiz

1. Does XNA use a right-handed or left-handed coordinate system?
2. What makes up a viewing frustum (or field of view) for a camera in XNA 3D?
3. What is culling?
4. What is a vertex declaration?
5. Fact or fiction: there is a difference between applying a rotation multiplied by a translation and applying a translation multiplied by a rotation.
6. What order of translation and rotation would be needed in order to simulate a planet spinning in place while orbiting the origin?
7. Fact or fiction: to map the lower-right corner of a texture that is 250 × 300 pixels in size to a vertex, you should specify the (U, V) coordinate (250, 300).
8. How many vertices are needed to draw three triangles using a triangle list?
9. How many vertices are needed to draw three triangles using a triangle strip?
10. How many polygons were used to draw Marcus in *Gears of War*?

Test Your Knowledge: Exercise

Building on the code that you wrote in this chapter, create a six-sided cube with different textures on each side that rotates on multiple axes.

CHAPTER 10

3D Models

In the previous chapter you went to work on some sweet triangles and rectangles, using fantastic colors and cool textures. You're ready to go out and create the next great game and make millions of dollars and retire when you're 23, right? Wrong. Unfortunately, I've got some bad news for you: there really isn't a market for 3D triangle and rectangle games right now. How will your *Attack of the Triangles* game compare against the latest shooters and role-playing games? Umm...it won't. So, how do those games get such cool-looking graphics when all you have is a simple triangle to work with? The answer lies with three-dimensional models.

Using 3D Models

In the last chapter, I mentioned that you can draw anything you want in XNA 3D if you use enough primitives (such as the triangle used in that chapter). Although that's true, it would be a severe pain in the neck to try to draw a spaceship or a dragon or whatever else you're thinking of by specifying each individual vertex in code and drawing hundreds or even thousands of triangles to create the object.

When drawing complicated objects, typically you'll use a *3D model*. Essentially, a 3D model is a collection of points that form vertices for primitives. In the model, colors and textures can be applied. These models are usually created outside of XNA in a third-party modeling application. Popular modeling tools you can use to create 3D models include 3D Studio Max, Maya, Blender, Lightwave, and Modo. Blender is a free tool that is pretty well done and typically is a favorite of the students in my XNA classes. You can download Blender from *http://www.blender.org*. Another popular free modeling tool is XSI Mod Tool, which has an XNA add-on available. You can download XSI Mod Tool at *http://www.softimage.com/products/modtool*.

Models created in these modeling applications can be saved into a number of different file formats for compatibility with different types of applications. XNA supports the *.X* file format as well as the *.FBX* file format for 3D models. Loading and drawing these model files in your XNA projects allows you to draw and manipulate detailed and complex graphics without having to worry about specifying every single vertex and texture. Instead, you can focus on moving, rotating, and manipulating the model and other gameplay-related issues.

Setting Up the Project

Before we get to loading and drawing a model, let's apply one of the lessons from the 2D section of this book: for this project, you'll work with some object-oriented design from the beginning. In the first half of this book, you implemented a `SpriteManager` class that handled the drawing of all sprites. You also created a base class for all sprites and derived specialized sprites from that base class. That approach seemed to work pretty well, so you'll implement the same type of design in your 3D game.

Start from scratch in this chapter by creating a new Windows Game (4.0) project. Name your game *3D Game*, as shown in Figure 10-1.

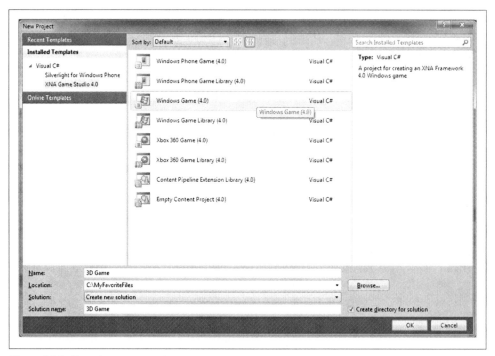

Figure 10-1. Creating a new project

The first thing you're going to need is a camera. You created a camera using a GameCom ponent in the previous chapter, and you'll need to do that again here. To simplify matters, you can copy the *Camera.cs* file from the previous chapter and paste it into this project; or, if you haven't already done so, you can download the source code for Chapter 9 and copy the *Camera.cs* file into your project now. You'll need to change the namespace from _3D_Madness to _3D_Game, though, in order to be able to use the Camera class in your project.

Alternatively, you can create a new GameComponent by right-clicking the solution in Solution Explorer, selecting Add→New Item…, and selecting the Game Component template from the list on the right. Name the file *Camera.cs* and click Add, as shown in Figure 10-2.

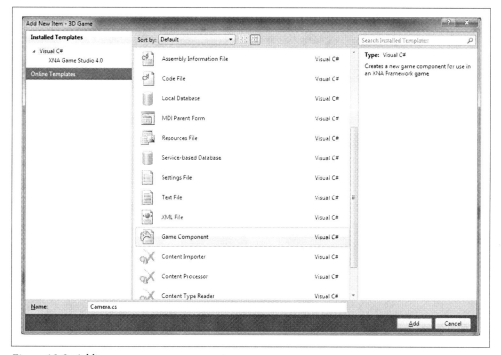

Figure 10-2. Adding a new game component

You'll need to modify the code generated for your GameComponent so it looks like this:

```
using System;
using System.Collections.Generic;
using System.Linq;
using Microsoft.Xna.Framework;
using Microsoft.Xna.Framework.Audio;
using Microsoft.Xna.Framework.Content;
using Microsoft.Xna.Framework.GamerServices;
using Microsoft.Xna.Framework.Graphics;
```

```
using Microsoft.Xna.Framework.Input;
using Microsoft.Xna.Framework.Media;
using Microsoft.Xna.Framework.Net;
using Microsoft.Xna.Framework.Storage;


namespace _3D_Game
{
    public class Camera : Microsoft.Xna.Framework.GameComponent
    {
        //Camera matrices
        public Matrix view { get; protected set; }
        public Matrix projection { get; protected set; }

        public Camera(Game game, Vector3 pos, Vector3 target, Vector3 up)
            : base(game)
        {
            view = Matrix.CreateLookAt(pos, target, up);

            projection = Matrix.CreatePerspectiveFieldOfView(
                MathHelper.PiOver4,
                (float)Game.Window.ClientBounds.Width /
                (float)Game.Window.ClientBounds.Height,
                1, 100);
        }

        public override void Initialize()
        {
            // TODO: Add your initialization code here

            base.Initialize();
        }

        public override void Update(GameTime gameTime)
        {
            // TODO: Add your update code here

            base.Update(gameTime);
        }
    }
}
```

Next, change the value for the far plane of your camera's field of view to 3000. You'll
be drawing your spaceships far off in the distance in the game that you build throughout
the next few chapters. To change the far plane, modify the last parameter in the call to
`Matrix.CreatePerspectiveFieldOfView`, which is in the constructor of your `Camera` class.
Change this code:

```
projection = Matrix.CreatePerspectiveFieldOfView(
    MathHelper.PiOver4,
    (float)Game.Window.ClientBounds.Width /
    (float)Game.Window.ClientBounds.Height,
    1, 100);
```

to this:

```
projection = Matrix.CreatePerspectiveFieldOfView(
    MathHelper.PiOver4,
    (float)Game.Window.ClientBounds.Width /
    (float)Game.Window.ClientBounds.Height,
    1, 3000);
```

 In the previous chapter, I cautioned you against having too large a distance between the near and far planes of your camera's field of view. Why am I now telling you to set the near plane to 1 and the far plane to 3000?

You're going to be drawing spaceships far in the distance in this game. However, you're not going to be drawing a huge number of objects. You do need to be aware of performance issues when making this call, but the impact on performance isn't down to the size of the field of view alone. Performance issues arise when the number of objects you draw within the field of view becomes too much for your PC to keep up with. In this case, you'll be perfectly fine.

Finally, you'll need to modify your Game1 class to use your camera. Add a class-level variable with the following auto-implemented properties to the Game1 class:

```
public Camera camera { get; protected set; }
```

Then, add the code in the Initialize method of the Game1 class to instantiate the Camera object and add it to the list of components for the Game1 class:

```
camera = new Camera(this, new Vector3(0, 0, 50),
    Vector3.Zero, Vector3.Up);
Components.Add(camera);
```

Adding a Model to Your Project

To draw a model in XNA, first you'll need to add that model to the project the same way that you did with textures, sounds, etc. The content pipeline will compile the model for you at compile time and will verify that it's a valid *.X*-format model.

Many models have texture files associated with them. Sometimes these files will be referenced in the model's *.X* file. If that's the case, you'll need to make sure that your texture files are in the directories specified in the *.X* file.

First, create a subfolder within the *Content* folder in your solution by right-clicking the *3D GameContent* project and selecting Add→New Folder. Name the folder *Models*.

If you haven't already done so, download the source code for this chapter. In the *3D Game\3D GameContent\Models* folder, you'll find a model of a spaceship named *spaceship.x*. This model was actually one of the models shipped with Microsoft's DirectX SDK.

Add the spaceship model to the project by right-clicking your *3D GameContent* *\Models* folder in Solution Explorer, selecting Add→Existing Item..., and browsing to and selecting the *spaceship.x* model.

Once the model is in your application, compile your project. If compilation succeeds, you'll know that XNA recognized the *.X* file and was able to compile it. Otherwise, the content pipeline would have thrown an error indicating that it could not recognize the file format.

 If your model requires additional texture files (the *spaceship.x* model doesn't), you will get a compilation error if the texture files are not in the correct location. This may not seem like anything special, but it's actually really helpful. Before XNA came along, we developers had to figure out if the model worked and the textures were in the correct places through a lot of tedious trial and error. The content pipeline definitely improves that aspect of development in 3D.

Drawing a Model Using a BasicModel Class

Following the design in the 2D game from previous chapters, you'll want to create a base class for all your models. Add a new class by right-clicking your project in Solution Explorer and selecting Add→Class.... Name the class *BasicModel.cs*, as shown in Figure 10-3.

Let's flesh out the `BasicModel` class. First, you'll need to add these namespaces:

```
using Microsoft.Xna.Framework;
using Microsoft.Xna.Framework.Graphics;
```

Next, add two class-level variables to the class:

```
public Model model { get; protected set; }
protected Matrix world = Matrix.Identity;
```

The first variable is of type `Model`. The `Model` class is used to represent 3D models in memory, much like you used the `Texture2D` class previously to represent 2D images in memory. We'll go into more depth on what a `Model` comprises in a few moments.

The next variable is the `Matrix` representing the world for this particular model. This matrix represents where to draw the model and how to rotate it, scale it, and so on. It should be fairly familiar if you've read the previous chapter.

Next, add a constructor for the `BasicModel` class. All this constructor needs to do is receive a parameter of type `Model` and set the model member to that value:

```
public BasicModel(Model m)
{
    model = m;
}
```

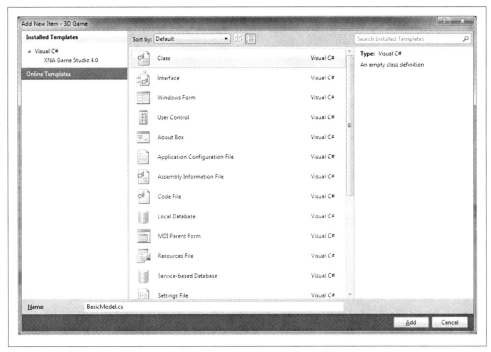

Figure 10-3. Adding a BasicModel class

Now, create an empty virtual `Update` method that can be overridden by classes that derive from `BasicModel` to customize the actions that should be performed during an update:

```
public virtual void Update( )
{

}
```

 In this case, the `Update` method in the base class does nothing. Contrast this with the base class in your 2D game, where, at a bare minimum, an animated sprite needs to move from one frame to another within a sprite sheet. This is a key difference between 2D and 3D development. Remember that 2D animation is much like a cartoon flipbook, where you constantly have to move from image to image. In contrast, 3D development is more like recording a home video; as objects move through the world, the camera automatically handles taking a "snapshot" of the viewing frustum every frame, and the successive snapshots are then drawn on the screen.

All that's left is the actual drawing of the model. Drawing a model is a somewhat tricky thing to do. To understand how models are drawn, it helps to understand what a model actually is. As mentioned previously, models are created in third-party modeling software applications. A model in XNA represents an entire scene from one of those tools that has been exported for use in XNA.

These scenes, which are exported into .X files, can each contain more than one object. These objects, called *meshes*, are stored within the model. The Model class in XNA represents these meshes as ModelMesh objects, and the Model class contains a list of ModelMesh objects in its Meshes property.

A mesh can contain materials or colors, textures, and so on for use in drawing that particular mesh. The various parts of a mesh do not need to be colored or textured the same way; you can have multiple materials on a single mesh. To store this data, the mesh is made up of multiple parts. The ModelMesh class stores a list of ModelMeshParts in a property called MeshParts. Each of these MeshParts contains materials for drawing the MeshPart as well as an Effect object that is used to draw the MeshPart.

By default, the Effect used in a Model's MeshPart is of the type BasicEffect. You should be familiar with the BasicEffect class from Chapter 9. BasicEffect derives from Effect and provides you with a way to draw objects in 3D without having to create your own custom HLSL effect files. You'll be writing your own effect files later in this book, but at this point, that's too advanced, so we'll stick with BasicEffects for now.

Finally, each ModelMesh has a transformation that will move that mesh to the appropriate location within the model.

To see how all this works, picture a car model with a movable steering wheel. The entire scene (car and steering wheel together) is represented by a Model. The Model may have two different ModelMesh objects in its Meshes property (one for the car and one for the steering wheel). Each of these Meshes will have a transformation that places the object in the correct place (the car will be placed at some location, such as the origin, while the steering wheel will be offset accordingly to put it in the appropriate place). In addition, each of the Meshes will have a material that modifies the way that mesh looks (for example, the car might use a material that makes it appear shiny red, whereas the steering wheel might use a material that makes it appear dull black) as well as an Effect that should be used to draw the ModelMesh.

Now that you understand what a model consists of, let's look at some typical code that can be used to draw a model (assume the model variable here is of the type Model):

```
Matrix[] transforms = new Matrix[model.Bones.Count];
model.CopyAbsoluteBoneTransformsTo(transforms);

foreach (ModelMesh mesh in model.Meshes)
{
    foreach (BasicEffect be in mesh.Effects)
    {
```

```
            be.EnableDefaultLighting( );
            be.Projection = camera.projection;
            be.View = camera.view;
            be.World = world * mesh.ParentBone.Transform;
        }

        mesh.Draw( );
    }
```

Notice that the first two lines of code deal with something called *bones*. These bones use transformations, which, as mentioned earlier, are used to place the objects in the appropriate locations within the model. Typically, your code won't be affected by these transformations, unless the model has multiple meshes (which your spaceship model does not). However, you'll want to include these first two lines just in case a given model has multiple parts.

Next, the code loops through each `ModelMesh` in the model and, for each of the `Basic Effect` objects associated with each `ModelMesh`, applies default lighting and sets the `Projection`, `View`, and `World` properties for the object being drawn using the camera for the projection and view matrices and the world matrix for the object's `World` property. The world matrix is multiplied by the transform here to ensure that the `ModelMesh` is placed in the appropriate location within the model.

If you're lost, don't worry about it; this is somewhat confusing, but all will become clear. Really, all you need to remember here is that you're looping through parts of a model, looping through effects for those model parts, and setting properties to draw the parts correctly.

The camera view and projection matrices were covered in the previous chapter, but as a reminder, they are essentially matrix variables that tell XNA where to place the camera (the view) and what the properties are that define the viewing frustum of the camera (the projection).

This might not all make sense at this point, but that's OK. The most important thing to remember about the model-drawing code is that you have to set your `BasicEffect`'s `Projection`, `View`, and `World` properties. Once you do that, the rest of the code will handle drawing the model for you.

You'll see later how to apply custom effects to your models. For now, notice that each model loaded into XNA uses `BasicEffect`s by default.

Go ahead and add the following two methods to your `BasicModel` class:

```
public void Draw(Camera camera)
{
    Matrix[] transforms = new Matrix[model.Bones.Count];
    model.CopyAbsoluteBoneTransformsTo(transforms);

    foreach (ModelMesh mesh in model.Meshes)
    {
        foreach (BasicEffect be in mesh.Effects)
        {
```

```
        be.EnableDefaultLighting( );
        be.Projection = camera.projection;
        be.View = camera.view;
        be.World = GetWorld( ) * mesh.ParentBone.Transform;
    }

    mesh.Draw( );
    }
}

public virtual Matrix GetWorld( )
{
    return world;
}
```

The `Draw` method is very similar to the code discussed previously that is used to draw a 3D model. The key difference is that a method is called to retrieve the object's world. The `GetWorld` method is `virtual`, and in the base class it simply returns the world matrix variable. This enables subclasses to override the `GetWorld` method and apply different scales, rotations, and translations as needed.

Adding a Model Manager

Again following the design from the 2D section of this game, you'll want to create a `GameComponent` that you'll use as a manager for all your models in this game. To add a new `GameComponent`, right-click the solution in Solution Explorer, select Add→New Item..., and then select the Game Component template from the list on the right. Name your class *ModelManager.cs*, as shown in Figure 10-4.

By default, the new `ModelManager` class will derive from `GameComponent`. Adding a Game Component to the list of components in your game will sync up the `GameComponent`'s `Update` method with your game's `Update` method (i.e., every time your game's `Update` method is called, your `GameComponent`'s `Update` method will also be called).

To connect your `ModelManager` to the game loop, add a class-level variable of type `ModelManager` to your `Game1` class:

```
ModelManager modelManager;
```

Next, in the `Initialize` method of your `Game1` class, instantiate the model manager and add it to the list of game components:

```
modelManager = new ModelManager(this);
Components.Add(modelManager);
```

Your model manager is now connected to your game loop. You want to have your `ModelManager`'s `Update` method synced with your game, but you'll also need to have a `Draw` method synced with your game's `Draw` method. To do this, you'll need to change the base class of your `ModelManager` to `DrawableGameComponent`, as shown here:

```
public class ModelManager : DrawableGameComponent
```

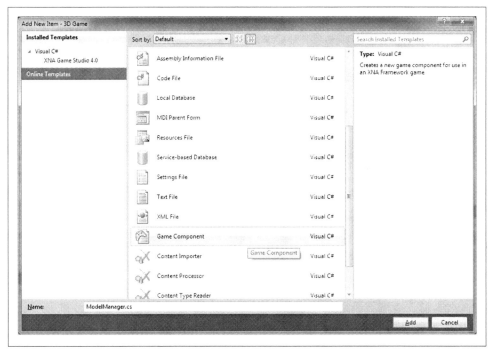

Figure 10-4. Adding the ModelManager class

You'll then need to override the `Draw` method in your `ModelManager` by adding the following method to that class:

```
public override void Draw(GameTime gameTime)
{
    base.Draw(gameTime);
}
```

Next, add to the `ModelManager` class a class-level variable that will store a list of `Basic Model` objects:

```
List<BasicModel> models = new List<BasicModel>( );
```

Then, add an overload of the `LoadContent` method to your `ModelManager` class. In that method, create a `BasicModel` using the spaceship model, and add it to the list of models:

```
protected override void LoadContent( )
{
    models.Add(new BasicModel(
        Game.Content.Load<Model>(@"models\spaceship")));

    base.LoadContent( );
}
```

Finally, you'll want to modify the `Update` and `Draw` methods of your `ModelManager` class to loop through the list of models and call their individual `Update` and `Draw` methods, respectively:

```
public override void Update(GameTime gameTime)
{
    // Loop through all models and call Update
    for (int i = 0; i < models.Count; ++i)
    {
        models[i].Update( );
    }

    base.Update(gameTime);
}

public override void Draw(GameTime gameTime)
{
    // Loop through and draw each model
    foreach (BasicModel bm in models)
    {
        bm.Draw(((Game1)Game).camera);
    }

    base.Draw(gameTime);
}
```

Compile and run your game, and you should see the model of the spaceship, as shown in Figure 10-5.

Very cool! Notice how much better your game is looking now than when you were dealing with triangles and textures in the previous chapter. 3D models enable you to quickly draw very detailed and highly realistic objects that would be almost impossibly difficult to draw by hand using only primitives.

Rotating Your Model

Great job! The model is looking good, and you're moving along. It's time to create your first subclass of the BasicModel class, to enable some basic rotation and movement. Right-click the project in Solution Explorer and select Add→Class..., and enter *SpinningEnemy.cs* as the class name.

Replace the code generated in the *SpinningEnemy.cs* class with the following code:

```
using System;
using System.Collections.Generic;
using System.Text;
using Microsoft.Xna.Framework;
using Microsoft.Xna.Framework.Graphics;


namespace _3D_Game
{
    class SpinningEnemy: BasicModel
    {
        Matrix rotation = Matrix.Identity;
```

```
public SpinningEnemy(Model m)
    : base(m)
{
}

public override void Update(  )
{
    rotation *= Matrix.CreateRotationY(MathHelper.Pi / 180);
}

public override Matrix GetWorld(  )
{
    return world * rotation;
}
```

So, what's going on here? The first thing to note is that the SpinningEnemy class derives from BasicModel. The constructor takes a Model and simply passes that model on to the constructor of the base class.

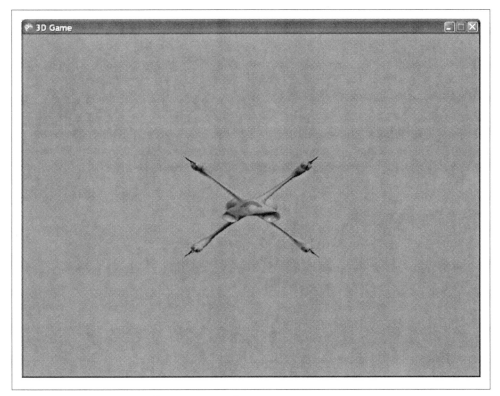

Figure 10-5. Menacing spaceship staring you down!

The key addition to this class lies in the class-level variable `rotation`. This variable allows you to rotate your object rather than just drawing it standing still, the way it was when you drew it using only the `BasicModel` class. In the `Update` method, you can see that the `rotation` variable is updated each frame with a rotation of 1 degree around the Y-axis (remember that angles are represented by radians in XNA; π is 180°, so $\pi/180$ equals 1 degree).

Finally, the `GetWorld` method that is called in the base class's `Draw` method to place the object appropriately in the world combines the `world` variable from the base class with the `rotation` variable from this class, giving the object a nice spinning effect.

That's all there is to it. When you have a solid design, programming becomes so much easier! All you need to do now is modify the `ModelManager` to demo your new class instead of the `BasicModel` class. In the `LoadContent` method of the `ModelManager` class, modify the line that creates a `BasicModel` and change it to use `SpinningEnemy`, as shown here:

```
models.Add(new SpinningEnemy(
    Game.Content.Load<Model>(@"models\spaceship")));
```

Compile and run your game now, and you'll see that the model spins around the Y-axis, as shown in Figure 10-6.

Wow! This is really looking good! You can easily derive classes from the `BasicModel` class, and by adding code to the `Update` and `GetWorld` overridden methods you can make your model spaceship move and rotate at will.

You may also notice that, using just the `BasicEffect` applied in your code, you've given the ship some decent lighting effects and made it look pretty sharp. In later chapters, you'll learn more about applying custom effects using HLSL, and you'll see how to make your models look even better by applying custom effects.

What You Just Did

We covered a lot of ground in this chapter. Let's recap for a minute:

- You imported a 3D model into your project in an .X file and loaded it into a `Model` object via the content pipeline.
- You created a model class hierarchy using a base class for drawing all models and a subclass for specialized rotating functionality.
- You created a `ModelManager` class that will be used to update, draw, and manage all models in your game.
- You drew a 3D model and applied a yaw rotation to the model.

Figure 10-6. Oh yeah! A spinning ship!

Summary

- 3D models contain vertex and sometimes texture information that together form some object that's typically larger and more detailed than a developer would ever want to attempt to build by hand.

- 3D models are created in third-party modeling software applications and exported to model files for use in other applications (in this case, your game).

- By default in XNA, models contain `BasicEffect`s. You can draw a model by looping through the meshes of the model and setting the properties of the `BasicEffect` class before drawing the model itself.

- Recent studies have shown that 9 out of 10 women prefer men who can develop in XNA.

Test Your Knowledge: Quiz

1. What model format(s) are supported in XNA?
2. Why use a model when you can just draw things on your own?
3. What type of effect are models loaded with by default when they're loaded into XNA?
4. Fact or fiction: if your model has separate texture files associated with it, but those files aren't in the location specified by the model file, your game will crash when it tries to load the model.
5. What number comes next in the sequence {4, 8, 15, 16, 23}?

Test Your Knowledge: Exercise

Take the code from this chapter and create a new subclass of `BasicModel` in which the ship moves back and forth between (0, 0, 0) and (0, 0, –400). Make the ship turn appropriately to always face the direction in which it is going.

CHAPTER 11

Creating a First-Person Camera

One of the most important things in a 3D game is the camera. Choosing the best type of camera and implementing it correctly can make or break a game. It matters as much as the storyline, audio, or graphics quality. Although the camera implementation is of paramount importance, in many ways it is a matter of personal preference—a camera that works well for some gamers may not be preferred by others. Many games, therefore, allow players to switch in and out of different camera angles, allowing them to choose the camera that best fits their style of play.

In this chapter, we'll implement a first-person camera and discuss issues related to moving that camera in 3D space (as in a flight simulator) versus moving a land-based camera.

Components of a Moving 3D Camera

In this chapter, you'll be starting with the code you finished in Chapter 10. Open that project for use throughout the rest of this chapter.

In Chapters 9 and 10, we discussed setting up a 3D camera and the basic components that make up a camera in XNA 3D. You created a camera GameComponent, which you added to your solutions in previous chapters to enable you to see the triangles and spaceship models you drew.

As a quick review, the camera is made up of two different matrices: the projection matrix and the view matrix. The projection matrix defines the camera's viewing frustum, or field of view. Remember that the field of view defines an area in front of the camera that is visible to the camera. The field of view has several components: a camera angle, an aspect ratio, and near and far clipping planes. The projection matrix typically will not change during your game. While your camera will move and rotate in 3D, the viewing frustum usually remains constant.

The view matrix defines where the camera sits in the world and how it is rotated. The view matrix is created from three vectors: the camera's position, the point the camera is looking at, and a vector indicating which direction is up for the camera. In contrast to the projection matrix, which does not need to change when a camera moves, the view matrix will change constantly to reflect new rotations and positions of the camera.

Let's take a look at your current Camera class:

```
using System;
using System.Collections.Generic;
using System.Linq;
using Microsoft.Xna.Framework;
using Microsoft.Xna.Framework.Audio;
using Microsoft.Xna.Framework.Content;
using Microsoft.Xna.Framework.GamerServices;
using Microsoft.Xna.Framework.Graphics;
using Microsoft.Xna.Framework.Input;
using Microsoft.Xna.Framework.Media;
using Microsoft.Xna.Framework.Net;
using Microsoft.Xna.Framework.Storage;


namespace _3D_Game
{
    public class Camera : Microsoft.Xna.Framework.GameComponent
    {
        //Camera matrices
        public Matrix view { get; protected set; }
        public Matrix projection { get; protected set; }

        public Camera(Game game, Vector3 pos, Vector3 target, Vector3 up)
            : base(game)
        {
            view = Matrix.CreateLookAt(pos, target, up);

            projection = Matrix.CreatePerspectiveFieldOfView(
                MathHelper.PiOver4,
                (float)Game.Window.ClientBounds.Width /
                (float)Game.Window.ClientBounds.Height,
                1, 3000);
        }

        public override void Initialize()
        {
            // TODO: Add your initialization code here

            base.Initialize();
        }



        public override void Update(GameTime gameTime)
        {
```

```
            // TODO: Add your update code here

            base.Update(gameTime);
        }
    }
}
```

Notice that you have specified two variables at the class level: one for the view matrix and one for the projection matrix. The camera represented by this class was designed to be stationary. As mentioned previously, the view matrix represents the location and rotation of the camera. If you're going to create a camera that can be moved through 3D space, you're going to have to be able to modify the view matrix.

In fact, rather than modifying the view matrix, you'll be rebuilding the matrix every frame. Remember that the view matrix is composed of a position vector, a direction vector, and an up vector. By creating class-level variables for each of those vectors, you can modify things like the position of the camera, the direction of the camera, and which direction is up for the camera by simply modifying the appropriate vector variable and then rebuilding the view matrix of the camera with the new vectors.

To move and rotate your camera, you'll need to add the following three class-level variables to your Camera class:

```
// Camera vectors
public Vector3 cameraPosition { get; protected set; }
Vector3 cameraDirection;
Vector3 cameraUp;
```

These three variables will be used to recreate your camera's view matrix each frame.

Note that the cameraDirection variable is not the same as the camera's target (or the actual point at which the camera is looking). The view matrix is created by the Matrix.CreateLookAt method, which takes three parameters: the position, target, and up vectors for the camera. The second parameter, the camera's target, represents the actual point at which your camera will be looking. In contrast, the cameraDirection variable represents a relative direction in which your camera is facing, rather than a target at which the camera is looking. In order to determine the actual target point that the camera is looking at, you need to add your cameraPosition and cameraDirection vectors together (see Figure 11-1).

This means two important things in relation to your cameraDirection vector. First, instead of passing cameraDirection as the second parameter of your Matrix.Create LookAt method, you'll need to pass cameraPosition + cameraDirection. Second, your cameraDirection vector cannot be (0, 0, 0); the variable must contain a value representing something other than the origin because it represents the direction in which your camera is looking, and the vector (0, 0, 0) has no direction.

OK, now that that's cleared up, go ahead and create a method in your Camera class that will define your new view matrix using your three new camera vectors:

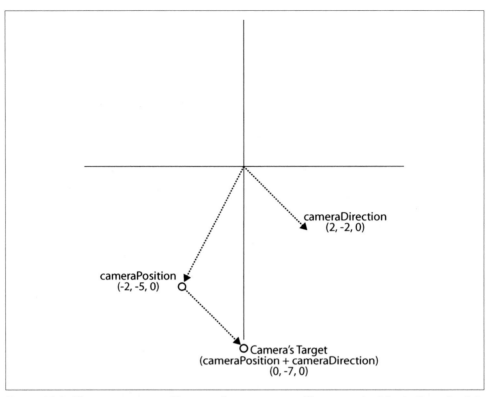

Figure 11-1. The camera target (the second parameter you'll pass to the Matrix.CreateLookAt method) is derived from adding the camera's direction to the camera's position

```
private void CreateLookAt( )
{
    view = Matrix.CreateLookAt(cameraPosition,
        cameraPosition + cameraDirection, cameraUp);
}
```

Next, you'll want to set your camera's Vector3 variables in your constructor. You're already accepting those three parameters in the constructor, but currently you're not storing them separately; you're just using them in the constructor to create a view matrix with the call to Matrix.CreateLookAt. Remove the line of code in the constructor that builds your view matrix:

```
view = Matrix.CreateLookAt(pos, target, up);
```

and replace it with the following code:

```
// Build camera view matrix
cameraPosition = pos;
cameraDirection = target - pos;
cameraDirection.Normalize( );
cameraUp = up;
CreateLookAt( );
```

This code sets the position and up vectors directly from the parameters received. The direction is derived from the target of the camera minus the position of the camera. Why? Because the target parameter that was passed in is currently treated as the actual camera target, whereas your direction variable represents the general direction in which the camera is facing. If you derive the target from the camera position plus the camera direction, you can also derive the camera direction from the camera target minus the camera position.

Notice that a call to `Normalize` is being used on the `cameraDirection`. The `Normalize` method takes any vector and converts it to a vector with a magnitude (or length) of one. Why this is done will become evident shortly. Basically, you'll be using this vector not only to represent the direction of the camera, but also to move the camera forward.

Finally, the call to `CreateLookAt` creates an initial view matrix based on the vectors specified.

Direction of Movement

Think about it—when you walk forward, what direction do you typically move in? Usually, you walk in the direction that you are facing. That is true of most game cameras as well. There are a few exceptions that allow the player to look in one direction and move in another, but as a general rule, you move a camera forward in the direction in which it faces.

What does that mean to you? Well, because you already have a vector that represents the direction in which the camera is facing, you can use that vector to move your camera forward. As you'll see shortly, you can move a camera forward by simply adding the direction vector to the position vector. This moves the position vector in the direction of the direction vector, and in turn moves the camera forward in the direction in which it's facing.

So, why normalize the direction vector? Remember that normalizing the vector will make it have a length or magnitude of one. Dealing with a vector with a length of one makes it much easier to apply things such as different speed values to the movement of the camera.

Moving in a First-Person Camera

With the `cameraDirection` vector being normalized and representing the direction in which the camera is looking, you can easily move the camera forward by simply adding the `cameraDirection` to the `cameraPosition`. Doing this will move the camera toward the camera's target in a straight line. Moving backward is just as easy: simply subtract the `cameraDirection` from the `cameraPosition`.

Because the `cameraDirection` vector is normalized (i.e., has a magnitude of one), the camera's speed will always be one. To allow yourself to change the speed of the camera, add a class-level `float` variable to represent speed:

```
float speed = 3;
```

Next, in your Camera class's Update method, add code to move the camera forward and backward with the W and S keys:

```
// Move forward/backward
if (Keyboard.GetState( ).IsKeyDown(Keys.W))
    cameraPosition += cameraDirection * speed;
if (Keyboard.GetState( ).IsKeyDown(Keys.S))
    cameraPosition -= cameraDirection * speed;
```

At the end of the Update method, you'll want to call your Camera's CreateLookAt method to rebuild the camera based on the changes you've made to its vectors. Add this line of code just above the call to base.Update:

```
// Recreate the camera view matrix
CreateLookAt( );
```

Compile and run the game at this point, and you'll see that when you press the W and S keys, the camera moves closer to and farther from the spaceship. It's important to note what's happening here: in our previous 3D examples, you've moved objects around by changing the world matrix for those objects, but in this example, instead of moving the object, you're moving the camera itself.

Now that you can move your camera forward and backward, you'll want to add other movement features. Any good 3D first-person camera also has *strafing* (or side-to-side movement) support. Your camera vectors are position, direction, and up, so how can you find a vector that will move your camera sideways? We might be able to solve this problem with a little bit of vector math. Think about what you need in order to move sideways: you'll need a vector that points in the direction that is sideways-on to your camera. If you had that vector, moving sideways would be just as easy as moving forward because you could simply add the sideways vector to the camera's position vector. As shown in Figure 11-2, you currently have a vector for the camera's up direction as well as a vector for the direction in which the camera is facing, but you don't have a vector representing the direction that is sideways-on to the camera.

Here's where the vector math can help: a *cross product* is a binary operation performed on two vectors in 3D space that results in another vector that is perpendicular to the two input vectors. Therefore, by taking the cross product of the up and direction vectors of your camera, you will end up with a vector perpendicular to those two vectors (i.e., coming from the side of your camera). This is illustrated in Figure 11-3. The cross product of your negative up and direction vectors will yield a perpendicular vector coming from the other direction (sideways-on to the other side of the camera).

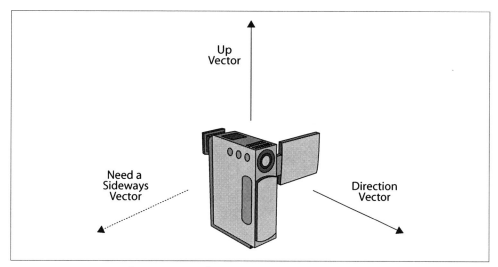

Figure 11-2. To move sideways in a strafe, you need a vector representing a sideways direction

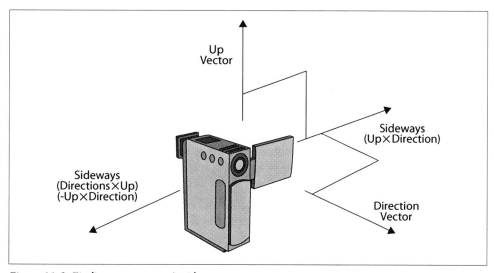

Figure 11-3. Finding your camera's sideways vector

 It's not critical that you understand how this vector math works, but if you're curious, feel free to investigate in some math textbooks. All you need to understand for now is that it does indeed work: the cross product of any two vectors yields a third vector perpendicular to the other two, and the cross product of the up and direction vectors of your camera yields a vector indicating the sideways direction for your camera.

It may help to picture a person standing and looking forward. The person's direction vector would be pointing straight ahead, whereas his up vector would be pointing straight up. The cross product of the up and direction vectors would essentially be the direction the person's left arm would be pointing in if it were held out perpendicular to both his up and direction vectors. The only vector that fits that criterion would be one that was pointing directly outward from the person's side.

XNA provides a method that will create a vector based on the cross product of two other vectors. It's a static method in the `Vector3` class called `Cross`. Pass in any two vectors to the `Cross` method, and the resulting vector will be the cross product of the two vectors passed in.

To enable the camera to move from side to side using the A and D keys, insert the following code immediately after the code you just added, which moves the camera forward and backward:

```
// Move side to side
if (Keyboard.GetState( ).IsKeyDown(Keys.A))
    cameraPosition += Vector3.Cross(cameraUp, cameraDirection) * speed;
if (Keyboard.GetState( ).IsKeyDown(Keys.D))
    cameraPosition -= Vector3.Cross(cameraUp, cameraDirection) * speed;
```

Compile and run the game, and you'll see that you now have full camera movement with the WASD keys. Very cool! You're ready to work on rotating your camera in 3D space.

Rotations in a First-Person Camera

All camera rotations are related to the same rotations that were discussed previously in relation to the rotation of 3D objects in XNA. Essentially, a camera can yaw, pitch, and roll just like an object can. As a reminder, yaw, pitch, and roll rotations are pictured in Figure 11-4.

In the classes in which I've taught XNA, one of the things that has traditionally been difficult for some students to understand is the fact that yaw, pitch, and roll rotations applied to objects or cameras that move and rotate in 3D don't necessarily correspond to rotations around the X-, Y-, and Z-axes.

For example, picture the camera you currently have in your game. The camera sits on the Z-axis and faces in the negative Z direction. If you wanted to rotate the camera in a roll, you could rotate the camera around the Z-axis. However, what would happen if the camera rotated to turn 90° and was now looking in the direction of positive X? If you performed a rotation around the Z-axis at this point, you'd rotate in a pitch rather than a roll.

It's easier to think of yaw, pitch, and roll as related to the vectors available to you in your camera. For example, a yaw, rather than rotating around the Y-axis, rotates around the camera's up vector. Similarly, a roll rotates around the camera's direction vector,

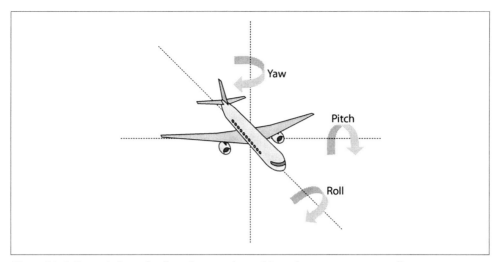

Figure 11-4. Yaw, pitch, and roll apply not only to objects, but to cameras as well

and a pitch rotates around a vector coming out of the side of the object, perpendicular to the up and direction vectors. Any idea how you'd get that perpendicular vector? That's right, you've used it before to add strafing ability: it's the cross product of the up and direction vectors. Figure 11-5 illustrates how yaw, pitch, and roll rotations are accomplished in a 3D camera.

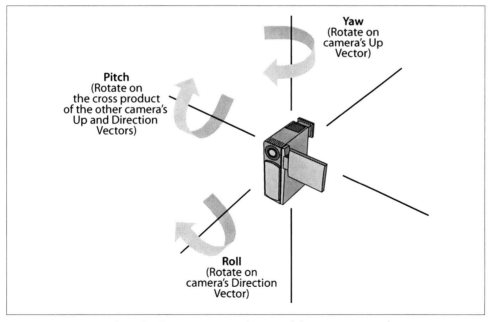

Figure 11-5. Yaw, pitch, and roll rotations using the up and direction vectors of a camera

Which of these rotations you choose to implement in your particular game completely depends on what type of experience you want to give the player. For example, a typical space simulator will have the ability to yaw, pitch, and roll in an unlimited fashion. A helicopter simulator may allow yaw, pitch, and roll to some extent, but might not allow you to perform a complete roll (a fairly difficult task in a helicopter). A land-based shooter may allow only a yaw and a pitch, though some games allow roll rotations for special moves such as tilting your head to look around a corner.

Once you've decided which of these rotations you'll allow in your camera, the next step is to implement them. Each of these camera rotations can be accomplished by rotating one or more of your camera's vectors. For a yaw, pitch, or roll, it helps to evaluate the rotation using these steps: first, determine which of the three camera vectors need to rotate; second, figure out what axis you will need to rotate those vectors around; and third, determine which methods will be needed to accomplish this.

Rotating a Camera in a Yaw

Let's start by creating a yaw for the camera. Of the three camera vectors (position, direction, and up), the only one that changes when performing a yaw is the direction vector. Picture a person standing up and performing a yaw rotation (moving her head from side to side). The person's up vector doesn't change, and neither does her position, but the direction vector (the direction in which she is looking) definitely changes.

The axis you want to rotate the direction vector around for a yaw is the camera's up vector. The method used to rotate a `Vector3` is `Vector3.Transform`, which takes two parameters: the source or original vector, and a matrix representing a rotation or translation to apply to the vector.

 When performing a yaw rotation for a camera, why rotate around the camera's up vector instead of the Y-axis?

The Y-axis might not always be up for a camera. It might be for a land-based shooter game, but consider a flight simulator that freely flies and rotates in three dimensions. In that case, you'd always want to yaw around the up vector of the camera.

Before you add the `Vector3.Transform` to perform the yaw, you'll want to add some code to allow your camera to capture mouse movement. A typical first-person configuration uses the WASD keys for movement and the mouse for rotating the camera. So, to capture mouse movement, add the following class-level variable to your `Camera` class:

```
MouseState prevMouseState;
```

Next, in the `Initialize` method of your `Camera` class, set the initial position of the mouse cursor to the middle of the screen. Also, add the code to initialize the new variable:

```
// Set mouse position and do initial get state
Mouse.SetPosition(Game.Window.ClientBounds.Width / 2,
    Game.Window.ClientBounds.Height / 2);
prevMouseState = Mouse.GetState( );
```

Remember that the `Mouse.GetState` call returns the mouse position. To find out how far the mouse has actually moved, you need to capture the state from the previous frame and compare it to the current state in each frame. You initialize the state variable in the `Initialize` method so that you have something to compare against in the first frame (the first time `Update` is called).

Now you're ready to code your yaw rotation. In the `Update` method of your `Camera` class, add the following code just above the call to `CreateLookAt`:

```
// Yaw rotation
cameraDirection = Vector3.Transform(cameraDirection,
    Matrix.CreateFromAxisAngle(cameraUp, (-MathHelper.PiOver4 / 150) *
    (Mouse.GetState( ).X - prevMouseState.X)));

// Reset prevMouseState
prevMouseState = Mouse.GetState( );
```

In this code, you're assigning the `cameraDirection` vector the value given in the `Vector3.Transform` call. By passing in `cameraDirection` as the first parameter, you ensure that the `Vector3.Transform` method will apply the rotation specified in the second parameter to the `cameraDirection` and return the resulting vector. The matrix specified in the second parameter is created from the `CreateFromAxisAngle` method, which creates a rotation around a specific axis (in this case, the camera's up vector). The angle of rotation is determined by how much the mouse has moved horizontally.

Compile and run the game at this point, and you'll see that not only can you move in 3D space, but now you can yaw the camera left and right. It may seem a bit awkward because you don't have full rotation of your camera yet, but that will come shortly.

 If your camera moves backward relative to your mouse (e.g., if you move the mouse right and it rotates the camera left), you've probably left off the negative sign in front of the `MathHelper.PiOver4` in the code. Add that, and it should work properly.

Rotating a Camera in a Roll

When rotating in a roll, follow the same steps to figure out what to do: ask yourself what vectors rotate when performing a roll, what axis you would rotate those vectors on, and what methods need to be used.

In a roll, the only camera vector that changes is the camera's up vector. The vector that you want to rotate your camera's up vector around is the camera's direction vector. Add the following code to the `Update` method of your `Camera` class, just before the `prevMouseState = Mouse.GetState( )` line:

```
// Roll rotation
if (Mouse.GetState(  ).LeftButton == ButtonState.Pressed)
{
    cameraUp = Vector3.Transform(cameraUp,
        Matrix.CreateFromAxisAngle(cameraDirection,
        MathHelper.PiOver4 / 45));
}
if (Mouse.GetState(  ).RightButton == ButtonState.Pressed)
{
    cameraUp = Vector3.Transform(cameraUp,
        Matrix.CreateFromAxisAngle(cameraDirection,
        -MathHelper.PiOver4 / 45));
}
```

Run the game now, and you'll see that with the left and right mouse buttons you can roll your camera left or right. It will probably look a little strange in this example because the only thing that you're drawing is the spaceship and it is rotating as well, which makes the rotation of your camera seem off.

Let's make the ship not spin anymore, so you can get a better sense of how your camera is working. In the ModelManager's LoadContent method, change the type of ship that's being created from a SpinningEnemy to a BasicModel:

```
models.Add(new BasicModel(
    Game.Content.Load<Model>(@"models\spaceship")));
```

Run the game again, and your camera rotations and movements should feel more accurate without the ship spinning on its own.

Rotating a Camera in a Pitch

Coding a pitch is slightly more complicated than coding a yaw or a roll. First, think of what needs to change when you pitch. You may think that just your direction changes, but here's a question: does your up vector change in a pitch?

This is one place where you'll need to stop and think about what kind of functionality you want in your camera. Typically, in a flight simulator, you'd rotate both your direction and your up vector in a pitch. The reason? Remember that in a yaw you rotate around your up vector. In a flight simulator, you'll want to have your up vector change in a roll and a pitch to make your yaw rotation more realistic.

What about pitching in a land-based shooter? Would you want to rotate your up vector in a pitch in that scenario? Again, remember that when you yaw, you do so around the up vector. Imagine hunting down an enemy and looking two or three stories up a wall to see if he's perched on a ledge. Then, you rotate in a yaw to scan the rest of that level of the building. You'd expect your rotation in that case to be based on the Y-axis— rotating around the up vector (if it was changed by your pitch) would cause an unexpected rotation.

One solution to this is to use the up vector for rotating in a yaw with a flight simulator and use the Y-axis for yaw rotations with land-based cameras. However, there's another thing to consider here: typically in a land-based shooter you can't pitch a full 360°. When looking up, typically you can't look straight up; you can pitch your camera until it is maybe 10–15° away from exactly up, but no further. One reason for this is that in XNA, if the angle between your up vector and your direction vector is small enough, XNA doesn't know how to draw what you're telling it to draw, and it will freak out on you a little bit. To avoid this, it's common to set a limit on how far you can pitch your camera. But if you're going to set a limit on how much you can pitch, you might as well just not rotate your up vector in a pitch on a game like this.

Either way, these are some things to think about. In this example, you're going to use a flight simulator approach, so you'll be rotating both the up and the direction vectors. Now that you know what you're going to rotate, you need to figure out which axis to rotate around. The pitch rotates around a vector that runs out from the side of your camera. Remember using `Vector3.Cross` to get a vector perpendicular to the up and direction vectors of your camera when strafing? You'll be using that same vector to rotate your direction and up vectors in a pitch.

In the `Update` method of the `Camera` class, add the following code just before the `prevMouseState = Mouse.GetState( )` line:

```
// Pitch rotation
cameraDirection = Vector3.Transform(cameraDirection,
    Matrix.CreateFromAxisAngle(Vector3.Cross(cameraUp, cameraDirection),
    (MathHelper.PiOver4 / 100) *
    (Mouse.GetState( ).Y - prevMouseState.Y)));

cameraUp = Vector3.Transform(cameraUp,
    Matrix.CreateFromAxisAngle(Vector3.Cross(cameraUp, cameraDirection),
    (MathHelper.PiOver4 / 100) *
    (Mouse.GetState( ).Y - prevMouseState.Y)));
```

Your camera now has full movement and full yaw, pitch, and roll rotation. Run the game and fly around the world to see different angles of the ship that weren't previously available, as shown in Figure 11-6.

Coding the Camera for the 3D Game

In the previous sections of this chapter, you created a free-flying 3D camera. You're now going to take that camera and change it to work for the game that you'll be building throughout the rest of this book. If you want to keep your free-flying camera code, you should make a copy of your project to save the existing code that you have written.

If you download the source code for this chapter, you'll find the free-flying camera code that you just created in the folder called *Flying Camera*. The code that will be written and used through the rest of this chapter is located with the source code as well, in the folder called *3D Game*.

Figure 11-6. Your camera is now freely mobile in 3D space—here's a view from above the spaceship

The game that you're going to build in the rest of this book will use a stationary camera that can rotate a total of 45° in a pitch and 45° in a yaw. Later, you'll add some code to send ships flying toward the camera, which you'll have to shoot down.

Because you won't be moving your camera and you won't be rotating in a roll, you can go into the `Camera` class's `Update` method and remove the code that enables that functionality.

To do this, remove the following code (which moves the camera forward and backward and side to side) from the `Update` method of the `Camera` class:

```
// Move forward/backward
if (Keyboard.GetState(  ).IsKeyDown(Keys.W))
    cameraPosition += cameraDirection * speed;
if (Keyboard.GetState(  ).IsKeyDown(Keys.S))
    cameraPosition -= cameraDirection * speed;
```

```
// Move side to side
if (Keyboard.GetState(   ).IsKeyDown(Keys.A))
    cameraPosition +=
        Vector3.Cross(cameraUp, cameraDirection) * speed;
if (Keyboard.GetState(   ).IsKeyDown(Keys.D))
    cameraPosition -=
        Vector3.Cross(cameraUp, cameraDirection) * speed;
```

Also remove the following code, which rolls the camera (also located in the Update method of the Camera class):

```
// Roll rotation
if (Mouse.GetState(   ).LeftButton == ButtonState.Pressed)
{
    cameraUp = Vector3.Transform(cameraUp,
        Matrix.CreateFromAxisAngle(cameraDirection,
        MathHelper.PiOver4 / 45));
}
if (Mouse.GetState(   ).RightButton == ButtonState.Pressed)
{
    cameraUp = Vector3.Transform(cameraUp,
        Matrix.CreateFromAxisAngle(cameraDirection,
        -MathHelper.PiOver4 / 45));
}
```

In addition, you can also remove the class-level speed variable from the Camera class, as you won't be using it anymore.

What you're left with is a camera that yaws and pitches 360° in each direction. However, you want to cap that at 22.5° in each direction (for a total of 45° in a yaw and 45° in a pitch).

To do this, you'll need to add four variables at the class level in the Camera class (two representing the total rotation allowed in pitch and yaw and two representing the current rotation in pitch and yaw):

```
// Max yaw/pitch variables
float totalYaw = MathHelper.PiOver4 / 2;
float currentYaw= 0;
float totalPitch = MathHelper.PiOver4 / 2;
float currentPitch = 0;
```

Next, you'll need to modify the code that performs the yaw and pitch rotations in the Update method of your Camera class. Each time you rotate, you'll need to add the angle of rotation to the currentYaw and currentPitch variables, respectively. Then, you'll perform the yaw rotation only if the absolute value of the currentYaw variable plus the new yaw angle is less than the value of the totalYaw variable. You'll place the same restriction on pitch rotation as well.

Replace the following yaw code in the Camera class's Update method:

```
// Yaw rotation
cameraDirection = Vector3.Transform(cameraDirection,
    Matrix.CreateFromAxisAngle(cameraUp, (-MathHelper.PiOver4 / 150) *
    (Mouse.GetState( ).X - prevMouseState.X)));
```

with this:

```
// Yaw rotation
float yawAngle = (-MathHelper.PiOver4 / 150) *
        (Mouse.GetState( ).X - prevMouseState.X);

if (Math.Abs(currentYaw + yawAngle) < totalYaw)
{
    cameraDirection = Vector3.Transform(cameraDirection,
        Matrix.CreateFromAxisAngle(cameraUp, yawAngle));
    currentYaw += yawAngle;
}
```

Next, replace the following pitch code in the Camera class's Update method:

```
// Pitch rotation
cameraDirection = Vector3.Transform(cameraDirection,
    Matrix.CreateFromAxisAngle(Vector3.Cross(cameraUp, cameraDirection),
    (MathHelper.PiOver4 / 100) *
    (Mouse.GetState( ).Y - prevMouseState.Y)));

cameraUp = Vector3.Transform(cameraUp,
    Matrix.CreateFromAxisAngle(Vector3.Cross(cameraUp, cameraDirection),
    (MathHelper.PiOver4 / 100) *
    (Mouse.GetState( ).Y - prevMouseState.Y)));
```

with this:

```
// Pitch rotation
float pitchAngle = (MathHelper.PiOver4 / 150) *
    (Mouse.GetState( ).Y - prevMouseState.Y);

if (Math.Abs(currentPitch + pitchAngle) < totalPitch)
{
    cameraDirection = Vector3.Transform(cameraDirection,
        Matrix.CreateFromAxisAngle(
            Vector3.Cross(cameraUp, cameraDirection),
        pitchAngle));

    currentPitch += pitchAngle;
}
```

Compile and run your game again, and you'll see that you can rotate the camera in pitch and yaw, but the angle is limited to 45° in the yaw and pitch directions.

What Happened to the Up Vector?

Why are you not modifying the camera's up vector in the pitch anymore?

You're going to be simulating a stationary camera now (not a 3D flying camera). Because of that, you're going to want your camera to always yaw around a stationary up vector. In this case, (0, 1, 0) is the up vector that you start with, and it never changes. If you were to modify the up vector in the pitch and then rotate in a yaw around that modified up vector, your camera would eventually rotate slightly off-center.

Try it—add the following code to the pitch rotation section of the Update method just before the line that reads currentPitch += pitchAngle:

```
cameraUp = Vector3.Transform(cameraUp,
    Matrix.CreateFromAxisAngle(
        Vector3.Cross(cameraUp, cameraDirection),
    pitchAngle));
```

Compile and run the game and move the mouse in all directions, and you'll see the camera begin to tilt. Make sure you remove the code that modifies the up vector of the camera when you've finished testing this, because you won't want it in your game.

In the next chapter, you'll take this camera setup and add some logic for the 3D game. But first, let's look at what you did in this chapter.

What You Just Did

You've made some real progress in this chapter. Here's a recap:

- You created a 3D flying camera that moves forward and backward as well as from side to side.
- You added rotations to the flying camera to rotate in yaw, pitch, and roll.
- You modified the 3D flying camera code to build a customized, stationary camera with 45° rotation limits in the yaw and pitch directions.

Summary

- Choosing the best type of camera for your game is often as important as creating great graphics, exciting plots, or any other aspect of the game.
- Certain cameras rotate differently (e.g., a 3D space simulator typically has complete rotation in all directions, a helicopter has some limited yaw and roll capabilities, and a land-based camera typically will always yaw around the Y-axis rather than the up vector).

- When moving a camera in 3D space, the projection matrix typically won't change, but the view matrix changes to reflect changing positions and rotations.
- Chuck Norris doesn't code XNA in 3D. Instead, he uses four dimensions: X, Y, Z, and Power.

Test Your Knowledge: Quiz

1. When performing a yaw rotation with a camera, what camera vector(s) rotate(s)? What axis would you rotate on?
2. When performing a roll rotation with a camera, what camera vector(s) rotate(s)? What axis would you rotate on?
3. When performing a pitch rotation with a camera, what camera vector(s) rotate(s)? What axis would you rotate on?
4. What famous holiday includes an event titled the "Airing of Grievances"?

Test Your Knowledge: Exercise

Remember that to move a 3D camera forward, you use the following code:

```
cameraPosition += cameraDirection * speed;
```

There is a small problem with this method, however, when it's applied to land-based cameras. Essentially, to eliminate the ability to "fly" when looking up, you remove the Y component of the `cameraDirection` vector prior to moving the camera with this line of code. This causes your camera to stay at the same Y value, which keeps the camera on the ground.

However, consequently the higher you pitch your camera, the slower you end up moving. For example, if your `cameraDirection` vector was (10, 2, 0) when you removed the Y component, you would end up with the vector (10, 0, 0) and you'd move at that speed. If your camera was pitched at a larger angle and your `cameraDirection` vector was (2, 10, 0), the resulting vector after removing the Y component would be (2, 0, 0) and you'd move forward at that speed.

Convert your 3D *Flying Camera* solution to a land-based camera and solve this problem so that when moving forward and backward your camera moves at the same speed, regardless of the pitch angle. Use the code you created in the first half of this chapter.

Hint: remember that `Vector3.Normalize` will take any `Vector3` and give it a magnitude or length of 1.

CHAPTER 12

3D Collision Detection and Shooting

OK, here we go. Fasten your seatbelts; we're coming to the final stretch. In the previous chapter, you built a flying camera and discussed differences between that and a land-based camera. Then, you took the code you've been building in this 3D section of the book and created a customized camera for your game. In this chapter, you'll add some game logic and support for shooting and collision detection. We've got a lot to do, so let's get to it.

This chapter picks up with the code that you finished with in Chapter 11. Open the *3D Game* project and use it for the examples and walkthroughs in this chapter.

 In the source code you've download for the book, you'll find that Chapter 11 has two projects: *Flying Camera*, which holds the code for the 3D flying camera you created in the first portion of that chapter, and *3D Game*, which holds the code for the stationary, customized camera you created in the second part of that chapter. Make sure you use the project called *3D Game* for this chapter.

Creating a Moving Enemy

Right now, you have a customized camera that rotates in yaw and pitch directions while looking at a spinning spaceship. That's pretty sweet, and you may be tempted to release your game now and see if you can pull some users away from *World of Warcraft*, making millions on monthly subscriptions. I'd caution you to take a step back for a minute, though, and realize that you still have some work to do before you get to that point.

In the game that you'll be building in the next few chapters, you'll have a stationary camera from which you'll shoot at enemies flying toward you. It would make sense, then, to add a new subclass of your BasicModel class to which you can add functionality to fly forward in a given direction. To add a sense of realism, you're also going to make the enemies roll randomly.

First, you'll need to modify the SpinningEnemy class. Add the following class-level variables to the SpinningEnemy class:

```
float yawAngle = 0;
float pitchAngle = 0;
float rollAngle = 0;
Vector3 direction;
```

Next, modify the constructor of the SpinningEnemy class as follows:

```
public SpinningEnemy(Model m, Vector3 Position,
    Vector3 Direction, float yaw, float pitch, float roll)
    : base(m)
{
    world = Matrix.CreateTranslation(Position);
    yawAngle = yaw;
    pitchAngle = pitch;
    rollAngle = roll;
    direction = Direction;
}
```

You previously had a parameter for a Model in the constructor, but you've now added several others. Let's look at each of the parameters you've added to the constructor and what they're used for:

Vector3 Position

The position parameter represents, strangely enough, the position of the object. Remember that in your BasicModel class, you have a world variable that is initially set to Matrix.Identity. In the constructor for the SpinningEnemy class, you're setting the world matrix of the base class to a Matrix.Translation using the passed-in position vector. This will make the initial position of the object be the point represented by the position vector parameter.

Vector3 Direction

The direction parameter represents the direction in which the object moves, as well as the speed at which it moves. In the constructor, you're simply assigning this parameter's value to a class variable to keep track of it for later use. In the Update method, notice that the world variable (which you're using to represent the position of the object) is multiplied by a new Matrix.Translation using the direction vector. This will move the object in the direction specified by the parameter at a speed equal to the magnitude of that vector every time Update is called.

float yaw, float pitch, float roll

The yaw, pitch, and roll angle parameters represent how many degrees, in radians, to rotate the object on a yaw, pitch, or roll every time Update is called. In the constructor, you assign the values to class variables. In the Update method, notice that you are multiplying a new matrix called rotation (which is a class-level variable initialized to Matrix.Identity) by a Matrix.CreateFromYawPitchRoll using the yaw, pitch, and roll angles as parameters. This will cause the object to rotate incrementally every time the Update method is called.

Next, modify the `Update` method of your `SpinningEnemy` class to rotate the model using the yaw, pitch, and roll variables passed into the constructor and then to move the model using the direction vector:

```
public override void Update( )
{
    // Rotate model
    rotation *= Matrix.CreateFromYawPitchRoll(yawAngle,
        pitchAngle, rollAngle);

    // Move model
    world *= Matrix.CreateTranslation(direction);
}
```

Finally, modify the `GetWorld` method as follows to return the rotation multiplied by the world matrix:

```
public override Matrix GetWorld( )
{
    return rotation * world;
}
```

Your newly modified `SpinningEnemy` class deals with two matrices to represent the position and rotation of the model the class represents. First, the rotation matrix is used to keep track of how much the object rotates. Second, the world matrix is used to keep track of how far the object is moved (using the `CreateTranslation` method). Returning the rotation matrix multiplied by the world matrix causes the object to spin in place while moving in the direction specified by the direction vector.

So, here's a question for you: what would be different if you returned `world * rotation` in the `GetWorld` method instead of `rotation * world`?

Whereas `rotation * world` will cause the object to spin in place while moving in the direction specified by the direction vector, `world * rotation` will cause the object to move in the direction specified by the direction vector while orbiting the origin. This small change to the matrix multiplication causes some very different functionality. A little later in this chapter, you'll have some objects of this class moving around the screen, and you can play with the `GetWorld` method to get different effects.

Adding Some Game Logic

Good times. Now that you have a class that will create a moving enemy, you need to add some game logic. As with nearly any game, there will be an element of randomness in this game, so you'll need to add a random number generator. Remember that you always want to have only one random number generator that you use throughout your entire game. If you have multiple random number generator variables, there's a possibility that some of the variables might end up with the same random seeds, in which case the number sequences will be the same (and will no longer be random). Add a Random object to your Game1 class and a public auto-property for that object:

```
public Random rnd { get; protected set; }
```

Then, initialize the rnd variable in the constructor of the Game1 class:

```
rnd = new Random( );
```

While you're working in the Game1 class, go ahead and change the background color of the game to black, to make it look more like we're in outer space (yay—outer space!!!). Remember that to change the background color, you change the parameter sent to the Clear method in Game1's Draw method:

```
GraphicsDevice.Clear(Color.Black);
```

Also, you'll probably want to make your game play in full-screen mode and in a decent resolution. Let's go with 1,280 × 1,024 (you'll want to make sure that your resolution is a standard resolution supported by most PC monitors, and the 1,280 × 1,024 resolution definitely passes that test). To change the screen size and specify full-screen mode, add the following code to the end of the constructor of the Game1 class:

```
graphics.PreferredBackBufferWidth = 1280;
    graphics.PreferredBackBufferHeight = 1024;
#if !DEBUG
    graphics.IsFullScreen = true;
#endif
```

The resolution you specify only indicates the *preferred* resolution. If for some reason the PC the game is played on can't support that resolution, your game will run in another resolution.

Also bear in mind that the Game.Window.ClientBounds method that you have been using in this book to detect the edges of the screen depends on your screen being large enough to accommodate the resolution you specify. For example, if you are running a widescreen monitor at a resolution of 1,400 × 900, you won't be able to fit a 1,280 × 1,024-sized window on your screen. This will cause issues with gameplay down the road. Make sure that the screen size you choose will fit the monitor you're using.

All right, now you're going to want to add some functionality to your ModelManager class that will periodically spawn enemies. You did something like this in your 2D game earlier in this book, but we're going to take it a step further this time and add increasingly difficult levels to the logic. The first thing you'll need to do is remove the line of code that creates the spinning ship that you have currently. This line is the call to the models.Add method in your ModelManager's LoadContent method. Remove the following code entirely:

```
models.Add(new BasicModel(
    Game.Content.Load<Model>(@"models\spaceship")));
```

Issues in Full-Screen Mode

In the code you've just added to the `Game1` class's constructor, notice the preprocessor directive indicating that the game should be run in full-screen mode only if it is not running in the debug configuration. Why is that? In XNA, Visual Studio has an extremely difficult time allowing you to debug and step through breakpoints when a game is running in full-screen mode. Because of this, you should always run your game in windowed mode when you're running in the debug configuration. However, when the game is in release mode, you should have no problems running in full-screen mode.

Also, when running in full-screen mode, you'll probably notice that you can't exit the game by clicking the red X in the upper-right corner of the window. That's because it doesn't exist—you're in full-screen mode! If you have a gamepad, you can use the back button to exit the game. Otherwise, use Alt-F4 to close the game when running in full-screen mode. You can also add some code in the `Update` method of your `Game1` class to quit when the player presses the Escape key if you want to do so.

Now, running your game will display a black screen with no objects visible whatsoever. That's weak sauce, and you can do better. In your game, you're going to be implementing a series of increasingly difficult levels in which enemies spawn and fly toward the player, and the player has to shoot them down to move to the next level. To begin, add a new class to your game called `LevelInfo`, and replace the code in that class with the following:

```
namespace _3D_Game
{
    class LevelInfo
    {
        // Spawn variables
        public int minSpawnTime { get; set; }
        public int maxSpawnTime { get; set; }

        // Enemy count variables
        public int numberEnemies { get; set; }
        public int minSpeed { get; set; }
        public int maxSpeed { get; set; }

        // Misses
        public int missesAllowed { get; set; }

        public LevelInfo(int minSpawnTime, int maxSpawnTime,
            int numberEnemies, int minSpeed, int maxSpeed,
            int missesAllowed)
        {
            this.minSpawnTime = minSpawnTime;
            this.maxSpawnTime = maxSpawnTime;
            this.numberEnemies = numberEnemies;
            this.minSpeed = minSpeed;
            this.maxSpeed = maxSpeed;
            this.missesAllowed = missesAllowed;
        }
```

```
        }
    }
```

Basically, you'll be creating an object of type `LevelInfo` for each level in your game. Let's take a look at what each of the variables in `LevelInfo` will be used for:

`int[] minSpawnTimes`
> This array of integers represents the minimum spawn time (in milliseconds) for a new enemy. The reason for the array? Each element in the array represents the minimum spawn time for a different level of the game.

`int[] maxSpawnTimes`
> This array of integers represents the maximum spawn time (in milliseconds) for a new enemy. Each element in the array represents the maximum spawn time for a different level.

`int[] numberEnemies`
> This represents how many enemies will spawn per level. Once this number is reached and all enemies are off the screen, the current level ends and the next level begins.

`int maxSpeed and int minSpeed`
> This represents the maximum speed of an enemy. This is an `int` instead of a `Vector3` because your enemies will move only in positive Z. When spawning a new enemy, you'll be using a direction vector of (0, 0) and some random value between `minSpeed` and `maxSpeed`.

`int[] missesAllowed`
> This will be used for your end-game logic. A player is allowed to let only a certain number of enemies get past her during each level. Once this number is reached in a given level, the game ends.

Now, add the following class-level variables to your `ModelManager` class. These variables are all used to help create increasingly difficult levels of enemies flying toward the camera:

```
// Spawn variables
Vector3 maxSpawnLocation = new Vector3(100, 100, -3000);
int nextSpawnTime = 0;
int timeSinceLastSpawn = 0;
float maxRollAngle = MathHelper.Pi / 40;

// Enemy count
int enemiesThisLevel = 0;

// Misses variables
int missedThisLevel = 0;

// Current level
int currentLevel = 0;
// List of LevelInfo objects
List<LevelInfo> levelInfoList = new List<LevelInfo>( );
```

Let's look at each of these variables and what you'll be using them for:

`Vector3 maxSpawnLocation`

This vector will be used to represent the starting location of the enemy ships. The Z value is a constant with all ships: all ships will start at –3,000. The X and Y values will be used as ranges from -X to +X and -Y to +Y, respectively. Essentially, when spawning an enemy, you'll place it at some random location between -X and +X, between -Y and +Y, and at –3,000 Z.

`int nextSpawnTime`

This variable will be used to identify when the next enemy should spawn. It will be generated as a random number between the `minSpawnTime` and `maxSpawnTime` for the current level.

`int timeSinceLastSpawn`

This variable will be used to track how much time has passed since the last enemy spawned and compared against the `nextSpawnTime` variable to determine when a new enemy should spawn.

`float maxRollAngle`

This value will represent the maximum roll angle to pass to your `SpinningEnemy` class. The value passed in will be some random value between `-maxRollAngle` and `+maxRollAngle`.

`int enemiesThisLevel`

This variable will be used to keep track of how many enemies have been spawned so far in the current level and compared against the `numberEnemies` array to determine when the level ends.

`int missedThisLevel`

This variable will be used to keep track of how many enemies have eluded the player in the current level and compared against the `missesAllowed` array to determine game-over conditions.

`int currentLevel`

This variable will hold the number reflecting the current level of the game. When the game starts, the value of `currentLevel` is 0, and the game is on level 1. This value is zero-based for easier access to the previously listed arrays.

`levelInfoList`

This variable will store a list of `LevelInfo` objects that will describe spawn times, speeds, and so on for each game level.

Once you have added those variables to your `ModelManager` class, you need to initialize your `levelInfoList` object with information for each of the game levels you'll be implementing. Add the following code to the constructor of the `ModelManager` class:

```
// Initialize game levels
levelInfoList.Add(new LevelInfo(1000, 3000, 20, 2,  6,  10));
levelInfoList.Add(new LevelInfo(900,  2800, 22, 2,  6,  9));
levelInfoList.Add(new LevelInfo(800,  2600, 24, 2,  6,  8));
```

```
levelInfoList.Add(new LevelInfo(700,   2400, 26,  3,   7,   7));
levelInfoList.Add(new LevelInfo(600,   2200, 28,  3,   7,   6));
levelInfoList.Add(new LevelInfo(500,   2000, 30,  3,   7,   5));
levelInfoList.Add(new LevelInfo(400,   1800, 32,  4,   7,   4));
levelInfoList.Add(new LevelInfo(300,   1600, 34,  4,   8,   3));
levelInfoList.Add(new LevelInfo(200,   1400, 36,  5,   8,   2));
levelInfoList.Add(new LevelInfo(100,   1200, 38,  5,   9,   1));
levelInfoList.Add(new LevelInfo(50,    1000, 40,  6,   9,   0));
levelInfoList.Add(new LevelInfo(50,    800,  42,  6,   9,   0));
levelInfoList.Add(new LevelInfo(50,    600,  44,  8,  10,   0));
levelInfoList.Add(new LevelInfo(25,    400,  46,  8,  10,   0));
levelInfoList.Add(new LevelInfo(0,     200,  48, 18,  20,   0));
```

This code creates 15 different levels, each represented by an instance of LevelInfo. In this code, you're setting the spawn times and speeds for each enemy created, as well as the number of enemies to create in each level and how many enemies the player can miss in each level before the game ends. You can see by the numbers that the game will get increasingly more difficult from level to level.

 How did I know to use these values for each of the levels? And how did I know to start the enemy ships at –3,000 Z? Mostly by trial and error. When creating a game like this, you start working on the concept and then, as you play the game, you get a feel for how things are working. If the enemies seem to be moving too quickly, slow them down. If they start too close to the camera, move them back. Getting other people's feedback on all of this is very important as well, because generally speaking, you'll want your game to appeal to a wider audience than just you as the developer.

Next, you need to start thinking about when you'll spawn your first enemy. Right now, there is no logic indicating when a new enemy will spawn. You'll need to create a method that sets the nextSpawnTime variable in order to spawn your first enemy. Add the following method to the ModelManager class:

```
private void SetNextSpawnTime(  )
{
    nextSpawnTime = ((Game1)Game).rnd.Next(
        levelInfoList[currentLevel].minSpawnTime,
        levelInfoList[currentLevel].maxSpawnTime);
    timeSinceLastSpawn = 0;
}
```

Note that in this method the nextSpawnTime variable is set to a random number using the Random object in the Game1 class. The resulting value is some number between the minSpawnTime and maxSpawnTime for the current level, using the levelInfoList list offset by the current level index. Then, the timeSinceLastSpawn variable is set to 0, which will let you count milliseconds from the time of this method call until the next spawn time has been reached.

Next, call the SetNextSpawnTime method in the Initialize method of your Model Manager class. This will set the nextSpawnTime and allow you to count down to the time you'll unleash your first enemy on the pitiful human player:

```
// Set initial spawn time
SetNextSpawnTime( );
```

Now you'll need to code a method that will actually spawn a new enemy:

```
private void SpawnEnemy( )
{
    // Generate random position with random X and random Y
    // between -maxX and maxX and -maxY and maxY. Z is always
    // the same for all ships.
    Vector3 position = new Vector3(((Game1)Game).rnd.Next(
        -(int)maxSpawnLocation.X, (int)maxSpawnLocation.X),
        ((Game1)Game).rnd.Next(
        -(int)maxSpawnLocation.Y, (int)maxSpawnLocation.Y),
        maxSpawnLocation.Z);

    // Direction will always be (0, 0, Z), where
    // Z is a random value between minSpeed and maxSpeed
    Vector3 direction = new Vector3(0, 0,
        ((Game1)Game).rnd.Next(
        levelInfoList[currentLevel].minSpeed,
        levelInfoList[currentLevel].maxSpeed));

    // Get a random roll rotation between -maxRollAngle and maxRollAngle
    float rollRotation = (float)((Game1)Game).rnd.NextDouble( ) *
        maxRollAngle - (maxRollAngle / 2);

    // Add model to the list
    models.Add(new SpinningEnemy(
        Game.Content.Load<Model>(@"models\spaceship"),
        position, direction, 0, 0, rollRotation));

    // Increment # of enemies this level and set next spawn time
    ++enemiesThisLevel;
    SetNextSpawnTime( );
}
```

This method creates a new SpinningEnemy and adds it to the list of models in your ModelManager. First, the position is generated as a Vector3 with random values between -maxSpawnLocation.X and +maxSpawnLocation.X, -maxSpawnLocation.Y and +maxSpawn Location.Y, and maxSpawnLocation.Z.

Then, the direction is calculated, using 0 for X and Y and a random value between minSpeed and maxSpeed for Z, which will move the objects toward the camera at different speeds in the direction of positive Z.

Next, the roll rotation is calculated as a random value between -maxRollAngle and +maxRollAngle. The enemy being created will not rotate in a pitch or a yaw, so the only rotation generated is for the roll.

The model is then created and added to the models list, the enemiesThisLevel variable is incremented, and the next spawn time is set via a call to SetNextSpawnTime.

When the next spawn time has been reached, you'll need to actually spawn your enemies. Add the following method to the ModelManager class to spawn a new enemy when the time is right:

```
protected void CheckToSpawnEnemy(GameTime gameTime)
{
    // Time to spawn a new enemy?
    if (enemiesThisLevel <
        levelInfoList[currentLevel].numberEnemies)
    {
        timeSinceLastSpawn += gameTime.ElapsedGameTime.Milliseconds;
        if (timeSinceLastSpawn > nextSpawnTime)
        {
            SpawnEnemy( );
        }
    }
}
```

Then, call the new method at the top of the Update method in your ModelManager class:

```
// Check to see if it's time to spawn
CheckToSpawnEnemy(gameTime);
```

The if statement at the beginning of this code will prevent enemies from spawning if all of the enemies allocated for the current level have already been spawned. Then, using the gameTime variable, you increment the timeSinceLastSpawn variable. When the value of the timeSinceLastSpawn variable is greater than the value of the nextSpawn Time variable, the time has come to launch a new enemy. Calling SpawnEnemy will both create a new enemy and reset the spawn timers, so that's all you need to do at this point.

Finally, because your game camera rotates only 45°, once an enemy has passed out of the camera's field of view, it's out of play and needs to be removed from the game. You currently have a public accessor for the Vector3 cameraPosition variable in your Camera class, which will allow your ModelManager to use that property to detect when an enemy has passed out of the camera's field of view.

The Matrix class has a Translation property that returns a Vector3 representing the net translations applied to the Matrix. You can use this property in the ModelManager class on all of the enemy ships that you create and compare it against the Z coordinate from your camera's cameraPosition auto-implemented property to determine whether the Z value of the ship's translation is greater than the Z value of the camera's position (indicating that the ship has passed out of view). If that is the case, the ship is out of bounds and should be removed from the game.

Modify the code that calls the Update method on each model in the models list (in the Update method of your ModelManager class) to remove models once they are out of play. Remove the following code from the Update method of your ModelManager class:

```
// Loop through all models and call Update
for (int i = 0; i < models.Count; ++i)
{
    models[i].Update( );
}
```

and add the following method, which will loop through your ship models, update them, and remove them when they are out of bounds:

```
protected void UpdateModels( )
{
    // Loop through all models and call Update
    for (int i = 0; i < models.Count; ++i)
    {
        // Update each model
        models[i].Update( );

        // Remove models that are out of bounds
        if (models[i].GetWorld( ).Translation.Z >
            ((Game1)Game).camera.cameraPosition.Z + 100)
        {
            models.RemoveAt(i);
            --i;
        }
    }
}
```

Next, call the UpdateModels method from the Update method of your ModelManager class, just before the call to base.Update:

```
// Update models
UpdateModels( );
```

Wow! You just made a huge amount of progress. At this point, you should be able to compile and run your game and see that you have enemies that move toward the camera and roll randomly left or right for a bit of realism, as seen in Figure 12-1. You're making some great strides in your game now. The next thing to do is add the ability to shoot down the enemies!

Figure 12-1. Enemies are coming at us in droves!

Firing Shots

Many types of games have some form of projectile that is thrown or shot toward other players or enemies. How would you go about adding the ability to shoot a projectile of some sort in your game? Think about it at its most basic level, and you'll realize that a projectile flying through the air or through space is just like the moving camera and moving objects you've already implemented in previous chapters of this book. Essentially, your shots (or bullets) will each consist of a model, a position, and a direction, and potentially some form of rotation as well. Seems like an easy enough concept. Let's see how you can add it to your game.

Your SpinningEnemy class already has all the components that a shot requires, so you can use that class for the shots as well as the enemy ships. Isn't it great to have a generic, multipurpose class that can be reused for different things? Think of all the time you just saved! You're already done coding your shot class...nice job!

The next step to creating a shot is to add the shot model to your project. If you haven't already, download the source code for this chapter of the book. With the source code for this chapter is a model file called *ammo.x* in the *3D Game\3D GameContent \Models* folder. In Visual Studio, add the *ammo.x* file to your project by right-clicking the *3D GameContent\Models* folder in Solution Explorer, selecting Add→Existing Item..., browsing to the location of the *ammo.x* file, and selecting it.

Once you've added the *ammo.x* file to your project, add a couple of class-level variables to your ModelManager class to help you keep track of the shots you fire:

```
List<BasicModel> shots = new List<BasicModel>( );
float shotMinZ = -3000;
```

The first variable is a new list of BasicModel objects. This list will contain all shots fired. Because the shots use the same class as the ships, you could store your shot objects in the same list as your enemy ships. Although that method would work, some added processor time would be required to identify which objects are ships and which ones are shots when it comes to collision detection (you don't care whether shots hit shots or ships hit ships; all you care about in this particular game is when a shot hits a ship). So, given that description of the game, the best route is to have a list for ships and another list for shots.

The second variable added in the preceding code is the minimum Z value for a shot. Once a shot travels beyond –3,000 in the Z direction, the shot is out of play and will be marked for removal from the list.

Next, you'll need to create a way to add shots to the ModelManager. Your model manager is responsible for adding enemy ships on its own because your enemies are autogenerated at random intervals. However, shots will be added based on user input, and that's really outside the scope of responsibilities of your ModelManager class; all that it should be responsible for is managing models, not handling user input.

So, you'll be adding shots from within your Game1 class, and you'll need to have a way to add shots to the ModelManager's shot list. Add the following method to your Model Manager to allow the Game1 class to add shots to the list:

```
public void AddShot(Vector3 position, Vector3 direction)
{
    shots.Add(new SpinningEnemy(
        Game.Content.Load<Model>(@"models\ammo"),
        position, direction, 0, 0, 0));
}
```

You'll also need to update and draw your shots every time your ModelManager's Update and Draw methods are called. You'll handle this in the same way that you did with your enemy ships. In addition, when updating your shots, you'll want to check to make sure that the shots are still in play (i.e., that they haven't passed the shotMinZ value indicating that they've traveled out of bounds). Any shots that are no longer in play should be removed. Add the following method to your ModelManager class to update each shot and remove those that are out of bounds:

```
protected void UpdateShots( )
{
    // Loop through shots
    for (int i = 0; i < shots.Count; ++i)
    {
        // Update each shot
        shots[i].Update( );

        // If shot is out of bounds, remove it from game
        if (shots[i].GetWorld( ).Translation.Z < shotMinZ)
        {
            shots.RemoveAt(i);
            --i;
        }
    }
}
```

Next, call the UpdateShots method from your ModelManager's Update method, just before the call to base.Update:

```
// Update shots
UpdateShots( );
```

Notice that you can use the Translation property of your shot's world matrix to determine the position of the object and compare it against the value of shotMinZ. You probably noticed this already, but this is basically the same way that you are comparing your enemy ships against the camera position to see whether they are out of bounds.

To draw your shots, add the following code to your ModelManager's Draw method, just before the base.Draw call:

```
// Loop through and draw each shot
foreach (BasicModel bm in shots)
{
    bm.Draw(((Game1)Game).camera);
}
```

All right, that's all for the `ModelManager` class for now. Let's move on to the `Camera` class.

What? Wait a minute. Why are we modifying the `Camera` class to add shooting ability?

Well, remember when I mentioned that a shot is basically the same as a moving camera or a moving object with a position and a direction? That's true, and the initial position of the shot will be the location where the shot originated (in your game's case, that will be the camera position). But what direction will you give each shot? The direction of a shot is the direction of the object that created the shot. For example, if you have a gun pointing in some direction and it shoots a bullet, the bullet will have a direction vector, and that direction vector will be the same as the gun's direction vector.

In your game, the camera will determine the direction of the shot, and therefore the `Game1` class needs to be able to get the direction vector of the camera. So, you'll need to add a `public` accessor for your `Camera` class's `cameraDirection` variable:

```
public Vector3 GetCameraDirection
{
    get { return cameraDirection; }
}
```

 Why create a traditional property accessor for the `cameraDirection` rather than using an auto-implemented property, like you do with the `cameraPosition`?

In the constructor of the `Camera` class, you call `Normalize` on the camera `Direction`. This will not work properly on an auto-implemented property, so it's best to leave the `cameraDirection` member alone and create a new, traditional accessor for that property.

Now, in your `Game1` class, let's take a look at what you'll need to add to generate shots. First, add three class-level variables to help with your shot logic:

```
float shotSpeed = 10;
int shotDelay = 300;
int shotCountdown = 0;
```

Let's look at these variables. First, you added a shot speed variable, which will be multiplied by the direction vector to give the shot some added power in the velocity department.

Next, you added shot delay and shot countdown variables. What are these for? Well, consider that you're going to be checking for user input in order to fire a shot. The player will be able to fire a shot by pressing the space bar or the left mouse button, and you'll be checking for that user input in your `Game1`'s `Update` method. Remember how many times a second the Update method is called? If all goes well, it'll be called around 60 times per second. Now, imagine if you simply fired a shot in the Update method every time the space bar was pressed or the left mouse button was clicked. If you hold down the space bar for a half a second, you've just fired around 30 shots! I'm all in favor of cool rapid-fire action, but that's a bit too much.

To prevent this overload, a common behavior for a weapon is to have a delay period after a shot is fired during which no more shots can be fired.

The shotDelay variable you added represents the duration of your weapon's shot delay, and the shotCountdown variable will be used to determine when the shot delay expires and another shot can be fired.

Add the following method to the Game1 class, which will cause shots to be fired when the player presses the left mouse button or the space bar, but only if the shot delay has expired:

```
protected void FireShots(GameTime gameTime)
{
    if (shotCountdown <= 0)
    {
        // Did player press space bar or left mouse button?
        if (Keyboard.GetState(  ).IsKeyDown(Keys.Space) ||
            Mouse.GetState(  ).LeftButton == ButtonState.Pressed)
        {
            // Add a shot to the model manager
            modelManager.AddShot(
                camera.cameraPosition + new Vector3(0, -5, 0),
                camera.GetCameraDirection * shotSpeed);

            // Reset the shot countdown
            shotCountdown = shotDelay;
        }
    }
    else
        shotCountdown -= gameTime.ElapsedGameTime.Milliseconds;
}
```

Next, call the FireShots method in your Game1's Update method, just before the call to base.Update:

```
// See if the player has fired a shot
FireShots(gameTime);
```

Essentially, you fire the weapon only when the shotCountdown has reached or passed zero. If that is the case, you check to see whether the space bar or the left mouse button is pressed. If one of them is pressed, you're ready to fire a shot. Yeah, get ready...and hide the children, this is getting very exciting!

First, you call the ModelManager's AddShot method, which you added earlier to add a shot to its list of shots. For the position parameter, you pass in the camera's position, but you also add a vector to that position that pushes the vector toward negative Y. This is because if you fired the shot from the actual camera position, you would see a huge blob of a model on the screen as the model moved away from the camera position. To prevent this and give a more realistic effect, you add some negative Y to the position so your shot will appear to come from just below the camera.

The direction of the shot is composed of the direction of the camera multiplied by the shotSpeed variable.

Once the shot is added, you assign the value of the shotDelay variable to the shotCount down variable, preventing another shot from being fired until the shotCountdown variable reaches zero again.

If the shotCountdown is not zero or less during a call to Update, the initial if statement in the FireShots method evaluates as false and the shotCountdown variable is decremented by the elapsed time in the else portion of that statement.

Compile and run your game, and you should see that shots are fired when you press the space bar or the left mouse button (see Figure 12-2). Also, notice that holding down the space bar or left mouse button causes the shots to be fired every 300 milliseconds (or the equivalent of the shot delay time). Who needs *Unreal Tournament* when you have this kind of sweet gameplay?

Figure 12-2. Dang…I'm kind of a bad shot

Well, great job getting to this point. The ships are flying and the shots are looking great. There's one problem, though: the shots don't do anything when they collide with a ship. Yeah, yeah, yeah...minor detail, right? It's probably worth fixing anyway. Let's look at how you can add some collision detection using XNA's BoundingSphere class.

3D Collision Detection and Bounding Spheres

In the 2D section of this book, we covered a bounding-box algorithm for collision detection. Essentially, the algorithm uses an invisible box that surrounds an object and is used to determine whether another object's box intersects with it. The bounding-box algorithm is one of the fastest collision-detection algorithms.

A similar approach is to use spheres surrounding the objects, rather than boxes. The same concept applies: you check an object's sphere to determine whether it has collided with another object's sphere.

When you use models in XNA, bounding spheres are generated for you as part of the model. Each model contains one or more ModelMesh objects, and each ModelMesh has a property called BoundingSphere that defines a sphere surrounding that part of the model.

The tricky part of this is that when you apply a translation or scale to the model, the BoundingSphere of the model is not affected. So, to use the BoundingSphere specified in the model, you have to apply the same translations and scales to it that you apply to your model.

To do this, you'll be adding a collision-detection method inside the BasicModel class, to which you'll pass another BasicModel's model and world to check for collisions against all of its ModelMesh's BoundingSpheres.

This collision-detection method will receive a different model and world matrix in its parameter list. The method will loop through all of its own ModelMeshes and then loop through the other Model's ModelMeshes and check its own ModelMesh's BoundingSpheres for collisions with the other model's BoundingSpheres. Before comparing the Bounding Spheres for each object, the method will have to apply the world matrix to the Boun dingSphere using the Transform method, which will move and rotate the Bounding Sphere to the same place that you have already moved and rotated its model.

 Although it's important to apply any translations or scaling operations that have been applied to the model's world matrix to the Bounding Sphere, any rotations applied to the model don't need to be applied to the BoundingSphere. This is because the BoundingSphere is a sphere: any rotation applied to it won't affect its shape. That said, it won't do any harm to apply the rotations to the BoundingSphere anyway.

Add the following method to your BasicModel class:

```
public bool CollidesWith(Model otherModel, Matrix otherWorld)
{
    // Loop through each ModelMesh in both objects and compare
    // all bounding spheres for collisions
    foreach (ModelMesh myModelMeshes in model.Meshes)
    {
        foreach (ModelMesh hisModelMeshes in otherModel.Meshes)
        {
            if (myModelMeshes.BoundingSphere.Transform(
                GetWorld( )).Intersects(
                hisModelMeshes.BoundingSphere.Transform(otherWorld)))
                return true;
        }
    }
    return false;
}
```

That's really all there is to it. Not too shabby, eh? Now you're going to have to add some code to your ModelManager to handle collisions.

In the UpdateShots method of your ModelManager class, you've already added some code to remove shots when they are out of bounds, using the shotMinZ variable as a gauge. Change your if statement that checks for shots that are out of bounds to an if/else statement. In the else portion of the statement, call the shot's CollidesWith method, passing in the model and world matrix of each enemy ship in a loop. If a collision is detected, remove the ship and the shot and exit the loop.

Change the UpdateShots method from the following:

```
protected void UpdateShots( )
{
    // Loop through shots
    for (int i = 0; i < shots.Count; ++i)
    {
        // Update each shot
        shots[i].Update( );

        // If shot is out of bounds, remove it from game
        if (shots[i].GetWorld( ).Translation.Z < shotMinZ)
        {
            shots.RemoveAt(i);
            --i;
        }
    }
}
```

to this:

```
protected void UpdateShots( )
{
    // Loop through shots
    for (int i = 0; i < shots.Count; ++i)
    {
        // Update each shot
        shots[i].Update( );
```

```
// If shot is out of bounds, remove it from game
if (shots[i].GetWorld(  ).Translation.Z < shotMinZ)
{
    shots.RemoveAt(i);
    --i;
}
else
{
    // If shot is still in play, check for collisions
    for (int j = 0; j < models.Count; ++j)
    {
        if (shots[i].CollidesWith(models[j].model,
            models[j].GetWorld(  )))
        {
            // Collision! remove the ship and the shot.
            models.RemoveAt(j);
            shots.RemoveAt(i);
            --i;
            break;
        }
    }
}
}
}
```

Bam! You have collision detection using BoundingSpheres! Run the game at this point and shoot at your enemies. You may find it difficult to keep track of where the enemies are spawning from and to keep your camera facing in that direction. We'll fix that shortly. Also, you may find the collision detection as it's currently implemented is good enough for you, or you may find it too forgiving or not forgiving enough. You can tweak the size of the BoundingSpheres by applying a uniform scale in addition to the world matrix to modify the size, which will make the collision detection more or less forgiving.

Also, if you find the ships are too fast and too hard to hit, you can tweak the speed of the ships using the minSpeed and maxSpeed variables in the list of LevelInfo objects. This is your game, and you want it to play the way that you like it, so you can really tweak whatever you want to fit your needs.

Adding a Crosshair

One other thing that you've probably noticed is missing at this point is some way to make sure you're aiming at the correct place. Typically, this is done by placing a cross-hair on the screen. Even though you're working in XNA 3D, you can still draw 2D sprites on the screen, just as you did earlier in this book. Drawing the crosshair on the screen in 2D rather than in the world in 3D will make it a lot easier to work with. Imagine if you wanted it to be drawn in the world in 3D. In this case you'd have to draw it a few units in front of the camera, and every time your camera rotated or moved, you'd have to adjust the crosshair accordingly.

When drawing a crosshair on the screen, you can basically "set it and forget it," just like in that annoying rotisserie chicken infomercial. However, this isn't annoying—this is pretty cool stuff. (Although, if you're interested in rotisserie chicken ovens, I can get you a sweet deal for five easy installments of only $29.99. But that's a different book— now back to XNA.)

The first thing you'll need to do is add an image of a crosshair to your project. To start, create a new folder under the *3D GameContent* project in Solution Explorer for textures. Right-click the *3D GameContent* project in Solution Explorer, select Add→New Folder, and name the new folder *Textures*.

With the source code for this chapter is a file called *crosshair.png* in the *3D Game\3D GameContent\Textures* folder. Add the file to your project by right-clicking the *3D GameContent\Textures* folder in Solution Explorer, choosing Add→Existing Item..., browsing to the *crosshair.png* file, and selecting it.

Next, in your `Game1` class, you'll need to add a `Texture2D` class-level variable to hold your image:

```
Texture2D crosshairTexture;
```

In the `LoadContent` method of your `Game1` class, you'll need to load the *crosshair.png* image into your new `crosshairTexture` variable via the content pipeline:

```
crosshairTexture = Content.Load<Texture2D>(@"textures\crosshair");
```

Now all you have to do is draw your texture on the screen using the `spriteBatch` provided. You'll have to use the screen size and the size of the texture to center the crosshair exactly in the middle of the screen (what good is a slightly off-center crosshair?). You'll add the code to draw the crosshair to the `Draw` method of the `Game1` class, after the call to `base.Draw`.

Add the following code at the end of the `Draw` method in the `Game1` class:

```
spriteBatch.Begin( );

spriteBatch.Draw(crosshairTexture,
    new Vector2((Window.ClientBounds.Width / 2)
        - (crosshairTexture.Width / 2),
        (Window.ClientBounds.Height / 2)
        - (crosshairTexture.Height / 2)),
        Color.White);

spriteBatch.End( );
```

Drawing After base.Draw?

Why do you need to add the code to draw the crosshair after the call to `base.Draw`?

You're now mixing two different methods of drawing (2D versus 3D). Remember that drawing in 3D is much like walking around with a video camera, whereas drawing in 2D is more like painting on a 2D canvas. Whichever method of drawing is used second will supersede the first, so objects drawn in 2D will be drawn on top of objects that were drawn previously in 3D (and vice versa).

Because you're drawing all your models in the `ModelManager`, which is a `GameCompo nent`, all that drawing doesn't actually take place until the `base.Draw` method is called. That `base.Draw` call will pump the `Draw` call through all `DrawableGameComponents`. You have to put your crosshair code after the `base.Draw` call to make sure your crosshair is always drawn after all the 3D models, because only then will it be drawn on top of the 3D models.

There you have it. Run the game now and see if adding a crosshair has helped your aim. You should see the crosshair in the center of the screen, as shown in Figure 12-3.

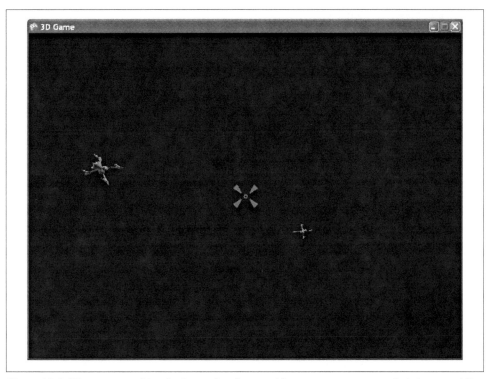

Figure 12-3. Those enemy ships don't stand a chance with your sweet new crosshair image guiding your shots!

Adding Sound

Another thing your game really lacks is the atmosphere and pizzazz that only audio can give. In this section, you'll add some sound effects and soundtracks to your game.

In Visual Studio, use the Solution Explorer to add a new folder under the *3D Game-Content* project called *Audio* (right-click the *3D GameContent* project and select Add→New Folder).

Launch the Microsoft Cross-Platform Audio Creation Tool (XACT) by clicking on your Windows Start button and selecting All Programs→Microsoft XNA Game Studio 4.0→Tools→Microsoft Cross-Platform Audio Creation Tool (XACT).

In XACT, select File→New Project, navigate to your project's *3D GameContent \Audio* directory, and save the file as *GameAudio.xap*. Once your project is ready, create a new wave bank and a new sound bank by right-clicking on the Wave Banks and Sound Banks tree items on the left and selecting New Wave Bank and New Sound Bank, respectively. Accept the default names for the wave and sound banks. Once both are created, select Window→Tile Horizontally to organize your windows for easier use.

There are six *.wav* files located in the *3D Game\3D GameContent\Audio* folder of the source code for this chapter. Copy those files to your project's *3D GameContent\Audio* folder in Windows Explorer. Here are the files:

- *Explosion1.wav*
- *Explosion2.wav*
- *Explosion3.wav*
- *Shot.wav*
- *Track1.wav*
- *Track2.wav*

Again, remember that when dealing with audio in XACT, you don't add the actual *.wav* files to your project in Visual Studio; you only copy the files to the project's *3D GameContent\Audio* folder in Windows Explorer. You'll add these files to an XACT project, and that project file is the only audio file that you'll need to add to the project from within Visual Studio.

In the Wave Bank window, right-click in an empty section and select Insert Wave File(s).... Browse to the six *.wav* files just listed, and add each of them to your wave bank. The files should show up in your Wave Bank window in red, indicating that they aren't currently used (see Figure 12-4).

Drag the *Shot* sound from the Wave Bank window to the Cue Name portion of the Sound Bank window. This will create both a cue and a sound for the *Shot* in the Sound Bank window, as pictured in Figure 12-5.

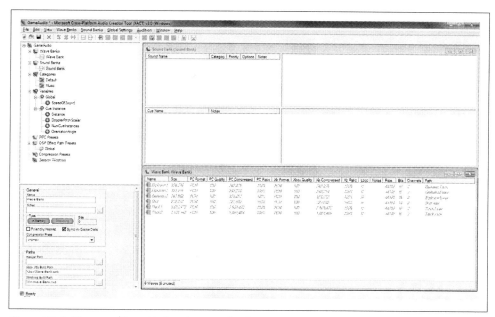

Figure 12-4. Six .wav files added to the wave bank

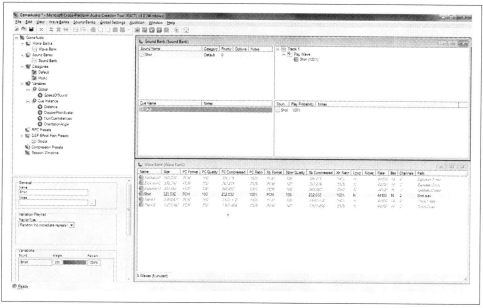

Figure 12-5. The Shot has a cue and a sound associated with it

Next, you're going to create a single cue that will play both of the sound files, with a 50% probability assigned to each. This will allow you to call that particular cue from code and have it play one track 50% of the time and the other track the rest of the time.

To do this, drag the *Track1.wav* and *Track2.wav* files from the Wave Bank window to the Sound Name section of the Sound Bank window. Until now, I've always told you to make sure that you drop the sounds into the Cue Name section of the Sound Bank window. In this case, however, you want to drop them into the Sound Name section because you don't want to create cue names for each of these sounds; instead, you'll be creating a single cue name for both of the sounds.

Next, right-click somewhere in the open space in the Cue Name section of the Sound Bank window and select New Cue. A new cue name will be created with the name "New Cue". Select the new cue and hit F2 to rename it. Name the new cue *Tracks*.

Next, drag the *Track1* and *Track2* sounds from the Sound Name section of the Sound Bank window and drop them onto the new *Tracks* cue that you've created in the Cue Name section of the Sound Bank window. This will add both sounds to the new *Tracks* cue and will give each track a 50% probability of playing. Basically what happens here is when you play the *Tracks* cue from XNA, it will play one of the sounds associated with that cue, selecting which one to play based on the probabilities listed here.

Your Sound Bank window should now look like Figure 12-6.

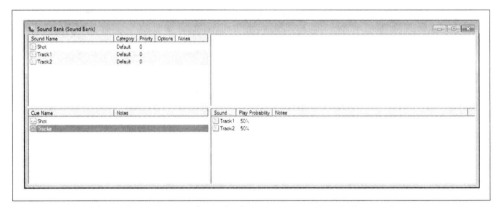

Figure 12-6. Track1 and Track2 sounds are both now associated with the Tracks cue name

You'll now need to do the same thing with the explosion sounds. You have three sounds for explosions loaded in your wave bank. Drag all three explosion sounds from the Wave Bank window and drop them into the Sound Name section of the Sound Bank window.

Right-click somewhere in the Cue Name section of the Sound Bank window and select New Cue. Select the new cue and hit F2 to rename it. Call the new cue *Explosions*.

Then, drag each of the explosion sounds from the Sound Name section of the Sound Bank window and drop them onto the new *Explosions* cue in the Cue Name section of the Sound Bank window. Notice that each of the explosion sounds is automatically assigned a 33% chance of being played when the *Explosions* cue is played.

Your Sound Bank window should now look something like Figure 12-7.

Before closing XACT, you'll want to set the looping properties of both the *Track1* and *Track2* sounds to infinite. First, select the *Track1* sound in the Sound Name section of the Sound Bank window. Then, in the lower-left corner of the screen, click the Infinite checkbox in the looping section, as shown in Figure 12-8. Repeat this step for *Track2* as well.

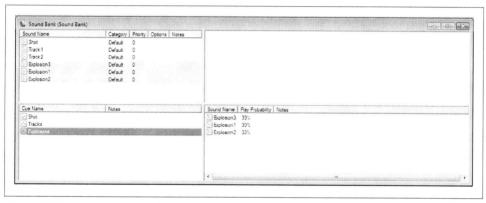

Figure 12-7. All sounds are ready to go

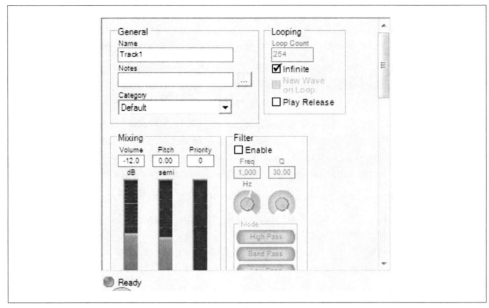

Figure 12-8. Setting the looping property of your Track1 and Track2 sounds to infinite

You're finished with XACT, so save your project, close XACT, and go back to Visual Studio.

In Visual Studio, you'll need to add the *.xap* file from XACT to your project. Right-click the *3D GameContent\Audio* folder in Solution Explorer, select Add→Existing Item..., and navigate to your *GameAudio.xap* file (which should be saved in your project's *3D GameContent\Audio* folder). Add the file to your solution by browsing to it and selecting it.

Once the *.xap* file is part of your solution, you'll need to add some code to your Game1 class. Add the following class-level variables:

```
AudioEngine audioEngine;
WaveBank waveBank;
SoundBank soundBank;
Cue trackCue;
```

Next, you'll need to initialize those variables via the content pipeline. Load the sounds from your XACT project by adding the following lines to the LoadContent method of your Game1 class:

```
// Load sounds and play initial sounds
audioEngine = new AudioEngine(@"Content\Audio\GameAudio.xgs");
waveBank = new WaveBank(audioEngine, @"Content\Audio\Wave Bank.xwb");
soundBank = new SoundBank(audioEngine, @"Content\Audio\Sound Bank.xsb");
trackCue = soundBank.GetCue("Tracks");
trackCue.Play( );
```

The first three lines load the sounds and cues from the XACT file, whereas the fourth line sets the trackCue variable by retrieving the cue for your soundtracks. This is done so that you can pause/resume/stop/restart the soundtrack music. The other sound effects do not need to be manipulated that way, so you don't need to save the cue information for those sounds.

Finally, the soundtrack cue is played with the last line of the code in the preceding listing.

To allow your ModelManager to play sounds when collisions occur, add the following method to your Game1 class:

```
public void PlayCue(string cue)
{
    soundBank.PlayCue(cue);
}
```

Before heading to the ModelManager, you'll need to call the PlayCue method from the FireShots method of your Game1 class when a shot is fired. To do that, add this line immediately after the call to modelManager.AddShot:

```
// Play shot audio
PlayCue("Shot");
```

In the ModelManager, you'll need to add a line of code that will call the PlayCue method when a collision occurs. In the UpdateShots method of your ModelManager, find the if/else statement that determines whether a collision has occurred. The current code should look something like this:

```
if (shots[i].CollidesWith(models[j].model,
    models[j].GetWorld()))
{
    // Collision! remove the ship and the shot.
    models.RemoveAt(j);
    shots.RemoveAt(i);
    --i;
    break;
}
```

Add a call to the PlayCue method of the Game1 class just before the break keyword that breaks from that for loop (the added line is shown in bold):

```
if (shots[i].CollidesWith(models[j].GetModel,
    models[j].GetWorld( )))
{
    // Collision! Remove the ship and the shot.
    models.RemoveAt(j);
    shots.RemoveAt(i);
    --i;
    ((Game1)Game).PlayCue("Explosions");
    break;
}
```

Nice! Fire up the game now and see how much difference the audio makes. You might want to tweak the volume levels of the different sounds—the explosions and shot sounds seemed a little weak to me, and I wanted to crank them up a little bit. Remember from Chapter 6 that you can do that by selecting the sound name in XACT and editing its volume properties in the window in the lower-left corner. This is all down to personal preference, however, and you can tweak the sounds in any way you prefer.

What You Just Did

You're cruising along now with some good game logic, shooting, and sound effects. Before we move on to explosions and particle effects and other fine-tunings, let's review what you did in this chapter:

- You created a moving model class, which you were able to use for both enemies and shots.
- You created a shooting projectile.
- You used the bounding spheres provided by XNA to perform 3D collision detection.
- You added a crosshair 2D image to a 3D game.
- You implemented sounds using single cues with multiple sounds based on probabilities.

Summary

- Moving objects through 3D space is very similar to moving a camera through 3D space. Your object typically will have a position and a direction (which also indicates its speed).
- Every ModelMesh has a BoundingSphere object associated with it, which defines a sphere for collision-detection purposes. The BoundingSphere does not move, scale, or rotate with the model, however, so you have to apply those matrices to the BoundingSphere separately to use it for collision detection.
- Adding 2D images to a 3D game is done exactly the same way it is done in a 2D game.
- With the XACT tool, you can specify a single cue to play numerous sounds based on given probabilities for those sounds.
- People who code in XNA not only are more popular and wealthy, but also live longer, happier lives.

Test Your Knowledge: Quiz

1. When firing a shot in a 3D (or 2D, for that matter) game, how do you determine the direction of the shot?

2. Fact or fiction: every model has a BoundingSphere object that surrounds the entire model and can be used for collision detection.

3. When using BoundingSpheres associated with a moving model for collision detection, what must be done to the BoundingSphere in order to accurately detect collisions?

4. What is the difference between drawing 2D images on screen in a 3D game and drawing 2D images on the screen in a 2D game?

5. Why does Kramer's advice to Elaine regarding his karate class and the power of the inner katra backfire on Elaine?

Test Your Knowledge: Exercise

To familiarize yourself further with what was covered in this chapter, customize the shot firing mechanism by modifying the code to do the following:

- Slow the shots down by 50%.
- Cut the shot delay in half (i.e., make shots fire twice as often when holding the space bar continuously).
- Every time a shot is fired, fire three shots in a spread (i.e., one shot down the center and two other shots, one to the left and one to the right).

CHAPTER 13

HLSL Basics

Let's take a break from developing the game for a minute and talk about High Level Shader Language (HLSL). Pre-XNA, DirectX allowed developers to send instructions directly to the graphics device through a mechanism called the Fixed Function Pipeline (FFP). This worked fine for a while, until graphics cards and hardware began to become incredibly complex. The more capabilities that were added to the hardware, the more detailed and complex the FFP needed to become to allow developers to take full advantage of that hardware.

 Even on modern cards, the FFP is implemented as a shader—just one that operates behind the scenes. This is very similar to the way that `BasicEffect` gives developers access to a simple version of the FFP.

Instead of continually adding features to the FFP and extending it, Microsoft decided instead to allow developers to talk directly to the hardware devices in a different language built specifically for those devices.

The first attempt to solve this problem was to allow developers to program directly to the hardware using assembly language. While this approach was functional, developers still needed a higher-level language to develop in. Enter HLSL. HLSL began as a joint project between Microsoft and NVIDIA. At some point, however, the development effort split, and NVIDIA's language (called C for Graphics, or Cg) went one route and Microsoft's language (called HLSL) went another.

HLSL allows developers to write in a language that is similar to C and that translates into assembly language on the graphics card itself. By using HLSL, developers can access all the functions of the graphics card without having to use an API such as the FFP.

As mentioned in previous chapters of this book, everything drawn in XNA 3D uses HLSL. The XNA development team at Microsoft was kind enough to add the `Basic Effect` class, which you've used in examples up until now, to enable developers to learn XNA without having to first study up on HLSL. However, even the `BasicEffect` class simply passes the data to an internal HLSL process.

 One thing that played into the decision to add the `BasicEffect` class to the XNA Framework was the fact that the FFP is not supported on the Xbox 360's Graphics Processing Unit (GPU). This meant that the developers at Microsoft were faced with a dilemma: should they support the FFP on the PC and force code rewrites for all Xbox 360 games, or invent a massive shader that implements the FFP? Ultimately, they decided to take an in-between approach that gives developers enough to get up and running without having to deal with shader code (the `BasicEffect` class).

In HLSL, developers write shaders that can access the most complex graphics hardware features. Graphics cards can support two different types of shaders: vertex shaders and pixel shaders. *Vertex shaders* are run once for every vertex in the viewing frustum, or field of view. *Pixel shaders* are run on every visible pixel in all visible objects drawn in the scene.

To understand a little more about the shader process in HLSL, look at Figure 13-1.

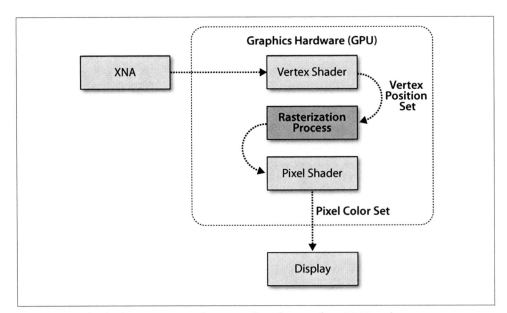

Figure 13-1. The shader process: an information flow diagram from XNA to the screen

The shader process first runs any vertex shaders, once for every vertex in the scene. The goal of a vertex shader is to set the positions of the vertices based on the world and camera settings. Once the position data is received from the vertex shader, a *rasterization* process takes place. Rasterization is the process that transforms a triangle into a set of pixels to be rendered on the screen.

After the scene has been rasterized, the pixel shader runs on each pixel that is drawn in the scene. The goal of a pixel shader is to define the color of each visible pixel.

 Before the pixel shader runs, a depth check is run on each pixel. This enables identification of pixels that are within the field of view but are hidden because another object is in front of them, so that the pixel shader is not unnecessarily run on them.

After the pixel shader runs, the data is output to the screen.

HLSL Syntax

HLSL is a language that resembles C. I will warn you before we get into this section that programming shaders in HLSL is very different than programming in XNA. If you don't get it and feel lost, don't get too stressed about it. In fact, in many game development shops it is not uncommon for there to be a team of game developers who write shaders and a separate team of game developers who write in DirectX or XNA—mainly because they really are two different skill sets.

That said, HLSL is an integral part of XNA development, and this book would be incomplete if it didn't cover it to some extent. In this chapter, we'll look at HLSL basics and go over some sample code, but this book is not meant to be an end-all, be-all HLSL resource. There are entire books devoted to that subject; if you're looking to get really deep into HLSL, you can pick up the basics here and then deepen your knowledge using those resources.

OK, that's my disclaimer. Let's get to the action.

Variables in HLSL are declared much the same way as in C#. In fact, many of the variables use the same keywords as in C# (e.g., HLSL has keywords such as int, float, bool, string, true, false, return, void, etc.).

More complex objects are typically represented as structs, which are also defined the same way that they are in C#. One very common way of representing data in 3D graphics is to use a vector. Vectors can be defined using a vector keyword, but they're more commonly defined as float3s for vectors with three elements and float4s for vectors with four elements.

`float3` and `float4` variables are essentially arrays of floating-point values. Vectors defined this way most commonly represent either colors or positions. As an example, you can define a new `float4` variable and initialize its value using the following line:

```
float4 color = float4(1, 0, 0, 1);
```

This defines a `float4` variable called `color`. You can access individual elements in the `float4` variable by using array notation, as shown here:

```
float red = color[0];
```

In addition to array notation, you can use special namespace accessors for the `float4` datatype. As mentioned earlier, a `float4` can represent a color or a position. As such, the four elements in the array can correspond to either `r`, `g`, `b`, and `a` or `x`, `y`, `z`, and `w`. To access a variable's elements using these namespaces, you can use code similar to the following:

```
float blue = color.b;
float z  = color.z;
```

Notice that you can use either `rgba` or `xyzw` to access the same variable. In fact, you can actually combine the elements of the array into a new array and access the elements in any order. The following code reverses the array by accessing the elements in reverse order:

```
float4 reverse = color.abgr;
```

Accessing multiple elements at one time, as shown in the previous line of code, is called *swizzling*. You can swizzle the elements in any order, but you cannot swizzle across color and position namespaces. For example, this code would result in a compilation error:

```
// This won't compile
float4 reverse = color.axgy;
```

Another important variable type worth noting is the matrix that is created using the `float`R`x`C keyword (where R equals the number of rows and C equals the number of columns). You can also use the `matrix` keyword to create matrix variables. Both of the following lines will create a 4 × 4 matrix:

```
float4x4 matrixFun;
matrix <float, 4, 4> matrixMadness;
```

Finally, as mentioned earlier, `structs` are created in HLSL the same way that they are created in C#, so you can use the following code to create a `struct` in HLSL:

```
struct myStruct
{
    float4 position;

};
```

Dissecting a Sample HLSL Effect File

In XNA, effects are created in effect files, which have an *.fx* extension. They are loaded via the content pipeline and are compiled just like other content resources. Therefore, the compiler will detect compilation errors in your HLSL code just like it will in your C# code, even though your effect files are stored with other content.

 Although your HLSL code will be compiled via the content pipeline, unfortunately you won't have access to IntelliSense when working with HLSL effect files.

Now that you have the basics of the HLSL language down, let's take a look at a sample effect file created using HLSL. In this section, we'll dissect the different sections of this example file:

```
float4x4 World;
float4x4 View;
float4x4 Projection;

struct VertexShaderInput
{
    float4 Position : POSITION0;
};

struct VertexShaderOutput
{
    float4 Position : POSITION0;
};

VertexShaderOutput VertexShaderFunction(VertexShaderInput input)
{
    VertexShaderOutput output;

    float4 worldPosition = mul(input.Position, World);
    float4 viewPosition = mul(worldPosition, View);
    output.Position = mul(viewPosition, Projection);

    return output;
}

float4 PixelShaderFunction(VertexShaderOutput input) : COLOR0
{
    return float4(1, 0, 0, 1);
}

technique Technique1
{
```

```
    pass Pass1
    {
        VertexShader = compile vs_2_0 VertexShaderFunction();
        PixelShader = compile ps_2_0 PixelShaderFunction();
    }
}
```

Don't be too scared by this code. It looks a bit different than what you're used to in XNA, but we'll explore each section of the code here so you can figure out what it's doing.

First, let's look at the top three lines of the file:

```
float4x4 World;
float4x4 View;
float4x4 Projection;
```

These three lines represent global variables in this file. All three variables are 4 × 4 matrices; they correspond to the world, the camera view, and the camera projection. These terms should be pretty familiar to you by now because they are the same world, view, and projection that you've used in previous examples in this book when drawing in 3D.

Look Familiar?

Remember where you've used the `World`, `View`, and `Projection` variables in the past?

You used them to set the `World`, `View`, and `Projection` properties of the `BasicEffect` class. The following code sets those variables, and it should be similar to what you have in the `Draw` method of your `BasicModel` class in the source code you completed in Chapter 12:

```
foreach (BasicEffect be in mesh.Effects)
{
    be.EnableDefaultLighting();
    be.Projection = camera.projection;
    be.View = camera.view;
    be.World = GetWorld() * mesh.ParentBone.Transform;
}
```

You're seeing the same `World`, `Projection`, and `View` variables in this HLSL file. It makes sense when you think about it. Remember that when drawing in 3D, everything in XNA uses HLSL. Until now, you've been using the `BasicEffect` class, which provides you with a way to draw, well, basic effects without having to know the underlying workings of HLSL. Behind the scenes, though, even the `BasicEffect` class is using HLSL.

Now that you're looking at branching out and using HLSL instead of the `BasicEffect` class, it probably won't surprise you to see some of the same properties you've used in the `BasicEffect` class show up in the HLSL file itself.

Variables that are in this global space can be set from your XNA code. (You'll see more about how to do that later, when you apply this code to an actual project.) When using an HLSL file in XNA, one of the first things to do is look for what variables need to be set from the XNA code.

Just like when you're programming in C or C++, in HLSL, variables and functions need to be defined before they are used. This means that a typical flow for an HLSL file will have variables at the top, followed by structs, functions, and finally the shader calls themselves.

When reading an HLSL file, it typically makes sense to read it in the order in which it will be executed. So, let's next skip to the bottom of the code in the sample file. Here's the section of the file that uses the technique keyword:

```
technique Technique1
{
    pass Pass1
    {
        VertexShader = compile vs_2_0 VertexShaderFunction();
        PixelShader = compile ps_2_0 PixelShaderFunction();
    }
}
```

Each HLSL effect file will have one or more techniques. In your XNA code, you'll specify which technique to run when applying an HLSL file by referring to the name of the technique, which in this case is Technique1.

Inside the technique section, notice that there is a subsection called a pass. Each technique has one or more passes. When you draw in XNA using a custom HLSL effect file, you'll set the technique as mentioned earlier and then loop through all the passes to draw each of them. This particular technique has only one pass (Pass1).

Each pass can contain a vertex and/or pixel shader. To implement a shader, your HLSL file must set the value of the VertexShader and/or PixelShader object(s) equal to a compiled vertex or pixel shader function.

Let's look at those two lines in more depth:

```
VertexShader = compile vs_2_0 VertexShaderFunction();
PixelShader = compile ps_2_0 PixelShaderFunction();
```

The VertexShader and PixelShader objects are HLSL objects whose names must be spelled exactly that way and are case-sensitive. The keyword compile tells XNA to compile the method that follows using a certain version of vertex shader or pixel shader (in this case, you're compiling using vertex shader version 2.0, as specified by vs_2_0, and pixel shader version 2.0, as specified by ps_2_0). The functions (VertexShader Function( ) and PixelShaderFunction( )) were defined earlier in the file. The first of those to be called is the vertex shader, so next we'll look at the vertex shader function.

The vertex shader function is listed in the file as:

```
VertexShaderOutput VertexShaderFunction(VertexShaderInput input)
{
    VertexShaderOutput output;
```

```
        float4 worldPosition = mul(input.Position, World);
        float4 viewPosition = mul(worldPosition, View);
        output.Position = mul(viewPosition, Projection);

        return output;
    }
```

The first thing you'll probably notice is that as an input type, the function accepts a struct of type VertexShaderInput (which was defined earlier in the file). The return type is also a struct and is of type VertexShaderOutput (which was also defined earlier in the file). Let's take another look at these two structs:

```
struct VertexShaderInput
{
    float4 Position : POSITION0;

};

struct VertexShaderOutput
{
    float4 Position : POSITION0;

};
```

There's really nothing unusual about these structs, other than one thing that you might not have seen before: an *HLSL semantic*. The POSITION0 code that appears after each of the variable definitions is an HLSL semantic.

HLSL code uses semantics to link data from the XNA game that is using the HLSL code. When a semantic is specified on a variable, HLSL will automatically assign a value to that variable based on the semantic given. This is essentially a way to connect variables in HLSL with certain data to which the XNA game has access.

In this case, the vertex shader method accepts a parameter of type VertexShaderInput, which contains a variable with a semantic of POSITION0. Specifying the POSITION0 semantic on the Position variable causes HLSL to automatically set that variable to a position value that is provided by the XNA game.

What position value will be automatically assigned? Remember that a vertex shader runs once for every visible vertex, so the position given via the POSITION0 semantic in a vertex shader is the position of the vertex.

There are several other possible vertex shader input semantics, in addition to POSITION0. These are listed in Table 13-1.

Table 13-1. Valid input semantics for vertex shaders

Semantic	Description	Type
BINORMAL[n]	Binormal	float4
BLENDINDICES[n]	Blend indices	uint
BLENDWEIGHT[n]	Blend weights	float

Semantic	Description	Type
COLOR[n]	Diffuse and specular color	float4
NORMAL[n]	Normal vector	float4
POSITION[n]	Vertex position in object space	float4
POSITIONT	Transformed vertex position	float4
PSIZE[n]	Point size	float
TANGENT[n]	Tangent	float4
TEXCOORD[n]	Texture coordinates	float4

You probably noticed that the vertex shader returns a struct as well, and that that struct also has a semantic of POSITION0 associated with it. Although the semantic is the same, the meaning is different in this case because it is used as a vertex shader output rather than an input. The meaning of different semantics varies depending on whether the variable using a particular semantic is being used for a pixel shader or a vertex shader and whether it is being specified as input or output in that shader.

For example, the semantics that can be applied to vertex shader output are different than those that can be applied to vertex shader input. Vertex shader output semantics are listed in Table 13-2.

Table 13-2. Valid output semantics for vertex shaders

Semantic	Description	Type
COLOR[n]	Diffuse or specular color.	float4
FOG	Vertex fog.	float
POSITION[n]	Position of a vertex in homogenous space. Compute position in screen-space by dividing (x, y, z) by w. Every vertex shader must write out a parameter with this semantic.	float4
PSIZE	Point size.	float
TESSFACTOR[n]	Tessellation factor.	float
TEXCOORD[n]	Texture coordinate.	float4

So, when the POSITION0 semantic is applied to an input parameter in the vertex shader, HLSL automatically assigns the vertex position to that parameter, but in contrast, a semantic specified on an output parameter is used to flag a variable as containing specific data.

Earlier, you read that the minimum job of any vertex shader is to set the positions of all vertices in the scene, which is done by specifying an output parameter with the POSITION[n] semantic. Essentially, your vertex output needs to set the position of each vertex. But how do you do this, given that there's no vertex.position variable or anything like that to set? That's where the output semantic comes in. By returning a value in a variable that has a semantic of POSITION0, you're specifying a return value that denotes a position.

Freaking out about this? Don't worry. Let's take a look at the actual vertex shader function. For your convenience, the function and the structs it uses are shown again here:

```
struct VertexShaderInput
{
    float4 Position : POSITION0;
};

struct VertexShaderOutput
{
    float4 Position : POSITION0;
};

VertexShaderOutput VertexShaderFunction(VertexShaderInput input)
{
    VertexShaderOutput output;

    float4 worldPosition = mul(input.Position, World);
    float4 viewPosition = mul(worldPosition, View);
    output.Position = mul(viewPosition, Projection);

    return output;
}
```

The first thing this code does is create a variable of type VertexShaderOutput so that it can return that datatype at the end of the function. Notice that that struct has a variable called Position that has a semantic of POSITION0. Again, the basic responsibility of a vertex shader is to set the position of each vertex. You can set the position by returning a value tied to a semantic of POSITION0. So, by returning an object of type Vertex ShaderOutput, you'll be setting the position of the vertex, assuming that you set the Position member of that VertexShaderOutput struct.

Next, the vertex shader function creates a variable called worldPosition and sets the value of that variable to the result of the mul function. What is the mul function? This is what's called an *intrinsic function* in HLSL: it's a function that HLSL provides for developers to manipulate data. A full list of intrinsic functions is provided later in this chapter. This particular function (mul) multiplies two matrices together.

First, the vertex shader function multiplies the position of the vertex (input.Position) by the World matrix. How do you know that input.Position represents the position of the vertex? Well, once again, this comes back to semantics. The input variable is of type VertexShaderInput, which is a struct defined prior to the definition of the vertex shader function. The VertexShaderInput struct has one member: Position. The Position member of that struct has a semantic of POSITION0. When the POSITION0 semantic is tied to a variable used for vertex shader input, the position of the vertex is automatically assigned to that variable.

Next, the vertex shader function multiplies the resulting matrix by the camera view. It then multiplies that resulting matrix by the camera projection and assigns that value to the output parameter, which it returns. All of that matrix multiplication sets the position of the vertex to the correct place, given the position and direction of the camera.

 I know what you're thinking: "Whoa...hold on a second. You're telling me that if you multiply the position of a vertex by the object's world matrix, then multiply that by the camera's view matrix, and then multiply that by the camera's projection matrix, it will magically set the position of the vertex to the correct place?"

Well, yes. And "magic" is really a good term for it. You don't really need to understand how all of this works, and such a discussion would go way deeper into matrix multiplication than we want to in this book. But yes, multiplying those matrices together in that order will yield the correct position for the vertex. That just goes to show how fascinating and how powerful matrix multiplication can be.

You might also be wondering how the code sets the position of each vertex in the scene when only one position variable is returned from the function. Remember that the vertex shader will be run for every vertex in the scene. For example, if you drew a triangle and then ran this HLSL file to render that triangle, your vertex shader would run once for each vertex (there are three vertices in a triangle, so the vertex shader would run three times).

The parameter passed into the vertex shader has a semantic of POSITION0, which will cause that variable to be filled automatically with the value representing the position of the vertex. So, if the vertices of the triangle you draw are (0, 1, 0), (1, 0, 0), and (–1, 0, 0), your vertex shader will run three times: the first time the input parameter value will be (0, 1, 0), the second time the input parameter value will be (1, 0, 0), and the third time the value will be (–1, 0, 0).

This might seem like a lot of confusing code, semantics, shaders, and so forth. Your head may be spinning. But that's OK. Here are the key points to remember so far:

- Global variables that aren't given semantics or initial values need to be set from XNA code.
- The name of the technique to run in your HLSL file needs to be set from XNA code.
- An input parameter with a semantic will automatically receive the data represented by that semantic when the HLSL effect is executed (for example, an input parameter in a vertex shader with a semantic of POSITION0 will automatically be set to a value representing the position of the vertex).

- An output variable with a semantic flags that variable as having a specific type of data for processing in the effect. This is how you "set" data in HLSL. If you need to "set" the position of a vertex in a vertex shader, you return a variable with a semantic of POSITION0.
- A vertex shader has different semantics for input and output.
- At a minimum, a vertex shader needs to specify a POSITION[n] semantic for output.

Once the vertex shader finishes, the pixel shader will run. Let's look at the pixel shader that was created in the effect file:

```
float4 PixelShaderFunction(VertexShaderOutput input) : COLOR0
{
    return float4(1, 0, 0, 1);
}
```

First, notice that the input parameter is the VertexShaderOutput, the same type that was the output from the VertexShaderFunction. This does not always have to be the case. In fact, because vertex shader output semantics are different than pixel shader input semantics, often they cannot be the same type. And sometimes (as in this case), you don't need to specify any input to your pixel shader function at all. Table 13-3 shows a list of valid pixel shader input semantics.

Table 13-3. Valid input semantics for pixel shaders

Semantic	Description	Type
COLOR[n]	Diffuse or specular color	float4
TEXCOORD[n]	Texture coordinates	float4
VFACE	Floating-point scalar that indicates a back-facing primitive; a negative value faces backward, whereas a positive value faces the camera	float
VPOS	Contains the current pixel (x, y) location	float2

Finally, notice the strange semantic on the function itself:

```
float4 PixelShaderFunction(VertexShaderOutput input) : COLOR0
```

This is another way of specifying a semantic for a return type. You can also specify an input semantic in the parameter list rather than using a struct. For example, the following method returns a color and accepts one as well:

```
float myShader(float COLOR0) : COLOR0
```

Valid output semantics for pixel shaders are shown in Table 13-4.

Table 13-4. Valid output semantics for pixel shaders

Semantic	Description	Type
COLOR[n]	Output color	float4
DEPTH[n]	Output depth	float

As mentioned earlier, the minimum job of a pixel shader is to set the color for each individual pixel. In this case, the pixel shader function is returning a `float` with the `COLOR0` semantic to accomplish that. The function contains only one line of code, and with that line, returns the color red:

```
return float4(1, 0, 0, 1);
```

Because the function itself has a semantic of `COLOR0`, returning a `float4` (which can represent color) will "set" the color for that pixel. You may be wondering how this function sets the color of each pixel in the scene. Remember that a pixel shader is run for each pixel in the scene. If you drew a triangle and then used this HLSL effect file to render that triangle, this pixel shader would run for every pixel that composes that part of the triangle. Depending on the size of the triangle and the size of the screen, that could be 10 times, 100 times, 1,000 times, or more. Each time the pixel shader returns a value, it returns that value with a semantic of `COLOR0`, indicating that the value being returned represents the new color of that particular pixel. In this example, the return value is always red (RGBA 1, 0, 0, 1), so every pixel will be colored red. You could change the color depending on the position of the pixel or based on some texture file or whatever else you might want to do, and that would let you color every pixel in the scene differently.

After running the pixel shader, the pass is finished. Because there was only one pass in this code, the HLSL file is now finished, and the data will be sent to the screen. The vertex shader set the positions of all the vertices in the world, and the pixel shader colored all the pixels red, so applying this effect file to a scene should result in everything in the scene being colored red. In the next section, we'll apply the file to some primitives to see whether that is actually the case.

Applying an HLSL Effect in C#

In this section, we'll be using the source code for the textured rectangle project from Chapter 9. You might remember this project as the one that created the cool rectangle with a tree image texture. Running the project will result in the familiar tree rectangle that you saw back when you first started the 3D section (see Figure 13-2).

Currently, the rectangle is drawn using the `BasicEffect` class. You're going to change that so it uses an effect created from an HLSL file that you generate. The first thing to do is create a subfolder under the *3DMadnessContent* project in your solution by right-clicking the *3DMadnessContent* project in Solution Explorer and selecting Add→New Folder. Name the new folder *Effects*.

Next, right-click the *3DMadnessContent\Effects* folder in Solution Explorer and select Add→New Item.... Select Effect File as the template on the right and name the file *Red.fx*, as shown in Figure 13-3.

Figure 13-2. Pretty, pretty rectangle…ahhhhh…

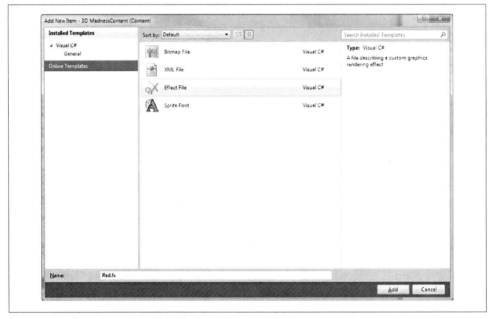

Figure 13-3. Creating a new effect file

Odds are that your sample effect file is the same as the code listed previously, but with comments added for your benefit. Just to be safe, make sure that your effect file contains the following code:

```
float4x4 World;
float4x4 View;
float4x4 Projection;

// TODO: add effect parameters here.

struct VertexShaderInput
{
    float4 Position : POSITION0;

    // TODO: add input channels such as texture
    // coordinates and vertex colors here.
};

struct VertexShaderOutput
{
    float4 Position : POSITION0;

    // TODO: add vertex shader outputs such as colors and texture
    // coordinates here. These values will automatically be interpolated
    // over the triangle, and provided as input to your pixel shader.
};

VertexShaderOutput VertexShaderFunction(VertexShaderInput input)
{
    VertexShaderOutput output;

    float4 worldPosition = mul(input.Position, World);
    float4 viewPosition = mul(worldPosition, View);
    output.Position = mul(viewPosition, Projection);

    // TODO: add your vertex shader code here.

    return output;
}

float4 PixelShaderFunction(VertexShaderOutput input) : COLOR0
{
    // TODO: add your pixel shader code here.

    return float4(1, 0, 0, 1);
}

technique Technique1
{
    pass Pass1
    {
        // TODO: set renderstates here.

        VertexShader = compile vs_2_0 VertexShaderFunction();
        PixelShader = compile ps_2_0 PixelShaderFunction();
```

```
        }
    }
```

You can verify that your effect code will compile by compiling your solution. If you get no compilation errors, you know that your code is at least syntactically correct (that's a good sign).

To use your effect in code, you need to create a variable of type Effect to store the effect in memory. You already have an effect variable in your Game1 class, but currently it is of type BasicEffect. Modify the declaration of the class-level effect variable in your Game1 class to be of type Effect, as shown here:

```
Effect effect;
```

Next, you'll need to load the effect into your Effect object via the content pipeline. Remove the following line from your LoadContent method, which initialized your BasicEffect:

```
effect = new BasicEffect(GraphicsDevice);
```

and replace it with the following code, which loads your effect from the content pipeline:

```
effect = Content.Load<Effect>(@"effects\red");
```

Finally, you'll need to remove the following code in your Draw method, which uses the BasicEffect class to draw:

```
//Set object and camera info
effect.World = worldRotation * worldTranslation * worldRotation;
effect.View = camera.view;
effect.Projection = camera.projection;
effect.Texture = texture;
effect.TextureEnabled = true;

// Begin effect and draw for each pass
foreach (EffectPass pass in effect.CurrentTechnique.Passes)
{
    pass.Apply();

    GraphicsDevice.DrawUserPrimitives<VertexPositionTexture>
        (PrimitiveType.TriangleStrip, verts, 0, 2);

}
```

 The second line of the code in this listing may be different in your project. This was because at the end of Chapter 9, I encouraged you to try different combinations of worldRotations and worldTranslations in the setting of the effect.World variable. Don't worry about that; just replace the preceding code section with the one listed next.

Replace that code with the following code, which uses your new `Effect` file instead of the `BasicEffect` class:

```
effect.CurrentTechnique = effect.Techniques["Technique1"];
effect.Parameters["World"].SetValue(Matrix.Identity);
effect.Parameters["View"].SetValue(camera.view);
effect.Parameters["Projection"].SetValue(camera.projection);

foreach (EffectPass pass in effect.CurrentTechnique.Passes)
{
    pass.Apply();
    GraphicsDevice.DrawUserPrimitives<VertexPositionTexture>
        (PrimitiveType.TriangleStrip, verts, 0, 2);
}
```

You'll notice that the core drawing `foreach` loop used is the same: you're looping through all the passes of the current technique and drawing your object. The main difference in the code lies in the fact that you are no longer using the `BasicEffect` class to draw.

The `BasicEffect` class has several properties to which you assigned the object's world matrix, the camera's view matrix, and the camera's projection matrix. When using HLSL, you still use that data, but you instead assign it to the global variables mentioned in your HLSL effect file by using the `effect.Parameters[].SetValue` method.

Passing Data from XNA to HLSL

There are two different ways to get data from XNA to your HLSL effect file. One way is by using semantics. As discussed earlier in this chapter, if you create a variable that is used as an input variable to a vertex shader or a pixel shader and assign a semantic to that variable, the appropriate data will automatically be set to that variable when the function is run.

The other way to get data to HLSL from XNA is to set parameters manually. As you saw earlier, only certain types of data can be passed via semantics (things such as positions, colors, texture coordinates, and so on). However, you can pass anything you want to an HLSL file via manual parameters. To do this, you define a global variable in your HLSL file and set the parameter using the `effect.Parameters[].SetValue` method shown in the preceding code.

If you've been playing with your code from Chapter 9 or tweaking it by following the exercises in this book, your code might be somewhat different than what I have used in this chapter thus far. To clarify, here's what your `Game1` class should look like at this point:

```
using System;
using System.Collections.Generic;
using System.Linq;
using Microsoft.Xna.Framework;
using Microsoft.Xna.Framework.Audio;
```

```
using Microsoft.Xna.Framework.Content;
using Microsoft.Xna.Framework.GamerServices;
using Microsoft.Xna.Framework.Graphics;
using Microsoft.Xna.Framework.Input;
using Microsoft.Xna.Framework.Media;

namespace _3D_Madness
{
    /// <summary>
    /// This is the main type for your game
    /// </summary>
    public class Game1 : Microsoft.Xna.Framework.Game
    {
        GraphicsDeviceManager graphics;
        SpriteBatch spriteBatch;

        // Game camera
        Camera camera;

        // Vertex data
        VertexPositionTexture[] verts;
        VertexBuffer vertexBuffer;

        // Effect
        Effect effect;

        // Movement and rotation stuff
        Matrix worldTranslation = Matrix.Identity;
        Matrix worldRotation = Matrix.Identity;

        // Texture info
        Texture2D texture;

        public Game1()
        {
            graphics = new GraphicsDeviceManager(this);
            Content.RootDirectory = "Content";
        }

        /// <summary>
        /// Allows the game to perform any initialization it needs to before
        /// starting to run. This is where it can query for any required services and
        /// load any non-graphic-related content.  Calling base.Initialize will
        /// enumerate through any components and initialize them as well.
        /// </summary>
        protected override void Initialize()
        {
            // Initialize camera
            camera = new Camera(this, new Vector3(0, 0, 5),
                Vector3.Zero, Vector3.Up);
            Components.Add(camera);

            base.Initialize();
        }
```

```csharp
/// <summary>
/// LoadContent will be called once per game and is the place to load
/// all of your content.
/// </summary>
protected override void LoadContent()
{
    // Create a new SpriteBatch, which can be used to draw textures.
    spriteBatch = new SpriteBatch(GraphicsDevice);

    // Initialize vertices
    verts = new VertexPositionTexture[4];
    verts[0] = new VertexPositionTexture(
        new Vector3(-1, 1, 0), new Vector2(0, 0));
    verts[1] = new VertexPositionTexture(
        new Vector3(1, 1, 0), new Vector2(1, 0));
    verts[2] = new VertexPositionTexture(
        new Vector3(-1, -1, 0), new Vector2(0, 1));
    verts[3] = new VertexPositionTexture(
        new Vector3(1, -1, 0), new Vector2(1, 1));

    // Set vertex data in VertexBuffer
    vertexBuffer = new VertexBuffer(GraphicsDevice,
        typeof(VertexPositionTexture), verts.Length,
        BufferUsage.None);
    vertexBuffer.SetData(verts);

    // Load texture
    texture = Content.Load<Texture2D>(@"Textures\trees");

    // Load the effect
    effect = Content.Load<Effect>(@"effects\red");
}

/// <summary>
/// UnloadContent will be called once per game and is the place to unload
/// all content.
/// </summary>
protected override void UnloadContent()
{
    // TODO: Unload any non-ContentManager content here
}

/// <summary>
/// Allows the game to run logic such as updating the world,
/// checking for collisions, gathering input, and playing audio.
/// </summary>
/// <param name="gameTime">Provides a snapshot of timing values.</param>
protected override void Update(GameTime gameTime)
{
    // Allows the game to exit
    if (GamePad.GetState(PlayerIndex.One).Buttons.Back ==
        ButtonState.Pressed)
        this.Exit();
```

```
            // Translation
            KeyboardState keyboardState = Keyboard.GetState();
            if (keyboardState.IsKeyDown(Keys.Left))
                worldTranslation *= Matrix.CreateTranslation(-.01f, 0, 0);
            if (keyboardState.IsKeyDown(Keys.Right))
                worldTranslation *= Matrix.CreateTranslation(.01f, 0, 0);

            // Rotation
            worldRotation *= Matrix.CreateFromYawPitchRoll(
                MathHelper.PiOver4 / 60,
                0,
                0);

            base.Update(gameTime);
        }

        /// <summary>
        /// This is called when the game should draw itself.
        /// </summary>
        /// <param name="gameTime">Provides a snapshot of timing values.</param>
        protected override void Draw(GameTime gameTime)
        {
            GraphicsDevice.Clear(Color.CornflowerBlue);


            // Set the vertex buffer on the GraphicsDevice
            GraphicsDevice.SetVertexBuffer(vertexBuffer);

            effect.CurrentTechnique = effect.Techniques["Technique1"];
            effect.Parameters["World"].SetValue(Matrix.Identity);
            effect.Parameters["View"].SetValue(camera.view);
            effect.Parameters["Projection"].SetValue(camera.projection);

            foreach (EffectPass pass in effect.CurrentTechnique.Passes)
            {
                pass.Apply();
                GraphicsDevice.DrawUserPrimitives<VertexPositionTexture>
                    (PrimitiveType.TriangleStrip, verts, 0, 2);
            }


            base.Draw(gameTime);
        }
    }
}
```

Compile and run the project, and you should see the same rectangle as before, but now in red (see Figure 13-4).

Now you may be thinking, "Hmmm...the rectangle looked way better when I was using BasicEffect. HLSL is lame!" I have to admit that the rectangle did look better before, but this is only the very beginning of what HLSL can do. Let's take a look at some more detailed HLSL code to see if we can make things any better.

Figure 13-4. A red rectangle using a custom effect file!

Applying HLSL Using Textures

Coloring a rectangle red requires only the simplest HLSL shader, and it's something you'll rarely find in the latest video games. Typically, you'll be applying a texture to an object and then tweaking the way the texture appears by applying shininess or fog or some other effect.

In this section, you'll apply a custom HLSL file to your rectangle while applying color from the trees texture as well.

Open your *Red.fx* file again and replace the code in the file with the code shown here:

```
float4x4 xWorldViewProjection;

Texture xColoredTexture;

sampler ColoredTextureSampler = sampler_state
{ texture = <xColoredTexture> ;
magfilter = LINEAR; minfilter = LINEAR; mipfilter=LINEAR;
AddressU = mirror; AddressV = mirror;};
```

```
struct VertexIn
{
    float4 position : POSITION;
    float2 textureCoordinates : TEXCOORD0;
};

struct VertexOut
{
    float4 Position : POSITION;
    float2 textureCoordinates : TEXCOORD0;
};

VertexOut VertexShaderFunction(VertexIn input)
{
    VertexOut Output = (VertexOut)0;
    Output.Position =mul(input.position, xWorldViewProjection);
    Output.textureCoordinates = input.textureCoordinates;

    return Output;
}

float4 PixelShaderFunction(VertexOut input) : COLOR0
{
    float4 output = tex2D(ColoredTextureSampler,
        input.textureCoordinates);
    return output;
}

technique Textured
{
    pass Pass0
    {
        VertexShader = compile vs_2_0 VertexShaderFunction( );
        PixelShader = compile ps_2_0 PixelShaderFunction( );
    }
}
```

Even though you're still new to HLSL, this file isn't incredibly complex, and for the most part it should make sense to you. Notice first that instead of using three variables to represent the world, view, and projection matrices, respectively, you have only one variable, called xWorldViewProjection. In your XNA code, you'll need to multiply the world, view, and projection matrices together and assign the resulting value to this variable. Because they are all multiplied together to set the vertex position, it doesn't matter whether you do that in the HLSL file or in XNA code. The advantage of doing the multiplication in XNA code rather than in the HLSL file is that you do the multiplication once per scene if you pass it into the HLSL code, whereas doing the multiplication within HLSL will cause it to be done once for every vertex.

Also, notice the new variable called xColoredTexture. This variable represents a texture object, and you'll need to assign it the value of your Texture object from your XNA code.

There's also a ColoredTextureSampler object that allows you to sample data from a texture to determine the color of a particular part of that texture. When the pixel shader runs, it will map each pixel on the object to the corresponding location in the texture by using the sampler object and will return the color that the pixel should have.

Notice that the pixel shader uses a `tex2D` method to accomplish this. `tex2D` is a function that is built into HLSL, much like `mul`, which you used previously to multiply together two matrices. `tex2D` looks up a color at a particular point in a texture using a sampler. Essentially, you'll be running your pixel shader for every pixel on the screen, right? Each time the pixel shader runs, you're going to receive a texture coordinate for that pixel (it's passed into the pixel shader via the `textureCoordinates` member of the `VertexOut struct`). The `tex2D` function will take those texture coordinates, look up the corresponding pixel in the texture at each coordinate, and return the color of that pixel. Using this method, the entire rectangle will be colored to look just like the texture you're passing to the HLSL effect file.

In addition to `mul` and `tex2D`, there are a number of other built-in functions (also called intrinsic functions) in HLSL. These functions are listed in Microsoft's MSDN library for help on DirectX and XNA. For your convenience, they are also shown in Table 13-5.

Table 13-5. Intrinsic functions in HLSL

Syntax	Description
abs(x)	Returns the absolute value (per component)
acos(x)	Returns the arccosine of each component of x
all(x)	Tests if all components of x are nonzero
any(x)	Tests if any component of x is nonzero
asfloat(x)	Converts the input type to a float
asin(x)	Returns the arcsine of each component of x
asint(x)	Converts the input type to an integer
asuint(x)	Converts the input type to an unsigned integer
atan(x)	Returns the arctangent of x
atan2(x, y)	Returns the arctangent of two values (x, y)
ceil(x)	Returns the smallest integer that is greater than or equal to x
clamp(x, min, max)	Clamps x to the range [min, max]
clip(x)	Discards the current pixel, if any component of x is less than zero
cos(x)	Returns the cosine of x
cosh(x)	Returns the hyperbolic cosine of x
cross(x, y)	Returns the cross product of two 3D vectors
D3DCOLORtoUBYTE4(x)	Swizzles and scales components of the 4D vector x to compensate for the lack of UBYTE4 support in some hardware
ddx(x)	Returns the partial derivative of x with respect to the screen-space X coordinate

Syntax	Description
ddy(x)	Returns the partial derivative of x with respect to the screen-space Y coordinate
degrees(x)	Converts x from radians to degrees
determinant(m)	Returns the determinant of the square matrix m
distance(x, y)	Returns the distance between two points
dot(x, y)	Returns the dot product of two vectors
exp(x)	Returns the base-e exponent
exp2(x)	Returns the base-2 exponent (per component)
faceforward(n, i, ng)	Returns -n * \<sign\>($\cdot$(i, ng))
floor(x)	Returns the greatest integer that is less than or equal to x
fmod(x, y)	Returns the floating-point remainder of x/y
frac(x)	Returns the fractional part of x
frexp(x, exp)	Returns the mantissa and exponent of x
fwidth(x)	Returns abs(ddx(x)) + abs(ddy(x))
GetRenderTargetSampleCount( )	Returns the number of render-target samples
GetRenderTargetSamplePosition(x)	Returns a sample position (x, y) for a given sample index
isfinite(x)	Returns true if x is finite, and false otherwise
isinf(x)	Returns true if x is +INF or -INF, and false otherwise
isnan(x)	Returns true if x is NAN or QNAN, and false otherwise
ldexp(x, exp)	Returns x * 2exp
length(v)	Returns the length of the vector v
lerp(x, y, s)	Returns x + s(y - x)
lit(n • l, n • h, m)	Returns a lighting vector (ambient, diffuse, specular, 1)
log(x)	Returns the base-e logarithm of x
log10(x)	Returns the base-10 logarithm of x
log2(x)	Returns the base-2 logarithm of x
max(x, y)	Selects the greater of x and y
min(x, y)	Selects the lesser of x and y
modf(x, out ip)	Splits the value x into fractional and integer parts
mul(x, y)	Performs matrix multiplication using x and y
noise(x)	Generates a random value using the Perlin-noise algorithm
normalize(x)	Returns a normalized vector
pow(x, y)	Returns xy
radians(x)	Converts x from degrees to radians
reflect(i, n)	Returns a reflection vector

Syntax	Description
`refract(i, n, R)`	Returns the refraction vector
`round(x)`	Rounds x to the nearest integer
`rsqrt(x)`	Returns `1 / sqrt(x)`
`saturate(x)`	Clamps x to the range [0, 1]
`sign(x)`	Computes the sign of x
`sin(x)`	Returns the sine of x
`sincos(x, out s, out c)`	Returns the sine and cosine of x
`sinh(x)`	Returns the hyperbolic sine of x
`smoothstep(min, max, x)`	Returns a smooth Hermite interpolation between 0 and 1
`sqrt(x)`	Returns the square root (per component)
`step(a, x)`	Returns `(x >= a) ? 1 : 0`
`tan(x)`	Returns the tangent of x
`tanh(x)`	Returns the hyperbolic tangent of x
`tex1D(s, t)`	1D texture lookup
`tex1Dbias(s, t)`	1D texture lookup with bias
`tex1Dgrad(s, t, ddx, ddy)`	1D texture lookup with a gradient
`tex1Dlod(s, t)`	1D texture lookup with LOD
`tex1Dproj(s, t)`	1D texture lookup with projective divide
`tex2D(s, t)`	2D texture lookup
`tex2Dbias(s, t)`	2D texture lookup with bias
`tex2Dgrad(s, t, ddx, ddy)`	2D texture lookup with a gradient
`tex2Dlod(s, t)`	2D texture lookup with LOD
`tex2Dproj(s, t)`	2D texture lookup with projective divide
`tex3D(s, t)`	3D texture lookup
`tex3Dbias(s, t)`	3D texture lookup with bias
`tex3Dgrad(s, t, ddx, ddy)`	3D texture lookup with a gradient
`tex3Dlod(s, t)`	3D texture lookup with LOD
`tex3Dproj(s, t)`	3D texture lookup with projective divide
`texCUBE(s, t)`	Cube texture lookup
`texCUBEbias(s, t)`	Cube texture lookup with bias
`texCUBEgrad(s, t, ddx, ddy)`	Cube texture lookup with a gradient
`tex3Dlod(s, t)`	Cube texture lookup with LOD
`texCUBEproj(s, t)`	Cube texture lookup with projective divide
`transpose(m)`	Returns the transpose of the matrix m
`trunc(x)`	Truncates floating-point value(s) to integer value(s)

So essentially, the new effect file that you've just created is going to set the vertex positions and then color the object by pulling pixel coordinates out of the associated texture using the sampler object. In other words, it will map the texture to the rectangle drawn on the screen.

Next, you'll need to change the code in your `Draw` method to use your new custom effect rather than the red custom effect used previously. Do you remember what data you need to set in order to use an HLSL effect in XNA?

You'll need to set the name of the effect to run, and you'll need to set all global variables in the effect file. Currently, you have the following code in the `Draw` method of your `Game1` class to do that, but you're setting data for the *red.fx* file:

```
effect.CurrentTechnique = effect.Techniques["Technique1"];
effect.Parameters["World"].SetValue(Matrix.Identity);
effect.Parameters["View"].SetValue(camera.View);
effect.Parameters["Projection"].SetValue(camera.Projection);
```

The first thing you'll need to change in order to use the new effect is the name of the technique. The technique in the *red.fx* file was called `Technique1`, whereas the new effect uses a technique called `Textured`.

Change the first line of the preceding code, which is in the `Draw` method of your `Game1` class, to this:

```
effect.CurrentTechnique = effect.Techniques["Textured"];
```

Next, you might have noticed that the global variables are different. Previously, you had three global variables in your HLSL effect: `World`, `View`, and `Projection`.

Your new effect has only two global variables: `xWorldViewProjection` (which should be set to the world matrix multiplied by the view matrix multiplied by the projection matrix) and `xColoredTexture` (which should be set to the `Texture2D` object you want to apply to the rectangle).

Remove the following three lines of code from the `Draw` method of your `Game1` class:

```
effect.Parameters["World"].SetValue(Matrix.Identity);
effect.Parameters["View"].SetValue(camera.View);
effect.Parameters["Projection"].SetValue(camera.Projection);
```

and replace them with this code:

```
effect.Parameters["xWorldViewProjection"].SetValue(
    Matrix.Identity * camera.view * camera.projection);
effect.Parameters["xColoredTexture"].SetValue(texture);
```

This new code should look pretty familiar because it's essentially the same as the code you added in the previous example to make your triangle draw in red. The only key difference here is that, as mentioned previously, you are setting the `World`, `View`, and `Projection` variables all at once rather than individually. When multiplied together, they give you the same result, so this works just as well as the method you used earlier.

Compile and run the game now, and you'll see the exact same textured rectangle, but this time it will be rendered using a custom HLSL shader (as seen in Figure 13-5).

Figure 13-5. Oh so pretty once again…

One thing that you've probably noticed is that your rectangle used to spin, but now it stands still. Why is that? The answer lies in the world matrix. Remember that an object's world matrix represents the position, rotation, scale, and so on for that particular object. Therefore, if the object isn't rotating properly, isn't scaled correctly, or is in the wrong location, there's probably a problem with the object's world matrix.

In this particular case, you're supposed to set the `xWorldViewProjection` HLSL variable to the world matrix multiplied by the view matrix multiplied by the projection matrix. The code you used to do that is listed here:

```
effect.Parameters["xWorldViewProjection"].SetValue(
    Matrix.Identity * camera.view * camera.projection);
```

Notice the value that you're using for the world portion of that multiplication: `Matrix.Identity`. Remember what the identity matrix does? When you multiply matrix A by the identity matrix, the product is matrix A. So in this case, you're multiplying the identity matrix by the view and the projection. That's exactly the same as just multiplying together the view and the projection; in other words, you're really not specifying anything special (no movement, no rotations, nothing) for the object's world matrix. That's why the object isn't rotating.

So, how do you fix that? When you built this code in Chapter 9, you used two class-level matrix variables to rotate the rectangle: worldTranslation and worldRotation. To make the object rotate, build a world matrix from the worldTranslation and world Rotation matrices, and use that world matrix instead of Matrix.Identity when setting the xWorldViewProjection HLSL variable.

That is, replace the following line in the Draw method of your Game1 class:

```
effect.Parameters["xWorldViewProjection"].SetValue(
    Matrix.Identity * camera.view * camera.projection);
```

with this:

```
Matrix world = worldRotation * worldTranslation;
effect.Parameters["xWorldViewProjection"].SetValue(
    world * camera.view * camera.projection);
```

Now the rotation and translation code you wrote in Chapter 9 will be applied to the rectangle. Run the game at this point and you should see a spinning rectangle, as shown in Figure 13-6.

Figure 13-6. Wow! HLSL is amazing!!!

The rectangle will move when you press the left and right arrow keys, just as you coded the original rectangle to do in Chapter 9. Again, feel free to play with the different rotations and translations and apply them in different orders, as you did in Chapter 9. Instead of setting the `World` property of the `BasicEffect` class, you're now creating a temporary world matrix variable and assigning that value to the variable in an HLSL effect file, but the end result is exactly the same.

Well...maybe HLSL isn't so amazing. You just put in a lot of extra work to end up with the exact same result that you had previously! That's not the end of the possibilities, though. Let's look at some different things you can do with this textured rectangle using HLSL.

HLSL Effects: Creating a Negative

Now that you have an effect file using a texture, there are any number of things you can do to your HLSL file to get some really interesting and cool effects. For instance, changing the code in the pixel shader to the following will result in a negative image being drawn:

```
float4 PixelShaderFunction(VertexOut input) : COLOR0
{
    float4 output = 1-tex2D(ColoredTextureSampler, input.textureCoordinates);
    return output;
}
```

The effect is shown in Figure 13-7.

HLSL Effects: Blur

Another very simple effect is blurring the image. To do this, you grab the color of each pixel in the texture and add to it the colors from the pixels adjacent to the target pixel. To try this, replace the pixel shader in your game with the following code:

```
float4 PixelShaderFunction(VertexOut input) : COLOR0
{
    float4 Color;
    Color =  tex2D(ColoredTextureSampler, input.textureCoordinates.xy);
    Color += tex2D(ColoredTextureSampler, input.textureCoordinates.xy + (0.01));
    Color += tex2D(ColoredTextureSampler, input.textureCoordinates.xy - (0.01));
    Color = Color / 3;

    return Color;
}
```

The result will be a blurred image, as shown in Figure 13-8.

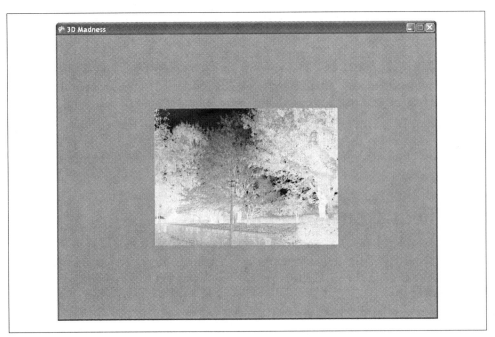

Figure 13-7. Negative image drawn using HLSL

Figure 13-8. Blurred image using HLSL

HLSL Effects: Grayscale

Rendering an image in grayscale is another very simple effect that can be added with little difficulty. By applying a standard grayscale equation, you can convert the colors of every pixel to a shade of gray using the dot function. Replace your pixel shader with this code:

```
float4 PixelShaderFunction(VertexOut input) : COLOR0
{
    float4 color;
    color = tex2D( ColoredTextureSampler, input.textureCoordinates.xy);
    return dot(color, float3(0.3, 0.59, 0.11));
}
```

What's this doing? First, the shader function retrieves the color of the pixel at the coordinate of the pixel. Then, the dot function retrieves a dot product using two vectors: the color of the pixel from the texture and a vector generated using (0.3, 0.59, 0.11). Why these numbers? Well, you could just use 0.33 for each of them and get an average color, which would look pretty decent in grayscale. However, a long time ago, somebody much smarter than myself figured out that these numbers much more closely approximate grayscale as seen by the human eye. I hate to quote Wikipedia in a book like this, but it's a great resource to read about these numbers (see *http://en.wikipedia .org/wiki/Grayscale*).

The resulting image will be drawn in grayscale, as shown in Figure 13-9.

Figure 13-9. Scary and spooky grayscale!!!

As you can see, there are endless possibilities when dealing with HLSL effects. These are only a few samples of the things you can do. As mentioned at the beginning of this chapter, this book isn't intended to be a definitive resource on HLSL. However, if this stuff interests you, there are a lot of resources on the Internet and other books that will take you deeper into the world of HLSL and effects.

What You Just Did

In the next chapter, we'll look at particle engines and how you can apply HLSL to particles to make them look realistic. But before we get to that, let's take a look back at this chapter and what you just did:

- You learned about HLSL syntax, including semantics, keywords, functions, vertex shaders, and pixel shaders.
- You implemented your first shader, which colored everything drawn on the screen in red.
- You implemented a texture map shader that colored a rectangle based on pixel coordinates in a texture.
- You created several different effects using HLSL.

Summary

- HLSL allows developers to make full use of the wide range of capabilities of the latest graphics cards.
- In HLSL, there are two kinds of shaders: vertex shaders (which are executed once for each visible vertex in the scene) and pixel shaders (which are executed once for each pixel drawn in the scene).
- The minimum requirement of a vertex shader is to set the position of each vertex. The minimum requirement of a pixel shader is to set the color of each pixel.
- In HLSL, data is run first through the vertex shader, then through a rasterization process, and then through a pixel shader before finally being sent to the screen.
- HLSL files are added to the project in the *Content* folder and are picked up by the content pipeline. The content pipeline compiles them, and any syntax errors will be caught at compile time.
- Pixel shader 2.0 can draw most objects, but pixel shader 928,217,661,293,721.12 is required to draw either of Chuck Norris's biceps.

Test Your Knowledge: Quiz

1. In HLSL, how can you access the first element in a `float4` object?
2. What is swizzling?
3. In HLSL, how do you specify which vertex and pixel shader versions to use?
4. What does HLSL do for you that you can't accomplish without it?
5. How do you multiply two matrices together in HLSL?
6. What is the role of a semantic in HLSL?
7. Who burninates the countryside, burninates the peasants, burninates all the people, and their thatch-roofed cottages?

Test Your Knowledge: Exercise

Take the code you built in this chapter and draw a six-sided cube using the trees image provided as the texture for each side of the cube. On each side of the cube, use one of the four texture effects you built in this chapter (normal texture, burred texture, negative texture, grayscale texture). Use each of the four effects at least once on the cube.

CHAPTER 14

Particle Systems

In this chapter, you'll get back to work on the 3D game you've been building throughout most of the 3D section of this book. Specifically, you'll be adding some particle effects to your game. Particle effects allow game developers to create exciting and realistic special effects such as smoke, fire, explosions, magic, and other effects that can make the gameplay experience more exciting and attractive.

To start with, let's talk about particles. What is a particle? In game development terms, a *particle* typically represents a single component in a particle effect. A single spark in a firework, a single element in a smoke plume, and a single flickering light in a magical effect are all examples of particles. The combination of multiple particles flowing in a single special effect is what's called a *particle effect*.

Particle engines are the driving mechanism behind particle effects. A particle engine manipulates multiple particles to create a particle effect by applying forces such as gravity and momentum to make the particles move and react in realistic ways.

Throughout this chapter, you'll create a particle engine that creates explosion particle effects that you'll plug into your game when a shot strikes an enemy ship.

Creating a Particle Engine

So let's get to it. First, let's examine what each individual particle will look like so we can get a better handle on what we're trying to do. Each individual particle will be represented by four vertices, forming a square. You've done this before, so it shouldn't be anything revolutionary. Also, you'll be drawing a texture onto that square. The texture you'll use is shown in Figure 14-1.

Figure 14-1. Texture for your particles

The actual texture file is simply a white shaded dot, as shown in Figure 14-1, but with a transparent background. The image in Figure 14-1 has a black background to give it some context in this book. If you haven't already, download the source code for this chapter of the book. In the *3D Game\3D GameContent\Textures* folder, you'll find an image file called *particle.png*. Add it to your project by right-clicking the *3D Game-Content\Textures* folder in Solution Explorer, selecting Add→Existing Item..., and then navigating to the *particle.png* file and selecting it.

Each of your particles will be a ball of light, shaded like the texture shown previously. But what fun is an explosion of white particles? You'll want to add some random color to each particle. To do this, you'll use another texture, which is shown in Figure 14-2.

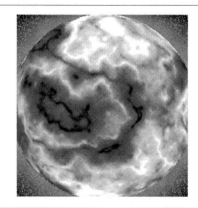

Figure 14-2. Texture containing random colors for your particles

This texture will be used as a color map representing all the possible colors of your particles. Each time a particle is created, you'll be pulling a random pixel from this texture, getting its color data, and assigning that to the new particle. Why use a picture of a red-hot sun? Simply because the reds, blacks, whites, and yellows in this texture represent a lot of colors you'd typically see in an explosion. In truth, you could swap this texture out for any texture you prefer and use those colors for your pixels. Go ahead and add this texture to your solution. In the *3D Game\3D GameContent\Textures* folder, you'll find an image file called *ParticleColors.png*. Add it to your project by right-clicking the *3D GameContent\Textures* folder in Solution Explorer, selecting Add→Existing Item…, and then navigating to the *ParticleColors.png* file and selecting it.

OK, now that we have an idea of how this will work, let's get to the code. You'll be creating three new classes in this section: `ParticleSettings`, which will hold settings for individual particles; `ParticleExplosionSettings`, which will hold settings for individual explosions; and `ParticleExplosion`, which represents a single explosion effect and will be responsible for moving, updating, and drawing all the particles involved in an explosion effect.

Create a new class within your project called `ParticleSettings`, and replace the contents of the *ParticleSettings.cs* file with the following code:

```
namespace _3D_Game
{
    class ParticleSettings
    {
        // Size of particle
        public int maxSize = 2;
    }

    class ParticleExplosionSettings
    {
        // Life of particles
        public int minLife = 1000;
        public int maxLife = 2000;

        // Particles per round
        public int minParticlesPerRound = 100;
        public int maxParticlesPerRound = 600;

        // Round time
        public int minRoundTime = 16;
        public int maxRoundTime = 50;

        // Number of particles
        public int minParticles = 2000;
        public int maxParticles = 3000;
    }
}
```

As you can see, the only setting at the particle level is the maximum size of each particle. When the `ParticleExplosion` class creates particles, it will create them with a size greater than zero and less than this maximum size.

In the `ParticleExplosionSettings` class, located in the same code file, there are more settings. (In C#, it's perfectly legal to have multiple classes within the same file, and because these two classes are so closely related, it makes sense to put them both in your *ParticleSettings.cs* file.) The settings in this class define different aspects of the particle effect, such as how long the effect lasts, how many particles are used in the effect, etc. All of this is explained in more detail in the following list.

Essentially, your `ParticleExplosion` class, when completed, will function as follows:

- Each particle in your explosion will be represented by four vertices, forming a square, with a colored texture drawn on the square.

- When an instance of `ParticleExplosion` is created, you'll fill a `VertexBuffer` which will contain the vertex data for your particles. The number of particles created by the explosion will be between the `minParticles` and `maxParticles` values you defined. Therefore, the size of your vertex array will be the number of particles times four (four vertices for each particle).

- Your `ParticleExplosion` class will function in what we'll call "rounds" of particles. A round is simply a time period indicating when new particles will be released from the explosion. Rounds will begin every X milliseconds, where X is between your `minRoundTime` and `maxRoundTime` settings. Every round, some number of particles between `minParticlesPerRound` and `maxParticlesPerRound` will be released from the explosion.

- Once the number of particles released by the `ParticleExplosion` class reaches the max number of particles, the explosion will not create any more particles.

- Every time the `Update` method is called in the `ModelManager` class, the `Update` method of the `ParticleExplosion` class will be called. This method will cycle through all active particles and update their positions. Because we're in outer space, there are no external forces such as gravity to deal with, so the particles will just move in a straight line designated by the direction stored in another array.

- A particle engine is also responsible for killing off particles once they expire. That is the purpose of the `minLife` and `maxLife` settings in your code. Each `Particle Explosion` will be given a lifetime value greater than `minLife` and less than `max Life`. Once the lifetime time limit has been reached for an explosion, it begins retiring particles in each round.

- Once all particles are retired, the explosion is over and will be deleted.

OK, now that you have an idea of how the `ParticleExplosion` class will work, let's throw it together. Create a new class within your project called `ParticleExplosion`. Make sure that you have the following namespaces at the top of the file:

```
using System;
using Microsoft.Xna.Framework;
using Microsoft.Xna.Framework.Graphics;
```

Next, add the following class-level variables:

```
// Particle arrays and vertex buffer
VertexPositionTexture[] verts;
Vector3[] vertexDirectionArray;
Color[] vertexColorArray;
VertexBuffer particleVertexBuffer;

// Position
Vector3 position;

// Life
int lifeLeft;

// Rounds and particle counts
int numParticlesPerRound;
int maxParticles;
static Random rnd = new Random();
int roundTime;
int timeSinceLastRound = 0;

// Vertex and graphics info
GraphicsDevice graphicsDevice;

// Settings
ParticleSettings particleSettings;

// Effect
Effect particleEffect;

// Textures
Texture2D particleColorsTexture;

// Array indices
int endOfLiveParticlesIndex = 0;
int endOfDeadParticlesIndex = 0;
```

Here's a rundown of what these variables will be used for:

verts

    An array of `VertexPositionTexture` objects that will store all vertices for all particles.

vertexDirectionArray

    An array of `Vector3` objects that will store the direction of each particle.

vertexColorArray

    An array of `Color` objects that will store the color of each particle.

particleVertexBuffer

    The vertex buffer you'll use to draw the particles.

position

    The position of the explosion, or the position from which new particles will emanate. This is also the position of the ship that was shot, triggering the explosion.

lifeLeft
How much life is left in the explosion before particles start being deleted.

numParticlesPerRound
How many particles to create each round, and how many to remove each round once the explosion has no more life left.

maxParticles
The total number of particles to be created by this explosion.

rnd
A random object from the Game1 class passed in via the constructor. This object is static because you want only one of these to exist for all explosion instances.

roundTime
The amount of time between particle rounds.

timeSinceLastRound
A counter to keep track of how much time is left until the next round begins.

graphicsDevice
The graphics device passed in from the Game1 class.

particleSettings
An instance of the ParticleSettings class, to apply those settings to particles being created.

particleEffect
The HLSL effect that you'll be using to draw your particles.

particleColorsTexture
This texture will contain a Texture2D object that is actually a picture of an explosion. It will be used to determine random colors for each of your particles.

endOfLiveParticlesIndex *and* endOfDeadParticlesIndex
Indices into the array of Particles. The entire array is instantiated when the explosion class is instantiated, but the only particles that are drawn are those that exist between the endOfDeadParticlesIndex and the endOfLiveParticlesIndex. As new particles are "created" each round, the endOfLiveParticlesIndex moves down the array. As new particles are "deleted" each round, the endOfDeadParticles Index moves down the list. Each time particles are drawn, the only ones being drawn are those that reside between the two indices.

Figure 14-3 provides a graphical explanation of how the array of Particles in the ParticleExplosion class functions. As the endOfDeadParticlesIndex and endOf LiveParticlesIndex move from left to right, particles between the two indices are drawn. Particles to the left of both indices are dead, whereas particles to the right of both indices are not yet alive.

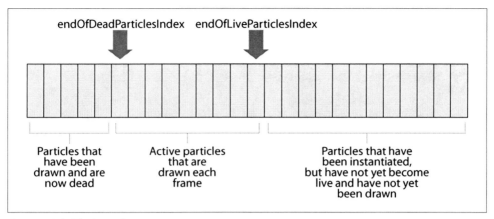

Figure 14-3. The Particle array

You'll also need to provide a way for the ModelManager class to determine when an explosion is finished. Add the following public property to the ParticleExplosion class:

```
public bool IsDead
{
    get { return endOfDeadParticlesIndex == maxParticles; }
}
```

Next, add a constructor to the ParticleExplosion class, as shown here:

```
public ParticleExplosion(GraphicsDevice graphicsDevice, Vector3 position,
    int lifeLeft, int roundTime, int numParticlesPerRound, int maxParticles,
    Texture2D particleColorsTexture, ParticleSettings particleSettings,
    Effect particleEffect)
{
    this.position = position;
    this.lifeLeft = lifeLeft;
    this.numParticlesPerRound = numParticlesPerRound;
    this.maxParticles = maxParticles;
    this.roundTime = roundTime;
    this.graphicsDevice = graphicsDevice;
    this.particleSettings = particleSettings;
    this.particleEffect = particleEffect;
    this.particleColorsTexture = particleColorsTexture;

    InitializeParticleVertices();

}
```

As you can see, there's not a lot of magic happening here. Most of the logic in the constructor is there just to copy the data from the parameters to the class-level variables. At the end of the constructor, there's a call to InitializeParticles. This method will instantiate the particle arrays and vertex buffer, setting positions, random directions, random colors, and random sizes for each particle. Add the InitializeParticles method next, as follows:

```
private void InitializeParticleVertices()
{
    // Instantiate all particle arrays
    verts = new VertexPositionTexture[maxParticles * 4];
    vertexDirectionArray = new Vector3[maxParticles];
    vertexColorArray = new Color[maxParticles];

    // Get color data from colors texture
    Color[] colors = new Color[particleColorsTexture.Width *
        particleColorsTexture.Height];
    particleColorsTexture.GetData(colors);

    // Loop until max particles
    for (int i = 0; i < maxParticles; ++i)
    {
        float size = (float)rnd.NextDouble() * particleSettings.maxSize;

        // Set position, direction and size of particle
        verts[i * 4] = new VertexPositionTexture(position, new Vector2(0, 0));
        verts[(i * 4) + 1] = new VertexPositionTexture(new Vector3(position.X,
            position.Y + size, position.Z), new Vector2(0, 1));
        verts[(i * 4) + 2] = new VertexPositionTexture(new Vector3(position.X + size,
            position.Y, position.Z), new Vector2(1, 0));
        verts[(i * 4) + 3] = new VertexPositionTexture(new Vector3(position.X + size,
            position.Y + size, position.Z), new Vector2(1, 1));

        // Create a random velocity/direction
        Vector3 direction = new Vector3(
            (float)rnd.NextDouble() * 2 - 1,
            (float)rnd.NextDouble() * 2 - 1,
            (float)rnd.NextDouble() * 2 - 1);
        direction.Normalize();

        // Multiply by NextDouble to make sure that
        // all particles move at random speeds
        direction *= (float)rnd.NextDouble();

        // Set direction of particle
        vertexDirectionArray[i] = direction;

        // Set color of particle by getting a random color from the texture
        vertexColorArray[i] = colors[(
            rnd.Next(0, particleColorsTexture.Height) * particleColorsTexture.Width) +
            rnd.Next(0, particleColorsTexture.Width)];
    }

    // Instantiate vertex buffer
    particleVertexBuffer = new VertexBuffer(graphicsDevice,
        typeof(VertexPositionTexture), verts.Length, BufferUsage.None);

}
```

There's a lot going on here, so let's walk through it.

First, you're instantiating the three arrays that will store the data for your particles (`verts`, `vertexDirectionArray`, and `vertexColorArray`). Note that the direction and color arrays are set to the size of `maxParticles`, whereas the vertex array is set to `maxParticles` * 4. This is because the vertex array will actually store four vertices for each particle.

Next, you're creating an array of `Color` objects and using the `GetData` method from the `particleColorsTexture` object to fill the array. The `GetData` method of the `Texture2D` object will copy the color data from the texture into an array of type `Color`. You'll be using this colors array later on to assign random colors to particles.

Then, in the `for` loop, you build four vertices for each particle, using a random size and setting the texture UV coordinates accordingly. You also build a random direction for each particle and assign it to the direction array.

You may have noticed the call to `Normalize` the direction vector, after the random XYZ values are generated. Why would you need to do that? If you didn't, instead of your explosion particles exploding in a nice sphere, they would explode in a cube formation. The reason? The range of random values used to create the vector in the first place is from –1 to 1 in X, Y, and Z. This will result in the longest vector horizontally being (1, 0, 0) and the longest vector diagonally being (1, 1, 1), which, when hundreds of particles are created using these random direction vectors, will result in a cube formation. Remember that `Normalize` will make all vectors have a length of 1, so normalizing the vectors will maintain the random directions, but will change the magnitude of all the vectors to 1. That means you'll have a nice spherical shape—but it also means that all the particles will have the same speed, which is not what you want. To fix that problem, you multiply the vectors by a call to the `NextDouble` method from the `Random` object, which will vary the lengths of the vectors.

Finally, at the end of the `for` loop you pull a random color from the texture color array you built earlier in the method and assign it to each particle via the `vertexColorArray`.

At the end of the `InitializeParticleVertices` method, you instantiate the vertex buffer you'll use to draw the particles.

Now you'll need to code the `Update` method of the `ParticleExplosion` class. This method will be responsible for moving the particles, as well as adding new particles each round and removing old particles each round. Add the method as follows:

```
public void Update(GameTime gameTime)
{
    // Decrement life left until it's gone
    if (lifeLeft > 0)
        lifeLeft -= gameTime.ElapsedGameTime.Milliseconds;

    // Time for new round?
    timeSinceLastRound += gameTime.ElapsedGameTime.Milliseconds;
    if (timeSinceLastRound > roundTime)
    {
        // New round - add and remove particles
        timeSinceLastRound -= roundTime;
```

```
            // Increment end of live particles index each
            // round until end of list is reached
            if (endOfLiveParticlesIndex < maxParticles)
            {
                endOfLiveParticlesIndex += numParticlesPerRound;
                if (endOfLiveParticlesIndex > maxParticles)
                    endOfLiveParticlesIndex = maxParticles;
            }
            if (lifeLeft <= 0)
            {
                // Increment end of dead particles index each
                // round until end of list is reached
                if (endOfDeadParticlesIndex < maxParticles)
                {
                    endOfDeadParticlesIndex += numParticlesPerRound;
                    if (endOfDeadParticlesIndex > maxParticles)
                        endOfDeadParticlesIndex = maxParticles;
                }
            }
        }

        // Update positions of all live particles
        for (int i = endOfDeadParticlesIndex;
            i < endOfLiveParticlesIndex; ++i)
        {
            verts[i * 4].Position += vertexDirectionArray[i];
            verts[(i * 4) + 1].Position += vertexDirectionArray[i];
            verts[(i * 4) + 2].Position += vertexDirectionArray[i];
            verts[(i * 4) + 3].Position += vertexDirectionArray[i];

        }
    }
```

Let's take a closer look at the logic in this method. The method first decrements the
lifeLeft variable by the amount of time that has passed since the last call to Update.
Remember that when the lifeLeft variable hits zero, you'll start removing particles
each round.

Next, the timeSinceLastRound counter is incremented and checked to determine
whether a new round should begin. If it is time for a new round, new particles are added
to the list of drawn particles by incrementing the value of the endOfLiveParticles
Index variable. If the index variable is already at the end of the array (designated by
maxParticles), no more particles are added to the list of particles to draw.

Then, the lifeLeft variable is checked to see whether its value is less than 1 (indicating
that the explosion's life is over). If that is the case, the endOfDeadParticlesIndex variable
is incremented, which will cause particles to be removed from the list of drawn particles.
Once the endOfDeadParticlesIndex variable reaches the end of the array, it will not
move any further, and the IsDead property you added earlier will return true (indicating
to the ModelManager that the explosion has run its course and is ready for deletion).

Finally, the method updates the positions of all particles that are in the list to be drawn (i.e., all particles between the endOfDeadParticlesIndex and endOfLiveParticlesIndex variables).

Very nice. We're getting close to the end! All you have to do now is code up a Draw method for the explosion. This code should be pretty straightforward, as it's no different than the code that you've written to draw with previously:

```
public void Draw(Camera camera)
{
    graphicsDevice.SetVertexBuffer(particleVertexBuffer);

    // Only draw if there are live particles
    if (endOfLiveParticlesIndex - endOfDeadParticlesIndex > 0)
    {
        for (int i = endOfDeadParticlesIndex; i < endOfLiveParticlesIndex; ++i)
        {
            particleEffect.Parameters["WorldViewProjection"].SetValue(
                camera.view * camera.projection);
            particleEffect.Parameters["particleColor"].SetValue(
                vertexColorArray[i].ToVector4());

            // Draw particles
            foreach (EffectPass pass in particleEffect.CurrentTechnique.Passes)
            {
                pass.Apply();

                graphicsDevice.DrawUserPrimitives<VertexPositionTexture>(
                    PrimitiveType.TriangleStrip,
                    verts, i * 4, 2);

            }
        }
    }
}
```

The camera data is passed into the method as the only parameter. The first thing the method does is assign the vertex buffer to the graphics device.

Then, you'll check to see whether there are any particles left to draw in this explosion. You'll want to draw only if there are actually particles that need to be drawn (meaning that there are some particles in the array between the two index variables). If there are particles to draw, you begin looping through all live particles in the array.

For each live particle, you set the parameters of the Effect. There are two effect parameters: one you should be familiar with by now, representing the world, view, and projection matrices; and another representing the color for that particle.

Next, you loop through each of the passes in the effect and begin the pass by calling Apply. Notice the call to DrawUserPrimitives and the fact that it uses PrimitiveType. TriangleStrip for drawing. Also, notice that the index of the particle (the variable i from your for loop) provides the key to find the spot where you should start pulling data from your vertex array. There are four vertices per particle, so i * 4 will give you the starting point for each particle. The final parameter is how many primitives (in this case, two) you want to draw.

That's all there is to it. You now have a custom vertex, some settings classes to help determine how things will function, and an explosion class to manipulate and draw your particles. Very impressive! Now it's time to create the effect file you'll use to draw your particles.

Adding a Particle Effect File

First, you'll want to create a folder for your effects. Right-click the *Content* node in Solution Explorer and select Add→New Folder. Name the folder *Effects*. Then, right-click the new *Content\Effects* folder and select Add→New Item.... Select the Effect File template on the right side of the window and name the file *Particle.fx*, as shown in Figure 14-4.

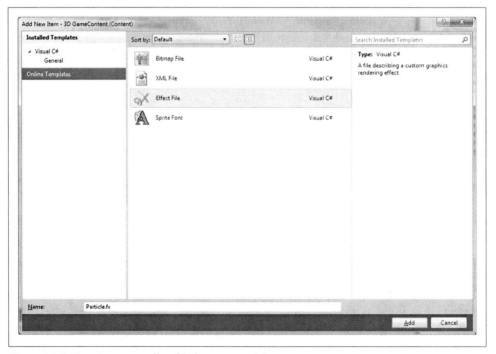

Figure 14-4. Creating a new effect file for your particles

Replace all of the code in your new *Particle.fx* file with the following effect code:

```
float4x4 WorldViewProjection;
Texture theTexture;
float4 particleColor;
```

```
sampler ColoredTextureSampler = sampler_state
{
    texture = <theTexture> ;
    magfilter = LINEAR;
    minfilter = LINEAR;
    mipfilter= POINT;
    AddressU = Clamp;
    AddressV = Clamp;
};

struct VertexShaderInput
{
    float4 Position : POSITION0;
    float2 textureCoordinates : TEXCOORD0;
};

struct VertexShaderOutput
{
    float4 Position : POSITION0;
    float2 textureCoordinates : TEXCOORD0;
};

struct PixelShaderInput
{
    float2 textureCoordinates : TEXCOORD0;
};

VertexShaderOutput VertexShaderFunction(VertexShaderInput input)
{
    VertexShaderOutput output;
    output.Position = mul(input.Position, WorldViewProjection);
    output.textureCoordinates = input.textureCoordinates;
    return output;
}

float4 PixelShaderFunction(PixelShaderInput input) : COLOR0
{
    float4 color = tex2D( ColoredTextureSampler, input.textureCoordinates);
    color.r = particleColor.r * color.a;
    color.g = particleColor.g * color.a;
    color.b = particleColor.b * color.a;
    return color;
}

technique Technique1
{
    pass Pass1
    {
        VertexShader = compile vs_2_0 VertexShaderFunction( );
        PixelShader = compile ps_2_0 PixelShaderFunction( );
    }
}
```

Most of this code should be somewhat familiar to you, as it's very similar to some of the examples in the previous chapter. Notice that you have a texture and a texture sampler. The texture coordinates are sent into the vertex shader input, then sent out to the vertex shader output, and finally into the pixel shader input.

Also notice the `particleColor` variable at the top of the file. This is the variable to which you assigned a random color for each particle. In your pixel shader function you can see that the method first pulls the color of the pixel from the texture for the particle. Remember earlier in the chapter when we discussed the two textures you'll use for each particle? The texture we're talking about now is the *particle.png* texture—the shaded white circle. Next, the pixel shader function modifies the color pulled from the *particle.png* texture by assigning it the RBG values from the color you passed into the effect (which was the random color you assigned it from the *particleColors.png* texture) and multiplying those values by the alpha value from the pixel. This allows you to keep the nice, round, shaded circle for each particle but also give the pixel the random color you wanted.

Why multiply the pixel color by the alpha value? Remember, your particles are square: you're just putting a circle-shaped texture on them so they don't look square. If you ignore the alpha (transparent) value for each pixel and simply slap a color on them, each pixel in the square will be drawn with that color, and you'd end up with lame-looking square particles. And come on, admit it, nobody wants square particles.

Adding Your Particle Engine to Your Game

Now that you have an effect and a particle engine, you need to modify your code to create explosions when ships are hit.

Open the `ModelManager` class, and let's get to work on adding some cool explosions to your game. Add the following class-level variables:

```
List<ParticleExplosion> explosions = new List<ParticleExplosion>();
ParticleExplosionSettings particleExplosionSettings = new ParticleExplosionSettings();
ParticleSettings particleSettings = new ParticleSettings();
Texture2D explosionTexture;
Texture2D explosionColorsTexture;
Effect explosionEffect;
```

These variables are all pretty self-explanatory: you have a list of `ParticleExplosions` so your class can update and draw them; an instance of both settings classes for your particles; and `Effect` and `Texture2D` objects for drawing your particles, an explosion texture, an explosion colors texture, and an effect.

Next, you'll need to load the resources for your particles, set the current technique of your particle effect, and set the texture for that effect as well. Modify the `LoadContent` method in your `ModelManager` class as follows:

```
protected override void LoadContent()
{
    // Load explosion textures and effect
    explosionTexture = Game.Content.Load<Texture2D>(@"Textures\Particle");
    explosionColorsTexture = Game.Content.Load<Texture2D>(@"Textures\ParticleColors");
    explosionEffect = Game.Content.Load<Effect>(@"effects\particle");

    // Set effect parameters that don't change per particle
    explosionEffect.CurrentTechnique = explosionEffect.Techniques["Technique1"];
    explosionEffect.Parameters["theTexture"].SetValue(explosionTexture);

    base.LoadContent();
}
```

In addition to loading your texture and effect, this code sets the current technique and the texture parameters of the effect, as those will not change throughout the course of the game.

Now, in the UpdateShots method of the ModelManager, you'll need to find the place where you determine whether a shot hits a ship. It's the only place in the class where you're calling the BasicModel CollidesWith method. The current code should look something like this:

```
if (shots[i].CollidesWith(models[j].GetModel,
    models[j].GetWorld(   )))
{
    // Collision! remove the ship and the shot.
    models.RemoveAt(j);
    shots.RemoveAt(i);
    --i;
    ((Game1)Game).PlayCue("Explosions");
    break;
}
```

Add the following lines of code at the top of the block, within that if(... Collides With...) statement (added lines are in bold):

```
if (shots[i].CollidesWith(models[j].GetModel,
    models[j].GetWorld(   )))
{
    // Collision! add an explosion.
    explosions.Add(new ParticleExplosion(GraphicsDevice,
        models[j].GetWorld().Translation,
        ((Game1)Game).rnd.Next(
            particleExplosionSettings.minLife,
            particleExplosionSettings.maxLife),
        ((Game1)Game).rnd.Next(
            particleExplosionSettings.minRoundTime,
            particleExplosionSettings.maxRoundTime),
        ((Game1)Game).rnd.Next(
            particleExplosionSettings.minParticlesPerRound,
            particleExplosionSettings.maxParticlesPerRound),
        ((Game1)Game).rnd.Next(
            particleExplosionSettings.minParticles,
            particleExplosionSettings.maxParticles),
```

```
        explosionColorsTexture, particleSettings,
        explosionEffect));

    // Remove the ship and the shot
    models.RemoveAt(j);
    shots.RemoveAt(i);
    --i;
    ((Game1)Game).PlayCue("Explosions");
    break;
}
```

This might look like a lot of code, but really all it's doing is creating a new ParticleEx plosion using the location of the ship (via the ship's world matrix Translation method) and using random values for the settings, as defined in your settings classes.

Although this will create an explosion, your class still needs to update the explosion and draw it in each frame. Add the following method to the ModelManager class to update explosions and remove them once they are finished:

```
protected void UpdateExplosions(GameTime gameTime)
{
    // Loop through and update explosions
    for (int i = 0; i < explosions.Count; ++i)
    {
        explosions[i].Update(gameTime);
        // If explosion is finished, remove it
        if (explosions[i].IsDead)
        {
            explosions.RemoveAt(i);
            --i;
        }
    }
}
```

Then, call the UpdateExplosions method at the end of the Update method, just before the call to base.Update:

```
// Update explosions
UpdateExplosions(gameTime);
```

This code will update each explosion in the list by calling the explosion's Update method. In addition, if an explosion is finished (determined by the IsDead accessor), it is removed from the list.

Finally, in the Draw method of your ModelManager class, add the following code to loop through all explosions and call their Draw methods immediately before the call to base.Draw:

```
// Loop through and draw each particle explosion
foreach (ParticleExplosion pe in explosions)
{
    pe.Draw(((Game1)Game).camera);
}
```

Boom! You're ready to go! Nice work. Compile and run the game and see what happens when you blow an enemy to oblivion. You should see a cool explosion effect like the one pictured in Figure 14-5.

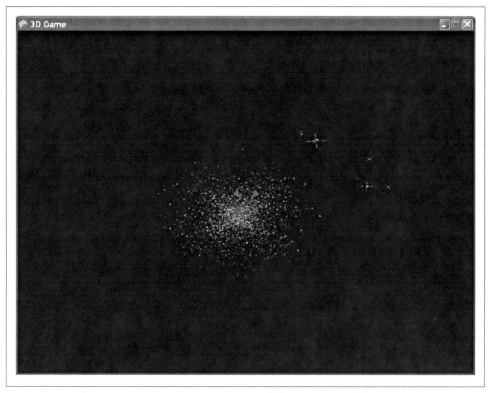

Figure 14-5. Luke: "Got 'im! I got 'im!" Han: "Great, kid. Don't get cocky."

Adding a Starfield

Given the way that you've created your particles and your particle engine, you're perfectly set up for creating a field of stars in the background to make this look more like outer space. To do this, you'll need to create a new version of your `Particle Explosion` class that treats the particles a little bit differently. For example, the particles you use for stars in the background won't move around the screen the way the ones in the explosions do. You also won't be deleting stars from the list of stars to draw, nor will your star particle engine die out at some time: the stars will be the same at the end of the game as they were at the beginning.

Add a new class to your project by right-clicking the solution and selecting Add→Class.... Name the class *ParticleStarSheet*. Then, replace the code in the file that is generated with the following:

```csharp
using System;
using Microsoft.Xna.Framework;
using Microsoft.Xna.Framework.Graphics;

namespace _3D_Game
{
    class ParticleStarSheet
    {
        // Particle arrays and vertex buffer
        VertexPositionTexture[] verts;
        Color[] vertexColorArray;
        VertexBuffer particleVertexBuffer;

        // Behavior variables
        Vector3 maxPosition;
        int maxParticles;
        static Random rnd = new Random();

        // Vertex and graphics info
        GraphicsDevice graphicsDevice;

        // Settings
        ParticleSettings particleSettings;

        // Effect
        Effect particleEffect;

        // Textures
        Texture2D particleColorsTexture;


        public ParticleStarSheet(GraphicsDevice graphicsDevice,
            Vector3 maxPosition, int maxParticles, Texture2D particleColorsTexture,
            ParticleSettings particleSettings, Effect particleEffect)
        {
            this.maxParticles = maxParticles;
            this.graphicsDevice = graphicsDevice;
            this.particleSettings = particleSettings;
            this.particleEffect = particleEffect;
            this.particleColorsTexture = particleColorsTexture;
            this.maxPosition = maxPosition;

            InitializeParticleVertices();

        }

        private void InitializeParticleVertices()
        {
            // Instantiate all particle arrays
            verts = new VertexPositionTexture[maxParticles * 4];
            vertexColorArray = new Color[maxParticles];
```

```
    // Get color data from colors texture
    Color[] colors = new Color[particleColorsTexture.Width *
        particleColorsTexture.Height];
    particleColorsTexture.GetData(colors);

    // Loop until max particles
    for (int i = 0; i < maxParticles; ++i)
    {
        float size = (float)rnd.NextDouble() * particleSettings.maxSize;

        Vector3 position = new Vector3(
            rnd.Next(-(int)maxPosition.X, (int)maxPosition.X),
            rnd.Next(-(int)maxPosition.Y, (int)maxPosition.Y),
            maxPosition.Z);

        // Set position and size of particle
        verts[i * 4] = new VertexPositionTexture(position, new Vector2(0, 0));
        verts[(i * 4) + 1] = new VertexPositionTexture(
            new Vector3(position.X, position.Y + size, position.Z),
            new Vector2(0, 1));
        verts[(i * 4) + 2] = new VertexPositionTexture(
            new Vector3(position.X + size, position.Y, position.Z),
            new Vector2(1, 0));
        verts[(i * 4) + 3] = new VertexPositionTexture(
            new Vector3(position.X + size, position.Y + size, position.Z),
            new Vector2(1, 1));

        // Set color of particle by getting a random color from the texture
        vertexColorArray[i] = colors[(rnd.Next(0,
            particleColorsTexture.Height) *
            particleColorsTexture.Width) +
            rnd.Next(0, particleColorsTexture.Width)];

    }

    // Instantiate vertex buffer
    particleVertexBuffer = new VertexBuffer(graphicsDevice,
        typeof(VertexPositionTexture), verts.Length, BufferUsage.None);

}


public void Draw(Camera camera)
{
    graphicsDevice.SetVertexBuffer(particleVertexBuffer);

    for (int i = 0; i < maxParticles; ++i)
    {
        particleEffect.Parameters["WorldViewProjection"].SetValue(
            camera.view * camera.projection);
        particleEffect.Parameters["particleColor"].SetValue(
            vertexColorArray[i].ToVector4());
```

```
            // Draw particles
            foreach (EffectPass pass in particleEffect.CurrentTechnique.Passes)
            {
                pass.Apply();

                graphicsDevice.DrawUserPrimitives<VertexPositionTexture>(
                    PrimitiveType.TriangleStrip,
                    verts, i * 4, 2);

            }
        }
    }
}
```

I won't go into a lot of detail about this class, because there's nothing here that you didn't see in the previous class you created. One key difference is that this class accepts a `Vector3` parameter called `maxPosition`. Whereas the `ParticleExplosion` class used the position of the exploding ship as an initial position for all its particles, this class will instead use random X and Y values and a constant Z value for the positions of all of its particles. This `maxPosition` variable is used in such a way that all star particles will have positions between `-maxPosition.X` and `+maxPosition.X`, `-maxPosition.Y` and `+maxPosition.Y`, and `maxPosition.Z`.

The other key difference between this class and the `ParticleExplosion` class is that this class draws all particles in the array and doesn't move or delete them (notice the `Update` method is missing altogether). All the logic for rounds is gone as well.

To use this class, you'll want to add a different texture for the stars. Stars will be more white and yellow than the particles in your explosions, which are often red and brown. In the *3D Game\3D GameContent\Textures* folder included with the source code for this chapter, there is a file called *Stars.png*. Add it to your project by right-clicking the *3D GameContent\Textures*folder in Solution Explorer, selecting Add→Existing Item..., and navigating to the *Stars.png* file and selecting it.

Now, add the following class-level variables to your `ModelManager` class:

```
ParticleStarSheet stars;
Effect starEffect;
Texture2D starTexture;
```

Next, in the LoadContent method of your ModelManager class, add the following code just before the call to base.LoadContent:

```
// Load star texture and effect
starTexture = Game.Content.Load<Texture2D>(@"textures\stars");
starEffect = explosionEffect.Clone();
starEffect.CurrentTechnique = starEffect.Techniques["Technique1"];
starEffect.Parameters["theTexture"].SetValue(explosionTexture);

// Initialize particle star sheet
stars = new ParticleStarSheet(
    GraphicsDevice,
    new Vector3(2000, 2000, -1900),
    1500, starTexture,
    particleSettings,
    starEffect);
```

In this code, you first load the texture into the Texture2D object, and then you take the explosion effect and make a copy of it using the Clone method. This will create a duplicate (but separate) effect. You do this so you can set the theTexture variable within the HLSL file differently for stars and explosions.

The other thing you're doing here is creating an initial starfield. This is done here because stars will exist throughout the game, rather than only at certain times such as with the explosions. Notice also that you're assigning the explosionTexture to the theTexture parameter of the star effect. This is because you'll still use that texture to create the round shape of the stars. You're using the new starTexture only for the color of the stars, which is why you pass it into the constructor of the ParticleStarSheet object.

Your stars never need to be updated because they won't ever move, so all that's left to do is to add a line of code that will draw the stars. Add the following line to the Draw method of your ModelManager class just before the call to base.Draw:

```
stars.Draw(((Game1)Game).camera);
```

Not bad at all. You're now using your Particle struct for stars and explosions. Compile and run the game and see how much better it looks with some stars in the background. You should see something like the image shown in Figure 14-6.

Well, you're almost done. The game is looking nice, and things are really coming together. All that's left now is to add some scoring and make your game levels work, and you'll have finished your first awesome XNA 3D game!

Figure 14-6. Stars make the game look much more realistic

What You Just Did

Before we get into all of that, let's review what you did this chapter:

- You learned about particles and particle systems.
- You created a particle engine that moves, adds, and removes particles to create a sphere-shaped explosion.
- You created an HLSL effect file that sets the shape of a particle based on one texture and the color based on a different texture.
- You created a starfield background using a modified particle engine that draws particles but doesn't remove them or move them around.

Summary

- A particle is simply a way of representing a single element within a group of elements that form a particle effect, such as an explosion or some magical spell effect.
- A particle engine is a mechanism that manipulates, adds, removes, and draws particles to make up a particle effect. Often, particle engines simulate gravity and other external forces to make particle effects look more realistic.
- Particle engines can be used for more than just cool effects. You can build things such as star sheets with a very similar model.
- Anyone who knows XNA and can create sweet particle effects will have more friends than they know what to do with.

Test Your Knowledge: Quiz

1. What is a particle engine?
2. Why were there two textures used for the particles in your explosion? What was the purpose of each?
3. What are texture (U, V) coordinates?
4. According to Napoleon Dynamite's Uncle Rico, how far could Uncle Rico throw a "pigskin" back in 1982?

CHAPTER 15

Wrapping Up Your 3D Game

Here we go—you're at the final stage in the development of your first 3D game. It looks good, sounds good, and plays well, and all that's left to do is to add some game logic and wrap it up. First things first: you need a splash screen when your game starts. In addition, you'll need to provide the player with some kind of an indicator when she reaches another level in the game. Why not use a splash screen between levels, too? Finally, you'll need to have a screen that displays the final score when the game is over. Sounds like a good solution to these problems would be to create a splash screen game component that will let you display text on the screen. That way, you can reuse the same class for all three purposes just mentioned—and let's face it, anytime you can reuse code, you're saving yourself all kinds of time and headaches.

This chapter picks up where Chapter 14 left off. Open the project that you were working on at the end of Chapter 14 and use it throughout this chapter.

Adding a Splash Screen Game Component

Before we jump in and code your splash screen component, let's step back and look at how this is going to work. Your Game1 class is going to manage different game states. Several states are possible: starting the game, playing the game, pausing the game between levels, and showing a game-over screen at the end of the game.

To help you manage these states, create an enum in your Game1 class that you will use to track changes from state to state during gameplay. Add the following lines of code at the class level of your Game1 class:

```
public enum GameState { START, PLAY, LEVEL_CHANGE, END}
GameState currentGameState = GameState.START;
```

In these lines, you first define an enum called GameState that enumerates all the possible game states, and then you create a variable that you'll use to track the current game state and initialize that variable to the START game state. That should be helpful as you move through this chapter.

You'll also need to add a way for the splash screen game component and the model manager game component to notify the Game1 class when a change in game state occurs. To that end, add the following method to the Game1 class:

```
public void ChangeGameState(GameState state, int level)
{
    currentGameState = state;
}
```

Later, you'll add more logic to this method that will make use of the second parameter and will perform different tasks based on the changed game state. For now, this will do.

To add a splash screen game component, first you'll need to create a blank game component class. Add a game component to your project and call the file *SplashScreen.cs*.

Remember that by default a game component does not have a Draw method and therefore will not draw anything. But what good would a splash screen component be if you couldn't use it to draw text? Change the base class of the new game component from GameComponent to DrawableGameComponent, which will let your game component tie into the game loop's Draw sequence.

Next, add the following class-level variables to your splash screen game component:

```
string textToDraw;
string secondaryTextToDraw;
SpriteFont spriteFont;
SpriteFont secondarySpriteFont;
SpriteBatch spriteBatch;
Game1.GameState currentGameState;
```

Your splash screen will have the ability to display a header in a larger font and some other text in a smaller font. The two SpriteFont variables and the SpriteBatch variable are included to facilitate the drawing of that text. Your currentGameState variable will track the current game state, so your splash screen will know what to do based on what state the game is currently in.

As you've probably guessed based on the SpriteFont variables you added, you now need to add a couple of spritefonts to your project. Right-click the *3D GameContent* node in Solution Explorer and select Add→New Folder. Name the new folder *Fonts*. Then, right-click the new *Fonts* folder and select Add→New Item.... Select the Sprite Font template on the right and name your font *SplashScreenFont.spritefont*, as shown in Figure 15-1.

Next, add another spritefont (following the same steps), and call this one *SplashScreen-FontLarge.spritefont*.

You're going to use the SplashScreenFontLarge spritefont for the larger title text in the window. Open that file, and you'll see that the content is XML-based. The second element of the font is a <Size> element. Change your SplashScreenFontLarge spritefont's size to 16 by modifying that element as follows:

```
<Size>16</Size>
```

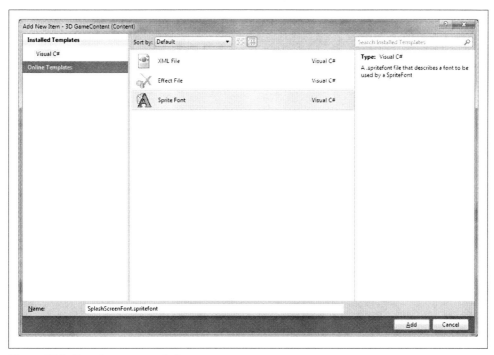

Figure 15-1. Creating a new spritefont

To make the larger text stand out a bit more, go ahead and modify the size of the SplashScreenFont spritefont as well. Open the *SplashScreenFont.spritefont* file and change the font to be smaller (size 10):

```
<Size>10</Size>
```

Next, in your SplashScreen class, you'll need to add an override for the LoadContent method so you can load the spritefonts and initialize your SpriteBatch object. Add the following code in the SplashScreen class:

```
protected override void LoadContent(  )
{
    // Load fonts
    spriteFont = Game.Content.Load<SpriteFont>(@"fonts\SplashScreenFontLarge");
    secondarySpriteFont = Game.Content.Load<SpriteFont>(@"fonts\SplashScreenFont");

    // Create sprite batch
    spriteBatch = new SpriteBatch(Game.GraphicsDevice);

    base.LoadContent(  );
}
```

Your splash screen will display at the beginning of the game, at the end of the game, and between levels. But how will you make the game transition from splash screen to gameplay or game exit? What's the best way to do that? That's a good question, and there really is no right answer. This is another aspect of game development that comes down to personal preference. Often, splash screens are time-based and will fade to the next game state after a few moments. Others may disappear when a key is pressed or a mouse button is clicked. Still others aren't even separate screens, but are just overlaid during gameplay and fade out slowly. Exactly how you want to do this is all up to you.

For the purposes of this book, we're going to make the screens transition by pressing the Enter key. To implement that, you'll need to catch any Enter key presses in the Update method of your SplashScreen class. If an Enter key press is detected, you'll either notify the Game1 class that a change in game state is needed or exit the game completely. Which of those you do depends on the current game state (i.e., is the SplashScreen component currently showing a start, level-change, or game-over screen?).

Change the Update method of your SplashScreen class to the following:

```
public override void Update(GameTime gameTime)
{
    // Did the player hit Enter?
    if (Keyboard.GetState( ).IsKeyDown(Keys.Enter))
    {
        // If we're not in end game, move to play state
        if (currentGameState == Game1.GameState.LEVEL_CHANGE ||
            currentGameState == Game1.GameState.START)
            ((Game1)Game).ChangeGameState(Game1.GameState.PLAY, 0);

        // If we are in end game, exit
        else if (currentGameState == Game1.GameState.END)
            Game.Exit( );
    }

    base.Update(gameTime);
}
```

Because the splash screen should never be displayed during the PLAY game state, the only states that you're checking for are START, LEVEL_CHANGE, and END. If the current state is either of the first two, you're going to transition to a PLAY state, so you call the Game1 class's ChangeGameState and notify the class of that change. If the current state is END, the game exits when the player presses the Enter key.

Next, you need to add the code that will actually draw the text. Of course, this is done in a Draw method, which you currently do not have. You'll need to create an override of the Draw method and add the code to draw the large title text and the smaller subtitle text:

```
public override void Draw(GameTime gameTime)
{
    spriteBatch.Begin( );

    // Get size of string
    Vector2 TitleSize = spriteFont.MeasureString(textToDraw);

    // Draw main text
    spriteBatch.DrawString(spriteFont, textToDraw,
```

```
            new Vector2(Game.Window.ClientBounds.Width / 2
                - TitleSize.X / 2,
                Game.Window.ClientBounds.Height / 2),
                Color.Gold);

        // Draw subtext
        spriteBatch.DrawString(secondarySpriteFont,
            secondaryTextToDraw,
            new Vector2(Game.Window.ClientBounds.Width / 2
                - secondarySpriteFont.MeasureString(
                    secondaryTextToDraw).X / 2,
                Game.Window.ClientBounds.Height / 2 +
                TitleSize.Y + 10),
                Color.Gold);

        spriteBatch.End( );

        base.Draw(gameTime);
    }
```

Notice that the first call to DrawString uses the larger SpriteFont object and centers the text using the screen width and height, as well as the TitleSize Vector2 object, which holds the size of the title text as given by the SpriteFont.MeasureString method. The second DrawString call also centers the text horizontally the same way, but it places the text vertically just below the title text by using the size of the title text as an offset.

The final piece of the SplashScreen class is a method that will enable the Game1 class to set the text that needs to be displayed and to set the current game state. Add this method to the SplashScreen class:

```
public void SetData(string main, Game1.GameState currGameState)
{
    textToDraw = main;
    this.currentGameState = currGameState;

    switch (currentGameState)
    {
        case Game1.GameState.START:
        case Game1.GameState.LEVEL_CHANGE:
            secondaryTextToDraw = "Press ENTER to begin";
            break;
        case Game1.GameState.END:
            secondaryTextToDraw = "Press ENTER to quit";
            break;
    }
}
```

The secondary text is set depending on the game state, whereas the primary text is passed into the method with the new game state. Now that your SplashScreen class is ready to go, all you need to do is hook up the component to your game. Add a Splash Screen variable at the class level of your Game1 class, together with a variable to keep track of scoring. You'll be adding scoring to the game later, and you'll want to display the player's score when the game is over:

```
SplashScreen splashScreen;
int score = 0;
```

Next, you'll need to initialize the SplashScreen component and add it to the list of game components in Game1's Initialize method. Currently, the method looks like this:

```
protected override void Initialize()
{
    // Initialize Camera
    camera = new Camera(this, new Vector3(0, 0, 50),
        Vector3.Zero, Vector3.Up);
    Components.Add(camera);

    // Initialize model manager
    modelManager = new ModelManager(this);
    Components.Add(modelManager);

    base.Initialize();
}
```

Modify the Initialize method as shown here (added lines are in bold):

```
protected override void Initialize( )
{
    // Initialize Camera
    camera = new Camera(this, new Vector3(0, 0, 50),
        Vector3.Zero, Vector3.Up);
    Components.Add(camera);

    // Initialize model manager
    modelManager = new ModelManager(this);
    Components.Add(modelManager);
    modelManager.Enabled = false;
    modelManager.Visible = false;

    // Splash screen component
    splashScreen = new SplashScreen(this);
    Components.Add(splashScreen);
    splashScreen.SetData("Welcome to Space Defender!",
        currentGameState);

    base.Initialize( );
}
```

The first two lines are added directly after the Components.Add(modelManager) line. These lines disable the modelManager component. Why are you doing this? Because you're going to begin your game with the splash screen. When the splash screen is active, the model manager needs to be inactive, and vice versa. Next, you initialize the SplashScreen component, add it to the list of components, and set its initial values via the SetData method.

The next thing you'll need to look at is the Update method. Currently, every time Update is called, you're checking the keyboard for a space bar key press and, if one occurs, firing a shot. You're going to want to do this now only if the current game state is set to PLAY.

The current `Update` method of your `Game1` class should look something like this:

```
protected override void Update(GameTime gameTime)
{
    // Allows the game to exit
    if (GamePad.GetState(PlayerIndex.One).Buttons.Back ==
        ButtonState.Pressed)
        this.Exit( );

    // See if the player has fired a shot
    FireShots(gameTime);

    base.Update(gameTime);
}
```

Surround the call to the `FireShots` method with an `if` statement so that new shots will be fired only if the game is in the PLAY state:

```
// Only check for shots if you're in the play game state
if (currentGameState == GameState.PLAY)
{
    // See if the player has fired a shot
    FireShots(gameTime);
}
```

Next, you'll need to do the same sort of thing in the `Draw` method, as you're currently drawing a crosshair every time that method is called. Surround that code with a similar `if` statement so that the crosshair is drawn only if the game is in the PLAY state (the added code is in bold):

```
protected override void Draw(GameTime gameTime)
{
    GraphicsDevice.Clear(Color.Black);

    base.Draw(gameTime);

    // Only draw crosshair if in play game state
    if (currentGameState == GameState.PLAY)
    {
        // Draw the crosshair
        spriteBatch.Begin( );

        spriteBatch.Draw(crosshairTexture,
            new Vector2((Window.ClientBounds.Width / 2)
                - (crosshairTexture.Width / 2),
                (Window.ClientBounds.Height / 2)
                - (crosshairTexture.Height / 2)),
                Color.White);

        spriteBatch.End( );
    }
}
```

Finally, you'll need to flesh out the `ChangeGameState` method. Currently, all it does is set the `currentGameState` variable. You'll need to add some action to stop or play the soundtrack music and enable/disable the splash screen and model manager components, based on the game state to which the game is transitioning. Modify the method as follows:

```
public void ChangeGameState(GameState state, int level)
{
    currentGameState = state;

    switch (currentGameState)
    {
        case GameState.LEVEL_CHANGE:
            splashScreen.SetData("Level " + (level + 1),
                GameState.LEVEL_CHANGE);
            modelManager.Enabled = false;
            modelManager.Visible = false;
            splashScreen.Enabled = true;
            splashScreen.Visible = true;

            // Stop the soundtrack loop
            trackCue.Stop(AudioStopOptions.Immediate);
            break;

        case GameState.PLAY:
            modelManager.Enabled = true;
            modelManager.Visible = true;
            splashScreen.Enabled = false;
            splashScreen.Visible = false;

            if (trackCue.IsPlaying)
                trackCue.Stop(AudioStopOptions.Immediate);

            // To play a stopped cue, get the cue from the soundbank again
            trackCue = soundBank.GetCue("Tracks");
            trackCue.Play();
            break;

        case GameState.END:
            splashScreen.SetData("Game Over.\nLevel: " + (level + 1) +
                "\nScore: " + score, GameState.END);
            modelManager.Enabled = false;
            modelManager.Visible = false;
            splashScreen.Enabled = true;
            splashScreen.Visible = true;

            // Stop the soundtrack loop
            trackCue.Stop(AudioStopOptions.Immediate);
            break;
    }
}
```

OK, we're almost there. You have a game that starts in a splash screen mode based on the START state. Your splash screen transitions to the PLAY state or exits the game, based on the current state. The last step in this process is to add the logic to transition from PLAY to LEVEL_CHANGE or END.

First, let's take care of the PLAY→LEVEL_CHANGE transition. Remember that you coded the game to spawn X number of enemy ships per level. The transition to a new level should take place when the final ship has passed the camera or been destroyed. To make the game flow a little better, let's also add the stipulation that all explosions should be finished as well. That way, when you destroy the final ship, the game won't immediately go to a splash screen but instead will let you witness the explosion, and then make the transition.

In the CheckToSpawnEnemy method of your ModelManager class, you have an if statement that checks to see whether the number of enemies spawned in this level is less than the number of enemies allowed in this level (if (enemiesThisLevel < levelInfoList [currentLevel].numberEnemies)). If this condition is true, there are more enemies to be spawned in this level, and you're checking to see whether it's time to spawn a new enemy. However, if it's false, that is your first indication that it's time to move to a new level. Add to that if statement the following else block, which will check to see whether all explosions have been wrapped up and, if so, transition to a new level (the entire method is shown here for clarity):

```
protected void CheckToSpawnEnemy(GameTime gameTime)
{
    // Time to spawn a new enemy?
    if (enemiesThisLevel <
        levelInfoList[currentLevel].numberEnemies)
    {
        timeSinceLastSpawn += gameTime.ElapsedGameTime.Milliseconds;
        if (timeSinceLastSpawn > nextSpawnTime)
        {
            SpawnEnemy( );
        }
    }
    else
    {
        if (explosions.Count == 0 && models.Count == 0)
        {
            // ALL EXPLOSIONS AND SHIPS ARE REMOVED AND THE LEVEL IS OVER
            ++currentLevel;
            enemiesThisLevel = 0;
            missedThisLevel = 0;
            ((Game1)Game).ChangeGameState(
                Game1.GameState.LEVEL_CHANGE,
                currentLevel);
        }
    }
}
```

If all ships and explosions have been removed from their respective lists and the number of enemies to be spawned in this level has been reached, you have nothing else to do in this level and it's time to move to the next. To move to the next level, you need to increment the currentLevel variable, reset a couple of counters (enemiesThisLevel and missedThisLevel), and notify the Game1 class of the change in game state.

That's all there is to it. Now, let's add a transition from the PLAY to the END game state.

In the UpdateModels method of the ModelManager class, you have two places where you remove ships from the list of ships using models.RemoveAt. One of these is the case where a player shoots a ship, and the other is the case where a ship gets past the camera and escapes. The game will end when more ships escape than are allowed per level. You have a variable set up to track that already (missedThisLevel), but you aren't doing anything with it. The current UpdateModels method looks like this:

```
protected void UpdateModels( )
{
    // Loop through all models and call Update
    for (int i = 0; i < models.Count; ++i)
    {
        // Update each model
        models[i].Update( );

        // Remove models that are out of bounds
        if (models[i].GetWorld( ).Translation.Z >
            ((Game1)Game).camera.cameraPosition.Z + 100)
        {
            models.RemoveAt(i);
            --i;
        }
    }
}
```

Modify the UpdateModels method to increment the missedThisLevel variable when a ship escapes and to move the game to an end-game state when the maximum number of missed ships is reached. The new method should look like this (added lines are in bold):

```
protected void UpdateModels( )
{
    // Loop through all models and call Update
    for (int i = 0; i < models.Count; ++i)
    {
        // Update each model
        models[i].Update( );

        // Remove models that are out of bounds
        if (models[i].GetWorld( ).Translation.Z >
            ((Game1)Game).camera.cameraPosition.Z + 100)
        {
```

```
        // If player has missed more than allowed, game over
        ++missedThisLevel;
        if (missedThisLevel >
            levelInfoList[currentLevel].missesAllowed)
        {
            ((Game1)Game).ChangeGameState(
                Game1.GameState.END, currentLevel);
        }

        models.RemoveAt(i);
        --i;
    }
  }
}
```

Basically, what's happening here is that every time a ship escapes, you increment the missedThisLevel variable. When that variable exceeds the number of misses allowed, the game is over and the Game1 class is notified.

OK, let's give it a shot. Compile and run your game, and you should be greeted with a nice intro splash screen (see Figure 15-2). You can also play the game now, and it should transition from level to level and display another splash screen when the game is over.

Figure 15-2. Nice welcoming intro splash screen

Because your splash screen is a game component, you can customize it just like you would when programming a game. Add a fancy background image, add sound...do whatever you want to make it more exciting and fun.

End-Game Logic

Note that there is only one way to end this game, and that is in failure. There is no logic to "win" the game. Why? What are the pros and cons of this model?

This is actually a common model for an arcade-style game. The idea is to make the game harder and harder until it is impossible for anybody to go further. One benefit of this approach is that players always have a reason to keep playing: there is no end, and the only goal is to beat the previous high score.

One drawback to this approach is that you're banking on the fact that nobody can ever get past the portion of the game that you deem "impossible." For example, in the game you're developing now, spawn times are shortened, more ships are spawned, and fewer escaped ships are allowed in each level. This continues until, in the final level, 48 ships are spawned, one every 0–200 milliseconds, and 0 missed ships are allowed. That's pretty close to impossible. However, it's important to note that your game would look really stupid if somebody actually beat that level. Essentially, your game would crash, and if it were a professionally developed game, that would be a hot topic on forums all over the Internet.

The stage where a game breaks because the player has reached the point at which there is no more logic to support continued gameplay is referred to as a "kill screen." Some of the more famous kill screens include *Pac-Man* crashing when the player reaches the 256th level, *Donkey Kong* crashing when the player reaches the 22nd stage or the 117th screen, and *Duck Hunt* crashing when the player reaches level 100. Look these up on the Internet, and you'll see how much buzz is generated when a player discovers how to break a video game. That's not exactly press that you want your game to receive, so it's a good idea to either add logic to your game to let the player ultimately win or make sure that it is literally impossible for anybody to reach the end of your game logic.

Keeping Score

You have levels and end-game logic now, but what's the fun when your score is always zero? In this section, you'll flesh out scoring for the game. You're already displaying the score at the end of the game, but you'll want to let players see their scores as they play. To do that, add a class-level `SpriteFont` variable to your `Game1` class, with which you'll draw the score:

```
SpriteFont scoreFont;
```

And yes, that's right: the next thing that you'll need to do is add a new spritefont to your project. Right-click the *3D GameContent\Fonts* folder in Solution Explorer and select Add→New Item.... Select the Sprite Font template on the right and name the file *ScoreFont.spritefont*.

To make your scoring font stand out a bit more, open the *ScoreFont.spritefont* file and find the `<Style>` element. This element lets you tweak properties such as setting the text in bold, italics, etc. Change the spritefont to use a bold font by changing the `<Style>` tag as follows:

```
<Style>Bold</Style>
```

 The `<Style>` tag entries are case-sensitive, as it says in the actual sprite-font file. Make sure you use the text `Bold` instead of `bold` or `BOLD`.

Next, in the `LoadContent` method of your `Game1` class, add the following code to load the font:

```
scoreFont = Content.Load<SpriteFont>(@"Fonts\ScoreFont");
```

Now you'll want to use that spritefont to draw the score on the screen. In addition to just drawing the score, though, it would be helpful for players to see how many more ships they can miss in each level.

To do that, you'll need to add a way for the `Game1` class to check how many misses are left (that data is stored in your `ModelManager` class). Add the following public accessor to the `ModelManager` class:

```
public int missesLeft
{
    get { return
        levelInfoList[currentLevel].missesAllowed
        - missedThisLevel; }
}
```

Now that you have the information you need to display on the screen, it's time to look at drawing the text on the screen. Being as brilliant as you are (yes, being smart enough to purchase this book denotes a certain level of brilliance), you've probably already realized that you need to do this in the `Draw` method of your `Game1` class. Remember that spritefonts are drawn with the `SpriteBatch.DrawString` method, and because they use a `SpriteBatch` object, that code must be between the `SpriteBatch.Begin` and `SpriteBatch.End` calls.

So, add the following code between the `SpriteBatch.Begin` and `SpriteBatch.End` calls in the `Draw` method of your `Game1` class:

```
// Draw the current score
string scoreText = "Score: " + score;
spriteBatch.DrawString(scoreFont, scoreText,
    new Vector2(10, 10), Color.Red);

// Let the player know how many misses he has left
spriteBatch.DrawString(scoreFont, "Misses Left: " +
    modelManager.missesLeft,
    new Vector2(10, scoreFont.MeasureString(scoreText).Y + 20),
    Color.Red);
```

Keep the Player Informed

Why is it such a big deal to show the number of misses left?

When developing any game, the more you can do to free the players of needless head-aches and worries, the better. That lets them focus on the gameplay and relax and enjoy the experience. It's not uncommon in more complex games for the screen to be riddled with indicators and notification methods to make the game experience better.

So, here's a question: if you add a text indicator to the screen showing how many misses are left, is that enough? That's a personal decision. Again, this is game development, and it's a creative process. But consider what else could be done. What if you added a sound effect that played whenever a miss occurred? Then a player could tell something negative had happened without having to look around. What if an alert sound played when the player has three or fewer misses left? Maybe the text could start flashing at that point, too. These are little changes and are easy to implement, but they can dra-matically improve gameplay and should be considered in your overall design.

Finally, there has to be a way to adjust the score. The `score` variable is part of your `Game1` class, but the means for detecting when a change in score should occur (i.e., when a shot hits a ship) lies in the `ModelManager` class. You'll need to add a method to your `Game1` class that will let your `ModelManager` adjust the score:

```
public void AddPoints(int points)
{
    score += points;
}
```

This very simple method will add points passed in as a parameter to the overall point total.

Now all that's left is to add the scoring mechanism to the `ModelManager` class itself. First, let's figure out how many points each kill is worth. This is another area where you can be creative and figure out a formula that works for you. A couple of common methods are using either a flat system (i.e., all ships are always worth X points) or an increased payoff method (i.e., ships are worth more and more points as the game progresses). For this game, you're going to implement the latter strategy. But first, you need a start-ing point. Add the following class-level variable to your `ModelManager` class:

```
const int pointsPerKill = 20;
```

You'll take this initial value and multiply it by the current level to give the actual point value for each kill (e.g., level-1 kills are worth 20, level-2 kills are worth 40, etc.). The last step here is to add the actual score change. Remember that in the `ModelManager` class there are two places where you call `models.RemoveAt` to remove an enemy ship: in the `UpdateModels` method, when a ship escapes and is out of bounds, and in the `UpdateShots` method, when a shot hits a ship.

You're going to need to add some code that will update the score when a shot hits a ship. At the end of the `UpdateShots` method there is a call to `models.RemoveAt` that removes the ship, followed by a call to `shots.RemoveAt` that removes the shot that hit the ship. Immediately before those calls to `RemoveAt`, add the following line, which will adjust the game score:

```
((Game1)Game).AddPoints(pointsPerKill * (currentLevel + 1));
```

Scoring Logic

Does scoring have to be this simple?

Absolutely not. Again, this is a very creative process, and the method for calculating the score can be whatever you want it to be. Can you think of something you could add to make scoring more interesting?

What about subtracting points for shots that weren't successful? This would make the game more interesting, in that it would discourage players from simply holding down the space bar and shooting steady streams of shots at the enemies.

However, remember that with more complicated scoring, more explanation is required. We're using a fairly straightforward method right now, and it's expected by the player, so no explanation is needed—you shoot ships, you get points. But imagine how surprised the player would be if the score started dropping for some reason, without any explanation! If you don't want your players to get extremely annoyed, they need to fully understand the rules of the game, and as the rules become more complex, more explanation is required.

There you have it. Now all that's left to do is play your game and challenge your friends to beat your score. The end-game screen is shown in Figure 15-3, with a stellar score.

Figure 15-3. 680! Simply amazing…

Adding a Power-Up

You've done well here: you've built your first 3D game, complete with scoring and increasingly difficult levels, and packed with a ton of fun! Before we end this chapter, though, let's do one more thing. Not that games are boring, but anything that breaks up the monotony of regular gameplay goes a long way toward making a game even more exciting and addicting.

In this section, you'll add a power-up feature that will be awarded when a player gets three consecutive kills. The power-up will let the player shoot in a rapid-fire mode for 10 seconds. I know...that sounds really exciting, so let's get to it.

First, you'll want to add a sound effect that you'll play when the rapid-fire power-up is awarded. With the source code for this chapter, in the *3D Game\3D GameContent \Audio* folder, you'll find a sound effect called *RapidFire.wav*. Copy that file to your project's *3D GameContent\Audio* directory in Windows Explorer. Remember not to add the file to your project in Visual Studio, because you'll be adding it to your XACT project file.

Open your XACT project file from within XACT, add the *RapidFire.wav* sound to the wave bank, and create a sound cue for that sound. Then, save the XACT project file and close XACT (see Chapter 6 if you need more help editing an XACT project file).

In addition to including an audio sound effect when the player receives the power-up, it would be a good idea to include a text indicator. This will help alleviate any confusion as to why all of a sudden the player can shoot so quickly. To do this, add a new spritefont to your project in Visual Studio by right-clicking the *3D GameContent\Fonts* folder and selecting Add→New Item.... Select the Sprite Font template on the right and name the file *PowerupFont.spritefont*.

Open the *PowerupFont.spritefont* file and change the size of the font by modifying the `<Size>` element as follows:

```
<Size>26</Size>
```

Also, modify the style to display in bold:

```
<Style>Bold</Style>
```

OK, now let's dig into the code and see how this will work. You're going to give the player a power-up when she hits three ships in a row without letting any ships get past her. To do this, you'll need to keep track of consecutive kills without letting a ship escape. The power-up decreases the delay between shots and expires after 10 seconds, so you'll have to keep that in mind as well. Open your `Game1` class and add the following class-level variables:

```
int originalShotDelay = 300;
public enum PowerUps { RAPID_FIRE }
int shotDelayRapidFire = 100;
int rapidFireTime = 10000;
int powerUpCountdown = 0;
```

```
string powerUpText = "";
int powerUpTextTimer = 0;
SpriteFont powerUpFont;
```

Let's look at these variables and what they're for:

originalShotDelay

When the power-up starts, you'll modify the shotDelay variable to give the rapid-fire functionality. After 10 seconds, you'll need to set it back to its original value. This variable simply holds the original value so you can reset it when the power-up expires.

PowerUps enum

This enumerates all possible power-ups, in case you want to add more later.

shotDelayRapidFire

This represents the shot delay in rapid-fire mode. Normally, it's 300, so you'll be firing three times as fast. Sweet!

rapidFireTime

This is the time (in milliseconds) that the power-up will last.

powerUpCountdown

This is the time counter that keeps track of how long the power-up has been in effect.

powerUpText

This is the text to display when a power-up is awarded.

powerUpTextTimer

This is the time counter that keeps track of how long the power-up text has been on the screen.

powerUpFont

This specifies the font with which to draw the power-up text.

Next, you'll need to load the spritefont you just created into your powerUpFont variable. Add the following line of code to the LoadContent method of your Game1 class:

```
powerUpFont = Content.Load<SpriteFont>(@"fonts\PowerupFont");
```

Now you need a way to turn off the power-up. All that happens when the power-up expires is that the shotDelay variable is set back to its original value. Add to your Game1 class the following method, which you'll use to cancel your power-up:

```
private void CancelPowerUps(  )
{
    shotDelay = originalShotDelay;
}
```

In the Update method of your Game1 class, you'll do the check to determine when a power-up expires. This is time-based, so you'll be using the gameTime variable to decrement your powerUpCountdown timer. Once that timer reaches zero, you'll cancel the power-up(s) by calling the CancelPowerUps method. Add to the Game1 class the following method, which will update your power-up timer and expire the power-up when needed:

```
protected void UpdatePowerUp(GameTime gameTime)
{
    if (powerUpCountdown > 0)
    {
        powerUpCountdown -= gameTime.ElapsedGameTime.Milliseconds;
        if (powerUpCountdown <= 0)
        {
            CancelPowerUps( );
            powerUpCountdown = 0;
        }
    }
}
```

Next, call the `UpdatePowerUp` method at the end of the `Update` method of your `Game1` class, just before the call to `base.Update`:

```
// Update power-up timer
UpdatePowerUp(gameTime);
```

You're going to need to add a `public` method to `Game1` that will let the model manager activate a power-up as well. Add the following method to your `Game1` class:

```
public void StartPowerUp(PowerUps powerUp)
{
    switch (powerUp)
    {
        case PowerUps.RAPID_FIRE:
            shotDelay = shotDelayRapidFire;
            powerUpCountdown = rapidFireTime;
            powerUpText = "Rapid Fire Mode!";
            powerUpTextTimer = 1000;
            soundBank.PlayCue("RapidFire");
            break;
    }
}
```

Why the `switch` statement using the `PowerUps` enum? It's just setting up the code to let you add other power-ups if you want. In the case of the rapid-fire power-up, first you set the new shot delay, and then you set the power-up countdown. Next, you set the power-up text to indicate rapid-fire mode and set the text timer to show that text for one second. Finally, you play the sound notifying the player that a power-up has been received.

Because the `shotDelay` variable is already being used to determine the delay between shots, there's nothing more to do in terms of enabling the rapid-fire functionality. However, you will want to draw the power-up text on the screen while the value of the `powerUpTextTimer` is greater than zero. To do that, add the following code to the `Draw` method of your `Game1` class, immediately before the call to `spriteBatch.End`:

```
// If power-up text timer is live, draw power-up text
if (powerUpTextTimer > 0)
```

```
    {
        powerUpTextTimer -= gameTime.ElapsedGameTime.Milliseconds;
        Vector2 textSize = powerUpFont.MeasureString(powerUpText);
        spriteBatch.DrawString(powerUpFont,
            powerUpText,
            new Vector2((Window.ClientBounds.Width / 2) -
            (textSize.X / 2),
            (Window.ClientBounds.Height / 2) -
            (textSize.Y / 2)),
            Color.Goldenrod);
    }
```

This isn't anything you haven't seen before. If the text timer is greater than zero, decrement it with the elapsed time and then draw the string. You center the string just as you've done previously, using the SpriteFont.MeasureString method to determine the size of the string being drawn.

The last thing you'll need to do in the Game1 class is cancel any power-ups that are in effect when a level ends. For example, you don't want somebody to get a power-up at the end of level 2 and then have that power-up continue into the beginning of level 3.

 Why shouldn't the power-up carry over from one level to the next? Well, like so many things in game development, this is a personal decision. Maybe you would prefer it to carry over, and maybe you wouldn't. In my opinion, it's better to cancel it between levels, so that's what we're doing in this book. However, feel free to create the world the way you want it. You can add different power-ups of your own and/or customize the current one. This is your world, and you get to do whatever you want with it.

Add a call to the CancelPowerUps method at the top of the ChangeGameState method in your Game1 class:

```
CancelPowerUps( );
```

Now let's move on to the ModelManager class. This class doesn't have a lot to do with this particular power-up because the power-up affects only shots, which are primarily handled in the Game1 class. However, you'll still need to keep track of when to start a power-up. Because this power-up is based on consecutive kills and kills are handled in the ModelManager, it makes sense to have this logic reside in this class.

Add the following class-level variables to your ModelManager class:

```
public int consecutiveKills = 0;
int rapidFireKillRequirement = 3;
```

The first variable will keep track of how many consecutive kills the player currently has, whereas the second variable tracks the number of consecutive kills required to grant the power-up. Note the first variable is public; that's because you'll be accessing it from the Game1 class to reset the count once a power-up has finished.

The only times when you're removing ships from the list of ships are when a ship escapes and when one is shot. In both cases, you'll be modifying the value of the consecutiveKills variable (when a ship escapes, consecutiveKills becomes 0, and when a ship is shot, consecutiveKills is incremented).

First, find the models.RemoveAt call at the end of the UpdateModels method that indicates a ship has escaped. In that same block of code, you're setting the game state to END with the Game1.ChangeGameState method if the game is over.

Add a line of code immediately before the call to models.RemoveAt, at the end of the UpdateModels method:

```
// Reset the kill count
consecutiveKills = 0;
```

The other place where you call models.RemoveAt indicates that a ship has been hit with a shot. This is at the end of the UpdateShots method. In this block, you're also playing the explosion sound with the Game1.PlayCue method. Add the following code immediately after the call to play the *Explosions* cue (the line reads PlayCue("Explosions")):

```
// Update consecutive kill count
// and start power-up if requirement met
++consecutiveKills;
if (consecutiveKills == rapidFireKillRequirement)
{
    ((Game1)Game).StartPowerUp(Game1.PowerUps.RAPID_FIRE);
}
```

After every kill, you increment the number of consecutive kills. If that counter ever equals the number required to grant the power-up, the power-up is granted via the Game1.StartPowerUp method.

Finally, you'll want to reset the kill count once a power-up has completed. Do this by adding the following line to the beginning of the CancelPowerUps method in your Game1 class:

```
modelManager.consecutiveKills = 0;
```

Oh yeah! You're ready to test it out. Compile and run the game. If your aim is good enough, you'll see that the power-up is granted after you've hit three ships in a row, as shown in Figure 15-4.

Not bad at all. The game is complete! Feel free to add other power-ups, notification indicators, sound effects, and whatever else you want to make this game yours and have it play exactly the way you want.

Figure 15-4. Oh yeah! All your base are belong to me!!!

What You Just Did

There's only one thing left to do to this game, and that's make the thing work on an Xbox 360. We'll look at how to do that in the next chapter. But first, let's review what you did here:

- You added a splash screen game component.
- You implemented game states and transitions between the start, play, level change, and end game states.
- You implemented a scoring system based on the current level.
- You added a rapid-fire power-up.
- You made all of your wildest dreams come true. (Well...at least a couple of them.)

Test Your Knowledge: Exercise

Create a multishot power-up that, when active, will fire four shots instead of one. Instead of shooting one shot in the center of the camera, when the multishot is active, shoot one shot from above and right of the camera, one from above and left, one from below and right, and one from below and left.

When the player shoots three ships in a row, the game will randomly choose which power-up to activate (rapid fire or multishot).

CHAPTER 16

Deploying to the Xbox 360

One of the most compelling reasons to learn XNA and write games using the XNA Framework is the fact that it enables developers to develop their own games and play them on the Xbox 360. Prior to XNA, it was nearly impossible for hobbyist developers to gain access to the tools needed to develop games for a next-generation console. Now, developers can either write specifically for the Xbox 360 or take code they've written for the PC and port it to the Xbox 360 (usually with few, if any, changes to the code required). Not only can developers write games for a next-gen console, but with the XNA Framework, they can write games that will run on the PC and the Xbox 360 in one environment and with one code base.

In addition, Xbox LIVE Marketplace now enables users to share games easily with users worldwide. Never before has the window of opportunity been opened so widely for console development. Members of the XNA Creator's Club who want to distribute games on Xbox LIVE Marketplace can submit games for review where testers preview them to ensure that they are safe to play. Once the game is approved by a group of peers within the Xbox Creators Club, the developer can set a price point for his game. The game is then made available to users worldwide as a purchasable download via Xbox LIVE Marketplace. What a great time to be an XNA game developer, eh? There are definitely some exciting times ahead of us!

This chapter covers the steps required to deploy a project to the Xbox 360, as well as specific topics that should be considered when targeting that platform.

Adding an Xbox 360 Device

To deploy a project to an Xbox 360, you need to let your PC know about the Xbox 360 machine. First, hook up your Xbox 360 to your PC's network with a LAN cable. (The Xbox 360 also has a wireless network adapter that you can purchase to connect your Xbox 360 to a wireless network.)

When you add your Xbox 360 as a device, your PC will require a connection key, which is generated by your Xbox 360. To get a connection key, you'll need to have at least a

Silver Xbox LIVE membership (which is free), an XNA Creators Club membership, and a hard drive for your Xbox 360. Both membership options are available in the Xbox LIVE Marketplace. The Xbox LIVE Silver membership is free of charge; the Creators Club license costs $99/year. Four-month memberships are also available, and the cost varies in different countries.

 Students can get a free trial membership through the DreamSpark program or through MSDNAA (the MSDN Academic Alliance). See *http:// forums.xna.com/forums/t/12661.aspx.*

Once you've obtained your memberships, you'll need to download XNA Game Studio Connect. You can get XNA Game Studio Connect in the Xbox LIVE Marketplace by selecting Game Marketplace→All Games→Browse→Genre→Other→Sort by Title→XNA Creators Club→Featured Downloads→XNA Game Studio Connect.

Now you're ready to generate your connection key. To generate the key, follow these steps:

1. Select the Games Library under My Xbox in the Xbox 360 dashboard.
2. Select Collections.
3. Select All Games.
4. Select XNA Game Studio Connect.
5. Select Launch.

You should see the XNA Game Studio Connect screen, which will look something like Figure 16-1. Note that the key listed in Figure 16-1 will not be the same as the one that you have on your screen. Make sure you use the key on your screen rather than the one shown in the figure.

Now that you have a connection key, you'll need to connect your PC to your Xbox 360 using this key. Start the XNA Game Studio Device Center on your PC. The Device Center is installed with XNA Game Studio 4.0; you can find it under Start→All Programs→Microsoft XNA Game Studio 4.0→XNA Game Studio Device Center.

Once you load the Device Center, it will display a list of known devices. Click Add Device to add your Xbox 360 to the Device Center (see Figure 16-2).

After clicking Add Device, XNA Game Studio Device Center will ask you which type of device you want to add by displaying the screen shown in Figure 16-3. Select Xbox 360 and click Next.

You'll then be asked to give your Xbox 360 a name to distinguish it from other Xbox 360 machines you might connect to your PC in the future. Enter a name for your Xbox 360 in the screen shown in Figure 16-4.

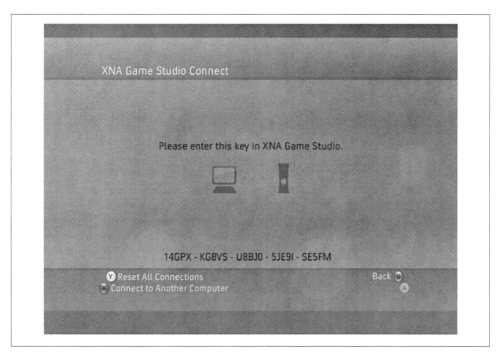

Figure 16-1. XNA Game Studio Connect screen

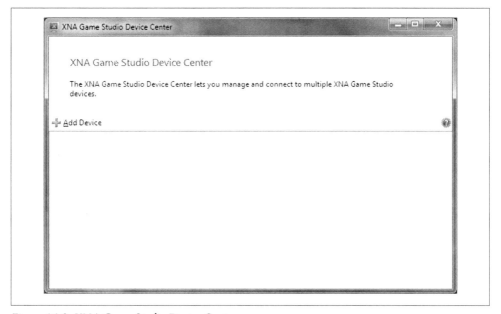

Figure 16-2. XNA Game Studio Device Center

Figure 16-3. Select the type of device to add (in this case, Xbox 360)

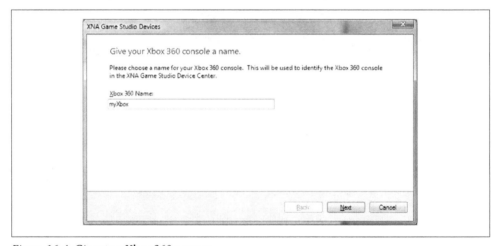

Figure 16-4. Give your Xbox 360 a name

Then, you'll be prompted to enter the connection key for the Xbox 360 you wish to associate with your PC, as you can see in Figure 16-5. Enter the connection key that appears on your XNA Game Studio Connect screen.

Once you've entered your connection key, the XNA Game Studio Device Center will search for the Xbox 360 and add it to the device list.

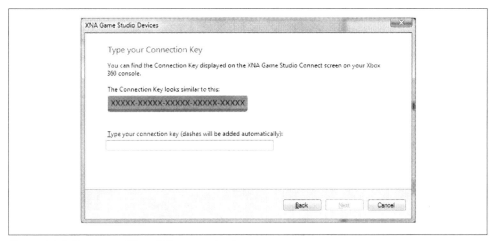

Figure 16-5. Enter your Xbox 360 connection key

Converting a Project to Run on the Xbox 360

Now that you have a connected Xbox 360, let's see just how easy it is to deploy an XNA Game Studio project to your Xbox 360 machine.

The rest of this chapter deals with converting the 3D game you finished building in the previous chapter and preparing it for deployment to the Xbox 360. Open the project from Chapter 15 and use that project throughout the rest of this chapter.

While 99% of the code that you write can be ported from the PC to the Xbox 360 without any changes, the projects are compiled differently depending on which platform you're targeting. As you created projects in previous chapters, you might have noticed that there were options to create projects for the Xbox 360. Using one of these options will generate the same type of project as its Windows counterpart, but the project will be wrapped in a project file that will compile the game to run on the Xbox 360.

A typical method for creating games for the Xbox 360 is to create the initial project for Windows and perform the majority of the coding, testing, and debugging in that project. Then, once the game is close to completion, you can create a copy of the project for development on the Xbox 360 and concentrate on Xbox 360–specific debugging.

This is the method that is laid out in this book. You have, from the previous chapter, a complete game written using XNA for Windows. Open that project, and then create a copy of the project for the Xbox 360 by right-clicking the project in Solution Explorer and selecting "Create Copy of Project for Xbox 360...", as shown in Figure 16-6.

Once you've chosen to create a copy of the project, XNA will create a new project within the same solution that shares the files with the original project. You'll find that changing a file in one of the projects affects both projects.

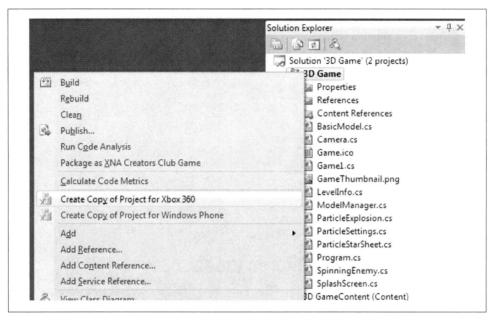

Figure 16-6. Creating a copy of a project for the Xbox 360

Once your duplicate project is created, your Solution Explorer window will look something like Figure 16-7. It will now have three projects: one for Windows, one for Xbox 360, and one for your game content.

Set the new project you added as the startup project by right-clicking the new project in Solution Explorer and selecting "Set as StartUp Project" (Figure 16-7).

Once you're ready to compile and test your game, you can start running the project the same way that you've done previously with Windows projects (by selecting the Debug→Start Debugging menu item in Visual Studio). Visual Studio will compile the project, and then, if the compilation was successful, it will begin a deployment step where it attempts to contact the Xbox 360 machine associated with your PC and install the project on that device. Once the project is installed, it will run on your Xbox 360.

 Your Xbox 360 must be connected to your PC's LAN, be on the same subnet as your PC, and be waiting at the XNA Game Studio Connect screen for Visual Studio to find the Xbox 360, copy the files, and run the project.

However, you'll probably find that your project in its current state is not ready for deployment to the Xbox 360. Remember that you're currently using the mouse to move the camera. You're probably going to want to modify that code to use the Xbox 360 gamepad instead.

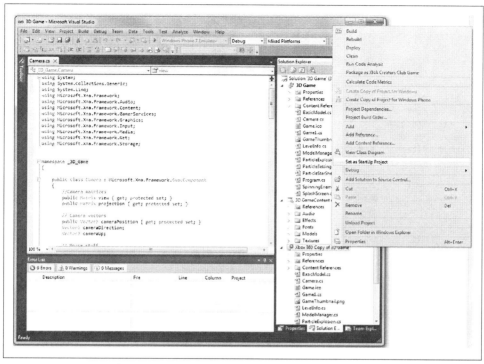

Figure 16-7. Set your Xbox 360 project as your StartUp Project

You might think there's an easy solution: you're using the mouse to move the camera and look around the world, so you can just remove the mouse stuff and add code to use the left thumbstick of the Xbox 360 gamepad, right?

Well, not exactly. Remember that the project files are shared between your Windows project and your Xbox 360 project. If you removed the mouse support in the Xbox 360 project, it would also be removed from the Windows project.

Luckily, XNA automatically defines two conditional compilation symbols (XBOX and XBOX360) in all Xbox 360 projects to help solve this problem.

Supporting Gamepad Input

The mouse is currently the only way to move the camera, and without support for the Xbox 360 gamepad, the camera will be immobile—which really won't increase the entertainment value of your game. To fix the Camera class, add support for the gamepad instead of the mouse anywhere that you see mouse support code being used. You can choose to surround the GamePad code with a preprocessor directive to have it compile only in the Xbox 360 project, but you might as well leave it in there for the Windows project as well because it's not uncommon to use a gamepad on a PC.

I've listed the modified Camera class here, with the changes highlighted in bold:

```
using System;
using System.Collections.Generic;
using System.Linq;
using Microsoft.Xna.Framework;
using Microsoft.Xna.Framework.Audio;
using Microsoft.Xna.Framework.Content;
using Microsoft.Xna.Framework.GamerServices;
using Microsoft.Xna.Framework.Graphics;
using Microsoft.Xna.Framework.Input;
using Microsoft.Xna.Framework.Media;
using Microsoft.Xna.Framework.Net;
using Microsoft.Xna.Framework.Storage;


namespace _3D_Game
{

    public class Camera : Microsoft.Xna.Framework.GameComponent
    {
        //Camera matrices
        public Matrix view { get; protected set; }
        public Matrix projection { get; protected set; }

        // Camera vectors
        public Vector3 cameraPosition { get; protected set; }
        Vector3 cameraDirection;
        Vector3 cameraUp;

#if (!XBOX360)
        // Mouse support
        MouseState prevMouseState;
#endif

        // Max yaw/pitch variables
        float totalYaw = MathHelper.PiOver4 / 2;
        float currentYaw = 0;
        float totalPitch = MathHelper.PiOver4 / 2;
        float currentPitch = 0;

        public Vector3 GetCameraDirection
        {
            get { return cameraDirection; }
        }

        public Camera(Game game, Vector3 pos, Vector3 target, Vector3 up)
            : base(game)
        {
            // Build camera view matrix
            cameraPosition = pos;
            cameraDirection = target - pos;
            cameraDirection.Normalize();
            cameraUp = up;
            CreateLookAt();
```

```
            projection = Matrix.CreatePerspectiveFieldOfView(
                MathHelper.PiOver4,
                (float)Game.Window.ClientBounds.Width /
                (float)Game.Window.ClientBounds.Height,
                1, 3000);
        }

        public override void Initialize()
        {
#if (!XBOX360)
            // Set mouse position and do initial get state
            Mouse.SetPosition(Game.Window.ClientBounds.Width / 2,
                Game.Window.ClientBounds.Height / 2);

            prevMouseState = Mouse.GetState();
#endif
            base.Initialize();
        }

        public override void Update(GameTime gameTime)
        {
            // Yaw rotation
            float yawAngle = 0;
#if (!XBOX360)
            yawAngle = (-MathHelper.PiOver4 / 150) *
                (Mouse.GetState( ).X - prevMouseState.X);
#endif

            if (yawAngle == 0)
            {
                yawAngle = (-MathHelper.PiOver4 / 150) *
                GamePad.GetState(PlayerIndex.One).ThumbSticks.Left.X;
            }

            if (Math.Abs(currentYaw + yawAngle) < totalYaw)
            {
                cameraDirection = Vector3.Transform(cameraDirection,
                    Matrix.CreateFromAxisAngle(cameraUp, yawAngle));
                currentYaw += yawAngle;
            }

            // Pitch rotation
            float pitchAngle = 0;
#if(!XBOX360)
            pitchAngle = (MathHelper.PiOver4 / 150) *
            (Mouse.GetState( ).Y - prevMouseState.Y);
#endif
            if (pitchAngle == 0)
            {
                pitchAngle = (MathHelper.PiOver4 / 150) *
                GamePad.GetState(PlayerIndex.One).ThumbSticks.Left.Y;
            }
```

```
            if (Math.Abs(currentPitch + pitchAngle) < totalPitch)
            {
                cameraDirection = Vector3.Transform(cameraDirection,
                    Matrix.CreateFromAxisAngle(
                        Vector3.Cross(cameraUp, cameraDirection),
                    pitchAngle));

                currentPitch += pitchAngle;
            }

#if(!XBOX360)
            //Reset mouse state
            prevMouseState = Mouse.GetState();
#endif

            // Recreate the camera view matrix
            CreateLookAt();

            base.Update(gameTime);
        }

        private void CreateLookAt()
        {
            view = Matrix.CreateLookAt(cameraPosition,
                cameraPosition + cameraDirection, cameraUp);
        }
    }
}
```

While you're working on input methods, you also have code that supports keyboard input in your game. There are only two places where you're currently supporting keyboard input: in the Game1 class, where you fire a shot when the space bar is pressed; and in the SplashScreen class, where you transition to a new game state when the Enter key is pressed.

First, let's look at the firing of shots. Currently, the FireShots method of the Game1 class contains shot-firing code with both keyboard and mouse support. That method looks something like this:

```
protected void FireShots(GameTime gameTime)
{
    if (shotCountdown <= 0)
    {
        // Did player press space bar or left mouse button?
        if (Keyboard.GetState().IsKeyDown(Keys.Space) ||
            Mouse.GetState().LeftButton == ButtonState.Pressed)
        {
            // Add a shot to the model manager
            modelManager.AddShot(
                camera.cameraPosition + new Vector3(0, -5, 0),
                camera.GetCameraDirection * shotSpeed);

            // Play shot audio
            PlayCue("Shot");
```

```
        // Reset the shot countdown
        shotCountdown = shotDelay;
    }
    }
    else
        shotCountdown -= gameTime.ElapsedGameTime.Milliseconds;
}
```

Using preprocessor directives just as you did in the Camera class, change the shot-firing code to use the keyboard and mouse only if you're not on the Xbox 360 and to always support the gamepad's A button. This code will do the trick (changes are in bold):

```
protected void FireShots(GameTime gameTime)
{
    if (shotCountdown <= 0)
    {
        // Did player press space bar or left mouse button?
        bool fireShot = false;
#if (!XBOX360)
        if (Keyboard.GetState( ).IsKeyDown(Keys.Space)||
            Mouse.GetState( ).LeftButton == ButtonState.Pressed)
            fireShot = true;
#endif
        if (fireShot || GamePad.GetState(PlayerIndex.One).Buttons.A ==
            ButtonState.Pressed)
        {
            // Add a shot to the model manager
            modelManager.AddShot(
                camera.cameraPosition + new Vector3(0, -5, 0),
                camera.GetCameraDirection * shotSpeed);

            // Play shot audio
            PlayCue("Shot");

            // Reset the shot countdown
            shotCountdown = shotDelay;
        }
    }
    else
        shotCountdown -= gameTime.ElapsedGameTime.Milliseconds;
}
```

If the XBOX360 symbol is defined, the keyboard input is skipped. If the symbol is not defined, both keyboard and gamepad input will be read.

Now let's look at the code in the SplashScreen class, which tracks Enter key presses. We'll modify this code in the same way. The Update method in your SplashScreen class contains a block of code similar to this:

```
// Did the player hit Enter?
if (Keyboard.GetState().IsKeyDown(Keys.Enter))
{
    // If we're not in end game, move to play state
    if (currentGameState == Game1.GameState.LEVEL_CHANGE ||
```

```
        currentGameState == Game1.GameState.START)
        ((Game1)Game).ChangeGameState(Game1.GameState.PLAY, 0);

    // If we are in end game, exit
    else if (currentGameState == Game1.GameState.END)
        Game.Exit();
}
```

You'll need to modify it using preprocessor directives, as follows:

```
// Did the player hit Enter or Start?
bool enterPressed = false;

#if (!XBOX360)

if (Keyboard.GetState( ).IsKeyDown(Keys.Enter))
    enterPressed = true;
#endif

if (enterPressed ||
    GamePad.GetState(PlayerIndex.One).Buttons.Start ==
    ButtonState.Pressed)
{
    // If we're not in end game, move to play state
    if (currentGameState == Game1.GameState.LEVEL_CHANGE ||
        currentGameState == Game1.GameState.START)
        ((Game1)Game).ChangeGameState(Game1.GameState.PLAY, 0);

    // If we are in end game, exit
    else if (currentGameState == Game1.GameState.END)
        Game.Exit();
}
```

Notice that this code will transition away from the SplashScreen class if the Enter key is pressed or if the user presses the Start button on the gamepad.

User Input Design

Why do you detect different buttons for firing a shot (A) and exiting the splash screen (Start)?

You could use the same button for both actions, but that might create some problems. Imagine a user trying desperately to destroy the final ship in a level. He's firing with the A button over and over, but the ship escapes and the level ends. If he hits the A button a millisecond too late, the SplashScreen will pick up that button press instead of the ModelManager class. If you're using that same key to exit the splash screen, the player will have just closed the splash screen as soon as it displayed and he wouldn't have had any time to read it or relax between levels.

This may seem like a minor issue, but the layout of game controls is a very important thing to consider. You can easily make a good game great by making the user input seem seamless and easy. You can also make a great game average by overcomplicating things and using an unintuitive input design.

So, your splash screen will now exit if the user presses the Start button on the gamepad, or, if the game is played on Windows, the user can also press the Enter key. Do you see any problems with this? Well, the code is fine, but your splash screen tells the user to press the Enter key to continue. This means the user won't have any idea that he needs to hit the Start button on an Xbox 360. The last thing you want is users resorting to trial and error and ending up getting frustrated, so let's fix that problem as well.

In the SplashScreen class, the SetData method sets the secondary text based on the game state that is passed into that method. Currently, the method looks like this:

```
public void SetData(string main, Game1.GameState currGameState)
{
    textToDraw = main;
    this.currentGameState = currGameState;

    switch (currentGameState)
    {
        case Game1.GameState.START:
        case Game1.GameState.LEVEL_CHANGE:
            secondaryTextToDraw = "Press ENTER to begin";
            break;
        case Game1.GameState.END:
            secondaryTextToDraw = "Press ENTER to quit";
            break;
    }
}
```

Add preprocessor directives, as shown next, to indicate to the user that on Windows the Enter key and the Start button are supported, whereas on the Xbox 360, the Start button is the only button supported:

```
public void SetData(string main, Game1.GameState currGameState)
{
    textToDraw = main;
    this.currentGameState = currGameState;

#if(XBOX360)
    string buttons = "START";
#else
    string buttons = "ENTER or the GamePad's START BUTTON";
#endif

    switch (currentGameState)
    {
        case Game1.GameState.START:
        case Game1.GameState.LEVEL_CHANGE:
            secondaryTextToDraw = "Press " + buttons + " to begin";
            break;
        case Game1.GameState.END:
            secondaryTextToDraw = "Press " + buttons + " to quit";
            break;
    }
}
```

Now that your text and input are Xbox 360-ready, you're ready to compile and run. Assuming you've followed the previous steps in this chapter to add your Xbox 360 machine to your PC via the XNA Game Studio Device Center, you should be ready to deploy your game to the Xbox 360. When you start debugging your Xbox 360 project, assuming there are no compilation errors, Visual Studio will find your Xbox 360 on the network, deploy the game to it, and start the game on that device.

Deploying to the Xbox 360

In order for your PC to find your Xbox 360, not only does it have to be added to the XNA Game Studio Device Center, but the Xbox 360 must be in a state where it expects input from the computer. Otherwise, if you deployed a game to an Xbox 360 on your network while somebody was using it, you could interrupt gameplay or some other activity.

Any time you want to deploy a game to the Xbox 360 from your PC, your Xbox 360 must be on the XNA Game Studio Connect screen with a status of "Waiting for computer connection", as shown in Figure 16-8.

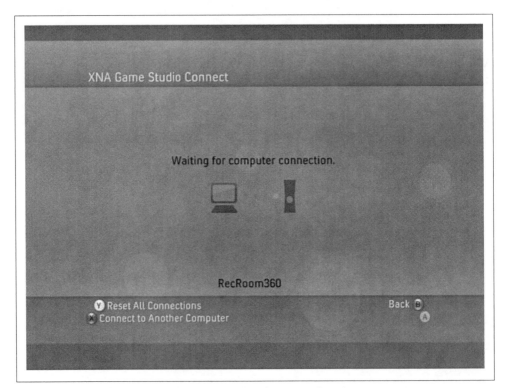

Figure 16-8. The Xbox 360 is ready to receive data from Visual Studio!

You can get to the XNA Game Studio Connect screen on your Xbox 360 by going to the Games tab in the Xbox 360 dashboard and selecting Games Library→Collections→All Games→XNA Game Studio Connect→Launch.

Once your Xbox 360 is displaying the XNA Game Studio Connect screen with a status of "Waiting for computer connection", you can compile and run your Xbox 360 project. You'll see that after the compilation step, Visual Studio's status bar indicates that it has entered a deployment stage. At that point, you can see some status updates on your Xbox 360's XNA Game Studio Connect screen, indicating that Visual Studio is copying over game content to the machine.

Once the copying and deployment stage has finished, the game will start.

But wait a minute—if you're running your game on a composite television set, there's a chance that you'll get an error when running this game. After deployment, your Xbox 360 might get stuck on a black screen. What's going on? Look over at your PC, and you'll probably see an exception generated on the PC itself within Visual Studio, as shown in Figure 16-9.

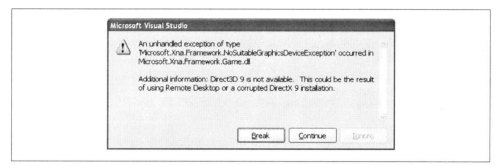

Figure 16-9. NoSuitableGraphicsDeviceException! Arrrggghhhh!!!!!!!!!!!

If instead of displaying this error your Xbox 360 went right back to the "Waiting for computer connection" stage, you're probably not running your project in debug mode. Start it in debug mode by selecting Debug→Start Debugging, and you should see the error.

When running in debug mode, the game executes on the Xbox 360, and the Visual Studio debug process attaches to that executing program, allowing you to debug just as if you were running the game on your PC. That's really helpful, not to mention just plain cool.

Debugging a Project on the Xbox 360

You can debug your Xbox 360 projects while they run on your Xbox 360 machine. Place a breakpoint in the code just as you would for debugging in Windows, and then run the project in debug mode. The project will again compile, deploy, and run on the Xbox 360, but it will stop execution at your breakpoint, allowing you to debug in Visual Studio on your PC while the project runs on your Xbox 360. Debugging a console application has never been this easy!

Xbox 360 Display Settings

The `NoSuitableGraphicsDeviceException` error is telling you that you don't have a graphics device that will run with the current settings. The problem? The resolution you're using. When you were writing the game for Windows, you used the following two lines in the constructor of the `Game1` class to set the resolution to 1,280 × 1,024:

```
graphics.PreferredBackBufferWidth = 1280;
graphics.PreferredBackBufferHeight = 1024;
```

You need to specify that those lines should be compiled only when the `XBOX360` symbol is not defined, as follows:

```
#if(!XBOX360)
    graphics.PreferredBackBufferWidth = 1280;
    graphics.PreferredBackBufferHeight = 1024;
#endif
```

With that change in place, you should be able to compile, run, and actually play your game on the Xbox 360.

Your resolution should now be set according to Table 16-1, following standards based on the display settings on your Xbox 360.

Table 16-1. Television display modes

Xbox 360 display setting	DisplayMode width and height
AV (Composite)	640 × 480
480p (Normal)	640 × 480
480p (Widescreen)	640 × 480
720p (Widescreen)	1,280 × 720
1,080i/1,080p (Widescreen)	1,920 × 1,080

You can detect the display settings by using the `DisplayMode` property of the `Graphics Device`. XNA sets this property before `Game1`'s `Initialize` method is called, so you can accurately read the property during and after this method.

The Title Safe Region

There's one more thing that you'll need to consider when developing for the Xbox 360: in standard-tube televisions, the actual display area is not a perfect rectangle. In fact, as much as 10% of the screen in any direction may or may not be visible, depending on the type of television you're using.

Because of this, when developing games for the Xbox 360, you should always display critical information within the inner 80% of the screen in both the vertical and horizontal directions (offset by 10% up, down, left, and right). This inner area is known as the *safe region*. You'll still want to draw the background and other objects on the whole screen, so that the screen doesn't have black edges if those areas are visible on a particular television, but anything that needs to be seen by the user or needs to be interacted with should be placed within the safe region.

So, how do you make your text display in the safe region on an Xbox 360? Luckily, the GraphicsDevice object has a member called Viewport that represents the viewport used to draw the current scene. This Viewport object has a member of type Rectangle called TitleSafeArea that represents the title safe region mentioned previously. In a Windows game, the Top and Left elements of the TitleSafeArea rectangle will be 0 (indicating that it is safe to draw at location 0, 0). In an Xbox 360 game, however, the Top and Left elements will reflect the upper-left corner of the title-safe region, as described earlier. So, you'll want to use these values as offset coordinates for the score text you draw in this game.

In the Draw method of your Game1 class, you should have two calls to SpriteBatch.Draw String that draw 2D text to display the score and the number of misses the player has left:

```
// Draw the current score
string scoreText = "Score: " + score;
spriteBatch.DrawString(scoreFont, scoreText,
    new Vector2(10, 10), Color.Red);

// Let the player know how many misses he has left
spriteBatch.DrawString(scoreFont, "Misses Left: " +
    modelManager.missesLeft,
    new Vector2(10, scoreFont.MeasureString(scoreText).Y + 20),
    Color.Red);
```

Modify those calls to use the TitleSafeArea member of the GraphicsDevice.Viewport instead of the hardcoded values, as shown here:

```
// Draw the current score
string scoreText = "Score: " + score;
spriteBatch.DrawString(scoreFont, scoreText,
    new Vector2(GraphicsDevice.Viewport.TitleSafeArea.Left,
        GraphicsDevice.Viewport.TitleSafeArea.Top), Color.Red);
```

```
// Let the player know how many misses he has left
spriteBatch.DrawString(scoreFont, "Misses Left: " +
    modelManager.missesLeft,
    new Vector2(GraphicsDevice.Viewport.TitleSafeArea.Left,
        scoreFont.MeasureString(scoreText).Y +
        GraphicsDevice.Viewport.TitleSafeArea.Top + 10),
    Color.Red);
```

Compile and run the game now, and you should always be able to see the game score, regardless of what type of television set is being used.

If you've run your game on the Xbox 360 already, you might have noticed that, depending on the type of television you're using, your crosshair may be off-center. When coding for the Xbox, you'll want to center 2D items on the screen using the `Viewport` member of the `GraphicsDevice class`.

In the `Draw` method of the `Game1` class, you're currently drawing the crosshair using the following code:

```
spriteBatch.Draw(crosshairTexture,
    new Vector2((Window.ClientBounds.Width / 2)
        - (crosshairTexture.Width / 2),
        (Window.ClientBounds.Height / 2)
        - (crosshairTexture.Height / 2)),
        Color.White);
```

Replace that code with the following code, which uses the `Viewport` to determine the position of the crosshair:

```
spriteBatch.Draw(crosshairTexture,
    new Vector2((GraphicsDevice.Viewport.Width / 2)
        - (crosshairTexture.Width / 2),
        (GraphicsDevice.Viewport.Height / 2)
        - (crosshairTexture.Height / 2)),
        Color.White);
```

Compile and run at this point. The crosshair should be centered, no matter what type of television is used. If your crosshair was off-center, most likely the text throughout the game that should be centered is also off-center. You'd fix those lines of text in the same way that you fixed the crosshair here.

After you've deployed a game to your Xbox 360, it will continue to be available on that device, and you won't have to redeploy the game every time you want to play it. You can find the games you've deployed to the Xbox 360 by going to the Games tab in the Xbox 360 dashboard and selecting Games Library→My Games.

Great job! You've just created your first game for the Xbox 360! Time to bring your friends over and show off your skills.

What You Just Did

Let's review what you accomplished in this chapter:

- You learned about requirements for deploying games to an Xbox 360.
- You connected your Xbox 360 to your PC for XNA game deployment.
- You created a copy of your Windows project and modified it to work on the Xbox 360.
- You learned how to write code for both the Xbox 360 and Windows in the same project by using preprocessor directives where differences occur.
- You learned how to debug Xbox 360 projects.
- You learned about some Xbox 360–specific considerations, such as user input, display resolutions, and title safe regions.
- You became the envy of most men, women, and children on our planet by developing a game for a next-gen console in your own living room. Nice work!

Summary

- To develop games in XNA, you need to install a version of Visual Studio 2010 (XNA supports the free Visual C# 2010 Express Edition) and XNA Game Studio 4.0.
- To deploy XNA games to an Xbox 360, you need to have a Silver (or higher) Xbox LIVE Membership *and* an Xbox Creators Club membership.
- By using the conditional symbol XBOX or XBOX360, you can modify code in a project targeting the Windows platform without affecting the code targeting the Xbox 360 platform, or vice versa.
- You can debug games on the Xbox 360 on the PC that is connected to the Xbox during deployment. Set a breakpoint in Visual Studio and start the game in debug mode, and the game will run on the Xbox 360 and pause at breakpoints in Visual Studio on your PC. (Yeah, that's really cool.)
- Some studies have shown that writing games for the Xbox 360 in XNA increases a person's life expectancy by an average of 8–10 years.

Test Your Knowledge: Quiz

1. What piece of information does a PC use to identify a specific Xbox 360 machine?
2. Fact or fiction: to debug a project that has been deployed on an Xbox 360, you have to load the code in the Xbox 360 code editor and place a breakpoint within the code on the Xbox 360 machine.
3. Fact or fiction: if you've created a Windows game project and you want to deploy that project to your Xbox 360, you need to create a new project in order to do so.

4. What is a preprocessor directive?

5. What does the following code do in a Windows project?

```
#if (XBOX360)
    int A = 5;
    int B = 4;
    int C = A - B;
#endif
```

6. What does "serenity now" lead to?

CHAPTER 17

Developing for Windows Phone 7

There has been a lot of hype and interest for years surrounding the release of Microsoft's Windows Phone 7 series. Microsoft has been in the mobile communications device market before with previous versions of Windows Phone operating systems, but Windows Phone 7 is aimed at putting Microsoft in the copilot seat of the market that has long been dominated by the iPhone.

For developers, Windows Phone 7 offers something that has previously never been available: the ability to write rich, interactive applications in Silverlight and create 2D and 3D games using XNA. With tons of features, such as 480 × 800 screen resolution, a slick touchscreen interface, and an internal accelerometer, the possibilities for development on Windows Phone 7 are virtually endless.

This chapter focuses on issues specific to developing games for Windows Phone 7. Instead of porting one of the games from previous chapters to Windows Phone 7, you'll be building a new game from scratch. Most of the code, however, will be similar to what you've done in previous chapters and, as a result, I'll skim over most of it fairly quickly and concentrate on the distinct features of Windows Phone 7 development.

In addition to the game in this book, there are a large number of Windows Phone 7 samples available on the XNA Creator's Club website (*http://creators.xna.com*) and on the MSDN website (*http://msdn.microsoft.com/en-us/library/ff431744(v=VS.92).aspx*).

Setting Up Your Windows Phone 7 Device

Visual Studio 2010 comes with an emulator for creating applications on Windows Phone 7 series devices. This emulator makes it possible to build applications for Windows Phone 7 without owning a Windows Phone 7 device. However, there are some aspects of Windows Phone 7 devices that are impossible to emulate (such as accelerometer input) and therefore are unavailable on the emulator.

This section will walk you through setting up your Windows Phone 7 device and getting it ready for development. If you don't have a device or you want to start developing right away on the emulator, go ahead and skip to "Creating a Windows Phone 7 Project" on page 370.

Registering for a Developer Account

The first step to setting up your Windows Phone 7 device is to register for a developer account with Microsoft. This account allows you to deploy, test, and debug your applications on your physical device and grants you the right to publish and distribute your applications. The steps you'll need to follow to register for an account are:

1. Create a Windows Live ID (or use a preexisting Windows Live ID account).
2. Sign the application provider agreement.
3. Choose an account type.
4. Pay the annual subscription fee.

 Note that students registered at Microsoft DreamSpark do not have to pay the subscription fee. To register as a student with DreamSpark, visit *https://www.dreamspark.com/*.

To begin the process of registering for a developer account, visit *http://developer.win dowsphone.com* and click "Register for the Marketplace". You'll see a screen that looks like Figure 17-1.

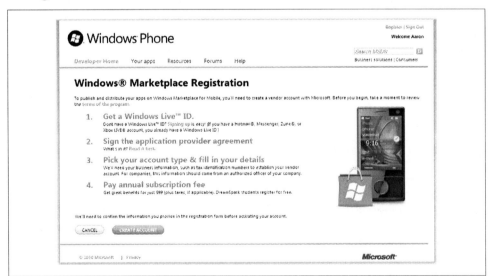

Figure 17-1. Starting the registration process

Once you click "Create Account", you'll be asked to sign the application provider agreement, as shown in Figure 17-2.

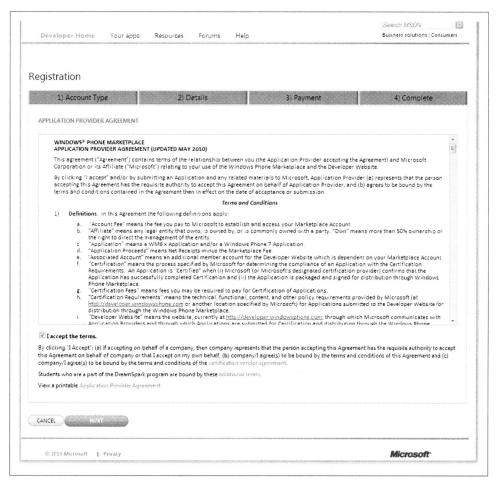

Figure 17-2. Signing the Application Provider Agreement

Next, you'll be asked to select an account type, as shown in Figure 17-3. You can register as a business, an individual, or a student. What's the difference between a business and an individual account, and why does it matter? One of the goals of the Windows Phone 7 marketplace is not only to create cool applications but also to earn a profit as a developer. The difference here in your account type really just comes down to how you want your profits to be taxed as a developer.

Figure 17-3. Selecting your account type

The next few screens will walk you through setting up the details on your account (contact info, etc.), selecting the payment method, and completing your registration. Once you've finished with the account registration, you'll see the Windows Phone developer dashboard, as shown in Figure 17-4. From this page you can view your registered phone devices, the applications you've built and submitted, payment schedules, and so on.

Note that the status of the account might be incomplete at this point (see the red X's at the top left under your account name). It takes a few days for the identity and bank verification to be processed. You'll be able to start working on your applications without finishing these steps, but you won't be able to proceed with publishing any applications until your account is completely set up.

Registering Your Windows Phone 7 Device

The next step is to register your Windows Phone 7 device. You do this from the computer on which you'll be developing your applications. Click Start→All Programs→Windows Phone Developer Tools→Windows Phone Developer Registration.

Figure 17-4. Windows Phone developer dashboard

This will bring up the screen shown in Figure 17-5. Enter the Windows Live ID you registered for as an application developer in the previous section. Also make sure your phone is plugged into your computer and that you're logged into the phone with your Windows Live ID. If you aren't, the status message at the bottom of the window will indicate that the system cannot communicate with your device.

Once you've entered your Live ID and password, you're ready to move on to the next section.

Unlocking Your Phone

The final step to setting up your Windows Phone 7 device is to download the Microsoft Zune software. Why the Zune software? Windows Phone 7 incorporates all the Zune HD functionality, and is a portable media device (Zune HD), not just a phone. You'll use the Zune software to add media files to your phone as well as transfer games you build in Visual Studio to your device. Download and install the Zune software from the Microsoft Zune website (*http://www.zune.net/en-us/products/software/download/default.htm*).

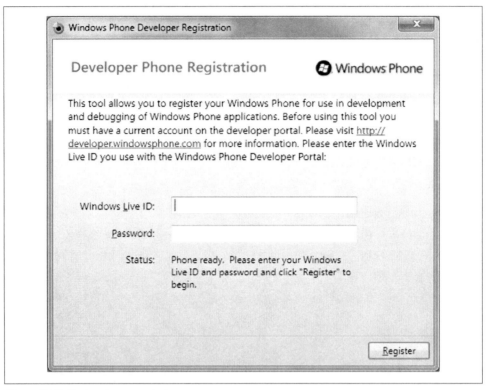

Figure 17-5. Registering your device

Once you've downloaded and installed your Zune software, plug your phone into your computer, and the phone registration page should appear (see Figure 17-6).

Follow the steps in the Zune Software to give your device a name and unlock it for development.

Creating a Windows Phone 7 Project

Once your device is unlocked via the Zune software, you can start writing your Windows Phone 7 game.

Open Visual Studio and create a new Windows Phone Game project by selecting Visual C#→XNA Game Studio 4.0 as the project type from the menu on the left side of the New Project window, and then select the Windows Phone Game (4.0) template on the right. Name your solution *PhoneAsteroids*, specify a directory for your game, and click OK (see Figure 17-7).

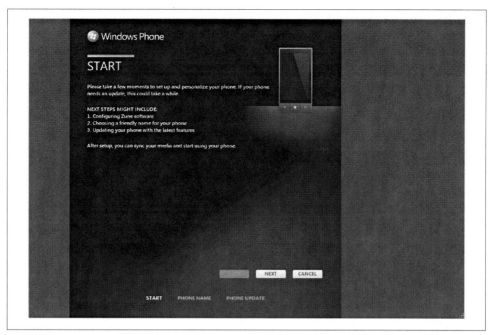

Figure 17-6. Unlocking your phone with the Zune software

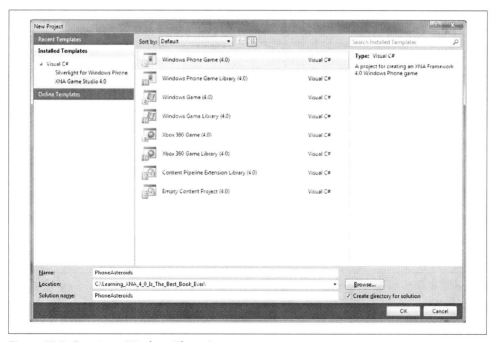

Figure 17-7. Creating a Windows Phone 7 game project

Once you click OK, your project will be created for you. Just like when you develop a game for Windows, the code generated will have a skeleton game application consisting of a `Game1` class with a constructor and `Initialize`, `LoadContent`, `UnloadContent`, `Update`, and `Draw` methods, as well as additional helper classes and content. The generated code will create the same familiar cornflower-blue screen that you saw when you first began developing your Windows game earlier in this book. The only difference of note thus far between your Windows Phone game and your Windows games is the following line in the constructor of your `Game1` class:

```
TargetElapsedTime = TimeSpan.FromTicks(333333);
```

Whereas the default framerate of a Windows or Xbox 360 game is 60 frames per second, the default framerate of a Windows Phone game is 30 frames per second. This is the line of code that sets that framerate.

The content pipeline also has the same behavior as that covered in previous chapters. In fact, the entire architecture of a Windows Phone game is essentially identical to that of a Windows or Xbox 360 game. Most of the code that you write for those platforms will be directly compatible with Windows Phone 7—with a few exceptions.

Resources

Let's get to it. You're going to build an *Asteroids*-style game in this chapter, and we'll call out some key differences in Windows Phone development in the process. The end game will look something like Figure 17-8.

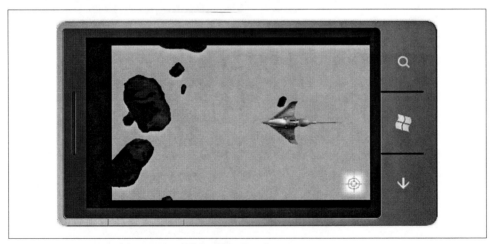

Figure 17-8. Preview of the game you'll build in this chapter

Let's go ahead and add all the resources you'll need for your game now. Under the `PhoneAsteroidsContent` project in Solution Explorer, create three subfolders called *Audio*, *Models*, and *Textures*.

If you haven't already, download the code for this chapter. Within that code you will find three files in the *PhoneAsteroids\PhoneAsteroidsContent\Audio* directory (*collision.wav*, *shot.wav* and *track.wav*). XACT is supported only in the HiDef profile and Windows Phone 7 supports only the Reach profile, so we won't be able to use XACT to manage these audio files. Add them directly to your project in your *PhoneAsteroids-Content\Audio* folder.

Next, look in the code for this chapter in the *PhoneAsteroids\PhoneAsteroidsContent \Models* folder, and you'll find four model files (*ammo.x*, *asteroid1.x*, *asteroid2.x*, and *p1_wedge.fbx*). Add each of those files to your project in your *PhoneAsteroidsContent \Models* folder.

Finally, in the code for this chapter in the *PhoneAsteroids\PhoneAsteroidsContent\Textures* folder, you'll find four texture files (*asteroid1.tga*, *asteroid2.tga*, *attack.png*, and *wedge_p1_diff_v1.tga*). Add those four files to your project in your *PhoneAsteroids-Content\Textures* folder.

I said we were going to go pretty quickly through all of this, right? You'll see what each of these files is used for as we move through the chapter, but by now none of this should be new, and most likely you can guess what they're for just by looking at the names of each file.

Please note that some of the content you just added to your project come from the online MSDN XNA samples available at *http://creators.xna .com* and *http://msdn.microsoft.com*. Review the license agreement for all such content at *http://creators.xna.com/downloads/?id=15*.

Digging In

Now let's get to the actual code. Developing a game for Windows Phone 7 is nearly identical to creating a game for Windows or Xbox 360. In this case, we're developing a 3D game, and just as in Windows and Xbox 360, you'll need a camera and some classes to handle your models. Add a *Camera.cs* class to your project and modify it to use the following code:

```
using System;
using System.Collections.Generic;
using System.Linq;
using Microsoft.Xna.Framework;
using Microsoft.Xna.Framework.Audio;
using Microsoft.Xna.Framework.Content;
using Microsoft.Xna.Framework.GamerServices;
using Microsoft.Xna.Framework.Graphics;
using Microsoft.Xna.Framework.Input;
using Microsoft.Xna.Framework.Media;

namespace PhoneAsteroids
{
```

```
public class Camera : Microsoft.Xna.Framework.GameComponent
{
    //Camera matrices
    public Matrix view { get; protected set; }
    public Matrix projection { get; protected set; }


    public Camera(Game game)
        : base(game)
    {
        // Build camera view matrix
        view = Matrix.CreateLookAt(new Vector3(0, 0, 200),
            Vector3.Zero, Vector3.Up);


        // Build camera projection matrix
        projection = Matrix.CreatePerspectiveFieldOfView(
            MathHelper.ToRadians(45.0f),
            1.6666f,
            1, 3000);

    }

    public override void Initialize()
    {

        base.Initialize();
    }

    public override void Update(GameTime gameTime)
    {

        base.Update(gameTime);
    }

}
}
```

This code is basically the same as all the 3D camera code you've created several times already in this book, and so none of this should be too much of a surprise at this point.

Next, add a *BasicModel.cs* class to your project, and replace the default code with the following:

```
using System;
using System.Collections.Generic;
using System.Linq;
using System.Text;
using Microsoft.Xna.Framework;
using Microsoft.Xna.Framework.Graphics;

namespace PhoneAsteroids
{
```

```
class BasicModel
{
    public Model model { get; protected set; }
    protected Matrix world = Matrix.Identity;

    public BasicModel(Model m)
    {
        model = m;
    }

    public virtual void Update()
    {

    }

    public void Draw(Camera camera)
    {
        Matrix[] transforms = new Matrix[model.Bones.Count];
        model.CopyAbsoluteBoneTransformsTo(transforms);

        foreach (ModelMesh mesh in model.Meshes)
        {
            foreach (BasicEffect be in mesh.Effects)
            {
                be.EnableDefaultLighting();
                be.Projection = camera.projection;
                be.View = camera.view;
                be.World = GetWorld() * mesh.ParentBone.Transform;
            }

            mesh.Draw();
        }
    }

    public virtual Matrix GetWorld()
    {
        return world;
    }

    public virtual Matrix GetWorldForBoundingSphere()
    {
        return world;
    }
}
```

Again, this `BasicModel` class is really...well...basic (ha!), and it's virtually the same base model class you've used several times in this book. All this one really does is draw the model and declare variables for moving the model about the 3D grid. There is a method called `GetWorldForBoundingSphere` that might have you scratching your head. It's a virtual method that derived classes can override to modify their bounding sphere for improved collision detection.

In this particular game, you'll have three types of models floating around the screen: the asteroids, the shots fired by the player, and the player itself. Next, you'll add the class you'll use to handle your asteroids. Add a class to your project called *Asteroid-Model.cs*, and replace the default code with the following:

```csharp
using System;
using System.Collections.Generic;
using System.Linq;
using System.Text;
using Microsoft.Xna.Framework;
using Microsoft.Xna.Framework.Graphics;
using Microsoft.Xna.Framework.Input.Touch;

namespace PhoneAsteroids
{
    class AsteroidModel : BasicModel
    {
        // Size of asteroids
        public enum AsteroidSize { SMALL, MEDIUM, LARGE }
        public AsteroidSize size;
        Vector3 scale;

        // Rotation stuff
        Vector3 rotationAxis = Vector3.Zero;
        Vector3 randomRotation;
        float maxRotationSpeed = MathHelper.Pi;

        // Misc
        Random random;
        Vector3 direction;
        public Vector3 position;

        public AsteroidModel(Model m, Random random, Vector3 direction,
            AsteroidSize size, Vector3 position)
            : this(m, random, direction, size)
        {
            this.position = position;
        }

        public AsteroidModel(Model m, Random random,
            Vector3 direction, AsteroidSize size)
            : base(m)
        {
            this.random = random;

            // Initialize random rotation speed
            randomRotation = new Vector3(
                (float)random.NextDouble() *
                maxRotationSpeed - (maxRotationSpeed / 2),
                (float)random.NextDouble() *
                maxRotationSpeed - (maxRotationSpeed / 2),
                (float)random.NextDouble() *
                maxRotationSpeed - (maxRotationSpeed / 2));

            this.size = size;
```

```csharp
    // Initialize random scale
    if (size == AsteroidSize.LARGE)
    {
        scale = new Vector3(((float)random.NextDouble() * .005f) + .035f,
            ((float)random.NextDouble() * .005f) + .035f,
            ((float)random.NextDouble() * .005f) + .035f);
    }
    else if (size == AsteroidSize.MEDIUM)
    {
        scale = new Vector3(((float)random.NextDouble() * .005f) + .015f,
            ((float)random.NextDouble() * .005f) + .015f,
            ((float)random.NextDouble() * .005f) + .015f);
    }
    else
    {
        scale = new Vector3(((float)random.NextDouble() * .005f) + .005f,
            ((float)random.NextDouble() * .005f) + .005f,
            ((float)random.NextDouble() * .005f) + .005f);
    }

    // Initialize random speed
    this.direction = direction * ((float)random.NextDouble() + 1f);

    position = new Vector3(-300, ((float)random.NextDouble() * 100) - 50, 0);

}


public override void Update()
{
    // Update rotation and position
    rotationAxis += randomRotation;
    position += direction;

    base.Update();
}

override public Matrix GetWorld()
{
    return world * Matrix.CreateScale(scale) *
        Matrix.CreateFromYawPitchRoll(MathHelper.ToRadians(rotationAxis.Y),
        MathHelper.ToRadians(rotationAxis.X),
            MathHelper.ToRadians(rotationAxis.Z)) *
        Matrix.CreateRotationY(MathHelper.PiOver2) *
        Matrix.CreateRotationX(MathHelper.PiOver2) *
        Matrix.CreateTranslation(position);
}

override public Matrix GetWorldForBoundingSphere()
{
    // Make the bounding sphere smaller but rotate the
    //same as the world is rotating
    return world * Matrix.CreateScale(scale / 2) *
```

```
                        Matrix.CreateFromYawPitchRoll(MathHelper.ToRadians(rotationAxis.Y),
                        MathHelper.ToRadians(rotationAxis.X),
                            MathHelper.ToRadians(rotationAxis.Z)) *
                        Matrix.CreateRotationY(MathHelper.PiOver2) *
                        Matrix.CreateRotationX(MathHelper.PiOver2) *
                        Matrix.CreateTranslation(position);
            }
        }
    }
```

Once again, there's nothing too new here. You have a model class that has a direction, a position, and a random rotation. One thing worth noting is the `AsteroidSize` enum and corresponding variable. Essentially, in this game you'll spawn larger asteroids to begin with. When the player shoots a large asteroid, you'll spawn a few medium-sized asteroids to simulate the asteroid blowing into pieces (nothing new here; if you've ever played any version of *Asteroids*, you know how this works). When the player shoots a medium asteroid, you'll spawn a few small asteroids. Finally, when the player shoots a small asteroid, you spawn nothing, and the asteroid chunk just disappears. The second constructor uses the `AsteroidSize` enum to set the size of the asteroid accordingly (large, medium, or small).

Also, you're going to build the game such that the large asteroids that spawn come from the left of the screen and move to the right. All other asteroids (medium and small ones) are created at the location of an exploded asteroid rather than at the top of the screen, and they will move in random directions all over the screen. That's why you have two constructors in this class. Notice the only difference in parameters is that the first constructor has a parameter for position. Also notice that the first constructor does nothing but set the position variable and call the other constructor (with the line `this(m, random, direction, size)`).

The second constructor sets the position to a coordinate off the left side of the screen (-300 X) and at a random point along the height of the screen (a random value between -50 and 50 Y). Any time you wish to create a new large asteroid to spawn and move across the screen, you'll call the second constructor. Any time you wish to create a medium or small asteroid at the point of an exploded asteroid, you'll call the first constructor and pass in the position of the exploded asteroid.

Screen Rotation and Resolution

So, hold on just a second. Isn't what I'm calling the "left" of the screen here technically the "top" of the screen on your Windows Phone 7? Actually, yes. But although the Windows Phone 7 device supports multiple rotations and can run games in landscape or portrait mode, XNA defaults to an 800 × 480 landscape left rotation for games. This means your game by default will appear as seen in Figure 17-9.

Figure 17-9. Landscape left rotation, the default for XNA

When rotating your device during gameplay, the display will automatically rotate for you. Input from the touchscreen is rotated for you as well, though input from the accelerometer must be rotated in your code.

Sometimes you might want to force your game to be played in a certain mode. This can be an advantage for you as a developer because you'll be able to predict more accurately what the user experience will be. However, you do have to keep in mind that a user might expect to have the ability to rotate the screen, and taking that away might be a negative.

You can force the rotation of the game by setting the `graphics.SupportedOrientations` property in the constructor of your `Game1` class. For this game, let's go ahead and force the game to be played in landscape left. To do this, add the following line in the constructor of your `Game1` class:

```
graphics.SupportedOrientations = DisplayOrientation.LandscapeLeft;
```

While we're talking about the screen, let's address the issues of screen resolution. The default Windows Phone 7 screen resolution is 480 × 800. However, the device will automatically scale other resolutions to fit within the screen. You can elect to use a different resolution by setting the `graphics.PreferredBackBufferWidth` and `graphics.PreferredBackBufferHeight` properties in the constructor of your `Game1` class. The device also will automatically scale input from the touchscreen, etc. to fit your desired resolution. This is a very powerful tool that will help developers working in nonstandard resolutions more easily build games for Windows Phone 7.

The default resolution of 480 × 800 is fine for your game, so you won't want to adjust it here.

More Model Classes

OK, so now you have a base model class and a class for your asteroids. Next, you'll want to add a class for the shots fired by the player. Add a new class to your project and call it *ShotModel.cs*. Replace the code with the following:

```
using System;
using System.Collections.Generic;
using System.Linq;
using System.Text;
using Microsoft.Xna.Framework;
using Microsoft.Xna.Framework.Graphics;
using Microsoft.Xna.Framework.Input.Touch;


namespace PhoneAsteroids
{
    class ShotModel : BasicModel
    {
        // Position and rotation
        public Vector3 translationVector;
        Vector3 rotationAxis = Vector3.Zero;
        Vector3 randomRotation;
        float maxRotationSpeed = MathHelper.Pi;

        // Speed, scale, and random
        Vector3 speed = new Vector3(-10, 0, 0);
        Vector3 scale = new Vector3(3, 3, 3);
        Random random;

        // Regular asteroid constructor
        public ShotModel(Model m, Random random, Vector3 initialPosition)
            : base(m)
        {
            this.random = random;

            // Initialize random rotation speed
            randomRotation = new Vector3(
                (float)random.NextDouble() *
                maxRotationSpeed - (maxRotationSpeed / 2),
                (float)random.NextDouble() *
                maxRotationSpeed - (maxRotationSpeed / 2),
                (float)random.NextDouble() *
                maxRotationSpeed - (maxRotationSpeed / 2));

            // Initialize position
            translationVector = new Vector3(initialPosition.X - 25,
                initialPosition.Y, initialPosition.Z);

        }


        public override void Update()
        {
            rotationAxis += randomRotation;
```

```
            translationVector += speed;

            base.Update();
        }

        override public Matrix GetWorld()
        {
            return world * Matrix.CreateScale(scale) *
                Matrix.CreateFromYawPitchRoll(MathHelper.ToRadians(rotationAxis.Y),
                MathHelper.ToRadians(rotationAxis.X),
                MathHelper.ToRadians(rotationAxis.Z)) *
                Matrix.CreateRotationY(MathHelper.PiOver2) *
                Matrix.CreateRotationX(MathHelper.PiOver2) *
                Matrix.CreateTranslation(translationVector);
        }

        public Matrix GetBoundingSphereWorld()
        {
            return world * Matrix.CreateScale(scale / 4f) *
                Matrix.CreateRotationY(MathHelper.PiOver2) *
                Matrix.CreateRotationX(MathHelper.PiOver2) *
                Matrix.CreateTranslation(new Vector3(50, 0, 0)) *
                Matrix.CreateTranslation(translationVector);
        }

        override public Matrix GetWorldForBoundingSphere()
        {
            return world * Matrix.CreateScale(scale / 2) *
                Matrix.CreateTranslation(translationVector);
        }
    }
}
```

This class is also very basic and nothing you haven't seen before. You're creating a shot at the position of the player's ship (offset slightly so it comes from the nose of the ship) and giving it a random rotation. The speed is set to (-10, 0, 0), which will make the shots move from right to left on the screen.

Finally, add one more model class to your game that will represent the player itself, and name it *PlayerModel.cs*. Replace the code in that file with the following:

```
using System;
using System.Collections.Generic;
using System.Linq;
using System.Text;
using Microsoft.Xna.Framework;
using Microsoft.Xna.Framework.Graphics;
using Microsoft.Xna.Framework.Input.Touch;
using Microsoft.Devices.Sensors;

namespace PhoneAsteroids
{
    class PlayerModel : BasicModel
    {
        Vector3 translationVector = Vector3.Zero;
```

```csharp
// Scale
float scale = .025f;

// Accelerometer stuff
Accelerometer accelerometer;
Vector3 accelerometerData = new Vector3();
int speed = 5;

public PlayerModel(Model m)
    : base (m)
{
    accelerometer = new Accelerometer();

    // Create an accelerometer event handler
    accelerometer.ReadingChanged +=
        new EventHandler<AccelerometerReadingEventArgs>(
        AccelerometerDataChanged);

    // Start the accelerometer
    accelerometer.Start();
}

public override void Update()
{
    // Move the ship based on accelerometer input
    translationVector.Y += accelerometerData.X * speed;
    translationVector.X += -accelerometerData.Y * speed;


    base.Update();
}

override public  Matrix GetWorld()
{
    return world * Matrix.CreateScale(scale) *
        Matrix.CreateRotationY(MathHelper.PiOver2) *
        Matrix.CreateRotationX(MathHelper.PiOver2) *
        Matrix.CreateTranslation(GetTranslationVector());
}

override public Matrix GetWorldForBoundingSphere()
{
    return world * Matrix.CreateScale(scale / 2) *
        Matrix.CreateRotationY(MathHelper.PiOver2) *
        Matrix.CreateRotationX(MathHelper.PiOver2) *
        Matrix.CreateTranslation(GetTranslationVector());
}


public Vector3 GetTranslationVector()
{
    // Return current translation vector plus offset
    // to start player at far right of screen
    return new Vector3(50, 0, 0) + translationVector;
```

```
    }

    public void AccelerometerDataChanged(object sender,
        AccelerometerReadingEventArgs e)
    {
        // Store accelerometer data
        accelerometerData.X = (float)e.X;
        accelerometerData.Y = (float)e.Y;
    }
  }
}
```

This class isn't really revolutionary either, and most of it should be very familiar to you by now. You have a translation vector used to store the player's position, and you're using the same methods you've used in the previous classes to get the world for the object and the bounding sphere. There is a `GetTranslationVector` method as well, which you'll use in other classes to get the current position of the player.

However, there is something new here that you haven't seen before: the `Accelerometer` class and supporting methods and variables to handle accelerometer input from your Windows Phone 7 device. In this game, the player will move about the screen by tilting the phone and using the accelerometer to control the player model's location.

The first thing you might have noticed is that in order to use the accelerometer, we've added a new namespace to the class via the following line of code:

```
using Microsoft.Devices.Sensors;
```

You might also notice that your game won't compile with this reference to the `Micro soft.Devices.Sensors` namespace. That's because you need to add a reference to this library in your project before you can access that namespace. To add the reference, right-click on the *PhoneAsteroids\References* node in Solution Explorer and select Add Reference. In the .NET tab of the resulting window, select the *Microsoft.Devices.Sensors* library and hit OK, as seen in Figure 17-10.

Now your code should at least compile. But before we see what happens when you run the game, let's discuss what's going on here with the accelerometer data. The `Acceler ometer` class provides the developer with access to the accelerometer on the device. The class has an event called `ReadingChanged` that fires when the accelerometer on the device receives new information. To access this data, you have wired up an event handler to a method called `AccelerometerDataChanged` with the following line of code, which is in the constructor for the `PlayerModel` class:

```
accelerometer.ReadingChanged += new EventHandler<AccelerometerReadingEventArgs>(
    AccelerometerDataChanged);
```

When the accelerometer device has new data to process, it will now call the `Accelero meterDataChanged` method. That method, shown again next for your review, stores the X and Y values from the accelerometer (representing how far the accelerometer sensed movement in each direction) in a `Vector3` variable called `accelerometerData`:

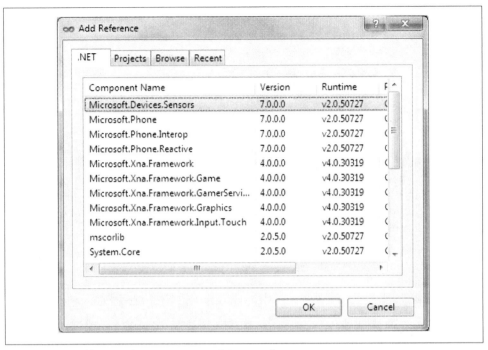

Figure 17-10. Adding a reference to Microsoft.Devices.Sensors

```
public void AccelerometerDataChanged(object sender,
    AccelerometerReadingEventArgs e)
{
    // Store accelerometer data
    accelerometerData.X = (float)e.X;
    accelerometerData.Y = (float)e.Y;
}
```

The last step in making all of this work is in your Update method, where you update the translation vector (representing the player's position) with the accelerometer data multiplied by a speed variable. That method currently looks like this:

```
public override void Update()
{
    // Move the ship based on accelerometer input
    translationVector.Y += accelerometerData.X * speed;
    translationVector.X += -accelerometerData.Y * speed;


    base.Update();
}
```

Not bad, eh? You should now be able to use your accelerometer to move the player around the screen in your game. Go ahead and compile and run your game, and see what happens. You should see something similar to the screen shown in Figure 17-11.

Figure 17-11. Best Windows Phone 7 game ever!!!

Wow. Now that is one sweet-looking game. You can thank me later for helping you make such an impressive piece of software. For now, let's look at what's happening... well...not much. Why? That's right, you have a bunch of models and model classes, but you aren't drawing them on the screen. You need a model manager like the one you built in past chapters. Let's tackle that next.

Adding a ModelManager

I hate to break it to you, but the hard part is over already for this chapter. Coding for Windows Phone 7 is so similar to coding for Windows and Xbox 360 that there really aren't that many key differences. That's awesome for developers wishing to build games across multiple platforms, but not too great for authors trying to explain the differences between those development platforms. That said, you still need to flesh out the rest of your game. To do that, add a class to your project called *ModelManager.cs*, and replace the default code with the following:

```
using System;
using System.Collections.Generic;
using System.Linq;
using Microsoft.Xna.Framework;
using Microsoft.Xna.Framework.Audio;
using Microsoft.Xna.Framework.Content;
using Microsoft.Xna.Framework.GamerServices;
using Microsoft.Xna.Framework.Graphics;
using Microsoft.Xna.Framework.Input;
using Microsoft.Xna.Framework.Media;

namespace PhoneAsteroids
{
    /// <summary>
    /// This is a game component that implements IUpdateable.
    /// </summary>
    public class ModelManager : DrawableGameComponent
    {
        // List of models
        List<AsteroidModel> asteroidList = new List<AsteroidModel>();
        List<ShotModel> shotList = new List<ShotModel>();
        PlayerModel player;

        // Spawning Asteroid stuff
        int timeSinceLastSpawn = 0;
        int nextSpawnTime = 0;
        int maxSpawnTime = 4000;
        int minSpawnTime = 2000;

        // Sounds
        SoundEffect trackSound;
        SoundEffect collisionSound;
        SoundEffectInstance trackSoundInstance;


        public ModelManager(Game game)
            : base(game)
        {
        }
```

```csharp
/// <summary>
/// Allows the game component to perform any initialization it needs to
/// before starting to run.  This is where it can query for any required
/// services and load content.
/// </summary>
public override void Initialize()
{
    SetNextSpawnTime();

    base.Initialize();
}

protected override void LoadContent()
{
    // Initialize player
    player = new PlayerModel(Game.Content.Load<Model>(@"models\p1_wedge"));

    // Load audio
    collisionSound = Game.Content.Load<SoundEffect>(@"audio\collision");
    trackSound = Game.Content.Load<SoundEffect>(@"audio\track");
    trackSoundInstance = trackSound.CreateInstance();
    trackSoundInstance.IsLooped = true;
    trackSoundInstance.Play();

    // Load all models
    Game.Content.Load<Model>(@"models\asteroid1");
    Game.Content.Load<Model>(@"models\asteroid2");
    Game.Content.Load<Model>(@"models\ammo");

    base.LoadContent();
}

/// <summary>
/// Allows the game component to update itself.
/// </summary>
/// <param name="gameTime">Provides a snapshot of timing values.</param>
public override void Update(GameTime gameTime)
{
    // Time to spawn?
    timeSinceLastSpawn += gameTime.ElapsedGameTime.Milliseconds;
    if (timeSinceLastSpawn > nextSpawnTime)
    {
        if(((Game1)Game).random.Next(2) == 0)
            asteroidList.Add(new AsteroidModel(Game.Content.Load<Model>(
                @"models\asteroid1"), ((Game1)Game).random,
                new Vector3(1, 0, 0), AsteroidModel.AsteroidSize.LARGE));
        else
            asteroidList.Add(new AsteroidModel(Game.Content.Load<Model>(
                @"models\asteroid2"), ((Game1)Game).random,
                new Vector3(1, 0, 0), AsteroidModel.AsteroidSize.LARGE));
        SetNextSpawnTime();
    }
```

```
// Update player
player.Update();

// Loop through all shots and call Update
for (int i = 0; i < shotList.Count; ++i)
{
    shotList[i].Update();
    if (shotList[i].translationVector.X < -300)
    {
        shotList.RemoveAt(i);
        --i;
    }
}

// Loop through all models and call Update
for (int i = 0; i < asteroidList.Count; ++i)
{
    asteroidList[i].Update();

    if (Collision(player, asteroidList[i]))
    {
        // Game over
        Game.Exit();
        --i;
        break;
    }

    // Check for asteroid out of bounds
    if (Math.Abs(asteroidList[i].position.X) > 300 ||
        Math.Abs(asteroidList[i].position.Y) > 300)
    {
        asteroidList.RemoveAt(i);
        --i;
        break;
    }

    // Check for shots hitting asteroids
    for (int j = 0; j < shotList.Count; ++j)
    {
        if(Collision(shotList[j], asteroidList[i]))
        {
            SpawnCollisionAsteroids(asteroidList[i].position,
                asteroidList[i].size);
            collisionSound.Play();
            shotList.RemoveAt(j);
            asteroidList.RemoveAt(i);
            i--;
            break;
        }
    }
}

base.Update(gameTime);
}
```

```csharp
private void SpawnCollisionAsteroids(Vector3 position,
    AsteroidModel.AsteroidSize asteroidSize)
{
    if (asteroidSize != AsteroidModel.AsteroidSize.SMALL)
    {
        // Spawn 2-4 smaller asteroids if collision was with a
        // large or medium asteroid
        int numberToSpawn = ((Game1)Game).random.Next(2, 5);
        for (int i = 0; i <= numberToSpawn; ++i)
        {
            if (((Game1)Game).random.Next(2) == 0)
                asteroidList.Add(new AsteroidModel(Game.Content.Load<Model>(
                    @"models\asteroid1"),
                    ((Game1)Game).random,
                    new Vector3(
                        ((float)((Game1)Game).random.NextDouble() * 2) - 1,
                        ((float)((Game1)Game).random.NextDouble() * 2) - 1,
                        0),
                    asteroidSize - 1, position));
            else
                asteroidList.Add(new AsteroidModel(Game.Content.Load<Model>(
                    @"models\asteroid2"),
                    ((Game1)Game).random,
                    new Vector3(
                        ((float)((Game1)Game).random.NextDouble() * 2) - 1,
                        ((float)((Game1)Game).random.NextDouble() * 2) - 1,
                        0),
                    asteroidSize - 1, position));
        }
    }
}

private bool Collision(BasicModel playerModel, BasicModel asteroidModel)
{
    // Check two models for collision using their bounding spheres
    foreach(ModelMesh playerMesh in playerModel.model.Meshes)
    {
        foreach (ModelMesh asteroidMesh in asteroidModel.model.Meshes)
        {
            if (asteroidMesh.BoundingSphere.Transform(
                asteroidModel.GetWorldForBoundingSphere()).
                Intersects(playerMesh.BoundingSphere.Transform(
                playerModel.GetWorldForBoundingSphere())))
                return true;
        }
    }
    return false;
}

public override void Draw(GameTime gameTime)
{
    // Draw player
    player.Draw(((Game1)Game).camera);
```

```csharp
        // Loop through and draw each asteroid
        foreach (AsteroidModel asteroid in asteroidList)
        {
            asteroid.Draw(((Game1)Game).camera);
        }

        // Loop through and draw each shot
        foreach (ShotModel shot in shotList)
        {
            shot.Draw(((Game1)Game).camera);
        }

        base.Draw(gameTime);
    }

    public void SetNextSpawnTime()
    {
        nextSpawnTime = ((Game1)Game).random.Next(minSpawnTime, maxSpawnTime);
        timeSinceLastSpawn = 0;
    }

    internal void FireShot()
    {
        shotList.Add(new ShotModel(Game.Content.Load<Model>(@"models\ammo"),
            ((Game1)Game).random, player.GetTranslationVector()));

    }

  }
}
```

As I mentioned previously, there isn't anything here that you haven't seen before. But that said, let's walk through it really quickly.

The first set of variables includes a list of asteroid models, a list of shot models, and a model for the player. Next, you have spawning variables for the asteroids (which are very similar to variables that you've used in previous chapters for random spawning of enemies). Finally, you have a few variables to handle some sound effects.

Notice the call to SetNextSpawnTime in your Initialize method. You've done this in previous chapters as well, and it sets the initial spawn time for your first enemy. The LoadContent method should be very straightforward by now, as all you're doing is loading resources and playing the soundtrack sound effect.

The Update method is a bit more complicated but still should be nothing new to you at this point. First, you're checking to see whether it's time to spawn a new enemy. If it is, you randomly create one of two models for asteroids (asteroid1 or asteroid2). Next, after calling Update on the player model, you loop through all the shots in the list of shots and call Update on each of them. Additionally, you're checking to see whether any of those shots are out of bounds and deleting any that are. Finally, you loop through all the asteroids and update them, check for game-over criteria (when the ship is hit with an asteroid), delete any asteroids that are out of bounds, and check for collisions between shots and asteroids. When a shot hits an asteroid, you spawn new asteroids, play an explosion sound effect, and remove both the shot and the asteroid.

The SpawnCollisionAsteroids method is called to create new, smaller asteroids when a shot hits an asteroid. This method randomly picks a number between two and four and creates that many asteroids of the next smaller size (with the asteroidSize - 1 parameter).

The Collision method uses the bounding spheres from each model to determine any collisions, and the Draw method does nothing more than loop through each model and call that model's Draw method. Finally, SetNextSpawnTime and FireShot are pretty self-explanatory.

Well, that's about it. All you have left is your Game1 class to tie it all together.

Finishing Details

The first thing you'll need to do in your Game1 class is add the following class-level variables:

```
ModelManager modelManager;
public Camera camera { get; protected set; }
public Random random { get; protected set; }
Texture2D attackTexture;
SoundEffect shotSound;
```

The first two variables are your model manager and camera game components. The random variable will be used for all the random calculations in your game. The attack Texture variable will be used to draw a small texture on the screen that the user will press to fire shots. The final variable added is the sound effect for firing shots.

Next, you'll want to initialize your random variable in the constructor of your Game1 class with the following code:

```
// Initialize random number generator
random = new Random();
```

Then add the following code to your Initialize method to initialize and add both of your game components:

```
// Initialize Camera
camera = new Camera(this);
Components.Add(camera);

// Initialize model manager
modelManager = new ModelManager(this);
Components.Add(modelManager);
```

Then you'll need to add the following code to your LoadContent method to load your texture and audio resources:

```
// Load textures
attackTexture = Content.Load<Texture2D>(@"textures\attack");
```

```
// Load audio
shotSound = Content.Load<SoundEffect>(@"audio\shot");
```

Now, in your `Update` method, add some code that will fire shots when the user presses the texture on the screen. Add the following code just before the call to `base.Update`:

```
// Did the user press the attack button on the touch panel?
TouchCollection touchCollection = TouchPanel.GetState();
foreach (TouchLocation touchLocation in touchCollection)
{
    if (touchLocation.State == TouchLocationState.Pressed &&
        GetAttackTextureRect().Contains(
        new Point((int)touchLocation.Position.X, (int)touchLocation.Position.Y)))
    {
        shotSound.Play();
        modelManager.FireShot();
    }
}
```

What's going on here? Let's take a closer look at touch panel input on the Windows Phone 7 to see how this works. First, you've used a method called `GetState` on the `TouchPanel` class. This method will return the current state of the touch panel from your Windows Phone 7 device in the form of a `TouchCollection`. This `TouchCollection` stores a list of `TouchLocation` objects that can be used to determine how and where the user has pressed the touch panel.

The `TouchLocation.State` property can be evaluated to figure out exactly how the user interacted with the touch panel. Possible state values are shown in Table 17-1:

Table 17-1. Possible TouchLocation states

State	Description
Invalid	This touch location position is invalid. Typically, you will encounter this state when a new touch location attempts to get the previous state of itself.
Moved	This touch location position was updated or pressed at the same position.
Pressed	This touch location position is new.
Released	This touch location position was released.

In this case, you're looking to see whether the `TouchLocation.State` property is `TouchLocationState.Pressed` (indicating a new touch location position, or in other words, the touch panel was pressed). If it is, you check the position of the touch location (via the `TouchLocation.Position` property) and see whether it is within the bounds of your attack texture. If it is, then the player intends to fire a shot, so you play the shot sound effect and call the `FireShot` method from the `ModelManager`.

Why do I keep saying that the user presses a texture to fire a shot? Isn't a texture just a 2D image? Absolutely, a texture is nothing more than a 2D image. However, when designing the user interface for a game (or any software, for that matter) it's important to make the interface as intuitive as possible. Gamers aren't used to simply pressing anywhere on a screen to get a weapon to fire, because traditionally you think of firing a weapon by hitting a button or pulling a trigger of some sort. So here you're keying off those typical senses of what's normal and drawing a button for them to press. Even though it's not a button, the user doesn't understand that—nor do they need to. You know when they hit that texture you're going to fire a shot, and they know when they see that texture that they should press it if they want to fire a shot.

All right, let's move on. You might have noticed you referenced a method that doesn't exist yet in your code: `GetAttackTextureRect`. This method is used to build a rectangle defining the location of the attack button texture. Add the method to your `Game1` class as shown here:

```
protected Rectangle GetAttackTextureRect()
{
    return new Rectangle(
        graphics.PreferredBackBufferWidth - attackTexture.Width - 10,
        graphics.PreferredBackBufferHeight - attackTexture.Height - 10,
        attackTexture.Width,
        attackTexture.Height);
}
```

Using the `GraphicsDevice.PreferredBackBufferWidth` and `GraphicsDevice.Preferred BackBufferHeight` properties as well as the size of the texture itself, you build a rectangle to represent the location of the button on the screen. You also subtract 10 from the X and Y coordinates of the rectangle so the button will not appear directly in the corner of the screen, but instead will be offset slightly.

Finally, modify your `Draw` method and add the `ResetGraphicsDevice` method as shown here:

```
protected override void Draw(GameTime gameTime)
{
    GraphicsDevice.Clear(Color.CornflowerBlue);

    spriteBatch.Begin();

    // Draw the attack texture on the screen
    spriteBatch.Draw(attackTexture,
        GetAttackTextureRect(),
        Color.White);

    spriteBatch.End();

    ResetGraphicsDevice();
```

```
        base.Draw(gameTime);
    }

    private void ResetGraphicsDevice()
    {
        GraphicsDevice.BlendState = BlendState.Opaque;
        GraphicsDevice.DepthStencilState = DepthStencilState.Default;
        GraphicsDevice.RasterizerState = RasterizerState.CullCounterClockwise;
        GraphicsDevice.SamplerStates[0] = SamplerState.LinearWrap;
    }
```

What's happening here? First, you're drawing the attackTexture using your sprite Batch variable. Then comes a call to the ResetGraphicsDevice method, which is added below the Draw method. What in the world is that doing? Well, you're mixing two very different drawing techniques here: 2D sprites and 3D models. XNA 4.0 uses a variety of state objects to tell the graphics device how to draw different types of data. When you use SpriteBatch.Begin and End to draw the sprites here, it modifies those state objects and sets the graphics device to a mode where it is prepared to draw 2D sprites. Drawing 3D objects while the graphics device is in that state can cause unpredictable results.

To counter that, after drawing 2D sprites you reset the graphics device with the code in the ResetGraphicsDevice method, which prepares the device to handle 3D models.

That's all there is to it. Congratulations! You just wrote your first ever 3D Windows Phone 7 game! Compile and run the game at this point, and you should see something similar to Figure 17-12.

Figure 17-12. Nice work! Asteroids aplenty!

What You Just Did

Well, congratulations! You've just done what very few people on this planet actually know how to do—program a game for a mobile device. You're in an elite club at this point, and your life is only going to get better. Let's review some of the highlights of what you just did:

- You learned how to register for a developer account, register your Windows Phone 7 device, and unlock your device using the Zune software.
- You created your first Windows Phone 7 game.
- You learned about changes required for development on Windows Phone 7 (accelerometer, touch panel input, screen size, and rotation issues).
- You wrote a killer asteroids app that will make your family happy for generations to come.

Summary

- To build games for your Windows Phone 7 device, you first need to register for a developer account.
- You use the Microsoft Zune software to unlock your Windows Phone 7 device and connect to it via Visual Studio.
- Developing on Windows Phone 7 is nearly identical to developing for Windows or Xbox 360, other than a few exceptions.
- The accelerometer on Windows Phone 7 is readable via event handlers.
- The touch panel on Windows Phone 7 devices is accessible via the TouchPanel class.
- Now that you've built a 3D game for Windows Phone 7, you're kind of a big deal. People know you. You're very important, and you have many leatherbound books, and your apartment smells of rich mahogany.

Test Your Knowledge: Quiz

1. What are the three types of developer accounts you can create for development on Windows Phone 7?
2. What software do you use to unlock your Windows Phone 7 device?
3. How do you read data from the Windows Phone 7 accelerometer?
4. What is the default screen resolution and screen rotation of a Windows Phone 7 game?
5. What are the possible states of a TouchLocation object?
6. Why does Brody the Bootlegger get angry with Jerry Seinfeld during the movie *Death Blow*?

CHAPTER 18

Multiplayer Games

In earlier sections of this book, we discussed the difficulty of creating true artificial intelligence. Although we dabbled in some light artificial intelligence earlier, the really complex algorithms used in the latest games are well beyond the scope of this book. You've probably realized by now how complicated it would be to really mimic a human player. It's so complicated that in many cases, depending on the game, it's downright impossible.

Chances are you've played a Real-Time Strategy (RTS) game where the computer player leaves his base too unguarded, or a football simulation game where there's one defensive play that stops the offense every single time, no matter what offensive play was called. This is one reason why multiplayer gaming is such an enjoyable experience; there really is nothing like playing against a real, live human opponent. Throw in the fun of trash talking and stat crunching and the general pride that typically results from winning these games, and multiplayer gaming can really become addicting.

In this chapter, we discuss different means of implementing multiplayer functionality in your games. First, we look at adding split-screen functionality to your game, and then we walk through building a new game using the XNA Framework networking API.

Split-Screen Functionality

One way to add multiplayer functionality to your games is to implement a split screen on a single monitor (for the PC) or television set (for the Xbox 360). Split screens will typically support one, two, three, or four players simultaneously playing on the same machine.

When implementing a split screen in your game, you need to consider several factors:

Input controls
> Typically, you'll want to support only the Xbox gamepad as input, because you won't want two, three, or four people huddled around a single keyboard.

Cameras and angles

> You'll probably have an independent camera for each player. You'll need to think about what camera angle gives each player the best view of the action from his perspective in the game.

Real estate

> Screen real estate will be at a premium when you're trying to squeeze multiple views into one screen. If you're implementing a two-player game, do the different views function more effectively side by side or top and bottom?

When drawing a scene in XNA, there's a property of the graphics device called `View port` that hasn't been mentioned in this book yet. The `Viewport` property is essentially a rectangle that represents the screen coordinates to which the graphics device will map its scene when drawing. By default, the `Viewport` is set to the size of the client window, which causes the graphics device to draw on the entire game window.

Split screens are implemented by modifying the `Viewport` of the graphics device and then drawing a particular scene multiple times (once for each player), using the camera for that player as the perspective from which to draw the scene.

That might sound like a lot of information, but don't let it scare you. Take a look at Figure 18-1 for a graphical view of a two-player split screen.

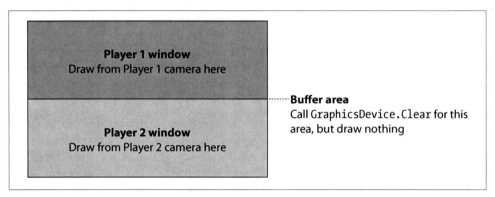

Figure 18-1. A typical two-player split-screen setup

To draw a screen with a typical vertically stacked two-player setup, as shown in Figure 18-1, you'd create a viewport for each of the players, which would contain screen coordinates representing the areas to be drawn for those players.

In your `Draw` method, you'd first want to call `GraphicsDevice.Clear` for the entire screen. This will clear the middle buffer area. The color that you specify in the `Clear` method will be the color of the border between the two split screens.

Why clear the entire screen just to clear the buffer area? Clearing the entire back buffer is a very fast and optimized operation for the GPU. It also resets other states that make rendering the scene very fast.

Next, you'd set the `GraphicsDevice.Viewport` property to the viewport for Player 1 and draw the scene from the perspective of Player 1's camera. You'd then do the same for Player 2.

So, how do you draw the scene from the perspective of Player 1's camera? You're most likely going to have a different camera for each player (after all, what use is a split screen if you draw the exact same thing on each player's section of the screen?). Remember that a camera has two matrices representing the view and the projection, respectively. These matrices are passed to your `BasicEffect` or your HLSL effect when you draw. To draw using Player 1's camera, you pass in the matrices representing that camera. To draw from a different camera's perspective, you just pass in the matrices corresponding to that camera instead.

That's the basic idea. Now, let's walk through the implementation of a two-player split screen. For this section, you're going to use the code that you built in Chapter 10. If you don't have this code any longer or you skipped Chapter 10, you can download the code for that chapter with the rest of the source code for this book.

Open the code for Chapter 10, and you'll see that in this project you've implemented a camera component, as you've done with all of the 3D examples in this book. Because all of the players will have their own cameras and their own viewports, and because a viewport represents the projection of what a camera sees in 3D to a rectangle on the game window in 2D, it makes sense to add the viewport to the `Camera` class.

Open the `Camera` class and add the following variable:

```
public Viewport viewport { get; set; }
```

Next, you'll need to make a few changes to the constructor of your `Camera` class. You'll need to accept a `Viewport` as a parameter and use that value to initialize the `viewport` variable you just added. In addition, the aspect ratio you're using in your constructor in the call to `CreatePerspectiveFieldOfView` is currently derived from the screen width and height. You're going to need to use the width and height of the viewport instead because the aspect ratio of each player's part of the split screen will no longer correspond to the size of the game window.

Your current constructor should look something like this:

```
public Camera(Game game, Vector3 pos, Vector3 target, Vector3 up) : base(game)
{
    view = Matrix.CreateLookAt(pos, target, up);

    projection = Matrix.CreatePerspectiveFieldOfView(
        MathHelper.PiOver4,
```

```
        (float)Game.Window.ClientBounds.Width /
        (float)Game.Window.ClientBounds.Height,
        1, 3000);
    }
```

Modify the constructor to accept a `Viewport` parameter and set the viewport variable as well, to use the viewport instead of the window size in the call to `CreatePerspecti veFieldOfView`, as shown here:

```
public Camera(Game game, Vector3 pos, Vector3 target,
    Vector3 up, Viewport viewport)
    : base(game)
{
    view = Matrix.CreateLookAt(pos, target, up);

    projection = Matrix.CreatePerspectiveFieldOfView(
        MathHelper.PiOver4,
        (float)viewport.Width /
        (float)viewport.Height,
        1, 3000);

    this.viewport = viewport;
}
```

Next, open the Game1 class. You've declared a `Camera` variable named `camera` at the class level. However, as you'll now be using two `Camera` objects (one for Player 1 and one for Player 2), remove the `camera` variable and add the following class-level variables instead:

```
public Camera camera1 { get; protected set; }
public Camera camera2 { get; protected set; }
```

Next, you'll need to initialize both of the new `Camera` objects. You're currently initializing the camera you just removed at the beginning of the `Initialize` method of the Game1 class with the following code:

```
// Camera component
camera = new Camera(this, new Vector3(0, 0, 50),
    Vector3.Zero, Vector3.Up);
Components.Add(camera);
```

Remove that code and replace it with the following code, which initializes the two new `Camera` objects after creating appropriate `Viewport` objects for each:

```
// Create viewports
Viewport vp1 = GraphicsDevice.Viewport;
Viewport vp2 = GraphicsDevice.Viewport;
vp1.Height = (GraphicsDevice.Viewport.Height / 2);

vp2.Y = vp1.Height;
vp2.Height = vp1.Height;


// Add camera components
camera1 = new Camera(this, new Vector3(0, 0, 50),
    Vector3.Zero, Vector3.Up, vp1);
Components.Add(camera1);
```

```
camera2 = new Camera(this, new Vector3(0, 0, -50),
    Vector3.Zero, Vector3.Up, vp2);
Components.Add(camera2);
```

Notice that when creating the new `Viewport` objects, you initially set them both equal to `GraphicsDevice.Viewport`. Remember that by default, the viewport of the graphics device is a rectangle encompassing the entire game window. Neither of your new viewports is significantly different from the rectangle representing the game window, so this is a good place to start. The `X`, `Y`, and `Width` properties of the top viewport (`vp1`) are all the same as those for the game window, so all you need to change for `vp1` is the height of the window. You're setting it to half the original viewport's height.

The `X` and `Width` properties of the `vp2` viewport are also the same as those of the game window, so you only need to change the `Y` property to make the top of the viewport be just below the bottom of the `vp1` viewport and change the height of the viewport to be the same as the height of the `vp1` viewport.

You then create each camera and pass the corresponding viewports to the constructor.

Next, you'll need to modify the code that draws the scene. You're drawing in two different places: within the `Game1` class and within the `ModelManager` class. Well, technically you don't draw in the `ModelManager` class, but you're calling `Draw` on each of the models in your models list and passing in a camera object from which to draw. You do so with the following code in your `ModelManager` class:

```
public override void Draw(GameTime gameTime)
{
    // Loop through and draw each model
    foreach (BasicModel bm in models)
    {
        bm.Draw(((Game1)Game).camera);
    }

    base.Draw(gameTime);
}
```

Remember that you're going to have to draw the scene once for every viewport. You can have the `Draw` method in your `ModelManager` class be called multiple times from within your `Game1` class (every time you call `base.Draw` in `Game1`, the `Draw` method in all game components is called as well). However, you're going to need to provide a way for the `ModelManager` class to know which camera to draw with. Add the following variable to the `Game1` class, which you'll use to set which camera is currently drawing:

```
public Camera currentDrawingCamera { get; protected set; }
```

Next, modify the `bm.Draw` call in the `Draw` method of your `ModelManager` class to use the `currentDrawingCamera` object from the `Game1` class to draw each model:

```
bm.Draw(((Game1)Game).currentDrawingCamera);
```

The last thing you'll need to do is modify the code that draws the scene in your Game1 class. Currently, the code in the Draw method of your Game1 class looks pretty bare:

```
protected override void Draw(GameTime gameTime)
{
    GraphicsDevice.Clear(Color.CornflowerBlue);

    // TODO: Add your drawing code here

    base.Draw(gameTime);
}
```

Modify the Draw method just shown as follows:

```
protected override void Draw(GameTime gameTime)
{
    // Clear border between screens
    GraphicsDevice.Clear(Color.Black);

    // Set current drawing camera for Player 1
    // and set the viewport to Player 1's viewport,
    // then clear and call base.Draw to invoke
    // the Draw method on the ModelManager component
    currentDrawingCamera = camera1;
    GraphicsDevice.Viewport = camera1.viewport;

    base.Draw(gameTime);

    // Set current drawing camera for Player 2
    // and set the viewport to Player 2's viewport,
    // then clear and call base.Draw to invoke
    // the Draw method on the ModelManager component
    currentDrawingCamera = camera2;
    GraphicsDevice.Viewport = camera2.viewport;

    base.Draw(gameTime);
}
```

It may seem kind of silly to implement all the logic of setting the camera and the viewport and then do nothing but clear the screen and call base.Draw, but remember that the ModelManager will actually be drawing the models, and when you call base.Draw the Draw method in the ModelManager will be called. The viewport that you set on the graphics device in the Draw method of the Game1 class will also be used until you set the viewport on the graphics device to something else. That means that by setting the viewport in the Draw method of the Game1 class, you are also affecting the Draw method of the ModelManager class.

Compile and run the game at this point, and you should see two ships in two different viewports, as shown in Figure 18-2.

It's important to note that you're not actually seeing two different ships. You're only drawing one model, so you're actually seeing the same ship from two different perspectives. When you created your two cameras, you placed one camera at (0, 0, 50)

Figure 18-2. I can't wait to play all my friends in this sweet two-player ship-watching game!

looking at the origin (where the ship is drawn) and the other at (0, 0, −50), also looking at the origin. This explains why one viewport shows the ship facing right and one shows it facing left—both are viewing the same ship, but from opposite sides.

There's still one problem with this game: it doesn't do anything. As exciting as it is to stare at a ship, you probably ought to offer the player a little bit more. We're not going to develop this example into an actual game, but it will help you to see the two different cameras moving independently in this example. Right now, you're drawing a ship at the origin and looking at it from one side with one camera and from the opposite side with a different camera. Each camera is used to draw the ship in a viewport the size of half the game window, which gives the split-screen look shown in Figure 18-2.

Because you're going to make the two cameras move in this example, you should first make the ship stop spinning. This will make it easier to see what's happening with each camera when you're moving it in 3D space. To stop the ship from spinning, use the `BasicModel` class instead of the `SpinningEnemy` class for the ship you create.

In the `LoadContent` method of the `ModelManager` class, change the line that creates the ship to use `BasicModel`, as follows:

```
models.Add(new BasicModel(
    Game.Content.Load<Model>(@"models\spaceship")));
```

If you compile and run the game now, you'll see the same ship with one view showing the front of the ship and the other view looking at the back of the ship. Now you'll need to add some code to move your cameras in 3D space. Add the following variables to the Camera class:

```
// Vectors for the view matrix
Vector3 cameraPosition;
Vector3 cameraDirection;
Vector3 cameraUp;

// Speed
float speed = 3;
```

The first three variables added here will be used to recreate the view matrix of the camera. This should be somewhat familiar, as this is the same technique used in Chapter 11 of this book. Because you're going to move your camera in 3D space, you need to be able to recreate your view matrix with a new camera position, direction, and up vector every time the Update method is called. These variables allow you to do that.

The final variable will be used to determine the speed of the camera movement.

Next, you'll need to add the following method to the Camera class to take care of recreating the view matrix:

```
private void CreateLookAt( )
{
    view = Matrix.CreateLookAt(cameraPosition,
        cameraPosition + cameraDirection, cameraUp);
}
```

Currently, the Camera class creates the view matrix only once, within the constructor, with the following line of code:

```
view = Matrix.CreateLookAt(pos, target, up);
```

Replace that line with the following code, which will set the position, direction, and up variables appropriately and create the view matrix by calling the method you just added:

```
// Create view matrix
cameraPosition = pos;
cameraDirection = target - pos;
cameraDirection.Normalize( );
cameraUp = up;
CreateLookAt( );
```

Again, this is the same technique used in Chapter 11. You're deriving a direction vector based on the difference between the position and the target of the camera. This vector will be used in the movement and rotation of the camera. The vector is normalized with the call to Normalize, which will give the vector a magnitude of one. This is done so that when the cameraDirection vector is multiplied by the speed variable, the resulting vector has a magnitude the size of the value represented by speed (meaning that your camera will move at the speed represented by the speed variable).

Because your camera now will need to recreate the view matrix every time the Update method is called, add the following line of code to the Update method of the Camera class:

```
    CreateLookAt( );
```

Next, add to the `Camera` class the following methods, which will let you move your camera forward and backward as well as strafe left and right:

```
public void MoveForwardBackward(bool forward)
{
    // Move forward/backward
    if (forward)
        cameraPosition += cameraDirection * speed;
    else
        cameraPosition -= cameraDirection * speed;
}

public void MoveStrafeLeftRight(bool left)
{

    // Strafe
    if (left)
    {
        cameraPosition +=
            Vector3.Cross(cameraUp, cameraDirection) * speed;
    }
    else
    {
        cameraPosition -=
            Vector3.Cross(cameraUp, cameraDirection) * speed;
    }
}
```

Now all that's left is to move the cameras. Add the following code to the `Update` method of the `Game1` class:

```
// Move the cameras
KeyboardState keyboardState = Keyboard.GetState( );

// Move camera1 with WASD keys
if (keyboardState.IsKeyDown(Keys.W))
    camera1.MoveForwardBackward(true);
if (keyboardState.IsKeyDown(Keys.S))
    camera1.MoveForwardBackward(false);
if (keyboardState.IsKeyDown(Keys.A))
    camera1.MoveStrafeLeftRight(true);
if (keyboardState.IsKeyDown(Keys.D))
    camera1.MoveStrafeLeftRight(false);

// Move camera2 with IJKL keys
if (keyboardState.IsKeyDown(Keys.I))
    camera2.MoveForwardBackward(true);
if (keyboardState.IsKeyDown(Keys.K))
    camera2.MoveForwardBackward(false);
if (keyboardState.IsKeyDown(Keys.J))
    camera2.MoveStrafeLeftRight(true);
if (keyboardState.IsKeyDown(Keys.L))
    camera2.MoveStrafeLeftRight(false);
```

This code will allow you to move the top view (camera 1) with the WASD keys and move the bottom view (camera 2) with the IJKL keys. Compile and run the game at this point, and you'll see that both cameras move independently of each other. If you want to add rotation to your camera, you can do so by using the camera rotation code discussed in previous chapters, implementing it in a way similar to how you just added the code to move each camera.

Where's the Camera?

When you move around with one camera, you'll be able to see where the other camera should be, but you won't see it. Why?

You don't see camera 2 sitting in 3D space when moving camera 1, because a camera isn't an object that is drawn. That is, in this example you can move each camera to look at the point where the other camera is located, but you won't see anything there, because the camera is not a visible object in the game.

Let's say you wanted to make this game into a space shooter where each player flies a ship in 3D space and shoots at the other. To implement this, you'd need to take the code you currently have and, for each camera, draw a ship at the camera's location, rotated to face the direction that that camera is facing. Only then will you see something in the game itself that represents the other player.

That's all there is to it! You can easily add split-screen functionality to any game this way. To add support for three players, use three viewports and three cameras. To add support for four players, use four viewports and four cameras.

Depending on the specifics of your game, you may also need to add functionality to move each camera independently as well as functionality to perform other actions to interact with the world independently, based on input from the player assigned to that camera.

Network Game Development

Networking has been a hot topic in graphics API circles at Microsoft for a long time. Since the days of DirectX and the DirectPlay libraries, there have been numerous iterations that have met with varying levels of success. However, DirectPlay was created before TCP/IP became the standard that it is today, so it was eventually deprecated. Instead of DirectPlay, DirectX developers were told that the Windows sockets libraries were ultimately going to be the tool of choice for developing games with network play functionality.

XNA 1.0 followed suit with no support for networking API outside of System.net and no support for network play on the Xbox 360. The result? A new and complete networking API was the XNA 1.0 developers' most requested feature. Because of that, beginning with XNA Game Studio 2.0, Microsoft allowed developers to use the Live for Windows APIs on Windows and the Xbox 360.

According to a presentation by Shawn Hargreaves (engineer on the XNA Community Game Platform team at Microsoft) at the Game Developers Conference in 2008, the design goals for the XNA team included:

- Enable networked multiplayer games
- Make the API easy to use
- Make the API handle lower-level networking details for the user
- Support both Xbox LIVE and Games for Windows LIVE
- Allow development with a single Xbox 360 and PC
- Don't require dedicated servers

The best thing about the XNA networking API is how simple it is to use. If you've ever dealt with networking code in other languages or libraries, you'll most likely find the XNA implementation a refreshing upgrade in terms of ease of use.

XNA uses the Xbox LIVE and Games for Windows LIVE platforms for multiplayer connections. You're probably somewhat familiar with how Xbox LIVE works, but you might be new to Games for Windows LIVE. Essentially, Games for Windows LIVE ties Windows games to gamertags and online identities the same way that Xbox LIVE does. In fact, they use the same online gamertags and identities. As you'll see later in this chapter, the Games for Windows LIVE platform even uses a series of screens that closely resembles the Xbox 360 dashboard for sign-in and other account maintenance activities.

A list of XNA Creators Club and LIVE membership requirements for different game types on the PC and the Xbox 360 is shown in Table 18-1.

Table 18-1. XNA Creators Club and LIVE Membership requirements

XNA Framework and network usage	Xbox 360	PC
Run an XNA Framework game	LIVE Silver membership and Creators Club membership	No membership requirements
Use SystemLink	LIVE Silver membership and Creators Club membership	No membership requirements
Sign on to Xbox LIVE and Games for Windows LIVE servers	LIVE Silver membership and Creators Club membership	LIVE Silver membership and Creators Club membership
Use Xbox LIVE Matchmaking	LIVE Gold membership and Creators Club membership	LIVE Gold membership and Creators Club membership

Amazingly, most of the code that you write for a PC game using Games for Windows LIVE will be compatible with the Xbox 360 and Windows Phone 7. The networking API will work with any of those platforms, although there are fewer details to worry about with Windows Phone 7 (e.g., no support for gamertags).

Network Configurations

One of the most important things to consider when writing a networked game is what type of network you'll be using (peer-to-peer, client/server, or a hybrid). The type of network you choose will have a big impact on how you handle your in-game network traffic, and on the performance of your application.

In a peer-to-peer network, all the participants are clients of each other. When something changes on one computer, that computer sends a message to all other computers telling them what's happened. In space shooter game terms, let's say you're playing a game with five participants. If one computer's player shoots a bullet, that computer sends a message to all other computers telling them that a bullet has been fired. A typical peer-to-peer architecture diagram is shown in Figure 18-3.

In contrast to a peer-to-peer network, a client/server network configuration typically has one server, and the rest of the machines are clients. All communication is run through the server. If you took the previous example of five people playing a space shooter game and one player firing a shot, in a client/server network that computer would send a message to the server (unless that computer is the server), and then the server would send the message out to all the clients.

A typical client/server configuration is shown in Figure 18-4.

You might think at first that a client/server configuration is a bit of a bottleneck because all communication runs through one machine. In some cases, it might be. However, look at all the arrows (representing network messages) in the peer-to-peer network diagram in Figure 18-3. Imagine this network being applied to a game like *World of Warcraft*, where hundreds or even thousands of players are playing simultaneously. With messages going back and forth between every single computer in that game, you can see how communications and handling messages would quickly get out of hand.

That's not to say that a peer-to-peer network is never a good idea, though. In a client/server model, if the server goes down, the game ends. In peer-to-peer networks that's less of an issue, and the "host" of the game can more easily transition from one computer to another. The best network configuration really depends on how much information you have to keep track of in a game and how many players are going to be involved at the same time.

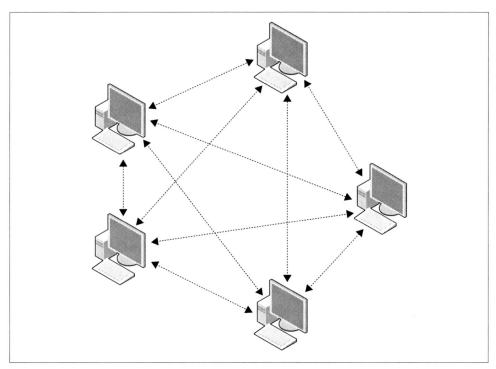

Figure 18-3. Typical peer-to-peer network—all computers interact with each other

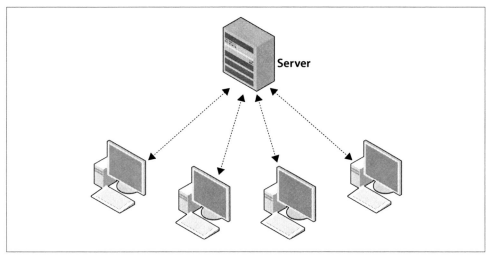

Figure 18-4. Typical client/server network—all messages are run through the server

Writing an XNA Network Game

Throughout the rest of this chapter, we'll be building a game that uses the XNA networking APIs to enable multiplayer functionality across a Windows network. The same code can be applied to the Xbox 360 system link networking functionality.

In this section, you'll start with a new project, but you'll be using some code and resources from the project you completed in Chapter 8 of this book. If you don't have the code for Chapter 8, it can be downloaded with the rest of the code for this book.

 I debated creating this chapter as a simple introduction to the networking API, and instead opted to demonstrate the API in a network game. However, because of that decision, this chapter has a large amount of code in it.

If you're weary of typing so much code, feel free to download the source code for this chapter and walk through it while reading the chapter. It might save you some headaches in the long run.

This chapter assumes that you've read through the book and are pretty familiar with Visual Studio 2010 and XNA Game Studio 4.0. If you find yourself not understanding those principles in this chapter, please refer back to the earlier chapters in this book.

Also, because all other games written in this book have used XACT for audio, I assume that by now you have a good feel for XACT and how it works. Hence, this chapter will instead implement sound using the simplified sound API provided with the XNA Framework 4.0. If you're looking to learn more about XACT, please refer to the other examples in this book.

To start things off, create a new XNA 4.0 Windows Game project in Visual Studio. Call your project *Catch*.

You're going to need to add two files to your project from the source code for Chapter 8 of this book. Right-click your project in Solution Explorer, select Add→Existing Item..., and navigate to the source code for Chapter 8. Select the following files to add to your project:

- *Sprite.cs*
- *UserControlledSprite.cs*

You're going to create a 2D networked game in which one player chases another player around the screen, with the goal of colliding with the other player. The player being chased will earn more points the longer he stays away from the chaser. You'll be modifying your existing sprite classes to handle the sprite objects in the multiplayer networked game.

Modifying the Sprite Class

The first thing you'll need to do in the `Sprite` class is change the namespace of the class from `AnimatedSprites` to `Catch`:

```
namespace Catch
```

In this game, players will take turns chasing each other. There will be two sprite objects: a gears sprite and a dynamite sprite. The dynamite sprite will always chase the gears sprite around the screen. Because players will be switching back and forth from gears sprites to dynamite sprites, you'll need to expose a few variables with auto-implemented properties. To do this, change the following class-level variables of your `Sprite` class to have public accessors, as shown here:

```
public Texture2D textureImage { get; set; }
public Point sheetSize { get; set; }
public Vector2 speed { get; set; }
public Vector2 originalSpeed { get; set; }
```

You're also going to need to set the positions of the sprites between rounds, so that the chaser and chased players don't start next to each other. Change the `GetPosition` property accessor to `Position` and add a `set` accessor:

```
public Vector2 Position
{
    get { return position; }
    set { position = value; }
}
```

Modifying the UserControlledSprite Class

Next let's work on changes to the `UserControlledSprite` class. First, change the namespace from `AnimatedSprites` to `Catch`:

```
namespace Catch
```

When you worked on the 2D game using these classes in previous chapters, you were dealing with a one-player game and the score was kept in the `Game1` class. You're now dealing with a two-player game. So, you'll need to either add a second score variable to the `Game1` class or figure out a better solution. Because a `UserControlledSprite` represents a player, it would make sense to add the score to this class. Add the following class-level variable to the `UserControlledSprite` class:

```
public int score { get; set; }
```

Also, as mentioned earlier, you're going to be swapping players back and forth between the chasing sprite and the chased sprite. That means you'll need to add a variable that will keep track of which role this particular player sprite is currently playing:

```
public bool isChasing { get; set; }
```

Then, modify both constructors of the UserControlledSprite class to receive the chasing parameter. Also add code in the bodies of both constructors to initialize the isChasing and score variables:

```
public UserControlledSprite(Texture2D textureImage, Vector2 position,
    Point frameSize, int collisionOffset, Point currentFrame, Point sheetSize,
    Vector2 speed, bool isChasing)
    : base(textureImage, position, frameSize, collisionOffset, currentFrame,
    sheetSize, speed, null, 0)
{
    score = 0;
    this.isChasing = isChasing;
}

public UserControlledSprite(Texture2D textureImage, Vector2 position,
    Point frameSize, int collisionOffset, Point currentFrame, Point sheetSize,
    Vector2 speed, int millisecondsPerFrame, bool isChasing)
    : base(textureImage, position, frameSize, collisionOffset, currentFrame,
    sheetSize, speed, millisecondsPerFrame, null, 0)
{
    score = 0;
    this.isChasing = isChasing;
}
```

Finally, modify the Update method of the UserControlledSprite class to accept a parameter indicating whether the Update method should move the sprite. Then, use that parameter to run the code that will move the sprite only if the parameter is true. Note that because the base class's Update method does not have this parameter, you'll have to remove the override keyword in the method definition.

The modified Update method should look like this:

```
public void Update(GameTime gameTime,
    Rectangle clientBounds, bool moveSprite)
{
    if (moveSprite)
    {
        // Move the sprite according to the direction property
        position += direction;

        // If the sprite is off the screen, put it back in play
        if (position.X < 0)
            position.X = 0;
        if (position.Y < 0)
            position.Y = 0;
        if (position.X > clientBounds.Width - frameSize.X)
            position.X = clientBounds.Width - frameSize.X;
        if (position.Y > clientBounds.Height - frameSize.Y)
            position.Y = clientBounds.Height - frameSize.Y;
    }

    base.Update(gameTime, clientBounds);
}
```

Now the `Update` method will only update the frame of the sprite, rather than moving it, when the `moveSprite` parameter is set to false. Why would you ever want to only update the frame and not move a `UserControlledSprite`?

This is a good time for a little discussion about network data. Passing data through a network is a bottleneck in terms of performance. Although performance over a network is extremely fast, it simply cannot keep up with the internal speed of your PC or Xbox 360. Because of this, you'll want to limit the amount of data that you pass around the network.

In this game, you'll be implementing a peer-to-peer network, which means that each PC will send data to the other PC letting it know what's happening in its instance of the game. A good example of this is when a player moves a sprite in his instance of the game. Let's say you have two computers playing this game. One player is chasing the other player around the screen. If the chasing player moves left by pressing a key on his keyboard or pressing the thumbstick on his gamepad, how will the other computer know that he moved? The answer is, it won't.

That's where the messaging comes in. When the chasing player moves left, the instance of the game that he is playing on needs to update that player's position and then notify the other instance of the game on the other computer that this player has moved to the left. One way to do that is to send over the entire `UserControlledSprite` object from the chasing player's computer to the other computer. The other computer could then pull it off the network and use it as the chasing player in its instance of the game.

However, while the `UserControlledSprite` may have all the data that the other computer would need, it also has a lot of other data (e.g., texture, frame size, sheet size, scale, and other information). The other computer already has all this information, and doesn't need to be given it again. A much more efficient way of doing things is to send the other computer a message that contains only the information that has changed (in this case, the player's position). The receiving computer can pull the chasing player's position off the network and use it as the new position of the chasing player in its instance of the game. This way, the chasing player will move around the screen on the chased player's computer, even though the chasing player is playing on a different computer.

The complication is that in addition to updating the position of the chasing player, the chased player's computer also needs to animate that sprite. Another way you could do this would be to pass not only the position of the sprite to the other computer, but also the current frame of the sprite. But why would you not want to do that?

There are two reasons: it would involve sending more data across the network, and it's not necessary. Will anybody notice if the chasing player's sprite is a frame or two behind in its animation sequence on the second computer? Not in this game. In other games it might matter, but in this game you have a single, continuous animation for each sprite, and nobody will notice if it is slightly out of sync. Consequently, it's not worth sending the extra data across the network.

Instead, you need a way to update the position of the `UserControlledSprite` that represents the other player and then update that player's animation without moving it based on user input—hence the parameter you just added that will cause the `Update` method to update the animation frame only.

Coding Your Game1 Class

The first thing you'll need to do in your `Game1` class is add an `enum` that you'll use to represent game states. We've discussed game states in previous chapters, but they're never more important than in networked games. Beyond the typical states in a game (a start state where you display instructions or splash screens, an in-game state, and an end-game state), in a networked game you'll usually also have a sign-in state where the player signs into Xbox LIVE or Games for Windows LIVE, a state where you find sessions of your game, and a state where you create sessions.

You'll actually want to add the following `enum` outside of the `Game1` class, between the `Catch` namespace declaration and the class declaration. This will allow any other classes you may add later to access the game states more easily:

```
namespace Catch
{
    // Represents different states of the game
    public enum GameState { SignIn, FindSession,
        CreateSession, Start, InGame, GameOver }

    public class Game1 : Microsoft.Xna.Framework.Game
    {
        ...
```

In addition, you'll need to add another `enum` that represents different types of messages that are sent across the network. Why? You need this because, as you'll see shortly, when your game reads data from the network, it needs to know in advance what type of data is coming in (an `int`, a `string`, a `Vector2`, etc.). You'll also need to know how much data is coming (two `int`s? three `int`s? one `int` and two `string`s?). That's not a problem if you're always sending the exact same datatypes and the same number of them in every message. However, your messaging will most likely be more complicated than that.

To solve this problem, you can send a value at the beginning of every message that tells the receiving computers what type of message is coming. In this case, you're going to be sending data telling other computers to either start the game, end the game, restart the game, rejoin the lobby, or update the player position. So, add the following `enum` immediately after the `GameState` enum:

```
// Represents different types of network messages
public enum MessageType { StartGame, EndGame, RestartGame,
    RejoinLobby, UpdatePlayerPos }
```

You'll be adding network code to your Game1 class, so add the following using statement at the top of the file:

```
using Microsoft.Xna.Framework.Net;
```

Next, add the following class-level variables to your Game1 class:

```
// Fonts
SpriteFont scoreFont;

// Current game state
GameState currentGameState = GameState.SignIn;

// Audio variables
SoundEffectInstance trackInstance;

// Sprite speeds
Vector2 chasingSpeed = new Vector2(4, 4);
Vector2 chasedSpeed = new Vector2(6, 6);

// Network stuff
NetworkSession networkSession;
PacketWriter packetWriter = new PacketWriter( );
PacketReader packetReader = new PacketReader( );
```

Most of these should look familiar to you. You're going to use the scoreFont variable to draw text on the screen. The currentGameState variable holds a value from the GameState enum indicating the current state of the game. The trackInstance variable holds the instance of the soundtrack sound, so you can stop it when the game ends. The two Vector2 variables hold data representing the speed of each sprite (the chasing sprite will move slightly slower than the chased sprite).

Three new variables that you've never seen before are listed at the end of that code block: networkSession, packetWriter, and packetReader.

The backbone of any networked game in XNA is the NetworkSession class. This class represents a single multiplayer session of your game. Through this class you can access all members of the session (via the AllGamers property, which is a collection of Gamer objects), the host of the game (via the Host member, which is a NetworkGamer object), and other properties pertinent to the multiplayer session.

The other two variables are used to send data across the network to other computers. The PacketWriter writes packets of information to the network, and the Packet Reader reads packets of information from the network.

Packets

What's a packet? Are we talking about those MSG-filled flavor packets that I use with my Top Ramen noodles?

Not quite. Networks and packets really are well beyond the scope of this book. I've touched on some high-level network configuration terminology, but I won't even try digging into packets and lower-level network communications. If you're interested in that sort of thing, there are tons of resources out there for you to learn more.

For the purposes of this book, just understand that when you send data to another computer, you send it in something called a "packet." Your packet can contain variable amounts of data (e.g., one packet might contain only an `int`, whereas another might contain a `string`, an `int`, two `Vector2`s, and five `float`s).

You write data to a packet and then send it, and when reading, you read a packet and then parse through the packet to find the data you need.

Imagine that you've hoarded tons of Top Ramen flavor packets, and you're communicating with your friends only through those packets (this is highly recommended). You'd write a note ("Hi, Brant!") and stick it in the packet and throw it at your friend. You'd wait a while and get another packet back. You'd open it and it would read, "Hi, Aaron. How are you?" Then you'd write another note ("Good. You? I'm so sorry that I destroyed you in racquetball today.") and stick it in another packet, and throw that one at your friend.

It's a great way to communicate, but kind of a waste of good MSG flavor packets....

The next thing you're going to need to do is add the following code to the `Initialize` method of your `Game1` class, just before the call to `base.Initialize`:

```
Components.Add(new GamerServicesComponent(this));
```

You're already familiar with game components, and as you can see, this code adds a game component of the type `GamerServicesComponent` to your list of components in this game. The obvious question is, what's a `GamerServicesComponent`? This component enables all networking and gamer services functionality. It will automatically enable your game to use Xbox LIVE and Games for Windows LIVE functions.

 If you use the gamer services component, any PC on which you run your game will have to have the full XNA Game Studio install because the basic redistributable for XNA does not support gamer services.

Next, add a new folder in Solution Explorer under the *CatchContent* project and name the folder *Fonts*. Add a new spritefont file to that folder called *ScoreFont.spritefont*. Then, load the font in the `LoadContent` method of the `Game1` class:

```
scoreFont = Content.Load<SpriteFont>(@"fonts\ScoreFont");
```

Adding Update Code

Now you'll need to modify the Update method of your Game1 class to call a different method based on the current game state (you'll add those methods shortly):

```
protected override void Update(GameTime gameTime)
{
    if (GamePad.GetState(PlayerIndex.One).Buttons.Back == ButtonState.Pressed)
        this.Exit( );

    // Only run the Update code if the game is currently active.
    // This prevents the game from progressing while
    // gamer services windows are open.
    if (this.IsActive)
    {
        // Run different methods based on game state
        switch (currentGameState)
        {
            case GameState.SignIn:
                Update_SignIn( );
                break;
            case GameState.FindSession:
                Update_FindSession( );
                break;
            case GameState.CreateSession:
                Update_CreateSession( );
                break;
            case GameState.Start:
                Update_Start(gameTime);
                break;
            case GameState.InGame:
                Update_InGame(gameTime);
                break;
            case GameState.GameOver:
                Update_GameOver(gameTime);
                break;
        }
    }

    // Update the network session and pump network messages
    if (networkSession != null)
        networkSession.Update( );

    base.Update(gameTime);
}
```

Besides the methods that you haven't coded yet, there are a couple of other things here that are worth mentioning. First, the game logic is surrounded by an if statement containing this.IsActive. This relates to the GamerServicesComponent you added earlier. That component will automatically render sign-in screens and account dashboards upon request. When it does so, your game becomes inactive (even though it is drawn in the same window). You don't want processing to take place while the player is working in the gamer services screens, so this is a way to essentially pause your game logic while those screens are visible.

Second, near the end of the method is a call to Update on the NetworkSession object. As mentioned earlier, the NetworkSession handles all session information, player information, and so on, related to the current session of the game. You have to call Update on that object in order to update the session and pump the network messages through the session. If you don't call Update on the NetworkSession object, you will not be able to receive messages sent from other players.

Updating While in the SignIn Game State

Next, add the Update_SignIn method to the Game1 class:

```
protected void Update_SignIn(  )
{
    // If no local gamers are signed in, show sign-in screen
    if (Gamer.SignedInGamers.Count < 1)
    {
        Guide.ShowSignIn(1, false);
    }
    else
    {
        // Local gamer signed in, move to find sessions
        currentGameState = GameState.FindSession;
    }
}
```

This method checks to see how many local gamers are signed into the game by using the Gamer.SignedInGamers property. If there are no gamers signed into the game, the gamer services sign-in screen (pictured in Figure 18-5) is shown by calling Guide.Show SignIn. Parameters for this method include the pane count, which indicates how many sign-in window panes to show (on Windows only one is allowed, but on the Xbox 360 one, two, or four are allowed), and the online only flag, which is a Boolean indicating whether the game will allow local players or force players to sign in online.

If you have never signed in with an account on this computer previously, the gamer services sign-in window will look something like Figure 18-5.

If you've signed in on this computer before, the Games for Windows Live screen will give you an option of either creating a new account or selecting a previously used profile.

 Games for Windows Live is provided on the PC only for the purpose of testing Xbox 360 games. As a result, when playing on your PC under Games for Windows Live, you must sign in with a premium XNA Creator's Club profile. Signing in with a nonpremium account may result in an unhandled GamerServicesNotAvailableException exception.

Once a gamer has signed in, the game state moves forward to the FindSession state.

Figure 18-5. Signing into Games for Windows LIVE for the first time

Updating While in the FindSession Game State

The next thing you'll need to do is add the `Update_FindSession` method:

```
private void Update_FindSession(  )
{
    // Find sessions of the current game
    AvailableNetworkSessionCollection sessions =
        NetworkSession.Find(NetworkSessionType.SystemLink, 1, null);
    if (sessions.Count == 0)
    {
        // If no sessions exist, move to the CreateSession game state
        currentGameState = GameState.CreateSession;
    }
    else
    {
        // If a session does exist, join it, wire up events,
        // and move to the Start game state
        networkSession = NetworkSession.Join(sessions[0]);
        WireUpEvents(  );
        currentGameState = GameState.Start;
    }

}
```

This method will search for a running session of the current game using the `Network Session.Find` method. Because you're using the `NetworkSessionType SystemLink` to create the game, the computer creating the session and the computer searching for the session must be on the same subnet in order to find each other. You're also specifying some specific criteria for finding another session by passing in parameters to the `Find` method: you're looking for games that use `SystemLink` and that allow only one local player.

If no session is found, the game state is moved to the `CreateSession` state, where a new session is created. If a session is found, the game joins that session. You then wire up some gamer events using the `WireUpEvents` method, which you'll write in a moment. Finally, the game state is then moved to the `Start` state.

Now, add the `WireUpEvents` method and the event-handler methods, as follows:

```
protected void WireUpEvents( )
{
    // Wire up events for gamers joining and leaving
    networkSession.GamerJoined += GamerJoined;
    networkSession.GamerLeft += GamerLeft;
}

void GamerJoined(object sender, GamerJoinedEventArgs e)
{
    // Gamer joined. Set the tag for the gamer to a new UserControlledSprite.
    // If the gamer is the host, create a chaser; if not, create a chased.
    if (e.Gamer.IsHost)
    {
        e.Gamer.Tag = CreateChasingSprite( );
    }
    else
    {
        e.Gamer.Tag = CreateChasedSprite( );
    }
}
```

The `WireUpEvents` method first wires up two events: when a gamer joins the session and when a gamer leaves the session. You're wiring these up because you'll need to add some special functionality in each scenario.

When a gamer joins the game, the `GamerJoined` method will be called. This method will assign a property named `Tag` for the player to a new `UserControlledSprite`. This `Tag` property is an object type, which means that you can use it to store virtually anything. Typically you'll use it to hold data representing a particular player in the game—in this case, a `UserControlledSprite`.

It's important to note that the `Tag` property of the `NetworkGamer` object will not be sent across the network. You don't use this property to sync up your objects. However, you can use this object to track each player locally in each instance of the game. What you'll be doing here is storing a `UserControlledSprite` in the `Tag` property of the `Network Gamer` object for each player. As one player moves, that player's computer will send a message to the other computer telling it the player's new position. That computer will then assign the `position` property of the `UserControlledSprite` object (stored in the `NetworkGamer.Tag` property) for that player to the position received over the network and will use the `NetworkGamer.Tag` property (which is a `UserControlledSprite`) to draw the opposing player.

If this doesn't make sense just yet, it's OK. Follow the code in the rest of this chapter, and hopefully it will become clearer as we move on.

The `NetworkGamer.Tag` property is set depending on whether the gamer who joined is the host, by using one of two methods:

```
private UserControlledSprite CreateChasedSprite(  )
{
    // Create a new chased sprite
    // using the gears sprite sheet
    return new UserControlledSprite(
            Content.Load<Texture2D>(@"Images/gears"),
            new Vector2((Window.ClientBounds.Width / 2) + 150,
                (Window.ClientBounds.Height / 2) + 150),
            new Point(100, 100), 10, new Point(0, 0),
            new Point(6, 8), chasedSpeed, false);
}

private UserControlledSprite CreateChasingSprite(  )
{
    // Create a new chasing sprite
    // using the dynamite sprite sheet
    return new UserControlledSprite(
            Content.Load<Texture2D>(@"Images/dynamite"),
            new Vector2((Window.ClientBounds.Width / 2) - 150,
                (Window.ClientBounds.Height / 2) - 150),
            new Point(100, 100), 10, new Point(0, 0),
            new Point(6, 8), chasingSpeed, true);
}
```

These should be pretty straightforward: you're creating a new sprite that will be chased using the gears sprite sheet in the `CreateChasedSprite` method and creating a sprite that will do the chasing using the dynamite sprite sheet in the `CreateChasingSprite` method.

You'll need to add these images to your project before moving on. The images are located with the source code for this chapter in the *Catch\CatchContent\Images* folder. Add a new folder under the *CatchContent* node in Solution Explorer called *Images*, and add the *dynamite.png* and *gears.png* files from the source code for this chapter to your project in the new folder.

Finally, if a gamer leaves, you'll want to check to see whether that gamer was the local gamer. If so, dispose of the session and move the game state to the `FindSession` state:

```
void GamerLeft(object sender, GamerLeftEventArgs e)
{
    // Dispose of the network session, set it to null.
    // Stop the soundtrack and go
    // back to searching for sessions.
    networkSession.Dispose(  );
    networkSession = null;
```

```
    trackInstance.Stop( );

    currentGameState = GameState.FindSession;
}
```

Updating While in the CreateSession GameState

Next, add the Update_CreateSession method:

```
private void Update_CreateSession( )
{
    // Create a new session using SystemLink with a max of 1 local player
    // and a max of 2 total players
    networkSession = NetworkSession.Create(NetworkSessionType.SystemLink, 1, 2);
    networkSession.AllowHostMigration = true;
    networkSession.AllowJoinInProgress = false;

    // Wire up events and move to the Start game state
    WireUpEvents( );
    currentGameState = GameState.Start;
}
```

This method creates a new session using the NetworkSession.Create method. The parameters are session type (in this case, SystemLink), max local players (one player allowed per computer), and max total players (two players allowed per session).

After it's created, the session is set to allow host migration (meaning if the host drops, the other player becomes the host), and not to allow gamers to join when the game is in progress.

The same events that you used for joining a session are then wired up, and the game state is set to Start.

Updating While in the Start Game State

Now you'll want to add the logic that will run when Update is called and the game is in the Start game state:

```
private void Update_Start(GameTime gameTime)
{
    // Get local gamer
    LocalNetworkGamer localGamer = networkSession.LocalGamers[0];

    // Check for game start key or button press
    // only if there are two players
    if (networkSession.AllGamers.Count == 2)
    {
        // If space bar or Start button is pressed, begin the game
        if (Keyboard.GetState( ).IsKeyDown(Keys.Space) ||
            GamePad.GetState(PlayerIndex.One).Buttons.Start ==
            ButtonState.Pressed)
        {
```

```
            // Send message to other player that we're starting
            packetWriter.Write((int)MessageType.StartGame);
            localGamer.SendData(packetWriter, SendDataOptions.Reliable);

            // Call StartGame
            StartGame( );
        }
    }

    // Process any incoming packets
    ProcessIncomingData(gameTime);
}
```

This method first gets the local gamer's `LocalNetworkGamer` object by using `networkSession.LocalGamers[0]`. You know that the local gamer you want is the first one in the list because you're allowing only one local gamer per computer. This `LocalNetworkGamer` object will be used later in the method to send network data to the other computers in the session.

The main purpose of this method is to determine whether the game will start. When you draw during the `Start` game state, you'll be drawing some text telling the player to wait for other players (if there is only one player in the session) or to hit the space bar or Start button on the gamepad to begin the game (if there are two players in the session).

There are two ways this game can start, for each instance of the game:

- The local player can hit the space bar or the Start button. In this method, you've added code to start the game if that happens.
- The other player (on the other computer) can start the game, in which case you'll receive a network message telling you that the other player has started the game and that you should start the game now (in this case, the local player doesn't need to hit the space bar or Start button to begin, as the other player has already done so).

When the local player starts the game

For the first scenario, you're looking for space bar or Start button presses in the `Update_Start` method, but only when there are two gamers in the session. If the local user starts the game that way, you send a message to the other computer by writing data to the `packetWriter` object using the `Write` method. As was discussed earlier in this chapter, you'll always start your packets with a `MessageType` enum value (in this case, `MessageType.StartGame`). This will tell the game instance that reads the packet that the packet is a start-game message. No other data is needed for a start-game message, so that's all that's written in this particular packet.

The packet is then sent using the local gamer object's `SendData` method. In this method, you pass the `packetWriter` and specify some `SendDataOptions`. The send options include:

None

Packet delivery is not guaranteed, and packets are not guaranteed to be delivered in any specific order (some packets sent after others may arrive before those others).

InOrder

Packet delivery is not guaranteed, but the order is guaranteed (packets that are delivered will not be delivered out of order).

Reliable

Packets are guaranteed to be delivered, but in no specific order. Because a little more work is being done to guarantee packet delivery, this is slower than None and InOrder.

ReliableInOrder

Packets are guaranteed to be delivered, and guaranteed to be in the correct order (this is the slowest way to send packets and should be used sparingly).

 Why did we use SendDataOptions.Reliable in the preceding code, when that's one of the slowest options?

These are critical messages—they must arrive. It's one thing to miss a packet that updates a sprite position. The next packet will also contain the sprite position, so it won't be a big deal. Missing a command telling the game to end or start or move from one state to another, however, would be a major problem.

Next, the StartGame method is called. That method should look like this:

```
protected void StartGame(  )
{
    // Set game state to InGame
    currentGameState = GameState.InGame;

    // Start the soundtrack audio
    SoundEffect se = Content.Load<SoundEffect>(@"audio\track");
    trackInstance = se.CreateInstance();
    trackInstance.IsLooped = true;
    trackInstance.Play();

    // Play the start sound
    se = Content.Load<SoundEffect>(@"audio\start");
    se.Play(  );
}
```

This method sets the current game state to InGame and then plays some sound effects to start the game. For these sounds to work, you'll need to include them in your project (remember, you'll be using the simplified audio API in this project rather than XACT).

Located with the source code for this chapter, in the *Catch\CatchContent\Audio* folder, are three audio files: *boom.wav*, *start.wav*, and *track.wav*. Create a folder under the *CatchContent* node in Solution Explorer called *Audio* and add these files to that folder.

When the remote player starts the game

To take care of the second way of starting a game (when the other player starts it and you receive a network message telling you to start the game), the Update_Start method calls another method: ProcessIncomingData. All game states that can receive data will use this method. Essentially, all the ProcessIncomingData method does is read the MessageType enum value from the start of the incoming packet and call the appropriate method to handle whatever type of message was received. Add the ProcessIncoming Data method, as follows:

```
protected void ProcessIncomingData(GameTime gameTime)
{
    // Process incoming data
    LocalNetworkGamer localGamer = networkSession.LocalGamers[0];

    // While there are packets to be read...
    while (localGamer.IsDataAvailable)
    {
        // Get the packet
        NetworkGamer sender;
        localGamer.ReceiveData(packetReader, out sender);

        // Ignore the packet if you sent it
        if (!sender.IsLocal)
        {
            // Read messagetype from start of packet
            // and call appropriate method
            MessageType messageType = (MessageType)packetReader.ReadInt32( );
            switch (messageType)
            {
                case MessageType.EndGame:
                    EndGame( );
                    break;
                case MessageType.StartGame:
                    StartGame( );
                    break;
                case MessageType.RejoinLobby:
                    RejoinLobby( );
                    break;
                case MessageType.RestartGame:
                    RestartGame( );
                    break;
                case MessageType.UpdatePlayerPos:
                    UpdateRemotePlayer(gameTime);
                    break;
            }
        }
    }
}
```

First, this method gets the local gamer object from the network session and uses the IsDataAvailable property to determine whether any other gamers in this session have sent any packets to this local gamer object. If so, the packet is read from the Packet Reader object. If the sender turns out to be the local gamer (i.e., if it was broadcast to all computers and thus was also sent to himself), the message is ignored. Otherwise, the PacketReader reads an int32 value from the packet, which represents the Message Type (assuming that the first thing you always write in your packets when you send them is a MessageType enum value). Based on this value, the appropriate method is called to handle the message.

In this particular case, the packet you wrote in the Update_Start method contained a message type of MessageType.StartGame. After sending the message, the method called the StartGame method. Notice also in the ProcessIncomingData method that when a message type of MessageType.StartGame is received, the StartGame method is called. This way, the StartGame method ends up being called on both computers.

Figure 18-6 shows a flow diagram indicating how this process works and how the StartGame method ends up being called on both PCs. When Player 1 starts the game, a message is sent to Player 2, and Player 1's computer then calls StartGame. Player 2's computer constantly looks for new messages. When a StartGame message is read, Start Game is called on Player 2's computer as well.

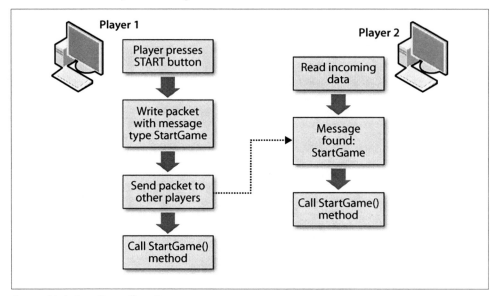

Figure 18-6. StartGame flow diagram

Before moving on to the other methods called in the Update method based on the different game states, let's add the rest of the methods referenced in the ProcessIncoming Data method. These methods will all function like the StartGame method, in that they'll be called on both computers using the messaging technique just described.

First, add the EndGame method:

```
protected void EndGame( )
{
    // Play collision sound effect
    // (game ends when players collide)
    SoundEffect se = Content.Load<SoundEffect>(@"audio\boom");
    se.Play( );

    // Stop the soundtrack music
    trackInstance.Stop( );

    // Move to the game-over state
    currentGameState = GameState.GameOver;
}
```

There's nothing really impressive going on here: you're playing the collision sound effect because the game will end when players collide, and then stopping the soundtrack music and setting the game state to GameOver.

 It's critical that methods such as StartGame and EndGame are called on *both* computers in the session because otherwise your data and game states will be out of sync. Why this is the case might be more obvious when you realize that both of these methods play audio effects.

If you have two computers in a session and EndGame is called on only one of them, the end-game sound effect would play on only that computer. Also, the soundtrack will stop on only that computer and the game state will not be set on the other computer, which means that the two computers will be in totally different game states. Not good!

The RejoinLobby and RestartGame methods are pretty similar:

```
private void RejoinLobby( )
{
    // Switch dynamite and gears sprites
    // as well as chaser versus chased
    SwitchPlayersAndReset(false);
    currentGameState = GameState.Start;
}

private void RestartGame( )
{
    // Switch dynamite and gears sprites
    // as well as chaser versus chased
    SwitchPlayersAndReset(true);
    StartGame( );
}
```

Both of these methods first switch the players and reset the game (scores, positions of players, etc.). The RejoinLobby method then sets the game state to Start, causing the

"Waiting for players" or "Press Spacebar or Start button to begin" message screen to be displayed.

The RestartGame method calls the StartGame method, which actually restarts the game.

Both of these methods use the SwitchPlayersAndReset method to switch the players. That method should look like this:

```
private void SwitchPlayersAndReset(bool switchPlayers)
{
    // Only do this if there are two players
    if (networkSession.AllGamers.Count == 2)
    {
        // Are we truly switching players or are we
        // setting the host as the chaser?
        if (switchPlayers)
        {
            // Switch player sprites
            if (((UserControlledSprite)networkSession.AllGamers[0].Tag).isChasing)
            {
                networkSession.AllGamers[0].Tag = CreateChasedSprite( );
                networkSession.AllGamers[1].Tag = CreateChasingSprite( );
            }
            else
            {
                networkSession.AllGamers[0].Tag = CreateChasingSprite( );
                networkSession.AllGamers[1].Tag = CreateChasedSprite( );
            }
        }
        else
        {
            // Switch player sprites
            if (networkSession.AllGamers[0].IsHost)
            {
                networkSession.AllGamers[0].Tag = CreateChasingSprite( );
                networkSession.AllGamers[1].Tag = CreateChasedSprite( );
            }
            else
            {
                networkSession.AllGamers[0].Tag = CreateChasedSprite( );
                networkSession.AllGamers[1].Tag = CreateChasingSprite( );
            }
        }

    }
}
```

This method will switch the gears and dynamite sprites for each player, switch the chasing/chased variable, and reset things such as the scores and positions of each player.

The last method called in the ProcessIncomingData method is one that updates the remote player. This process is similar to the one followed when calling StartGame, EndGame, and other such methods. What happens here is that when a local player moves, that player's UserControlledSprite object on the local computer is updated. A message is then sent to the other computer with the new position of that player's sprite. On the other end, the message is read and the following method is called:

```
protected void UpdateRemotePlayer(GameTime gameTime)
{
    // Get the other (nonlocal) player
    NetworkGamer theOtherGuy = GetOtherPlayer( );

    // Get the UserControlledSprite representing the other player
    UserControlledSprite theOtherSprite = ((UserControlledSprite)theOtherGuy.Tag);

    // Read in the new position of the other player
    Vector2 otherGuyPos = packetReader.ReadVector2( );

    // If the sprite is being chased,
    // retrieve and set the score as well
    if (!theOtherSprite.isChasing)
    {
        int score = packetReader.ReadInt32( );
        theOtherSprite.score = score;
    }

    // Set the position
    theOtherSprite.Position = otherGuyPos;

    // Update only the frame of the other sprite
    // (no need to update position because you just did!)
    theOtherSprite.Update(gameTime, Window.ClientBounds, false);
}

protected NetworkGamer GetOtherPlayer( )
{
    // Search through the list of players and find the
    // one that's remote
    foreach (NetworkGamer gamer in networkSession.AllGamers)
    {
        if (!gamer.IsLocal)
        {
            return gamer;
        }
    }

    return null;
}
```

This method will retrieve the remote player by calling the GetOtherPlayer method (also shown in the preceding code), which searches through all gamers in the session and finds the one that is not local. Next, the method retrieves the UserControlledSprite object for that player from the Tag property and reads a Vector2 from the packet reader, which you send for all UpdatePlayerPos MessageTypes. You'll also be sending the score for the player if the remote player was the player being chased. The method reads that data and sets the appropriate members in the UserControlledSprite. Then, the method updates the animation frame of the remote player's sprite.

Updating While in the InGame Game State

Now you'll need to add the `Update_InGame` method that the `Update` method will call when the game is in the InGame game state:

```
private void Update_InGame(GameTime gameTime)
{
    // Update the local player
    UpdateLocalPlayer(gameTime);

    // Read any incoming data
    ProcessIncomingData(gameTime);


    // Only host checks for collisions
    if (networkSession.IsHost)
    {
        // Only check for collisions if there are two players
        if (networkSession.AllGamers.Count == 2)
        {
            UserControlledSprite sprite1 =
                (UserControlledSprite)networkSession.AllGamers[0].Tag;
            UserControlledSprite sprite2 =
                (UserControlledSprite)networkSession.AllGamers[1].Tag;

            if (sprite1.collisionRect.Intersects(
                sprite2.collisionRect))
            {
                // If the two players intersect, game over.
                // Send a game-over message to the other player
                // and call EndGame.
                packetWriter.Write((int)MessageType.EndGame);
                networkSession.LocalGamers[0].SendData(packetWriter,
                    SendDataOptions.Reliable);

                EndGame( );
            }
        }
    }
}
```

First, this method updates the local player. This method, which will be shown shortly, will update the animation frame as well as the movement of the player based on local player input. Then, any incoming data is read in the `ProcessIncomingData` method.

Next, the end-game collision check is run, but only when the player is the host. Why have only the host check for collisions? If both players checked for collisions, they'd probably both send messages saying there was a collision at the same time—or even worse, one might think there was a collision when the other didn't. You could add some code to parse the messages to avoid that problem, but that would still involve more work than doing it this way. It's often useful to have one client be the master of things such as collision detection, game start, game stop, and so on.

So, the host checks for collisions and, if one occurs, sends a message to the other player saying that the game is over. It then calls EndGame.

The method that updates the local player (which was called at the beginning of Update_InGame) is listed here. Add this method to your Game1 class next:

```
protected void UpdateLocalPlayer(GameTime gameTime)
{
    // Get local player
    LocalNetworkGamer localGamer = networkSession.LocalGamers[0];

    // Get the local player's sprite
    UserControlledSprite sprite = (UserControlledSprite)localGamer.Tag;

    // Call the sprite's Update method, which will process user input
    // for movement and update the animation frame
    sprite.Update(gameTime, Window.ClientBounds, true);

    // If this sprite is being chased, increment the score
    // (score is just the num milliseconds that the chased player
    // survived)
    if(!sprite.isChasing)
        sprite.score += gameTime.ElapsedGameTime.Milliseconds;

    // Send message to other player with message tag and
    // new position of sprite
    packetWriter.Write((int)MessageType.UpdatePlayerPos);
    packetWriter.Write(sprite.Position);

    // If this player is being chased, add the score to the message
    if (!sprite.isChasing)
        packetWriter.Write(sprite.score);

    // Send data to other player
    localGamer.SendData(packetWriter, SendDataOptions.InOrder);

}
```

This method gets the local player and then the local player's sprite. It then calls Update on that sprite, which will process user input and update the animation frame.

If this player is being chased, the score (which is just the number of milliseconds he has survived) is incremented. Then, a message is sent to the other player with the new position of the player and the score.

Updating While in the GameOver Game State

The last part of the Update code is for the GameOver game state. Add this method to the Game1 class:

```
private void Update_GameOver(GameTime gameTime)
{
    KeyboardState keyboardState = Keyboard.GetState( );
    GamePadState gamePadSate = GamePad.GetState(PlayerIndex.One);
```

```
// If player presses Enter or A button, restart game
if (keyboardState.IsKeyDown(Keys.Enter) ||
    gamePadSate.Buttons.A == ButtonState.Pressed)
{
    // Send restart game message
    packetWriter.Write((int)MessageType.RestartGame);
    networkSession.LocalGamers[0].SendData(packetWriter,
        SendDataOptions.Reliable);

    RestartGame( );
}
// If player presses Escape or B button, rejoin lobby
if (keyboardState.IsKeyDown(Keys.Escape) ||
    gamePadSate.Buttons.B == ButtonState.Pressed)
{
    // Send rejoin lobby message
    packetWriter.Write((int)MessageType.RejoinLobby);
    networkSession.LocalGamers[0].SendData(packetWriter,
        SendDataOptions.Reliable);

    RejoinLobby( );
}

// Read any incoming messages
ProcessIncomingData(gameTime);
}
```

This method will read player input and, if the player indicates she wants to restart the game, sends a message to the other player and calls RestartGame. The same is done for RejoinLobby. Then, any incoming data is read.

Adding Draw Code

The final step is adding code to draw the game. Replace your existing Draw method in the Game1 class with the following:

```
protected override void Draw(GameTime gameTime)
{
    // Only draw when game is active
    if (this.IsActive)
    {
        // Based on the current game state,
        // call the appropriate method
        switch (currentGameState)
        {
            case GameState.SignIn:
            case GameState.FindSession:
            case GameState.CreateSession:
                GraphicsDevice.Clear(Color.DarkBlue);
                break;
```

```
            case GameState.Start:
                DrawStartScreen( );
                break;


            case GameState.InGame:
                DrawInGameScreen(gameTime);
                break;

            case GameState.GameOver:
                DrawGameOverScreen( );
                break;

        }

    }

    base.Draw(gameTime);
}
```

This method, like the `Update` method, will perform certain actions only when the game is active. This is to prevent drawing when the gamer services windows are open. The method then calls other methods based on the game state.

Notice that the `SignIn`, `FindSession`, and `CreateSession` game states do nothing but draw a blank screen by calling `GraphicsDevice.Clear`. This is because other gamer services activities are going on during these game states, and no drawing on the screen is needed.

So, let's start with the next one. Add the following `DrawStartScreen` method to your `Game1` class:

```
private void DrawStartScreen( )
{
    // Clear screen
    GraphicsDevice.Clear(Color.AliceBlue);

    // Draw text for intro splash screen
    spriteBatch.Begin( );

    // Draw instructions
    string text = "The dynamite player chases the gears\n";
    text += networkSession.Host.Gamertag +
        " is the HOST and plays as dynamite first";
    spriteBatch.DrawString(scoreFont, text,
        new Vector2((Window.ClientBounds.Width / 2)
        - (scoreFont.MeasureString(text).X / 2),
        (Window.ClientBounds.Height / 2)
        - (scoreFont.MeasureString(text).Y / 2)),
        Color.SaddleBrown);

    // If both gamers are there, tell gamers to press space bar or Start to begin
    if (networkSession.AllGamers.Count == 2)
    {
```

```
            text = "(Game is ready. Press Spacebar or Start button to begin)";
            spriteBatch.DrawString(scoreFont, text,
                new Vector2((Window.ClientBounds.Width / 2)
                - (scoreFont.MeasureString(text).X / 2),
                (Window.ClientBounds.Height / 2)
                - (scoreFont.MeasureString(text).Y / 2) + 60),
                Color.SaddleBrown);
        }
        // If only one player is there, tell gamer you're waiting for players
        else
        {
            text = "(Waiting for players)";
            spriteBatch.DrawString(scoreFont, text,
                new Vector2((Window.ClientBounds.Width / 2)
                - (scoreFont.MeasureString(text).X / 2),
                (Window.ClientBounds.Height / 2) + 60),
                Color.SaddleBrown);
        }

        // Loop through all gamers and get their gamertags,
        // then draw list of all gamers currently in the game
        text = "\n\nCurrent Player(s):";
        foreach (Gamer gamer in networkSession.AllGamers)
        {
            text += "\n" + gamer.Gamertag;
        }
        spriteBatch.DrawString(scoreFont, text,
            new Vector2((Window.ClientBounds.Width / 2)
            - (scoreFont.MeasureString(text).X / 2),
            (Window.ClientBounds.Height / 2) + 90),
            Color.SaddleBrown);

        spriteBatch.End( );
}
```

This method shouldn't include anything you haven't seen before, apart from at the end of the method where you're looping through all gamers in the network session and pulling their gamertags to display on the screen. The rest of the method draws simple instructions that the player should read at the start splash screen.

Next, add the following method to draw the screen during the game:

```
private void DrawInGameScreen(GameTime gameTime)
{
    // Clear device
    GraphicsDevice.Clear(Color.White);

    spriteBatch.Begin( );

    // Loop through all gamers in session
    foreach (NetworkGamer gamer in networkSession.AllGamers)
    {
        // Pull out the sprite for each gamer and draw it
        UserControlledSprite sprite = ((UserControlledSprite)gamer.Tag);
        sprite.Draw(gameTime, spriteBatch);
```

```
    // If the sprite is being chased, draw the score for that sprite
    if (!sprite.isChasing)
    {
        string text = "Score: " + sprite.score.ToString( );
        spriteBatch.DrawString(scoreFont, text,
            new Vector2(10, 10),
            Color.SaddleBrown);
    }
}

spriteBatch.End( );
}
```

This method loops through all gamers in the session and pulls out their UserControl
ledSprite objects, which it then draws. If the sprite being drawn is the one being chased,
the score for that sprite is also drawn on the screen.

Finally, add the DrawGameOverScreen method, which will loop through all the sprites,
find the one that was chased, and draw its score on the screen. It will then draw instructions to the players for further input:

```
private void DrawGameOverScreen( )
{
    // Clear device
    GraphicsDevice.Clear(Color.Navy);

    spriteBatch.Begin( );

    // Game over. Find the chased sprite and draw his score.
    string text = "Game Over\n";
    foreach (NetworkGamer gamer in networkSession.AllGamers)
    {
        UserControlledSprite sprite = ((UserControlledSprite)gamer.Tag);
        if (!sprite.isChasing)
        {
            text += "Score: " + sprite.score.ToString( );
        }
    }

    // Give players instructions from here
    text += "\nPress ENTER or A button to switch and play again";
    text += "\nPress ESCAPE or B button to exit to game lobby";

    spriteBatch.DrawString(scoreFont, text,
        new Vector2((Window.ClientBounds.Width / 2)
        - (scoreFont.MeasureString(text).X / 2),
        (Window.ClientBounds.Height / 2)
        - (scoreFont.MeasureString(text).Y / 2)),
        Color.WhiteSmoke);

    spriteBatch.End( );
}
```

Wow. That's a lot of code! You're now ready to give it a whirl, though. Grab a friend and run the game on two different computers that are on the same domain, subnet, and workgroup. You might need to turn off the firewalls on both computers as well.

Once the game is running, you should see a sign-in screen similar to that shown previously in Figure 18-5.

After you've both signed in, the first computer to get to that point should create a session, which the other computer will join. At that point you'll see a screen similar to Figure 18-7.

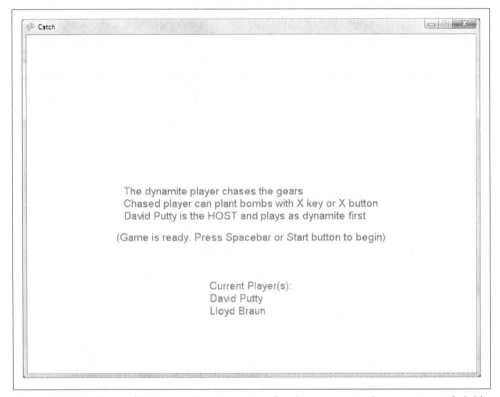

Figure 18-7. You have a full game and you're waiting for play to start. In the meantime, it feels like an Arby's night!

The game will begin after someone hits the space bar or the Start button on either computer. Both players will be able to move on their own computers and have that movement reflected on the other player's computer through the network messaging you've implemented. Your game will look something like Figure 18-8.

Finally, when the sprites collide, the game-over screen will display (as shown in Figure 18-9).

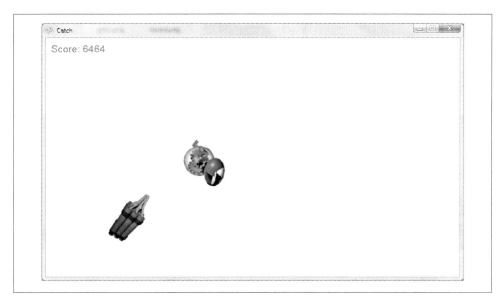

Figure 18-8. Chasing sprites…yay!

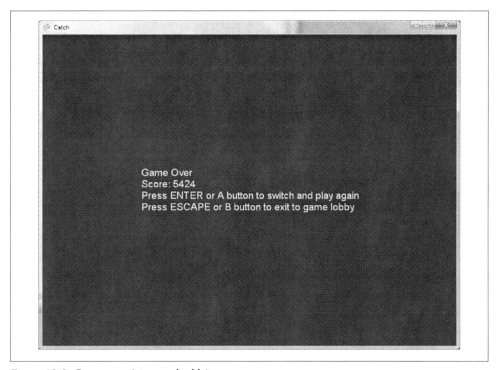

Figure 18-9. Game over (nice try, buddy)

Adding Biohazard Bombs of Insanity!

Let's modify this game to make things a little more interesting. Rather than just having one player chase another player around the screen, we'll let the chased player drop biohazard bombs every 5 seconds, which will cut the movement speed of the chasing sprite by 50% for 5 seconds. That should spice things up a bit.

First, you'll need to add a few more resources. Add the *hazardhit.wav* and *hazard-plant.wav* files to your *CatchContent\Audio* folder in Visual Studio (the files are located with the source code for this chapter in the *Catch\CatchContent\Audio* folder), and then add the *hazard.png* image to your project's *CatchContent\Images* folder (that file is located with the source code for this chapter in the *Catch\CatchContent\Images* folder).

Next, you're going to need to send two new message types between the two computers, for when the chased sprite plants a bomb and when the chasing sprite hits a bomb. Add two new message types to the `MessageTypes` enum:

```
// Represents different types of network messages
public enum MessageType { StartGame, EndGame, RestartGame,
    RejoinLobby, UpdatePlayerPos, DropBomb, ChaserHitBomb }
```

Next, add the following class-level variables to the `Game1` class:

```
// Bomb variables
int bombCooldown = 0;
List<UserControlledSprite> bombList = new List<UserControlledSprite>( );
int bombEffectCooldown = 0;
```

The `bombCooldown` will be a cooldown timer indicating when the next bomb can be planted. The `bombList` is a list of bomb objects. The `bombEffectCooldown` will tell you when the effect of the bomb expires.

Because you added two new message types for bombs, you'll need to go to the `ProcessIncomingData` method and add some code to do something when those messages are received. Add the following `case` statements to the `switch` statement in that method:

```
case MessageType.DropBomb:
    AddBomb(packetReader.ReadVector2( ));
    break;
case MessageType.ChaserHitBomb:
    ChaserHitBomb(packetReader.ReadInt32( ));
    break;
```

Then, add the `AddBomb` method, as follows:

```
protected void AddBomb(Vector2 position)
{
    // Add a bomb to the list of bombs
    bombList.Add(new UserControlledSprite(
        Content.Load<Texture2D>(@"images\hazard"),
        position, new Point(100, 100), 10, new Point(0, 0),
        new Point(6, 8), Vector2.Zero, false));
```

```
        // Play plant bomb sound effect
        SoundEffect se = Content.Load<SoundEffect>(@"audio\hazardplant");
        se.Play( );
    }
```

This method will add a bomb to the bomb list and then play the appropriate sound. The position of the bomb (read in from the packet in the ProcessIncomingData method) is passed in as a parameter.

Next, add the following methods:

```
    private void ChaserHitBomb(int index)
    {
        // Get the chaser player
        NetworkGamer chaser = GetChaser( );

        // Set the chaser's speed to 50% its current value
        ((UserControlledSprite)chaser.Tag).speed *= .5f;

        // Set the effect cooldown to 5 seconds
        bombEffectCooldown = 5000;

        // Remove the bomb
        bombList.RemoveAt(index);

        // Play the hazardhit sound
        SoundEffect se = Content.Load<SoundEffect>(@"audio\hazardhit");
        se.Play( );
    }

    protected NetworkGamer GetChaser( )
    {
        // Loop through all gamers and find the one that is chasing
        foreach (NetworkGamer gamer in networkSession.AllGamers)
        {
            if (((UserControlledSprite)gamer.Tag).isChasing)
            {
                return gamer;
            }
        }

        return null;
    }
```

The ChaserHitBomb method first gets the chasing sprite by calling a method called GetChaser, which is also defined in the preceding code. GetChaser loops through all gamer sprites and finds the one that is currently chasing. Then, the ChaserHitBomb method reduces the chaser's speed by 50%, sets the timer, removes the bomb, and plays a deadly sound effect. (Yeah...scary!)

Next, you'll need to have a way for the player to set a bomb. You'll want your local player to set the bombs, and then that computer will send a message telling the other computer that a bomb was set. To do this, add the following block of code at the end of your UpdateLocalPlayer method:

```
// If the sprite is being chased, he can plant bombs
if (!sprite.isChasing)
{
    // If it's time to plant a bomb, let the user do it;
    // otherwise, subtract gametime from the timer
    if (bombCooldown <= 0)
    {
        // If user pressed X or X button, plant a bomb
        if (Keyboard.GetState(  ).IsKeyDown(Keys.X) ||
            GamePad.GetState(PlayerIndex.One).Buttons.X == ButtonState.Pressed)
        {
            // Add a bomb
            AddBomb(sprite.Position);
            bombCooldown = 5000;

            packetWriter.Write((int)MessageType.DropBomb);
            packetWriter.Write(sprite.Position);
            localGamer.SendData(packetWriter, SendDataOptions.InOrder);
        }
    }
    else
        bombCooldown -= gameTime.ElapsedGameTime.Milliseconds;

}
```

This section of code will execute only if the player is being chased (only that player can plant bombs). It checks to see whether the bomb cooldown timer has expired, and then it checks to see whether the player has pressed a key or button that plants a bomb. If the cooldown timer has not expired, the cooldown timer is decreased by the amount of game time that has elapsed.

If the player plants a bomb, AddBomb is called, the bomb cooldown timer is set to 5 seconds, and a message is sent to the other player with the position of the bomb.

Next, because you can restart the game after it's ended, you'll want to clear the bomb list in the StartGame method so you start with a clean game window each time you play. Add the following code at the beginning of the StartGame method:

```
// Remove all bombs from previous game played
// during this instance of the application
bombList.Clear(  );
```

You'll then need to update the animation frames of each bomb. In the Update_InGame method, add the following code immediately after the call to UpdateLocalPlayer:

```
// Loop through each bomb and update only the animation
foreach (UserControlledSprite bomb in bombList)
    bomb.Update (gameTime, Window.ClientBounds, false);
```

Now you need to check to see whether the chaser has hit a bomb. Because this is collision detection, let one computer handle it. You're already using the host to handle collision detection between the two players, so you might as well add the bomb collision-detection logic there as well. In the `Update_InGame` method, you check for player versus player collisions with the following code:

```
// Only host checks for collisions
if (networkSession.IsHost)
{
    // Only check for collisions if there are two players
    if (networkSession.AllGamers.Count == 2)
    {
        UserControlledSprite sprite1 =
            (UserControlledSprite)networkSession.AllGamers[0].Tag;
        UserControlledSprite sprite2 =
            (UserControlledSprite)networkSession.AllGamers[1].Tag;

        if (sprite1.collisionRect.Intersects(
            sprite2.collisionRect))
        {
            // If the two players intersect, game over.
            // Send a game-over message to the other player
            // and call EndGame.
            packetWriter.Write((int)MessageType.EndGame);
            networkSession.LocalGamers[0].SendData(packetWriter,
                SendDataOptions.Reliable);

            EndGame( );
        }
    }
}
```

Add some code at the end of that block to be executed after the comparison for player versus player collisions. The same block of code is shown again here, with the added lines in bold:

```
// Only host checks for collisions
if (networkSession.IsHost)
{
    // Only check for collisions if there are two players
    if (networkSession.AllGamers.Count == 2)
    {
        UserControlledSprite sprite1 =
            (UserControlledSprite)networkSession.AllGamers[0].Tag;
        UserControlledSprite sprite2 =
            (UserControlledSprite)networkSession.AllGamers[1].Tag;

        if (sprite1.collisionRect.Intersects(
            sprite2.collisionRect))
        {
            // If the two players intersect, game over.
            // Send a game-over message to the other player
            // and call EndGame.
```

```
        packetWriter.Write((int)MessageType.EndGame);
        networkSession.LocalGamers[0].SendData(packetWriter,
            SendDataOptions.Reliable);

        EndGame( );
    }

    // Check for collisions between chaser and bombs.
    // First, get chaser.
    UserControlledSprite chaser =
        (UserControlledSprite)GetChaser( ).Tag;

    // Loop through bombs
    for (int i = 0; i < bombList.Count; ++i)
    {
        UserControlledSprite bomb = bombList[i];

        // If bombs and chaser collide, call ChaserHitBomb
        // and send message to other player passing the index
        // of the bomb hit
        if (bomb.collisionRect.Intersects(
            chaser.collisionRect))
        {
            ChaserHitBomb(i);

            packetWriter.Write((int)MessageType.ChaserHitBomb);
            packetWriter.Write(i);
            networkSession.LocalGamers[0].SendData(packetWriter,
                SendDataOptions.Reliable);
        }
    }

    }
}
```

You'll also need to add some code in the Update_InGame method that will check to see
whether the bomb effect has expired. Add the following methods to the Game1 class:

```
private void ExpireBombEffect(GameTime gameTime)
{
    // Is there a bomb effect in place?
    if (bombEffectCooldown > 0)
    {
        // Subtract game time from the timer
        bombEffectCooldown -= gameTime.ElapsedGameTime.Milliseconds;

        // If the timer has expired, expire the bomb effect
        if (bombEffectCooldown <= 0)
        {
            ExpireBombEffect( );
        }
    }
}
```

```
private void ExpireBombEffect( )
{
    // Get the chaser and restore the speed
    // to the original speed
    NetworkGamer chaser = GetChaser( );
    ((UserControlledSprite)chaser.Tag).speed =
        ((UserControlledSprite)chaser.Tag).originalSpeed;
}
```

The first method checks to see whether the bomb effect has expired. If it has, it calls the second method, which gets the chaser sprite and restores its original speed.

Now, call the first method at the end of your Update_InGame method:

```
ExpireBombEffect(gameTime);
```

Next, you'll need to draw the bombs. In the DrawInGameScreen method, add the following code immediately after the call to spriteBatch.Begin:

```
// Loop through and draw bombs
foreach (UserControlledSprite sprite in bombList)
    sprite.Draw(gameTime, spriteBatch);
```

Finally, you need to let the players know that hitting the X key or X button will plant a bomb. You're currently drawing instructions on the start screen during the Draw StartScreen method. The first instructions given to the user are stored in the text variable in the following line of code:

```
string text = "The dynamite player chases the gears\n";
```

Add another line of code below that one to tell the player that the chased sprite can plant bombs:

```
string text = "The dynamite player chases the gears\n";
text += "Chased player can plant bombs with X key or X button\n";
```

There you have it. Compile and run the game now, and your chased sprite should be able to plant bombs that will reduce the speed of the chaser by 50% for 5 seconds. Your game window should look something like Figure 18-10.

As you can see, the team at Microsoft did a great job with the networking API. It's easy to use, and once you get a handle on what type of network you need to simulate, what type of data you'll be sending across it, and how you're going to represent players and other objects in your game, you'll be well on your way to creating the next great networked XNA game.

Although the code in this chapter focused on creating a network game in Windows using Games for Windows LIVE, the same code that sends messages back and forth from PC to PC can be used on the Xbox 360 and Windows Phone 7. You can also apply the same concepts to those platforms with regard to network architecture, game states, and so on.

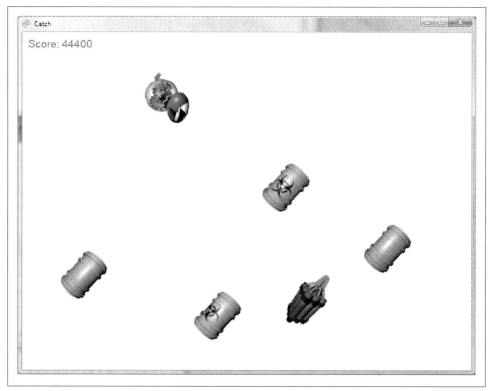

Figure 18-10. Hazard bombs galore…

What You Just Did

We covered an awful lot in this chapter. Let's take a look back at what you just did:

- You created a split-screen two-player game.
- You learned about network architectures (peer-to-peer versus client/server).
- You learned about critical networking classes in XNA, including the `Network Session`, `PacketWriter`, and `PacketReader` classes.
- You implemented a 2D networked game using Games for Windows LIVE.
- You made use of the gamer services windows for signing in and managing gamer identities in your networked game.
- You implemented game states and peer-to-peer messaging in your networked game.
- You added a cool slow-down bomb to the game.

Summary

- You can easily add multiplayer functionality to a game by allowing multiple players to play on the same machine and implementing a split screen. Each split-screen view will typically have its own camera and be independent of the other views.

- The `Viewport` class represents the area on the 2D screen to which the projection of the camera will be mapped. To implement a split screen, you modify the `View port` property of the graphics device to draw each camera's view and projection on only a portion of the game window rather than the entire surface of the game window.

- An important decision to make when developing networked games is to determine which type of network architecture to implement (peer-to-peer, client/server, or a hybrid). Factors that go into determining which is the best choice include the number of players and the number of objects that need to be updated or continually tracked.

- The `NetworkSession` class represents a single session of a network game. This class keeps track of all players in the session, the host of the session, and other properties related to the session itself.

- Communication between PCs, Xbox 360s, or Windows Phone 7 devices is done by writing packets using the `PacketWriter` class and reading packets using the `PacketReader` class.

- A packet is a single communication (which may contain a variable amount of data) sent from one entity to another on a network.

- The `GamerServicesComponent` allows your networked game to make use of gamer services windows and messaging throughout the game.

- A key part of network game development is determining how to store the data for player and nonplayer objects and deciding what types of messages should be sent between machines to update each machine's copies of those objects. It's better to minimize the data sent by sending only critical data that has changed on one machine and needs to be updated on the other machine(s) in the game (such as a player's position, whether a collision occurred, etc.).

- You've finished the book! Great job. You are now flowing with XNA power from head to toe. You're probably realizing the responsibility you have with such power and thinking, "I wish XNA had never come to me. I wish none of this had happened." Well, let me give you some advice: "So do all who live to see such times in XNA. But that is not for them to decide. All XNA developers have to decide is what to do with the time that is given us."

Test Your Knowledge: Quiz

1. If you create a two-player split screen, what should you use for the camera's aspect ratio to ensure that your graphics don't look squished?

2. Fact or fiction: networked games in XNA use a networking API that works on the PC and Xbox 360 but is different on Windows Phone 7.

3. What's the difference between a peer-to-peer and a client/server network architecture?

4. Which network type (peer-to-peer or client/server) is better?

5. What will happen if you don't call `NetworkSession.Update` in your game?

6. How do you force a user to sign in using the gamer services sign-in windows?

7. How do you send a message to another player in a networked XNA game?

8. How do you read a message from another player?

9. When receiving a network message in XNA, how do you know what type of data is going to be read from the `PacketReader` and what that data means?

10. What, according to Harry Dunne, is worse than his roommate, Lloyd Christmas, getting robbed by an old lady?

Answers to Quizzes and Exercises

Chapter 1: What's New in XNA 4.0?

Quiz Answers

1. What significant change was made to the XNA folder structure in XNA 4.0?

   The Content node within your solution, which was previously a subfolder of your game project, is now its own project within your solution. This enables you to easily share content across multiplatform projects.

2. What game platforms are supported with XNA 4.0?

   XNA 4.0 supports development on Windows, Xbox 360, and Windows Phone 7 series.

3. What is the difference between the Reach and HiDef profiles in XNA 4.0?

   HiDef is designed for high-powered, top-of-the-line hardware, whereas Reach is designed to support a wider range of hardware devices. The Reach profile offers a limited set of graphic features and is a subset of the HiDef profile.

4. Why do the Japanese tourists end up sleeping in a chest of drawers in Kramer's apartment?

   Because Kramer spent all their money, thinking that fifty-thousand yen was a huge sum of money they had at their disposal:

   Elaine: Fifty-thousand yen? Isn't that only a few hundred dollars?

   Kramer: Evidently. Oh, by the way, tell Brett that his chest of drawers are a big hit. My guests are very comfortable in them.

   Elaine: In them?!

   Jerry: You have them sleeping in drawers?!

   Kramer: Jerry, have you ever seen the business hotels in Tokyo? They sleep in tiny stacked cubicles all the time. They feel right at home.

Jerry: This has "international incident" written all over it.

Kramer: Oh yeah, yeah.

Chapter 2: Getting Started

Quiz Answers

1. XNA Game Studio 4.0 allows you to write games for which platforms?

   XNA 4.0 supports development for Windows Vista, Windows 7, the Xbox 360, and Windows Phone 7.

2. Which versions of Visual Studio support XNA Game Studio 4.0?

   Either Visual Studio 2010 Standard Edition or higher (with C# language support installed) or Visual C# 2010 Express Edition.

Chapter 3: Fun with Sprites

Quiz Answers

1. What are the steps in an XNA game loop?

   The XNA game loop consists of only two methods: `Update` and `Draw`.

2. If you wanted to load a `Texture2D` object, in which method should you do that?

   `LoadContent`.

3. What line of code should you use to change the framerate of an XNA game to 20 fps?

   Either of these lines will do the trick:

   ```
   TargetElapsedTime = TimeSpan.FromMilliseconds(50);
   TargetElapsedTime = new TimeSpan(0, 0, 0, 0, 50);
   ```

4. What should you pass in as the parameter of `Content.Load` when loading a `Texture2D` object?

   The asset name of the texture image you want to load. You can find an image's asset name by viewing its properties in Solution Explorer.

5. Fact or fiction: the content pipeline will let you know at compile time if you add an image to your project that it cannot parse.

   Fact. The content pipeline runs a compilation step on all content (textures, models, sounds, etc.) and then outputs the result as an XNA-compatible formatted object. If this step fails during compilation, the result is a compilation error.

6. You're drawing a sprite, and you want the background to be transparent. What steps do you need to take to draw it with a transparent background?

   There are two ways to draw transparent images in XNA. The first option has two requirements. First, the background of your image itself must be transparent. If it isn't, you'll need to edit the image in an image editor and give it a transparent background. Second, `BlendState.AlphaBlend` must be used (this is the default if no parameters are specified in `SpriteBatch.Begin`).

   The second option is to make sure that the transparent portion of the image is solid magenta (255, 0, 255).

7. You have two sprites (A and B), and when they collide, you always want A to be drawn on top of B. What do you need to do?

   There are two possible solutions: using `SpriteSortMode.FrontToBack`, you can set the layer depth of A to a value greater than that of B (both must be within the range of 0 to 1); or, using `SpriteSortMode.BackToFront`, you can set the layer depth of A to a value lower than that of B.

8. What are the things you need to keep track of to cycle through a sprite sheet?

   Current frame to draw, size of each individual frame, and number of columns and rows in your sprite sheet.

9. What was the first television series to command more than $1 million per minute for advertising?

   Only the best show in this history of television: *Seinfeld*.

Exercise Answer

In this chapter, you built an example where two XNA logo images moved around the screen and bounced off the edges. Take the animated sprite example that you built at the end of this chapter and make the animated sprite move and bounce in a similar fashion—but in this case, make the animated sprite move in both X and Y directions and bounce off of all four edges of the screen.

This exercise is fairly straightforward, as it involves taking two examples from the chapter and merging pieces together. The animation aspect of the exercise is covered at the end of the chapter, and the movement and bouncing off screen edges is covered in the middle of the chapter.

One thing that might be tricky is moving in both X and Y directions at the same time. In the previous moving example, you used a float variable for the speed and added it to either the X or the Y coordinate, depending on which sprite you were moving (they both moved in only one direction).

Now I'd recommend using a `Vector2` to represent speed. That way you can have different values for speed in the X direction and the Y direction. Also, you can add your `Vector2` speed to your `Vector2` position by simply adding the two together (you can add `Vector2` objects just as you would add integer or float values).

The other catch to this exercise is that in the previous moving example you used the size of the `Texture2D` object to determine how far from the edge of the screen to bounce in the other direction, but now the size of your `Texture2D` object will be inaccurate because you're using a sprite sheet. Instead, you'll want to use the size of an individual frame within that sprite sheet to detect when the image has hit the edge of the screen.

Here is one possible solution for this exercise:

```
using System;
using System.Collections.Generic;
using System.Linq;
using Microsoft.Xna.Framework;
using Microsoft.Xna.Framework.Audio;
using Microsoft.Xna.Framework.Content;
using Microsoft.Xna.Framework.GamerServices;
using Microsoft.Xna.Framework.Graphics;
using Microsoft.Xna.Framework.Input;
using Microsoft.Xna.Framework.Media;
using Microsoft.Xna.Framework.Net;
using Microsoft.Xna.Framework.Storage;

namespace AnimatedSprites
{
    public class Game1 : Microsoft.Xna.Framework.Game
    {
        GraphicsDeviceManager graphics;
        SpriteBatch spriteBatch;
        Texture2D texture;
        Point frameSize = new Point(75, 75);
        Point currentFrame = new Point(0, 0);
        Point sheetSize = new Point(6, 8);

        //Framerate stuff
        int timeSinceLastFrame = 0;
        int millisecondsPerFrame = 16;

        //Speed and movement
        Vector2 speed = new Vector2(5, 2);
        Vector2 position = Vector2.Zero;

        public Game1()
        {
            graphics = new GraphicsDeviceManager(this);
            Content.RootDirectory = "Content";
        }

        protected override void Initialize()
        {
            // TODO: Add your initialization logic here
```

```
        base.Initialize();
}

protected override void LoadContent()
{
    // Create a new SpriteBatch, which can be used to draw textures.
    spriteBatch = new SpriteBatch(GraphicsDevice);

    texture = Content.Load<Texture2D>(@"Images\threerings");
}

protected override void UnloadContent()
{
    // TODO: Unload any non-ContentManager content here
}

protected override void Update(GameTime gameTime)
{
    // Allows the game to exit
    if (GamePad.GetState(PlayerIndex.One).Buttons.Back ==
      ButtonState.Pressed)
        this.Exit();

    //Update time since last frame and only
    //change animation if framerate expired
    timeSinceLastFrame += gameTime.ElapsedGameTime.Milliseconds;
    if (timeSinceLastFrame > millisecondsPerFrame)
    {
        timeSinceLastFrame -= millisecondsPerFrame;

        ++currentFrame.X;
        if (currentFrame.X >= sheetSize.X)
        {
            currentFrame.X = 0;
            ++currentFrame.Y;
            if (currentFrame.Y >= sheetSize.Y)
                currentFrame.Y = 0;
        }
    }

    //Move sprite
    position += speed;

    //If the sprite hit a wall, reverse direction
    if (position.X > Window.ClientBounds.Width - frameSize.X ||
        position.X < 0)
        speed.X *= -1;
    if (position.Y > Window.ClientBounds.Height - frameSize.Y ||
        position.Y < 0)
        speed.Y *= -1;

    base.Update(gameTime);
}
```

```
protected override void Draw(GameTime gameTime)
{
    GraphicsDevice.Clear(Color.White);

    spriteBatch.Begin(SpriteSortMode.FrontToBack, BlendState.AlphaBlend);

    spriteBatch.Draw(texture, position,
        new Rectangle(currentFrame.X * frameSize.X,
            currentFrame.Y * frameSize.Y,
            frameSize.X,
            frameSize.Y),
            Color.White, 0, Vector2.Zero,
            1, SpriteEffects.None, 0);

    spriteBatch.End();

    base.Draw(gameTime);
}
}
}
```

Chapter 4: User Input and Collision Detection

Quiz Answers

1. What object is used to read input from a mouse?

   Mouse.

2. Fact or fiction: the X and Y coordinates from a mouse as read in an XNA application represent how much the mouse has moved since the previous frame.

   Fiction. The input is given in actual screen coordinates based off the upper-left corner of the game window. To get the distance moved since the previous frame, you have to compare the value from the current frame against the value of the previous frame.

3. What is the difference between an analog input control and a digital input control?

   A digital input yields a Boolean yes/no, on/off status, whereas an analog input gives a range of inputs based on how far the button has been pressed.

4. Describe the bounding-box collision-detection algorithm.

   The bounding-box algorithm is a simple collision-detection algorithm in which you "draw" imaginary boxes around objects and then run collision checks on the boxes themselves to see whether any objects are colliding.

5. Describe the pros and cons of the bounding-box collision-detection algorithm.

   The two biggest pros of the algorithm are its speed and simplicity. The biggest drawback is its inherent inaccuracy—not all objects are square or rectangular, and as such, the algorithm has accuracy issues.

6. What is the ratio of unicorns to leprechauns?

According to Stanley Hudson of *The Office*, the ratio of unicorns to leprechauns equals the ratio of Stanley nickels to Schrute bucks.

> Dwight: Don't you want to earn Schrute bucks?
>
> Stanley: No. In fact, I'll give you a billion Stanley nickels if you never talk to me again.
>
> Dwight: What's the ratio of Stanley nickels to Schrute bucks?
>
> Stanley: Same as the ratio of unicorns to leprechauns.

Exercise Answer

Let's combine some aspects of this chapter and the previous one. Take the code where we left off at the end of this chapter and modify it to include another nonuser-controlled sprite (use the *plus.png* image, which is located with the source code for this chapter in the *AnimatedSprites\AnimatedSprites\AnimatedSpritesContent\Images* folder). Add movement to both nonuser-controlled sprites, as you did in Chapter 3, so that each sprite moves in the X and Y directions and bounces off the edges of the screen. Add collision detection to the newly added sprite as well. The end result will be a game where you try to avoid two moving sprites. When you hit either sprite, the game ends.

For clarity in working with the *plus.png* image, the frame size of the sprite sheet is 75 × 75 pixels, and it has six columns and four rows (note that the rings and skull ball sprite sheets both had six columns and eight rows).

This exercise takes principles from Chapters 3 and 4 and combines them to create a very basic game where you try to avoid two sprites that move around the screen. The addition of a new animated sprite is a bit of a challenge, especially the way the code is currently written (in Chapter 5 you learned how to fine-tune the object-oriented design of the system you're building). Other than that, collision detection and object movement and edge bouncing are handled the same way as in previous examples and should be fairly straightforward at this point. Here's some sample code for this exercise:

```
using System;
using System.Collections.Generic;
using System.Linq;
using Microsoft.Xna.Framework;
using Microsoft.Xna.Framework.Audio;
using Microsoft.Xna.Framework.Content;
using Microsoft.Xna.Framework.GamerServices;
using Microsoft.Xna.Framework.Graphics;
using Microsoft.Xna.Framework.Input;
using Microsoft.Xna.Framework.Media;
using Microsoft.Xna.Framework.Net;
using Microsoft.Xna.Framework.Storage;

namespace AnimatedSprites
{
    public class Game1 : Microsoft.Xna.Framework.Game
    {
```

```csharp
GraphicsDeviceManager graphics;
SpriteBatch spriteBatch;

//Rings variables
Texture2D ringsTexture;
Point ringsFrameSize = new Point(75, 75);
Point ringsCurrentFrame = new Point(0, 0);
Point ringsSheetSize = new Point(6, 8);
int ringsTimeSinceLastFrame = 0;
int ringsMillisecondsPerFrame = 50;


//Skull variables
Texture2D skullTexture;
Point skullFrameSize = new Point(75, 75);
Point skullCurrentFrame = new Point(0, 0);
Point skullSheetSize = new Point(6, 8);
int skullTimeSinceLastFrame = 0;
const int skullMillisecondsPerFrame = 50;

//Plus variables
Texture2D plusTexture;
Point plusFrameSize = new Point(75, 75);
Point plusCurrentFrame = new Point(0, 0);
Point plusSheetSize = new Point(6, 4);
int plusTimeSinceLastFrame = 0;
const int plusMillisecondsPerFrame = 50;

//Rings movement
Vector2 ringsPosition = Vector2.Zero;
const float ringsSpeed = 6;
MouseState prevMouseState;

//Skull position
Vector2 skullPosition = new Vector2(100, 100);
Vector2 skullSpeed = new Vector2(4, 2);

//Plus position
Vector2 plusPosition = new Vector2(200, 200);
Vector2 plusSpeed = new Vector2(2, 5);

//Collision detection variables
int ringsCollisionRectOffset = 10;
int skullCollisionRectOffset = 10;
int plusCollisionRectOffset = 10;


public Game1()
{
    graphics = new GraphicsDeviceManager(this);
    Content.RootDirectory = "Content";
}

protected override void Initialize()
{
```

```
    // TODO: Add your initialization logic here

    base.Initialize();
}

protected override void LoadContent()
{
    // Create a new SpriteBatch, which can be used to draw textures
    spriteBatch = new SpriteBatch(GraphicsDevice);

    ringsTexture = Content.Load<Texture2D>(@"images \threerings");
    skullTexture = Content.Load<Texture2D>(@"images\skullball");
    plusTexture = Content.Load<Texture2D>(@"images\plus");
}

protected override void UnloadContent()
{
    // TODO: Unload any non-ContentManager content here
}

protected override void Update(GameTime gameTime)
{
    // Allows the game to exit
    if (GamePad.GetState(PlayerIndex.One).Buttons.Back ==
      ButtonState.Pressed)
        this.Exit();

    //Update time since last frame and only
    //change animation if framerate expired
    ringsTimeSinceLastFrame +=
        gameTime.ElapsedGameTime.Milliseconds;
    if (ringsTimeSinceLastFrame > ringsMillisecondsPerFrame)
    {
        ringsTimeSinceLastFrame -= ringsMillisecondsPerFrame;

        ++ringsCurrentFrame.X;
        if (ringsCurrentFrame.X >= ringsSheetSize.X)
        {
            ringsCurrentFrame.X = 0;
            ++ringsCurrentFrame.Y;
            if (ringsCurrentFrame.Y >= ringsSheetSize.Y)
                ringsCurrentFrame.Y = 0;
        }
    }

    //Then do the same to update the skull animation
    skullTimeSinceLastFrame +=
        gameTime.ElapsedGameTime.Milliseconds;
    if (skullTimeSinceLastFrame > skullMillisecondsPerFrame)
    {
        skullTimeSinceLastFrame -= skullMillisecondsPerFrame;

        ++skullCurrentFrame.X;
        if (skullCurrentFrame.X >= skullSheetSize.X)
```

```
        {
            skullCurrentFrame.X = 0;
            ++skullCurrentFrame.Y;
            if (skullCurrentFrame.Y >= skullSheetSize.Y)
                skullCurrentFrame.Y = 0;
        }
    }

    //Then do the same to update the plus animation
    plusTimeSinceLastFrame +=
        gameTime.ElapsedGameTime.Milliseconds;
    if (plusTimeSinceLastFrame > plusMillisecondsPerFrame)
    {
        plusTimeSinceLastFrame -= plusMillisecondsPerFrame;

        ++plusCurrentFrame.X;
        if (plusCurrentFrame.X >= plusSheetSize.X)
        {
            plusCurrentFrame.X = 0;
            ++plusCurrentFrame.Y;
            if (plusCurrentFrame.Y >= plusSheetSize.Y)
                plusCurrentFrame.Y = 0;
        }
    }

    //Move position of rings based on keyboard input
    KeyboardState keyboardState = Keyboard.GetState();
    if (keyboardState.IsKeyDown(Keys.Left))
        ringsPosition.X -= ringsSpeed;
    if (keyboardState.IsKeyDown(Keys.Right))
        ringsPosition.X += ringsSpeed;
    if (keyboardState.IsKeyDown(Keys.Up))
        ringsPosition.Y -= ringsSpeed;
    if (keyboardState.IsKeyDown(Keys.Down))
        ringsPosition.Y += ringsSpeed;

    //Move the skull
    skullPosition += skullSpeed;
    if (skullPosition.X >
        Window.ClientBounds.Width - skullFrameSize.X ||
        skullPosition.X < 0)
        skullSpeed.X *= -1;
    if (skullPosition.Y >
        Window.ClientBounds.Height - skullFrameSize.Y ||
        skullPosition.Y < 0)
        skullSpeed.Y *= -1;

    //Move the plus
    plusPosition += plusSpeed;
    if (plusPosition.X >
        Window.ClientBounds.Width - plusFrameSize.X ||
        plusPosition.X < 0)
        plusSpeed.X *= -1;
```

```
        if (plusPosition.Y >
            Window.ClientBounds.Height - plusFrameSize.Y ||
            plusPosition.Y < 0)
            plusSpeed.Y *= -1;

        //Move rings based on mouse movement
        MouseState mouseState = Mouse.GetState();
        if (mouseState.X != prevMouseState.X ||
        mouseState.Y != prevMouseState.Y)
            ringsPosition = new Vector2(mouseState.X, mouseState.Y);
        prevMouseState = mouseState;

        //Move rings based on gamepad input
        GamePadState gamepadState = GamePad.GetState(PlayerIndex.One);
        if (gamepadState.Buttons.A == ButtonState.Pressed)
        {
            //A is pressed, double speed and vibrate
            ringsPosition.X +=
                ringsSpeed * 2 * gamepadState.ThumbSticks.Left.X;
            ringsPosition.Y -=
                ringsSpeed * 2 * gamepadState.ThumbSticks.Left.Y;
            GamePad.SetVibration(PlayerIndex.One, 1f, 1f);
        }
        else
        {
            //A is not pressed, normal speed and stop vibration
            ringsPosition.X += ringsSpeed * gamepadState.ThumbSticks.Left.X;
            ringsPosition.Y -= ringsSpeed * gamepadState.ThumbSticks.Left.Y;
            GamePad.SetVibration(PlayerIndex.One, 0, 0);
        }

        //Adjust position of rings to keep it in the game window
        if (ringsPosition.X < 0)
            ringsPosition.X = 0;
        if (ringsPosition.Y < 0)
            ringsPosition.Y = 0;
        if (ringsPosition.X >
            Window.ClientBounds.Width - ringsFrameSize.X)
            ringsPosition.X =
                Window.ClientBounds.Width - ringsFrameSize.X;
        if (ringsPosition.Y >
            Window.ClientBounds.Height - ringsFrameSize.Y)
            ringsPosition.Y =
                Window.ClientBounds.Height - ringsFrameSize.Y;

        //If objects collide, exit the game
        if (Collide())
            Exit();

        base.Update(gameTime);
    }
```

```
protected bool Collide()
{
    Rectangle ringsRect = new Rectangle(
        (int)ringsPosition.X + ringsCollisionRectOffset,
        (int)ringsPosition.Y + ringsCollisionRectOffset,
        ringsFrameSize.X - (ringsCollisionRectOffset * 2),
        ringsFrameSize.Y - (ringsCollisionRectOffset * 2));

    Rectangle skullRect = new Rectangle(
        (int)skullPosition.X + skullCollisionRectOffset,
        (int)skullPosition.Y + skullCollisionRectOffset,
        skullFrameSize.X - (skullCollisionRectOffset * 2),
        skullFrameSize.Y - (skullCollisionRectOffset * 2));

    Rectangle plusRect = new Rectangle(
        (int)plusPosition.X + plusCollisionRectOffset,
        (int)plusPosition.Y + plusCollisionRectOffset,
        plusFrameSize.X - (plusCollisionRectOffset * 2),
        plusFrameSize.Y - (plusCollisionRectOffset * 2));

    return ringsRect.Intersects(skullRect) ||
        ringsRect.Intersects(plusRect);
}

protected override void Draw(GameTime gameTime)
{
    GraphicsDevice.Clear(Color.White);

    spriteBatch.Begin(SpriteSortMode.FrontToBack, BlendState.AlphaBlend);


    //Draw the rings
    spriteBatch.Draw(ringsTexture, ringsPosition,
        new Rectangle(ringsCurrentFrame.X * ringsFrameSize.X,
            ringsCurrentFrame.Y * ringsFrameSize.Y,
            ringsFrameSize.X,
            ringsFrameSize.Y),
            Color.White, 0, Vector2.Zero,
            1, SpriteEffects.None, 0);

    //Draw the skull
    spriteBatch.Draw(skullTexture, skullPosition,
        new Rectangle(skullCurrentFrame.X * skullFrameSize.X,
            skullCurrentFrame.Y * skullFrameSize.Y,
            skullFrameSize.X,
            skullFrameSize.Y),
            Color.White, 0, Vector2.Zero,
            1, SpriteEffects.None, 0);

    //Draw the plus
    spriteBatch.Draw(plusTexture, plusPosition,
        new Rectangle(plusCurrentFrame.X * plusFrameSize.X,
            plusCurrentFrame.Y * plusFrameSize.Y,
            plusFrameSize.X,
            plusFrameSize.Y),
```

```
                    Color.White, 0, Vector2.Zero,
                    1, SpriteEffects.None, 0);

            spriteBatch.End();

            base.Draw(gameTime);
        }
    }
}
```

Chapter 5: Applying Some Object-Oriented Design

Quiz Answers

1. What class does a game component derive from?

   GameComponent.

2. If you want to be able to draw on the screen with your game component, what class do you need to derive from?

   DrawableGameComponent.

3. Fact or fiction: time spent building a solid object-oriented design should not count as time spent developing software, because it is unnecessary and superfluous.

   Absolutely fiction. Creating a proper design up front will help you avoid countless headaches and maintenance issues down the road. Always, no matter what the project, plan ahead and code around a solid design.

4. What is spontaneous dental hydroplosion?

   As explained by Pam and Jim in *The Office* episode "Health Care", spontaneous dental hydroplosion occurs when a person's teeth turn to liquid and proceed to drip down the back of their throat.

Exercise Answer

Modify the code that you worked on this chapter to create four sprites which move and bounce off all four edges of the screen. To accomplish this, create a new class called BouncingSprite that derives from AutomatedSprite. BouncingSprite should do the same thing that AutomatedSprite does, with the exception that it will check during the Update method to determine whether the sprite has gone off the edge of the screen. If it has, reverse the direction of the sprite by multiplying the speed variable by –1.

Also, make two of the bouncing sprites use the skull image and two of them use the plus image (located with the source code for this chapter in the *AnimatedSprites\AnimatedSprites\AnimatedSpritesContent\Images* directory).

Note that when running this game after making these changes, you'll have four sprites moving around the screen and the game will exit when any of them collide with the user-controlled sprite. This could cause some issues in testing the game because the sprites may be colliding when the game first loads. Try moving your mouse to a far corner of the screen when loading the game to make sure your user-controlled sprite is out of the way to begin with.

Creating a bouncing sprite should be fairly straightforward at this point. You've already created a sprite that bounces off the edges of the game window in a previous chapter (more than once if you did the exercises for the previous chapters). All you'll need to do is check in the Update method whether the sprite has gone off the edge of the game window and, if it has, reverse its direction. You'll then need to update the code in your SpriteManager class that creates the automated sprites to have it create Bouncing Sprites with both the skullball and plus sprites.

Here's the BouncingSprite class:

```
using System;
using System.Collections.Generic;
using System.Linq;
using System.Text;
using Microsoft.Xna.Framework;
using Microsoft.Xna.Framework.Graphics;

namespace AnimatedSprites
{
    class BouncingSprite: AutomatedSprite
    {
        public BouncingSprite(Texture2D textureImage, Vector2 position,
            Point frameSize, int collisionOffset, Point currentFrame,
            Point sheetSize, Vector2 speed)
            : base(textureImage, position, frameSize, collisionOffset,
            currentFrame, sheetSize, speed)
        {
        }
        public BouncingSprite(Texture2D textureImage, Vector2 position,
            Point frameSize, int collisionOffset, Point currentFrame,
            Point sheetSize, Vector2 speed, int millisecondsPerFrame)
            : base(textureImage, position, frameSize, collisionOffset,
            currentFrame, sheetSize, speed, millisecondsPerFrame)
        {
        }

        public override void Update(GameTime gameTime, Rectangle clientBounds)
        {
            position += direction;

            //Reverse direction if hit a side
            if (position.X > clientBounds.Width - frameSize.X ||
                position.X < 0)
                speed.X *= -1;
```

```
                    if (position.Y > clientBounds.Height - frameSize.Y ||
                        position.Y < 0)
                        speed.Y *= -1;

                    base.Update(gameTime, clientBounds);
            }
        }
    }
```

And you should update the code that creates your automated sprites in your Sprite Manager class's LoadContent method to look something like this:

```
//Load several different automated sprites into the list
spriteList.Add(new BouncingSprite(
    Game.Content.Load<Texture2D>(@"Images/skullball"),
    new Vector2(150, 150), new Point(75, 75), 10, new Point(0, 0),
    new Point(6, 8), new Vector2(1,1)));
spriteList.Add(new BouncingSprite(
    Game.Content.Load<Texture2D>(@"Images/plus"),
    new Vector2(300, 150), new Point(75, 75), 10, new Point(0, 0),
    new Point(6, 4), new Vector2(1,0)));
spriteList.Add(new BouncingSprite(
    Game.Content.Load<Texture2D>(@"Images/plus"),
    new Vector2(150, 300), new Point(75, 75), 10, new Point(0, 0),
    new Point(6, 4), new Vector2(0,1)));
spriteList.Add(new BouncingSprite(
    Game.Content.Load<Texture2D>(@"Images/skullball"),
    new Vector2(600, 400), new Point(75, 75), 10, new Point(0, 0),
    new Point(6, 8), new Vector2(-1,-1)));
```

Chapter 6: Sound Effects and Audio

Quiz Answers

1. What do you use to reference a sound that has been included in an XACT audio file?

   To play a sound in an XACT audio file, you reference the sound by its associated cue name.

2. What are the pros and cons of using the simple sound API available in XNA 4.0 instead of using XACT?

   Pros: simple and fast, and supported on the Reach game profile. Cons: no design-time modification of sound properties.

3. Fact or fiction: the only way to get a soundtrack to loop during gameplay is to manually program the sound in code to play over and over.

   Fiction. You can set the looping property of a particular sound in XACT by specifying a certain number of times for the sound to play or by specifying the sound to play in an infinite loop.

4. Fact or fiction: you can adjust the volume of your sounds using XACT.

   Fact. You can adjust the volume, pitch, and other properties of a sound file using XACT.

5. How do you pause and restart a sound in XNA when using XACT audio files?

   If you capture the `Cue` object from the `GetCue` method and play the sound from the `Cue` object, you can call `Pause`, `Stop`, `Play`, and other methods on the `Cue` object to manipulate playback of that particular sound.

6. What was the best-selling video game of 2009?

   Call of Duty: Modern Warfare 2 was the best-selling game of 2009, selling just under 12 million copies globally.

Exercise Answer

Try experimenting with different sounds and sound settings in XNA using XACT. Find a few *.wav* files and plug them into the game. Experiment with different settings in XACT by grouping multiple sounds in a single cue.

There's really no right or wrong answer to this exercise. Follow the steps from earlier in the chapter, add some different sounds, and play with the settings in XACT. It doesn't need to sound pretty; just use this as a chance to become more familiar with XACT and all that it can do.

Chapter 7: Basic Artificial Intelligence

Quiz Answers

1. What is the Turing Test?

   Developed by Alan Turing, the Turing Test involved having a human interact with a computer and another human, asking questions to determine which was which. The test was designed to determine whether a computer was intelligent. If the interrogator was unable to determine which was the computer and which was the human, the computer was deemed "intelligent."

2. Why is artificial intelligence so difficult to perfect?

   Because intelligence itself is so difficult to define. It's something that currently is not truly understood and therefore is ambiguous by nature.

3. What constitutes irrelevancy for an object in a video game? What should be done with irrelevant objects, and why?

   An object is irrelevant if it can no longer affect the game. Irrelevant objects should be deleted because otherwise they will continue to be updated and drawn in each frame, which will negatively affect performance.

4. If you have a player whose position is stored in a `Vector2` object called `PlayerPos` and a chasing object whose position is stored in a `Vector2` object called `ChasePos`, what algorithm will cause your chasing object to chase after your player?

```
if(PlayerPos.X < ChasePos.X)
    --ChasePos.X;
else
    ++ChasePos.X;
if(PlayerPos.Y < ChasePos.Y)
    --ChasePos.Y;
else
    ++ChasePos.Y;
```

5. In the beginning, what was created that made a lot of people very angry and has been widely regarded as a bad move?

According to *The Restaurant at the End of the Universe*, the second book in Douglas Adams' hilarious *The Hitchhiker's Guide to the Galaxy* series: "In the beginning the Universe was created. This has made a lot of people very angry and has been widely regarded as a bad move."

Exercise Answer

Take what you've learned in this chapter and make yet another type of sprite object, one that moves randomly around the screen. To do this, you'll want to create a random timer that signifies when the object should change directions. When the timer expires, have the object move in a different direction, and then reset the random timer to a new random time at which the object will again shift its direction.

When dealing with a random object, you need to figure out when it will randomly change direction. Ideally, it will randomly change direction at random intervals. The actual values that are used to determine the thresholds of the random variables can be customized to get the desired functionality, but the underlying code is the same. Here is a randomly moving sprite class:

```
using System;
using Microsoft.Xna.Framework;
using Microsoft.Xna.Framework.Graphics;

namespace AnimatedSprites
{
    class RandomSprite : Sprite
    {
        SpriteManager spriteManager;

        //Random variable to determine when to change directions
        int minChangeTime = 500;
        int maxChangeTime = 1000;
        int changeDirectionTimer;
        Random rnd;
```

```
public RandomSprite(Texture2D textureImage, Vector2 position,
    Point frameSize, int collisionOffset, Point currentFrame,
    Point sheetSize, Vector2 speed, string collisionCueName,
    SpriteManager spriteManager, Random rnd)
    : base(textureImage, position, frameSize, collisionOffset,
    currentFrame, sheetSize, speed, collisionCueName)
{
    this.spriteManager = spriteManager;
    this.rnd = rnd;
    ResetTimer();
}

public RandomSprite(Texture2D textureImage, Vector2 position,
    Point frameSize, int collisionOffset, Point currentFrame,
    Point sheetSize, Vector2 speed, int millisecondsPerFrame,
    string collisionCueName, SpriteManager spriteManager,
    Random rnd)
    : base(textureImage, position, frameSize, collisionOffset,
    currentFrame, sheetSize, speed, millisecondsPerFrame,
    collisionCueName)
{
    this.spriteManager = spriteManager;
    this.rnd = rnd;
    ResetTimer();
}

public override Vector2 direction
{
    get { return speed; }
}

public override void Update(GameTime gameTime, Rectangle clientBounds)
{
    //Move forward
    position += speed;
    Vector2 player = spriteManager.GetPlayerPosition();

    //Is it time to change directions?
    changeDirectionTimer -= gameTime.ElapsedGameTime.Milliseconds;
    if (changeDirectionTimer < 0)
    {
        //Pick a new random direction
        float Length = speed.Length();
        speed = new Vector2((float)rnd.NextDouble() - .5f,
            (float)rnd.NextDouble() - .5f);
        speed.Normalize();
        speed *= Length;

        ResetTimer();
    }

    base.Update(gameTime, clientBounds);
}
```

```
        private void ResetTimer()
        {
            changeDirectionTimer = rnd.Next(
                minChangeTime, maxChangeTime);
        }

    }
}
```

Chapter 8: Putting It All Together

Quiz Answers

1. What type of object is used to draw 2D text in XNA?

   You need a `SpriteFont` object to draw 2D text in XNA.

2. How is a background image different from an image used to represent a player or object in the game?

   It really isn't any different. The underlying concept is exactly the same: you're drawing a 2D image on the game window. The background image in this case doesn't animate, and the file containing the background image contains only that image (in contrast to the player sprites, which are animated; the files used for those objects contain sprite sheets with multiple images forming an animation sequence).

3. What are game states and how are they used?

   Game states represent a way to indicate the current status of the game as a whole or some activity within the game. Game states are used to transition from splash screens to gameplay, from gameplay to end-game screens, and so on.

4. In the *Flight of the Conchords* episode "Mugged," what do the muggers steal from Jemaine?

   The muggers steal Jemaine's camera-phone—which was actually a gift to him from Bret and is also really just Jemaine's phone glued to a camera.

Exercise Answer

Change the behavior of the skull power-up (or power-down, if you prefer) to freeze the player for 2 seconds rather than reduce the player's speed by 50% for 5 seconds. Use different power-up timers for the skull, bolt, and plus sprites.

There really isn't anything too complicated involved in adding a new power-up (or power-down), now that you've fleshed out the core logic. You already have a built-in way to modify the speed of the player via a power-up (the bolt power-up increases the speed by 100%, and the skull currently slows the player by 50%). To freeze the player, all you'll need to do is reduce the player's speed to zero while the power-up is in effect. The other thing to think about is that this power-up will last only two seconds, whereas the others lasted five seconds. So, you'll need to add a new variable to track when this freeze power-up expires.

The modified SpriteManager class is shown here:

```
using System;
using System.Collections.Generic;
using System.Linq;
using Microsoft.Xna.Framework;
using Microsoft.Xna.Framework.Audio;
using Microsoft.Xna.Framework.Content;
using Microsoft.Xna.Framework.GamerServices;
using Microsoft.Xna.Framework.Graphics;
using Microsoft.Xna.Framework.Input;
using Microsoft.Xna.Framework.Media;


namespace AnimatedSprites
{
    /// <summary>
    /// This is a game component that implements IUpdateable.
    /// </summary>
    public class SpriteManager : Microsoft.Xna.Framework.DrawableGameComponent
    {
        // SpriteBatch for drawing
        SpriteBatch spriteBatch;

        // A sprite for the player and a list of automated sprites
        UserControlledSprite player;
        List<Sprite> spriteList = new List<Sprite>();

        // Variables for spawning new enemies
        int enemySpawnMinMilliseconds = 1000;
        int enemySpawnMaxMilliseconds = 2000;
        int enemyMinSpeed = 2;
        int enemyMaxSpeed = 6;
        int nextSpawnTime = 0;

        // Chance of spawning different enemies
        int likelihoodAutomated = 75;
        int likelihoodChasing = 20;
        int likelihoodEvading = 5;

        // Scoring
        int automatedSpritePointValue = 10;
        int chasingSpritePointValue = 20;
        int evadingSpritePointValue = 0;

        // Lives
        List<AutomatedSprite> livesList = new List<AutomatedSprite>();

        //Spawn time variables
        int nextSpawnTimeChange = 5000;
        int timeSinceLastSpawnTimeChange = 0;
```

```csharp
// Powerup stuff
int powerUpExpiration = 0;
int powerUpFreezeExpiration = 0;

public SpriteManager(Game game)
    : base(game)
{
    // TODO: Construct any child components here
}

/// <summary>
/// Allows the game component to perform any initialization it
/// needs to before starting to run.  This is where it can query for
/// any required services and load content.
/// </summary>
public override void Initialize()
{
    // Initialize spawn time
    ResetSpawnTime();

    base.Initialize();
}

protected override void LoadContent()
{
    spriteBatch = new SpriteBatch(Game.GraphicsDevice);

    player = new UserControlledSprite(
        Game.Content.Load<Texture2D>(@"Images/threerings"),
        new Vector2(Game.Window.ClientBounds.Width / 2,
            Game.Window.ClientBounds.Height / 2),
        new Point(75, 75), 10, new Point(0, 0),
        new Point(6, 8), new Vector2(6, 6));


    // Load player lives list
    for (int i = 0; i < ((Game1)Game).NumberLivesRemaining; ++i)
    {
        int offset = 10 + i * 40;
        livesList.Add(new AutomatedSprite(
            Game.Content.Load<Texture2D>(@"images\threerings"),
            new Vector2(offset, 35), new Point(75, 75), 10,
            new Point(0, 0), new Point(6, 8), Vector2.Zero,
            null, 0, .5f));
    }

    base.LoadContent();
}

/// <summary>
/// Allows the game component to update itself.
/// </summary>
/// <param name="gameTime">Provides a snapshot of timing values.</param>
public override void Update(GameTime gameTime)
{
```

```
    // Time to spawn enemy?
    nextSpawnTime -= gameTime.ElapsedGameTime.Milliseconds;
    if (nextSpawnTime < 0)
    {
        SpawnEnemy();

        // Reset spawn timer
        ResetSpawnTime();
    }

    UpdateSprites(gameTime);

    // Adjust sprite spawn times
    AdjustSpawnTimes(gameTime);

    // Expire Powerups?
    CheckPowerUpExpiration(gameTime);

    base.Update(gameTime);
}

protected void UpdateSprites(GameTime gameTime)
{
    // Update player
    player.Update(gameTime, Game.Window.ClientBounds);

    // Update all nonplayer sprites
    for (int i = 0; i < spriteList.Count; ++i)
    {
        Sprite s = spriteList[i];

        s.Update(gameTime, Game.Window.ClientBounds);

        // Check for collisions
        if (s.collisionRect.Intersects(player.collisionRect))
        {
            // Play collision sound
            if (s.collisionCueName != null)
                ((Game1)Game).PlayCue(s.collisionCueName);

            // If collided with AutomatedSprite
            // remove a life from the player
            if (s is AutomatedSprite)
            {
                if (livesList.Count > 0)
                {
                    livesList.RemoveAt(livesList.Count - 1);
                    --((Game1)Game).NumberLivesRemaining;
                }
            }
            else if (s.collisionCueName == "pluscollision")
            {
                // Collided with plus - start plus power-up
                powerUpExpiration = 5000;
                player.ModifyScale(2);
```

```
            }
            else if (s.collisionCueName == "skullcollision")
            {
                // Collided with skull - start skull power-up
                powerUpExpiration = 2000;
                player.ModifySpeed(0f);
            }
            else if (s.collisionCueName == "boltcollision")
            {
                // Collided with bolt - start bolt power-up
                powerUpExpiration = 5000;
                player.ModifySpeed(2);
            }

            // Remove collided sprite from the game
            spriteList.RemoveAt(i);
            --i;
        }

        // Remove object if it is out of bounds
        if (s.IsOutOfBounds(Game.Window.ClientBounds))
        {
            ((Game1)Game).AddScore(spriteList[i].scoreValue);
            spriteList.RemoveAt(i);
            --i;
        }

    }

    // Update lives-list sprites
    foreach (Sprite sprite in livesList)
        sprite.Update(gameTime, Game.Window.ClientBounds);
}

public override void Draw(GameTime gameTime)
{
    spriteBatch.Begin(SpriteSortMode.FrontToBack, BlendState.AlphaBlend);

    // Draw the player
    player.Draw(gameTime, spriteBatch);

    // Draw all sprites
    foreach (Sprite s in spriteList)
        s.Draw(gameTime, spriteBatch);

    // Draw player lives
    foreach (Sprite sprite in livesList)
        sprite.Draw(gameTime, spriteBatch);

    spriteBatch.End();
    base.Draw(gameTime);
}

private void ResetSpawnTime()
{
```

```
            // Set the next spawn time for an enemy
            nextSpawnTime = ((Game1)Game).rnd.Next(
                enemySpawnMinMilliseconds,
                enemySpawnMaxMilliseconds);
        }

        private void SpawnEnemy()
        {
            Vector2 speed = Vector2.Zero;
            Vector2 position = Vector2.Zero;

            // Default frame size
            Point frameSize = new Point(75, 75);

            // Randomly choose which side of the screen to place enemy,
            // then randomly create a position along that side of the screen
            // and randomly choose a speed for the enemy
            switch (((Game1)Game).rnd.Next(4))
            {
                case 0: // LEFT to RIGHT
                    position = new Vector2(
                        -frameSize.X, ((Game1)Game).rnd.Next(0,
                        Game.GraphicsDevice.PresentationParameters.
                        BackBufferHeight - frameSize.Y));
                    speed = new Vector2(((Game1)Game).rnd.Next(
                        enemyMinSpeed,
                        enemyMaxSpeed), 0);
                    break;
                case 1: // RIGHT to LEFT
                    position = new
                        Vector2(
                        Game.GraphicsDevice.PresentationParameters.
                        BackBufferWidth,
                        ((Game1)Game).rnd.Next(0,
                        Game.GraphicsDevice.PresentationParameters.
                        BackBufferHeight - frameSize.Y));

                    speed = new Vector2(-((Game1)Game).rnd.Next(
                        enemyMinSpeed, enemyMaxSpeed), 0);
                    break;
                case 2: // BOTTOM to TOP
                    position = new Vector2(((Game1)Game).rnd.Next(0,
                    Game.GraphicsDevice.PresentationParameters.
                        BackBufferWidth - frameSize.X),
                        Game.GraphicsDevice.PresentationParameters.
                        BackBufferHeight);

                    speed = new Vector2(0,
                        -((Game1)Game).rnd.Next(enemyMinSpeed,
                        enemyMaxSpeed));
                    break;
                case 3: // TOP to BOTTOM
                    position = new Vector2(((Game1)Game).rnd.Next(0,
                        Game.GraphicsDevice.PresentationParameters.BackBufferWidth
                        - frameSize.X), -frameSize.Y);
```

```
            speed = new Vector2(0,
                ((Game1)Game).rnd.Next(enemyMinSpeed,
                enemyMaxSpeed));
            break;
    }

    // Get random number between 0 and 99
    int random = ((Game1)Game).rnd.Next(100);
    if (random < likelihoodAutomated)
    {
        // Create an AutomatedSprite.
        // Get new random number to determine whether to
        // create a three-blade or four-blade sprite.
        if (((Game1)Game).rnd.Next(2) == 0)
        {
            // Create a four-blade enemy
            spriteList.Add(
            new AutomatedSprite(
                Game.Content.Load<Texture2D>(@"images\fourblades"),
                position, new Point(75, 75), 10, new Point(0, 0),
                new Point(6, 8), speed, "fourbladescollision",
                automatedSpritePointValue));
        }
        else
        {
            // Create a three-blade enemy
            spriteList.Add(
            new AutomatedSprite(
                Game.Content.Load<Texture2D>(@"images\threeblades"),
                position, new Point(75, 75), 10, new Point(0, 0),
                new Point(6, 8), speed, "threebladescollision",
                automatedSpritePointValue));
        }
    }
    else if (random < likelihoodAutomated +
    likelihoodChasing)
    {
        // Create a ChasingSprite.
        // Get new random number to determine whether
        // to create a skull or a plus sprite.
        if (((Game1)Game).rnd.Next(2) == 0)
        {
            // Create a skull
            spriteList.Add(
            new ChasingSprite(
                Game.Content.Load<Texture2D>(@"images\skullball"),
                position, new Point(75, 75), 10, new Point(0, 0),
                new Point(6, 8), speed, "skullcollision", this,
                chasingSpritePointValue));
        }
        else
        {
```

```
                // Create a plus
                spriteList.Add(
                new ChasingSprite(
                    Game.Content.Load<Texture2D>(@"images\plus"),
                    position, new Point(75, 75), 10, new Point(0, 0),
                    new Point(6, 4), speed, "pluscollision", this,
                    chasingSpritePointValue));
            }
        }
        else
        {
            // Create an EvadingSprite
            spriteList.Add(
            new EvadingSprite(
                Game.Content.Load<Texture2D>(@"images\bolt"),
                position, new Point(75, 75), 10, new Point(0, 0),
                new Point(6, 8), speed, "boltcollision", this,
                .75f, 150, evadingSpritePointValue));
        }
    }

    // Return current position of the player sprite
    public Vector2 GetPlayerPosition()
    {
        return player.GetPosition;
    }

    protected void AdjustSpawnTimes(GameTime gameTime)
    {
        // If the spawn max time is > 500 milliseconds
        // decrease the spawn time if it is time to do
        // so based on the spawn-timer variables
        if (enemySpawnMaxMilliseconds > 500)
        {
            timeSinceLastSpawnTimeChange +=
                gameTime.ElapsedGameTime.Milliseconds;
            if (timeSinceLastSpawnTimeChange > nextSpawnTimeChange)
            {
                timeSinceLastSpawnTimeChange -= nextSpawnTimeChange;
                if (enemySpawnMaxMilliseconds > 1000)
                {
                    enemySpawnMaxMilliseconds -= 100;
                    enemySpawnMinMilliseconds -= 100;
                }
                else
                {
                    enemySpawnMaxMilliseconds -= 10;
                    enemySpawnMinMilliseconds -= 10;
                }
            }
        }
    }

    protected void CheckPowerUpExpiration(GameTime gameTime)
    {
```

```
// Is a power-up active?
if (powerUpExpiration > 0)
{
    // Decrement power-up timer
    powerUpExpiration -= gameTime.ElapsedGameTime.Milliseconds;
    if (powerUpExpiration <= 0)
    {
        // If power-up timer has expired, end all power-ups
        powerUpExpiration = 0;
        player.ResetScale();
        player.ResetSpeed();
    }
}

// Is a freeze power-up active?
if (powerUpFreezeExpiration > 0)
{
    // Decrement power-up timer
    powerUpFreezeExpiration -=
        gameTime.ElapsedGameTime.Milliseconds;
    if (powerUpFreezeExpiration <= 0)
    {
        // If power-up timer has expired, end all power-ups
        powerUpFreezeExpiration = 0;
        player.ResetSpeed();
    }
}
        }
    }
}
```

Chapter 9: 3D Game Development

Quiz Answers

1. Does XNA use a right-handed or left-handed coordinate system?

   XNA uses a right-handed coordinate system, which means that if you looked at the origin down the Z axis with positive X moving to your right, the Z axis would be positive in the direction coming toward you.

2. What makes up a viewing frustum (or field of view) for a camera in XNA 3D?

   The viewing frustum is made up of a camera angle and near and far clipping planes.

3. What is culling?

   Culling is the process of not drawing objects that are not facing the camera. For example, you never need to see the inside of a soccer ball when playing a soccer game in XNA, so the processor doesn't draw that side of the object, which saves valuable processor time.

4. What is a vertex declaration?

 A vertex declaration lets the graphics device know what type of data you are about to send so it knows how to process that data.

5. Fact or fiction: there is a difference between applying a rotation multiplied by a translation and applying a translation multiplied by a rotation.

 Fact. A `rotation * translation` will cause an object to spin in place, whereas a `translation * rotation` will cause an object to orbit.

6. What order of translation and rotation would be needed in order to simulate a planet spinning in place while orbiting the origin?

 To spin in place, you first need a rotation. Then to orbit, you need a translation and a rotation, in that order. So, the answer is `rotation * translation * rotation`.

7. Fact or fiction: to map the lower-right corner of a texture that is 250 × 300 pixels in size to a vertex, you should specify the (U, V) coordinate (250, 300).

 Fiction. (U, V) coordinates must be between 0 and 1. To specify the upper-left corner of a texture, you use the coordinate (0, 0). To specify the lower-right corner, you use the coordinate (1, 1).

8. How many vertices are needed to draw three triangles using a triangle list?

 A triangle list uses three vertices for each triangle. To draw three triangles, nine vertices are required.

9. How many vertices are needed to draw three triangles using a triangle strip?

 A triangle strip builds a triangle out of the first three vertices and a new triangle with every additional vertex, using the new vertex and the two previous vertices. Five vertices are required to draw three triangles using a triangle strip.

10. How many polygons were used to draw Marcus in *Gears of War*?

 According to *d'Artiste: Character Modeling 2* (Ballistic Publishing, 2010), Marcus took a whopping 15,000 polygons to draw. Crazy to think of how fast the computer and the graphics card are working to bring something that complex to life. Luckily, we don't have to draw complex models by hand like you did to create the triangle and rectangle in this chapter. In Chapter 10, you'll see how much easier it is to draw complex objects using models.

Exercise Answer

Building on the code that you wrote in this chapter, create a six-sided cube with different textures on each side that rotates on multiple axes.

To create the six-sided cube with different textures on each side, first you'll need to add five extra images to your project. Then, you'll have to figure out the coordinates to draw 12 triangles: 2 for each side of the cube. Next, create vertices for the sides of the cube in your vertex array, and then draw each side in your `Draw` method. One thing to be aware of is that you'll need to begin and end the effect for each side of the cube because you'll need to reset the texture for each side (which must be done before `BasicEffect.Begin` is called).

The `Game1` class is the only thing that changes in the solution. It's listed here:

```
using System;
using System.Collections.Generic;
using System.Linq;
using Microsoft.Xna.Framework;
using Microsoft.Xna.Framework.Audio;
using Microsoft.Xna.Framework.Content;
using Microsoft.Xna.Framework.GamerServices;
using Microsoft.Xna.Framework.Graphics;
using Microsoft.Xna.Framework.Input;
using Microsoft.Xna.Framework.Media;

namespace _3D_Madness
{
    /// <summary>
    /// This is the main type for your game
    /// </summary>
    public class Game1 : Microsoft.Xna.Framework.Game
    {
        GraphicsDeviceManager graphics;
        SpriteBatch spriteBatch;

        // Game camera
        Camera camera;

        // Vertex data
        VertexPositionTexture[] verts;
        VertexBuffer vertexBuffer;

        // Effect
        BasicEffect effect;

        // Movement and rotation stuff
        Matrix worldTranslation = Matrix.Identity;
        Matrix worldRotation = Matrix.Identity;

        // Texture info
        List<Texture2D> textureList = new List<Texture2D>();

        public Game1()
        {
            graphics = new GraphicsDeviceManager(this);
            Content.RootDirectory = "Content";
        }

        /// <summary>
        /// Allows the game to perform any initialization it
        /// needs to before starting to run. This is where it can query for
        /// any required services and load any content.
        /// </summary>
```

```
protected override void Initialize()
{
    // Initialize camera
    camera = new Camera(this, new Vector3(0, 0, 5),
        Vector3.Zero, Vector3.Up);
    Components.Add(camera);

    base.Initialize();
}

/// <summary>
/// LoadContent will be called once per game and is the place to load
/// all of your content.
/// </summary>
protected override void LoadContent()
{
    // Create a new SpriteBatch, which can be used to draw textures.
    spriteBatch = new SpriteBatch(GraphicsDevice);

    //initialize vertices
    verts = new VertexPositionTexture[24];
    //FRONT
    verts[0] = new VertexPositionTexture(
        new Vector3(-1, 1, 1), new Vector2(0, 0));
    verts[1] = new VertexPositionTexture(
        new Vector3(1, 1, 1), new Vector2(1, 0));
    verts[2] = new VertexPositionTexture(
        new Vector3(-1, -1, 1), new Vector2(0, 1));
    verts[3] = new VertexPositionTexture(
        new Vector3(1, -1, 1), new Vector2(1, 1));

    //BACK
    verts[4] = new VertexPositionTexture(
        new Vector3(1, 1, -1), new Vector2(0, 0));
    verts[5] = new VertexPositionTexture(
        new Vector3(-1, 1, -1), new Vector2(1, 0));
    verts[6] = new VertexPositionTexture(
        new Vector3(1, -1, -1), new Vector2(0, 1));
    verts[7] = new VertexPositionTexture(
        new Vector3(-1, -1, -1), new Vector2(1, 1));

    //LEFT
    verts[8] = new VertexPositionTexture(
        new Vector3(-1, 1, -1), new Vector2(0, 0));
    verts[9] = new VertexPositionTexture(
        new Vector3(-1, 1, 1), new Vector2(1, 0));
    verts[10] = new VertexPositionTexture(
        new Vector3(-1, -1, -1), new Vector2(0, 1));
    verts[11] = new VertexPositionTexture(
        new Vector3(-1, -1, 1), new Vector2(1, 1));

    //RIGHT
    verts[12] = new VertexPositionTexture(
        new Vector3(1, 1, 1), new Vector2(0, 0));
```

```
    verts[13] = new VertexPositionTexture(
        new Vector3(1, 1, -1), new Vector2(1, 0));
    verts[14] = new VertexPositionTexture(
        new Vector3(1, -1, 1), new Vector2(0, 1));
    verts[15] = new VertexPositionTexture(
        new Vector3(1, -1, -1), new Vector2(1, 1));

    //TOP
    verts[16] = new VertexPositionTexture(
        new Vector3(-1, 1, -1), new Vector2(0, 0));
    verts[17] = new VertexPositionTexture(
        new Vector3(1, 1, -1), new Vector2(1, 0));
    verts[18] = new VertexPositionTexture(
        new Vector3(-1, 1, 1), new Vector2(0, 1));
    verts[19] = new VertexPositionTexture(
        new Vector3(1, 1, 1), new Vector2(1, 1));

    //BOTTOM
    verts[20] = new VertexPositionTexture(
        new Vector3(-1, -1, 1), new Vector2(0, 0));
    verts[21] = new VertexPositionTexture(
        new Vector3(1, -1, 1), new Vector2(1, 0));
    verts[22] = new VertexPositionTexture(
        new Vector3(-1, -1, -1), new Vector2(0, 1));
    verts[23] = new VertexPositionTexture(
        new Vector3(1, -1, -1), new Vector2(1, 1));


    // Set vertex data in VertexBuffer
    vertexBuffer = new VertexBuffer(GraphicsDevice,
        typeof(VertexPositionTexture), verts.Length,
        BufferUsage.None);
    vertexBuffer.SetData(verts);

    // Initialize the BasicEffect
    effect = new BasicEffect(GraphicsDevice);

    //load all textures
    textureList.Add(Content.Load<Texture2D>(@"Textures\Trees"));
    textureList.Add(Content.Load<Texture2D>(@"Textures\t1"));
    textureList.Add(Content.Load<Texture2D>(@"Textures\t2"));
    textureList.Add(Content.Load<Texture2D>(@"Textures\t3"));
    textureList.Add(Content.Load<Texture2D>(@"Textures\t4"));
    textureList.Add(Content.Load<Texture2D>(@"Textures\t5"));
}


/// <summary>
/// UnloadContent will be called once per game and is the
/// place to unload all content.
/// </summary>
protected override void UnloadContent()
{
    // TODO: Unload any non-ContentManager content here
}
```

```csharp
/// <summary>
/// Allows the game to run logic such as updating the world,
/// checking for collisions, gathering input, and playing audio.
/// </summary>
/// <param name="gameTime">Provides a snapshot of timing values.</param>
protected override void Update(GameTime gameTime)
{
    // Allows the game to exit
    if (GamePad.GetState(PlayerIndex.One).Buttons.Back ==
        ButtonState.Pressed)
        this.Exit();

    // Translation
    KeyboardState keyboardState = Keyboard.GetState();
    if (keyboardState.IsKeyDown(Keys.Left))
        worldTranslation *= Matrix.CreateTranslation(-.01f, 0, 0);
    if (keyboardState.IsKeyDown(Keys.Right))
        worldTranslation *= Matrix.CreateTranslation(.01f, 0, 0);

    // Rotation
    worldRotation *= Matrix.CreateFromYawPitchRoll(
        MathHelper.PiOver4 / 60,
        MathHelper.PiOver4 / 360,
        MathHelper.PiOver4 / 180);

    base.Update(gameTime);
}

/// <summary>
/// This is called when the game should draw itself.
/// </summary>
/// <param name="gameTime">Provides a snapshot of timing values.</param>
protected override void Draw(GameTime gameTime)
{
    GraphicsDevice.Clear(Color.CornflowerBlue);


    // Set the vertex buffer on the GraphicsDevice
    GraphicsDevice.SetVertexBuffer(vertexBuffer);

    //Set object and camera info
    effect.World = worldRotation * worldTranslation * worldRotation;
    effect.View = camera.view;
    effect.Projection = camera.projection;
    effect.TextureEnabled = true;

    // Draw front
    effect.Texture = textureList[0];
    foreach (EffectPass pass in effect.CurrentTechnique.Passes)
    {
        pass.Apply();
```

```
            GraphicsDevice.DrawUserPrimitives<VertexPositionTexture>
                (PrimitiveType.TriangleStrip, verts, 0, 2);

    }

    //draw back
    effect.Texture = textureList[1];
    foreach (EffectPass pass in effect.CurrentTechnique.Passes)
    {
        pass.Apply();

        GraphicsDevice.DrawUserPrimitives<VertexPositionTexture>
            (PrimitiveType.TriangleStrip, verts, 4, 2);

    }


    //draw left
    effect.Texture = textureList[2];
    foreach (EffectPass pass in effect.CurrentTechnique.Passes)
    {
        pass.Apply();

        GraphicsDevice.DrawUserPrimitives<VertexPositionTexture>
            (PrimitiveType.TriangleStrip, verts, 8, 2);

    }

    //draw right
    effect.Texture = textureList[3];
    foreach (EffectPass pass in effect.CurrentTechnique.Passes)
    {
        pass.Apply();

        GraphicsDevice.DrawUserPrimitives<VertexPositionTexture>
            (PrimitiveType.TriangleStrip, verts, 12, 2);

    }

    //draw top
    effect.Texture = textureList[4];
    foreach (EffectPass pass in effect.CurrentTechnique.Passes)
    {
        pass.Apply();

        GraphicsDevice.DrawUserPrimitives<VertexPositionTexture>
            (PrimitiveType.TriangleStrip, verts, 16, 2);

    }

    //draw bottom
    effect.Texture = textureList[5];
    foreach (EffectPass pass in effect.CurrentTechnique.Passes)
    {
```

```
          pass.Apply();

          GraphicsDevice.DrawUserPrimitives<VertexPositionTexture>
              (PrimitiveType.TriangleStrip, verts, 20, 2);

      }


      base.Draw(gameTime);
    }
  }
}
```

Chapter 10: 3D Models

Quiz Answers

1. What model format(s) are supported in XNA?

   XNA supports *.x* and *.fbx* model files.

2. Why use a model when you can just draw things on your own?

   Models allow you to build a model or design in a third-party tool specifically designed for artistically modeling and molding three-dimensional objects. It would be nearly impossible to develop objects by hand in XNA 3D using primitives and attain the same level of detail and complexity that is achievable using a model.

3. What type of effect are models loaded with by default when they're loaded into XNA?

   By default, models in XNA use `BasicEffects`.

4. Fact or fiction: if your model has separate texture files associated with it, but those files aren't in the location specified by the model file, your game will crash when it tries to load the model.

   Fiction. Your game would not compile if textures were missing. The content pipeline would throw a compilation error.

5. What number comes next in the sequence {4, 8, 15, 16, 23}?

   42. These are the numbers that haunted Hurley in one of the greatest television series of all time, ABC's *Lost (http://abc.go.com/primetime/lost/index?pn=index)*.

Exercise Answer

Take the code from this chapter and create a new subclass of `BasicModel` in which the ship moves back and forth between (0, 0, 0) and (0, 0, –400). Make the ship turn appropriately to always face the direction in which it is going.

There are numerous solutions that will give you the effect described here. The following solution uses a variable to indicate how far the ship can go in the background and a direction Vector3 variable to indicate the ship's current direction. When the ship reaches a point where it must turn around, the Direction's Z value is multiplied by –1 and the ship is rotated on a 180 degree yaw to make it face the direction it is heading. The code for a subclass of BasicModel that solves this exercise is shown here (note that you'll have to create this class and then also modify the ModelManager to create an object of this type rather than the SpinningEnemy type):

```
using System;
using System.Collections.Generic;
using System.Text;
using Microsoft.Xna.Framework;
using Microsoft.Xna.Framework.Graphics;


namespace _3D_Game
{
    class FlyingShip : BasicModel
    {

        Matrix rotation = Matrix.CreateRotationY(MathHelper.Pi);
        Matrix translation = Matrix.Identity;

        float maxDistance = -400;
        Vector3 direction = new Vector3(0, 0, -1);

        public FlyingShip(Model m)
            : base(m)
        {
        }

        public override void Update()
        {
            //if the object has traveled past the max distance
            //or in front of the origin, reverse direction
            //and rotate ship 180 degrees
            if (translation.Translation.Z < maxDistance ||
                translation.Translation.Z > 0)
            {
                direction.Z *= -1;
                rotation *= Matrix.CreateRotationY(MathHelper.Pi);
            }

            translation *= Matrix.CreateTranslation(direction);
        }

        public override Matrix GetWorld()
        {
            return world * rotation * translation;
        }
    }
}
```

Chapter 11: Creating a First-Person Camera

Quiz Answers

1. When performing a yaw rotation with a camera, what camera vector(s) rotate(s)? What axis would you rotate on?

   In a yaw, the only vector that changes is the camera direction. You rotate the direction vector around the camera's up vector.

2. When performing a roll rotation with a camera, what camera vector(s) rotate(s)? What axis would you rotate on?

   In a roll, the only vector that changes is the camera's up vector. You rotate the up vector around the camera's direction vector.

3. When performing a pitch rotation with a camera, what camera vector(s) rotate(s)? What axis would you rotate on?

   In a pitch, the direction vector always changes and, depending on whether you're creating a land-based camera or a flight-simulator camera, you may also rotate the up vector. You rotate both of these vectors around the cross product of the camera's up and direction vectors.

4. What famous holiday includes an event titled the "Airing of Grievances"?

   Festivus (a holiday invented by Frank Costanza on the greatest show of all time, *Seinfeld*) includes the "Airing of Grievances," which takes place immediately after the Festivus feast and consists of all participants letting everybody know how much they have disappointed you that year.

Exercise Answer

Remember that to move a 3D camera forward, you use the following code:

```
cameraPosition += cameraDirection * speed;
```

There is a small problem with this method, however, when it's applied to land-based cameras. Essentially, to eliminate the ability to "fly" when looking up, you remove the Y component of the `cameraDirection` vector prior to moving the camera with this line of code. This causes your camera to stay at the same Y value, which keeps the camera on the ground.

However, consequently the higher you pitch your camera, the slower you end up moving. For example, if your `cameraDirection` vector was (10, 2, 0) when you removed the Y component, you would end up with the vector (10, 0, 0) and you'd move at that speed. If your camera was pitched at a larger angle and your `cameraDirection` vector was (2, 10, 0), the resulting vector after removing the Y component would be (2, 0, 0) and you'd move forward at that speed.

Convert your 3D *Flying Camera* solution to a land-based camera and solve this problem so that when moving forward and backward your camera moves at the same speed, regardless of the pitch angle. Use the code you created in the first half of this chapter.

Hint: remember that `Vector3.Normalize` will take any `Vector3` and give it a magnitude or length of 1.

The solution to this problem is fairly straightforward. First, you remove the Y component of the direction vector, and then you normalize the resulting vector, which gives the vector a magnitude (or length) of 1. Once you do this, you can multiply the vector by the speed of the camera and add it to your camera position. The code that moves the camera forward and backward is found in the `Update` method of the `Camera` class. The solution to the problem affects only that code and is shown here:

```
//Remove the Y component of the camera direction
Vector3 movementDirection = cameraDirection;
movementDirection.Y = 0;

//Normalize the vector to ensure constant speed
movementDirection.Normalize();

// Move forward/backward
if (Keyboard.GetState().IsKeyDown(Keys.W))
    cameraPosition += movementDirection * speed;
if (Keyboard.GetState().IsKeyDown(Keys.S))
    cameraPosition -= movementDirection * speed;
```

Chapter 12: 3D Collision Detection and Shooting

Quiz Answers

1. When firing a shot in a 3D (or 2D, for that matter) game, how do you determine the direction of the shot?

   Typically, the thing that's firing a shot (a camera, a gun, etc.) has a direction of its own. When firing a shot, you give the bullet or projectile the same direction vector as the item from which it emanates.

2. Fact or fiction: every model has a `BoundingSphere` object that surrounds the entire model and can be used for collision detection.

   Fiction. The `BoundingSphere` object belongs to a `ModelMesh` object. Every `Model` has one or more `ModelMesh` objects. The `BoundingSphere` therefore may cover the entire model, but a `Model` may also have several meshes, and in that case, the `Model` will have multiple `BoundingSphere` objects that each surround portions of the `Model`.

3. When using `BoundingSphere`s associated with a moving model for collision detection, what must be done to the `BoundingSphere` in order to accurately detect collisions?

   `BoundingSphere`s do not automatically move, rotate, and scale with the model that owns them. You need to apply the movement, rotation, and scale matrices to the `BoundingSphere` before using them for collision detection.

4. What is the difference between drawing 2D images on screen in a 3D game and drawing 2D images on the screen in a 2D game?

   Nothing. Drawing in 2D is the same, regardless of whether there are also 3D graphics in the game.

5. Why does Kramer's advice to Elaine regarding his karate class and the power of the inner katra backfire on Elaine?

   After Kramer encourages Elaine to run the J. Peterman catalog by relaying stories of his dominance of the karate dojo, Elaine gains new perspective and excitement for the task ahead. But everything falls apart when she finds out that Kramer is dominating the dojo because his peers are 8-year-old children:

   Elaine: Kramer!

   Kramer: Oh, hey.

   Elaine: What are you doing?

   Kramer: Oh, well, I-I-I'm dominating.

   Elaine: You never said you were fighting children.

   Kramer: Well, it's not the size of the opponent, Elaine, it's, uh, the ferocity.

   Elaine: This is what you used to build me up? This is where you got all that stupid katra stuff?

   Kramer: No, no. That's from, uh, *Star Trek III...The Search for Spock*.

   Elaine: Search...for Spock?!

   Kramer: Yeah, I know Jerry will tell you that *The Wrath of Khan* is the better picture, but for me, I always....

   Elaine: (pushes him) You doofus!

Exercise Answer

To familiarize yourself further with what was covered in this chapter, customize the shot firing mechanism by modifying the code to do the following:

- Slow the shots down by 50%.
- Cut the shot delay in half (i.e., make shots fire twice as often when holding the space bar continuously).
- Every time a shot is fired, fire three shots in a spread (i.e., one shot down the center and two other shots, one to the left and one to the right).

Well, the first two problems here are easy: by changing the initial values for the variables representing the shot speed and the shot delay, you can solve each of those problems with minimal coding. To fire three shots in a spread, you'll have to find the code where a single shot is fired and add two more shots to the model manager (one to the right of the original shot and one to the left).

The Game1 class is the only one that needs modification. Here is a sample solution:

```
using System;
using System.Collections.Generic;
using System.Linq;
using Microsoft.Xna.Framework;
using Microsoft.Xna.Framework.Audio;
using Microsoft.Xna.Framework.Content;
using Microsoft.Xna.Framework.GamerServices;
using Microsoft.Xna.Framework.Graphics;
using Microsoft.Xna.Framework.Input;
using Microsoft.Xna.Framework.Media;
using Microsoft.Xna.Framework.Net;
using Microsoft.Xna.Framework.Storage;

namespace _3D_Game
{
    public class Game1 : Microsoft.Xna.Framework.Game
    {
        GraphicsDeviceManager graphics;
        SpriteBatch spriteBatch;

        public Camera camera { get; protected set; }
        ModelManager modelManager;

        //Randomness
        public Random rnd { get; protected set; }

        //Shots
        float shotSpeed = 5;
        int shotDelay = 150;
        int shotCountdown = 0;

        //Crosshair
        Texture2D crosshairTexture;

        //Audio
        AudioEngine audioEngine;
        WaveBank waveBank;
        SoundBank soundBank;
        Cue trackCue;

        public Game1()
        {
            graphics = new GraphicsDeviceManager(this);
            Content.RootDirectory = "Content";

            graphics.PreferredBackBufferWidth = 1280;
            graphics.PreferredBackBufferHeight = 1024;
```

```
#if !DEBUG
        graphics.IsFullScreen = true;
#endif

        rnd = new Random();
    }

    protected override void Initialize()
    {
        //Initialize camera
        camera = new Camera(this, new Vector3(0, 0, 50),
            Vector3.Zero, Vector3.Up);
        Components.Add(camera);

        //Initialize model manager
        modelManager = new ModelManager(this);
        Components.Add(modelManager);

        base.Initialize();
    }

    protected override void LoadContent()
    {
        // Create a new SpriteBatch, which can be used to draw textures.
        spriteBatch = new SpriteBatch(GraphicsDevice);

        //Load crosshair
        crosshairTexture = Content.Load<Texture2D>(@"textures\
crosshair");

        // Load sounds and play initial sounds
        audioEngine = new AudioEngine(
            @"Content\Audio\GameAudio.xgs");
        waveBank = new WaveBank(audioEngine,
            @"Content\Audio\Wave Bank.xwb");
        soundBank = new SoundBank(audioEngine,
            @"Content\Audio\Sound Bank.xsb");

        trackCue = soundBank.GetCue("Tracks");
        trackCue.Play();
    }

    protected override void UnloadContent()
    {
        // TODO: Unload any non-ContentManager content here
    }

    protected override void Update(GameTime gameTime)
    {
        // Allows the game to exit
        if (GamePad.GetState(PlayerIndex.One).Buttons.Back ==
            ButtonState.Pressed)
            this.Exit();
```

```csharp
        // See if the player has fired a shot
        FireShots(gameTime);

        base.Update(gameTime);
    }

    protected override void Draw(GameTime gameTime)
    {
        GraphicsDevice.Clear(Color.Black);

        // TODO: Add your drawing code here

        base.Draw(gameTime);

        //Draw crosshair
        spriteBatch.Begin();

        spriteBatch.Draw(crosshairTexture,
            new Vector2((Window.ClientBounds.Width / 2)
                - (crosshairTexture.Width / 2),
                (Window.ClientBounds.Height / 2)
                - (crosshairTexture.Height / 2)),
                Color.White);

        spriteBatch.End();
    }

    protected void FireShots(GameTime gameTime)
    {
        if (shotCountdown <= 0)
        {
            // Did player press space bar or left mouse button?
            if (Keyboard.GetState().IsKeyDown(Keys.Space) ||
                Mouse.GetState().LeftButton == ButtonState.Pressed)
            {
                // Add a shot to the model manager
                modelManager.AddShot(
                    camera.cameraPosition + new Vector3(0, -5, 0),
                    camera.GetCameraDirection * shotSpeed);

                //Add shot in spread to the right
                Vector3 initialPosition = camera.cameraPosition +
                    Vector3.Cross(camera.GetCameraDirection,
                    camera.cameraUp) * 5;

                modelManager.AddShot(
                    initialPosition + new Vector3(0, -5, 0),
                    camera.GetCameraDirection * shotSpeed);

                //Add shot in spread to the left
                initialPosition = camera.cameraPosition -
                    Vector3.Cross(camera.GetCameraDirection,
                    camera.cameraUp) * 5;
```

```
                modelManager.AddShot(
                    initialPosition + new Vector3(0, -5, 0),
                    camera.GetCameraDirection * shotSpeed);


                // Play shot audio
                PlayCue("Shot");

                // Reset the shot countdown
                shotCountdown = shotDelay;
            }
        }
        else
            shotCountdown -= gameTime.ElapsedGameTime.Milliseconds;
    }

    public void PlayCue(string cue)
    {
        soundBank.PlayCue(cue);
    }
}
}
```

Chapter 13: HLSL Basics

Quiz Answers

1. In HLSL, how can you access the first element in a float4 object?

   If you want to access the first element in a float4 object called color, you can use array notation (color[0]), or you can use the namespaces for color and position (color.r or color.x).

2. What is swizzling?

   The term swizzling refers to accessing multiple elements of a float4 or similar datatype at the same time by using two or more elements from the color or position namespaces (e.g., color.rb or color.xyz).

3. In HLSL, how do you specify which vertex and pixel shader versions to use?

   In the pass block of the technique for an HLSL effect file, you specify a Vertex Shader and/or a PixelShader by providing the compile keyword followed by a shader version. For vertex shaders, you use vs_2_0 syntax, and for pixel shaders, you use ps_2_0 syntax.

4. What does HLSL do for you that you can't accomplish without it?

   HLSL allows developers to access hardware functions that aren't available via the XNA Framework. The reason: graphics hardware has become more and more complex, and if the XNA Framework were expanded to handle all capabilities of graphics cards, the framework would be enormous. Instead, HLSL works with XNA and allows you to write code for the graphics card itself.

5. How do you multiply two matrices together in HLSL?

   The `mul` function in HLSL will multiply together two matrices.

6. What is the role of a semantic in HLSL?

   A semantic marks a variable as being used for a certain purpose. For input parameters, the semantic means that the parameter will automatically be given a value specified by the semantic. For output parameters, it is a way to flag certain variables as containing certain information that is required for processing that takes place after the shader is finished executing.

7. Who burninates the countryside, burninates the peasants, burninates all the people, and their thatch-roofed cottages?

   Trogdor, the man...er...dragon man...er...the dragon, of course.

Exercise Answer

Take the code you built in this chapter and draw a six-sided cube using the trees image provided as the texture for each side of the cube. One each side of the cube, use one of the four texture effects you built in this chapter (normal texture, burred texture, negative texture, grayscale texture). Use each of the four effects at least once on the cube.

This exercise is very similar to the one from Chapter 9 in which you built a six-sided cube with different textures on each side. The difference here is that you'll be applying the same texture to each side of the cube and then applying different HLSL effects to those sides.

First, create the different effect files as shown in this chapter, and then use something similar to the following code to create the cube and apply the effects:

```
using System;
using System.Collections.Generic;
using System.Linq;
using Microsoft.Xna.Framework;
using Microsoft.Xna.Framework.Audio;
using Microsoft.Xna.Framework.Content;
using Microsoft.Xna.Framework.GamerServices;
using Microsoft.Xna.Framework.Graphics;
using Microsoft.Xna.Framework.Input;
using Microsoft.Xna.Framework.Media;

namespace _3D_Madness
{
    /// <summary>
    /// This is the main type for your game.
    /// </summary>
    public class Game1 : Microsoft.Xna.Framework.Game
    {
```

```
GraphicsDeviceManager graphics;
SpriteBatch spriteBatch;

// Game camera
Camera camera;

// Vertex data
VertexPositionTexture[] verts;
VertexBuffer vertexBuffer;

// Effect
Effect normalEffect;
Effect blurEffect;
Effect negativeEffect;
Effect grayscaleEffect;

// Movement and rotation stuff
Matrix worldTranslation = Matrix.Identity;
Matrix worldRotation = Matrix.Identity;

// Texture info
Texture2D texture;

public Game1()
{
    graphics = new GraphicsDeviceManager(this);
    Content.RootDirectory = "Content";
}

/// <summary>
/// Allows the game to perform any initialization it
/// needs to before starting to run. This is where it can query for
/// any required services and load content.
/// </summary>
protected override void Initialize()
{
    // Initialize camera
    camera = new Camera(this, new Vector3(0, 0, 5),
        Vector3.Zero, Vector3.Up);
    Components.Add(camera);

    base.Initialize();
}

/// <summary>
/// LoadContent will be called once per game and is the place to load
/// all of your content.
/// </summary>
protected override void LoadContent()
{
    // Create a new SpriteBatch, which can be used to draw textures.
    spriteBatch = new SpriteBatch(GraphicsDevice);

    //initialize vertices
    verts = new VertexPositionTexture[24];
```

```
//FRONT
verts[0] = new VertexPositionTexture(
    new Vector3(-1, 1, 1), new Vector2(0, 0));
verts[1] = new VertexPositionTexture(
    new Vector3(1, 1, 1), new Vector2(1, 0));
verts[2] = new VertexPositionTexture(
    new Vector3(-1, -1, 1), new Vector2(0, 1));
verts[3] = new VertexPositionTexture(
    new Vector3(1, -1, 1), new Vector2(1, 1));

//BACK
verts[4] = new VertexPositionTexture(
    new Vector3(1, 1, -1), new Vector2(0, 0));
verts[5] = new VertexPositionTexture(
    new Vector3(-1, 1, -1), new Vector2(1, 0));
verts[6] = new VertexPositionTexture(
    new Vector3(1, -1, -1), new Vector2(0, 1));
verts[7] = new VertexPositionTexture(
    new Vector3(-1, -1, -1), new Vector2(1, 1));

//LEFT
verts[8] = new VertexPositionTexture(
    new Vector3(-1, 1, -1), new Vector2(0, 0));
verts[9] = new VertexPositionTexture(
    new Vector3(-1, 1, 1), new Vector2(1, 0));
verts[10] = new VertexPositionTexture(
    new Vector3(-1, -1, -1), new Vector2(0, 1));
verts[11] = new VertexPositionTexture(
    new Vector3(-1, -1, 1), new Vector2(1, 1));

//RIGHT
verts[12] = new VertexPositionTexture(
    new Vector3(1, 1, 1), new Vector2(0, 0));
verts[13] = new VertexPositionTexture(
    new Vector3(1, 1, -1), new Vector2(1, 0));
verts[14] = new VertexPositionTexture(
    new Vector3(1, -1, 1), new Vector2(0, 1));
verts[15] = new VertexPositionTexture(
    new Vector3(1, -1, -1), new Vector2(1, 1));

//TOP
verts[16] = new VertexPositionTexture(
    new Vector3(-1, 1, -1), new Vector2(0, 0));
verts[17] = new VertexPositionTexture(
    new Vector3(1, 1, -1), new Vector2(1, 0));
verts[18] = new VertexPositionTexture(
    new Vector3(-1, 1, 1), new Vector2(0, 1));
verts[19] = new VertexPositionTexture(
    new Vector3(1, 1, 1), new Vector2(1, 1));

//BOTTOM
verts[20] = new VertexPositionTexture(
    new Vector3(-1, -1, 1), new Vector2(0, 0));
verts[21] = new VertexPositionTexture(
    new Vector3(1, -1, 1), new Vector2(1, 0));
```

```
verts[22] = new VertexPositionTexture(
    new Vector3(-1, -1, -1), new Vector2(0, 1));
verts[23] = new VertexPositionTexture(
    new Vector3(1, -1, -1), new Vector2(1, 1));

// Set vertex data in VertexBuffer
vertexBuffer = new VertexBuffer(GraphicsDevice,
    typeof(VertexPositionTexture), verts.Length,
    BufferUsage.None);
vertexBuffer.SetData(verts);

//Load effect
normalEffect = Content.Load<Effect>(@"effects\Red");
grayscaleEffect = Content.Load<Effect>(@"effects\Grayscale");
negativeEffect = Content.Load<Effect>(@"effects\Negative");
blurEffect = Content.Load<Effect>(@"effects\Blur");

// Load texture
texture = Content.Load<Texture2D>(@"Textures\trees");

}

/// <summary>
/// UnloadContent will be called once per game and is
/// the place to unload all content.
/// </summary>
protected override void UnloadContent()
{
    // TODO: Unload any non-ContentManager content here
}

/// <summary>
/// Allows the game to run logic such as updating the world,
/// checking for collisions, gathering input, and playing audio.
/// </summary>
/// <param name="gameTime">Provides a snapshot of timing values.</param>
protected override void Update(GameTime gameTime)
{
    // Allows the game to exit
    if (GamePad.GetState(PlayerIndex.One).Buttons.Back ==
        ButtonState.Pressed)
        this.Exit();

    // Translation
    KeyboardState keyboardState = Keyboard.GetState();
    if (keyboardState.IsKeyDown(Keys.Left))
        worldTranslation *= Matrix.CreateTranslation(-.01f, 0, 0);
    if (keyboardState.IsKeyDown(Keys.Right))
        worldTranslation *= Matrix.CreateTranslation(.01f, 0, 0);

    // Rotation
    worldRotation *= Matrix.CreateFromYawPitchRoll(
        MathHelper.PiOver4 / 60,
        0,
        0);
```

```csharp
        base.Update(gameTime);
    }

    /// <summary>
    /// This is called when the game should draw itself.
    /// </summary>
    /// <param name="gameTime">Provides a snapshot of timing values.
    /// </param>
    protected override void Draw(GameTime gameTime)
    {
        GraphicsDevice.Clear(Color.CornflowerBlue);


        // Set the vertex buffer on the GraphicsDevice
        GraphicsDevice.SetVertexBuffer(vertexBuffer);

        //Draw front
        DrawVerts(normalEffect, 0, 2);
        //Draw back
        DrawVerts(blurEffect, 4, 2);
        //Draw left
        DrawVerts(grayscaleEffect, 8, 2);
        //Draw right
        DrawVerts(negativeEffect, 12, 2);
        //Draw top
        DrawVerts(blurEffect, 16, 2);
        //Draw bottom
        DrawVerts(grayscaleEffect, 20, 2);

        base.Draw(gameTime);
    }

    protected void DrawVerts(Effect effect, int start, int end)
    {
        effect.CurrentTechnique = effect.Techniques["Textured"];
        Matrix world = worldRotation * worldTranslation;
        effect.Parameters["xWorldViewProjection"].SetValue(
            world * camera.view * camera.projection);
        effect.Parameters["xColoredTexture"].SetValue(texture);

        foreach (EffectPass pass in effect.CurrentTechnique.Passes)
        {
            pass.Apply();
            GraphicsDevice.DrawUserPrimitives<VertexPositionTexture>
                (PrimitiveType.TriangleStrip, verts, start, end);
        }

    }
  }
}
```

Chapter 14: Particle Systems

Quiz Answers

1. What is a particle engine?

   A particle engine is a mechanism that manipulates, moves, adds, removes, and draws particles to create a particle effect.

2. Why were there two textures used for the particles in your explosion? What was the purpose of each?

   The first texture you added to the project (*particle.png*) represents the shape of each particle. It is simply a shaded, round circle, all white, with a transparent background. The second texture (*particleColors.png*) is used to get random colors with which to color each particle. The same technique was used with the stars using the *particle.png* file for the shape and the *stars.png* file for the colors.

3. What are texture (U, V) coordinates?

   (U, V) coordinates map texture sizes into a coordinate system that ranges from 0 to 1 horizontally (U) and 0 to 1 vertically (V).

4. According to Napoleon Dynamite's Uncle Rico, how far could Uncle Rico throw a "pigskin" back in 1982?

   In the movie *Napoleon Dynamite*, Uncle Rico often reminisces of the good ol' days in '82:

   > Uncle Rico: Back in '82, I used to be able to throw a pigskin a quarter mile.
   > Kip: Are you serious?
   > Uncle Rico: I'm dead serious.

Chapter 15: Wrapping Up Your 3D Game

Exercise Answer

Create a multishot power-up that, when active, will fire four shots instead of one. Instead of shooting one shot in the center of the camera, when multishot is active, shoot one shot from above and right of the camera, one from above and left, one from below and right, and one from below and left.

When the player shoots three ships in a row, the game will randomly choose which power-up to activate (rapid fire or multishot).

You have all the code fleshed out to create a power-up. Now you'll need to take that code and add a new multishot power-up. Start with adding a new value to the PowerUps enum to represent multishot mode.

Once that's done, there are really only two other steps: add code when a power-up is triggered that randomly picks the multishot or rapid fire mode, and add the code to fire multiple shots in multishot mode.

The difficult part will be in the FireShots method of the Game1 class, where you'll need to add the code for multiple shots. Here is one possible solution for that part of the problem:

```
protected void FireShots(GameTime gameTime)
{
    if (shotCountdown <= 0)
    {
        // Did player press space bar or left mouse button?
        if (Keyboard.GetState().IsKeyDown(Keys.Space) ||
            Mouse.GetState().LeftButton == ButtonState.Pressed)
        {
            if (currentPowerUp != PowerUps.MULTI_SHOT)
            {
                //Normal mode - fire one shot

                // Add a shot to the model manager
                modelManager.AddShot(
                    camera.cameraPosition + new Vector3(0, -5, 0),
                    camera.GetCameraDirection * shotSpeed);
            }
            else
            {
                //Multi-shot mode!

                //Add shot in spread to the top right
                Vector3 initialPosition = camera.cameraPosition +
                    Vector3.Cross(camera.GetCameraDirection, camera.
                        cameraUp) * 5
                        + (camera.cameraUp * 5);
                modelManager.AddShot(
                    initialPosition + new Vector3(0, -5, 0),
                    camera.GetCameraDirection * shotSpeed);

                //Add shot in spread to the bottom right
                initialPosition = camera.cameraPosition +
                    Vector3.Cross(camera.GetCameraDirection, camera.
                        cameraUp) * 5
                        - (camera.cameraUp * 5);
                modelManager.AddShot(
                    initialPosition + new Vector3(0, -5, 0),
                    camera.GetCameraDirection * shotSpeed);

                //Add shot in spread top left
                initialPosition = camera.cameraPosition -
                    Vector3.Cross(camera.GetCameraDirection, camera.
                        cameraUp) * 5
                        + (camera.cameraUp * 5);
                modelManager.AddShot(
                    initialPosition + new Vector3(0, -5, 0),
                    camera.GetCameraDirection * shotSpeed);
```

```
            //Add shot in spread bottom left
            initialPosition = camera.cameraPosition -
                Vector3.Cross(camera.GetCameraDirection, camera.
                    cameraUp) * 5
                    - (camera.cameraUp * 5);
            modelManager.AddShot(
                initialPosition + new Vector3(0, -5, 0),
                camera.GetCameraDirection * shotSpeed);
        }

        // Play shot audio
        PlayCue("Shot");

        // Reset the shot countdown
        shotCountdown = shotDelay;
        }
    }
    else
        shotCountdown -= gameTime.ElapsedGameTime.Milliseconds;
}
```

Chapter 16: Deploying to the Xbox 360

Quiz Answers

1. What piece of information does a PC use to identify a specific Xbox 360 machine?

   XNA uses a connection key to identify an Xbox 360 machine on a PC.

2. Fact or fiction: to debug a project that has been deployed on an Xbox 360, you have to load the code in the Xbox 360 code editor and place a breakpoint within the code on the Xbox 360 machine.

   Fiction. To debug projects that are deployed on an Xbox 360, place a breakpoint in the code on the PC used to deploy the project. If you then start the project in debug mode, it will run on the Xbox 360 and allow you to debug on the connected PC.

3. Fact or fiction: if you've created a Windows game project and you want to deploy that project to your Xbox 360, you need to create a new project in order to do so.

   Fact. Creating a Windows project allows you to run your game on Windows only, and creating an Xbox 360 project allows you to run your game on an Xbox 360 only. To facilitate multiplatform development, you can create a project for one platform and then create a copy of it for another platform and share files between the two.

4. What is a preprocessor directive?

   Preprocessor directives give developers a way to write code intended for the preprocessor rather than the compiler. Developers can perform logic that affects what code is compiled and how it is compiled using these directives.

5. What does the following code do in a Windows project?

```
#if (XBOX360)
    int A = 5;
    int B = 4;
    int C = A - B;
#endif
```

   Because the XBOX360 symbol is not defined for a Windows project, this code not only does nothing, but it will not even compile in the game. The end result of the project will be exactly the same as if the code did not exist.

6. What does "serenity now" lead to?

   According to Lloyd Braun, a childhood neighbor of George Costanza, serenity now leads to insanity later.

Chapter 17: Developing for Windows Phone 7

Quiz Answers

1. What are the three types of developer accounts you can create for development on Windows Phone 7?

   You can register for an account as a business, an individual, or a student.

2. What software do you use to unlock your Windows Phone 7 device?

   You use the Microsoft Zune software to unlock your Windows Phone 7 as well as to connect to the device through Visual Studio.

3. How do you read data from the Windows Phone 7 accelerometer?

   You handle the ReadingChanged event on the accelerometer and capture the X, Y, and/or Z values in that method's AccelerometerReadingEventArgs parameter.

4. What is the default screen resolution and screen rotation of a Windows Phone 7 game?

   The default screen rotation is LandscapeLeft, and the resolution is 800 × 480.

5. What are the possible states of a TouchLocation object?

   Invalid (indicating an error occurred), Moved (indicating a single touch has changed position), Pressed (indicating a new touch location was pressed), and Released (indicating that the touch location was released).

6. Why does Brody the Bootlegger get angry with Jerry Seinfeld during the movie *Death Blow*?

Because Jerry made a comment about the large bag of candy that Brody was chowing down on all by himself:

> Kramer: There's Brody. Brody! Over here...
>
> Brody: Hey, Kramer. And you must be Jerry. Thanks for the ticket.
>
> Jerry: That's quite a feed bag you're workin' on there.
>
> Brody: It's for all of us. Is there a problem?
>
> Kramer: Brody, c'mon. He's just kidding. He's a joke maker. Tell him, Jerry.
>
> Jerry: I'm a joke maker.

Chapter 18: Multiplayer Games

Quiz Answers

1. If you create a two-player split screen, what should you use for the camera's aspect ratio to ensure that your graphics don't look squished?

Instead of using the width and height of the game window for your aspect ratio, you should use the width and height of the viewport for that split-screen view.

2. Fact or fiction: networked games in XNA use a networking API that works on the PC and Xbox 360 but is different on the Zune.

Fiction. The networking API in XNA is compatible with all three platforms (PC, Xbox 360, and Zune)—although each platform can communicate only with devices of its own type.

3. What's the difference between a peer-to-peer and a client/server network architecture?

Peer-to-peer networks have no server, and all machines send data to all other machines in the network. Client/server networks have a server and one or more clients. All clients send data to the server, and the server broadcasts all messages to all clients.

4. Which network type (peer-to-peer or client/server) is better?

That totally depends on the type of game you're creating. You'll need to consider the number of players involved as well as how much information needs to be updated throughout the game.

5. What will happen if you don't call `NetworkSession.Update` in your game?

The `NetworkSession.Update` call updates your session and pumps all network messages through the session. If you don't call this method, the machines on the network will not be able to communicate and sync up in order for the game to be played.

6. How do you force a user to sign in using the gamer services sign-in windows?

   Calling `Guide.ShowSignIn` makes the game window render a series of gamer services windows that allow players to sign into their online gamertags or local accounts.

7. How do you send a message to another player in a networked XNA game?

   You'll first need to write the data to a `PacketWriter` object using the `PacketWriter.Write` method. You'll then send the data via the local gamer's `SendData` method.

8. How do you read a message from another player?

   You use a `PacketReader` object in the local gamer's `ReceiveData` method to pull the packet from the network. You then use different methods of the `PacketReader` to pull out different types of data (for example, `ReadInt32`).

9. When receiving a network message in XNA, how do you know what type of data is going to be read from the `PacketReader` and what that data means?

   You'll typically want to create an `enum` indicating the type of each message. You'll then send that `enum` value as the first item in every packet. When reading packets, you'll read the message type and perform the action appropriate for that message type.

10. What, according to Harry Dunne, is worse than his roommate, Lloyd Christmas, getting robbed by an old lady?

    In the movie *Dumb and Dumber*—one of the greatest films of our time—Harry and Lloyd go from bad to worse when Harry's pet parakeet comes down with a sudden illness:

    > Lloyd: I got robbed by a sweet old lady on a motorized cart. I didn't even see it coming.
    > Harry: Oh, no, no.
    > Lloyd: Come on, Harry.
    > Harry: It gets worse. My parakeet, Petey.
    > Lloyd: Yeah?
    > Harry: He's dead.
    > Lloyd: Oh, man, I'm sorry. What happened?
    > Harry: His head fell off.
    > Lloyd: His head fell off?
    > Harry: Yeah. He was pretty old.

Index

Symbols

2D games
  animation, 39
  compared to 3D games, 171, 207
  sprites, 17
  types of objects in, 67
  X, Y screen coordinates, 27
2D graphics compared to 3D graphics, 171
2D images, 129, 484
2D text, 126–131, 465
3D cameras
  components of a moving 3D camera, 217–221
  creating, 176
3D collision detection, 251–253
3D games, 323–344
  coding for cameras for, 229–233
  drawing images, 484
  keeping score, 334–337
  power-ups, 338–342
  splash screens, 323–334
3D graphics
  textures, 191
  vectors, 267
3D models, 201–216
  adding a model manager, 210
  adding models to projects, 205
  drawing using a BasicModel class, 206–210
  rotating, 212
  setting up projects, 202
  using, 201

A

abs function, 287

accounts, developer accounts, 366
accuracy, collision detection, 64
acos function, 287
adding
  3D models to projects, 205
  audio, 96–100, 256–262
  background images, 139
  biohazard bombs of insanity, 438–443
  crosshairs, 253
  drawing code in multiplayer games, 432–436
  game logic, 237–245
  model managers, 210, 386–391
  particle engines to games, 312
  power-downs, 465
  power-ups, 338–342, 465
  splash screens, 323–334
  starfields, 315
  update code to multiplayer games, 417–432
    while in CreateSession game state, 422
    while in FindSession game state, 419–421
    while in GameOver game state, 431
    while in InGame game state, 430
    while in SignIn game state, 418
    while in Start game state, 422–429
  variety to sprites, 133–139
  Xbox 360 device, 345
all function, 287
alpha test effects, 4
analog controls
  about, 58
  versus digital, 452
animation

We'd like to hear your suggestions for improving our indexes. Send email to *index@oreilly.com*.

random objects, 463
random values, 106
randomly generating different sprite types, 132
randomly spawning sprites, 106
randomness, 237
rasterization, 267
RasterizerState class, 5
Reach
    compared to HiDef, 447
    configurable effects, 4
Real-Time Strategy (RTS) games, 397
Rectangle parameter, 71
rectangles
    creating, 41
    drawing using the BasicEffect class, 277
    drawing with triangles, 192
    intersection of, 61
reflect function, 288
refract function, 289
registering
    for developer accounts, 366
    for events, 18, 52
    Windows Phone 7, 368
remote players, adding update code while in Start game state, 425
rendering
    portions of images transparently, 28
    targets, 4
resolution, screens in Windows Phone 7, 378
RightButton property, 55
rolls, rotating a camera in, 227
Rotation parameter, 32
rotations, 184, 188–191
    3D models, 212
    cameras and, 482
    in a first-person camera, 224–229
        in a pitch, 228
        in a roll, 227
        in a yaw, 226
    screen rotations of a Windows Phone 7 game, 497
    screens in Windows Phone 7, 378
    and translations, 474
round function, 289
rsqrt function, 289
RTS (Real-Time Strategy) games, 397

S

safe region, Xbox 360, 361
SamplerState class, 5
saturate function, 289
scalars, 5
Scale parameter, 32
scoring
    3D games, 334–337
    about, 140–147, 337
    rules and calculations, 141
screens
    game-over screen, 153–160
    height, 177
    orientation, 5
    resolution, 238, 378, 497
    rotation, 378, 497
    splash screens, 323–334
    split screens in multiplayer games, 397–406
    width, 177
    X, Y coordinates in 2D games, 27
ScrollWheelValue property, 55
semantics, role in HLSL, 489
send options, 423
SetPosition() method, 54
SetVibration method, 58
shader Model, support for, 3
shaders, 267
sheetSize method, 68
shooting
    about, 246–251
    direction of, 483
    shots, 484
shut down, Xbox 360, 19
sign function, 289
sign-in, gamer services sign-in windows, 499
SignIn game state, adding update code, 418
Silver Xbox LIVE membership, 346
sin function, 289
sincos function, 289
sinh function, 289
skinned effects, 5
skull ball image, 136, 164
smoothstep function, 289
Song.FromUri method, 6
sound API
    compared to XACT, 86
    file types, 94
    using, 94

About the Author

Aaron Reed has extensive software development experience and, more importantly, experience in software development education. He has taught many courses at Neumont University on topics such as .NET, web development and web services, DirectX, XNA, and systems design and architecture.

Aaron's experience in teaching DirectX and XNA for several years to university-level students helps him understand what topics are easily understood and which ones need more depth and emphasis. Through his experiences in the classroom, he has developed a good understanding of what format and sequence makes the most sense when presenting the material. This book follows that format and is meant to present game development concepts in the most efficient and comprehensible way, as proven in the classroom. When he's not teaching, writing, or developing, Aaron can usually be found playing with his wife and kids, preferably in the mountains of Utah.

Colophon

The animal on the cover of *Learning XNA 4.0* is a sea robin fish (*Chelidonichthys lucernus*), otherwise known as a sapphirine gurnard. While the body of the fish is usually a somewhat bland color mix of browns, reds, and whites, its eyes are a striking peacock blue.

The sea robin fish is so named because it swims across the ocean floor and opens and closes its fins in a manner reminiscent of a flying bird. Some species of the fish also use their fins to fly above water for short distances.

In addition to having "wings," the sea robin fish also has six "legs" (three on each side of its body) that were once part of its pectoral fin. These legs—which are really flexible spines—allow the sea robin fish to stir up and detect food from the ocean floor while walking.

The sea robin fish occasionally brings to mind yet another creature: when caught, the fish croaks like a frog. Chefs say the sea robin fish can replace scorpion fish in bouillabaisse, and add that the fish has firm and tender flesh when cooked.

The cover image is from *Lydekker's Natural History*. The cover font is Adobe ITC Garamond. The text font is Linotype Birka; the heading font is Adobe Myriad Condensed; and the code font is LucasFont's TheSansMonoCondensed.

CPSIA information can be obtained at www.ICGtesting.com
Printed in the USA
BVOW081426290212

284122BV00007B/40/P